I0828430

HISTORIC PHOTOS OF
SARASOTA COUNTY

TEXT AND CAPTIONS BY STEVE RAJTAR

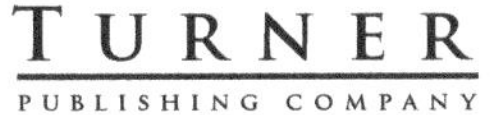

Here is a 1912 view of the Belle Haven Inn, originally the DeSoto Hotel, after renovation and the addition of a large wing. To the far left, beyond the Main Street pier, is the Halton Sanitarium opened by Dr. Jack Halton in 1909. The sanitarium also provided housing for Bertha Palmer of Chicago when she visited for the first time, and later was the Admiral Bayfront Hotel; the building was torn down in the 1960s.

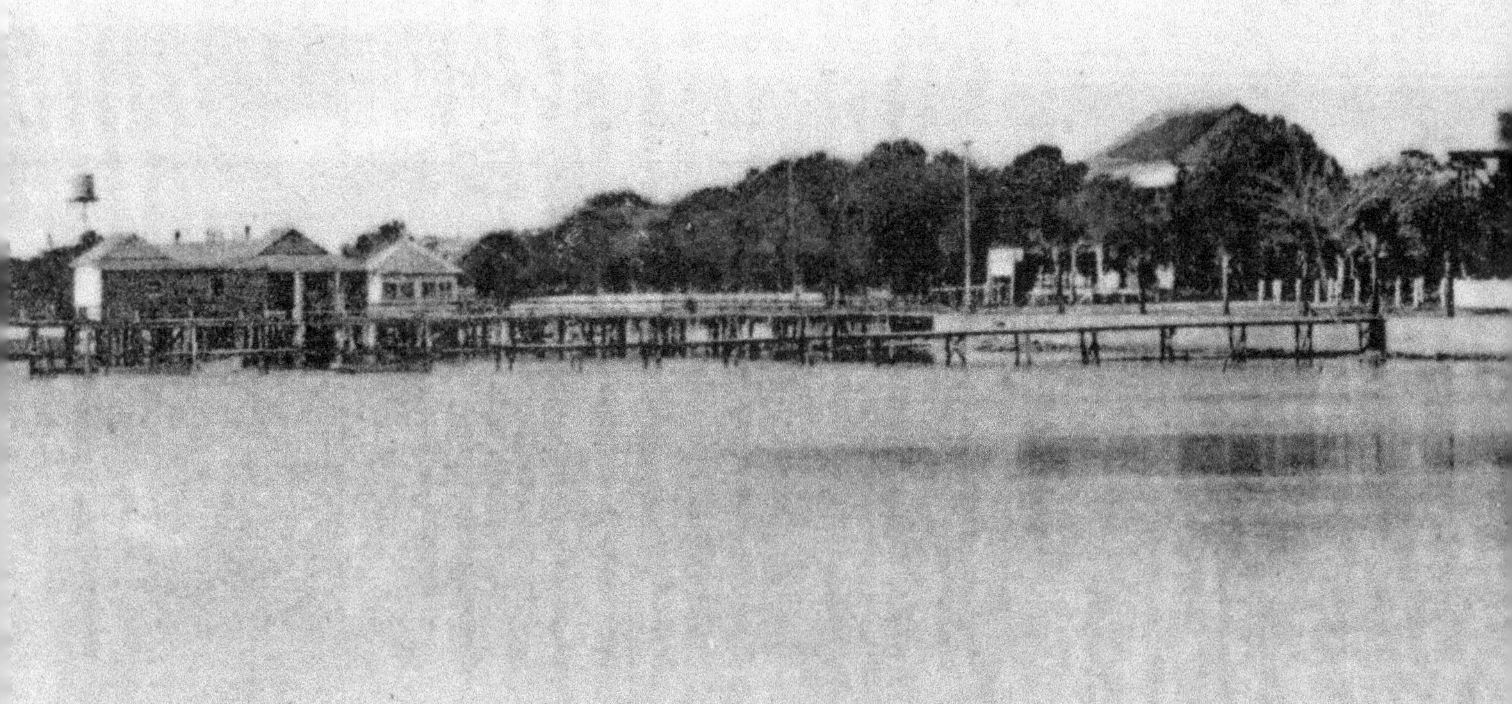

HISTORIC PHOTOS OF
SARASOTA COUNTY

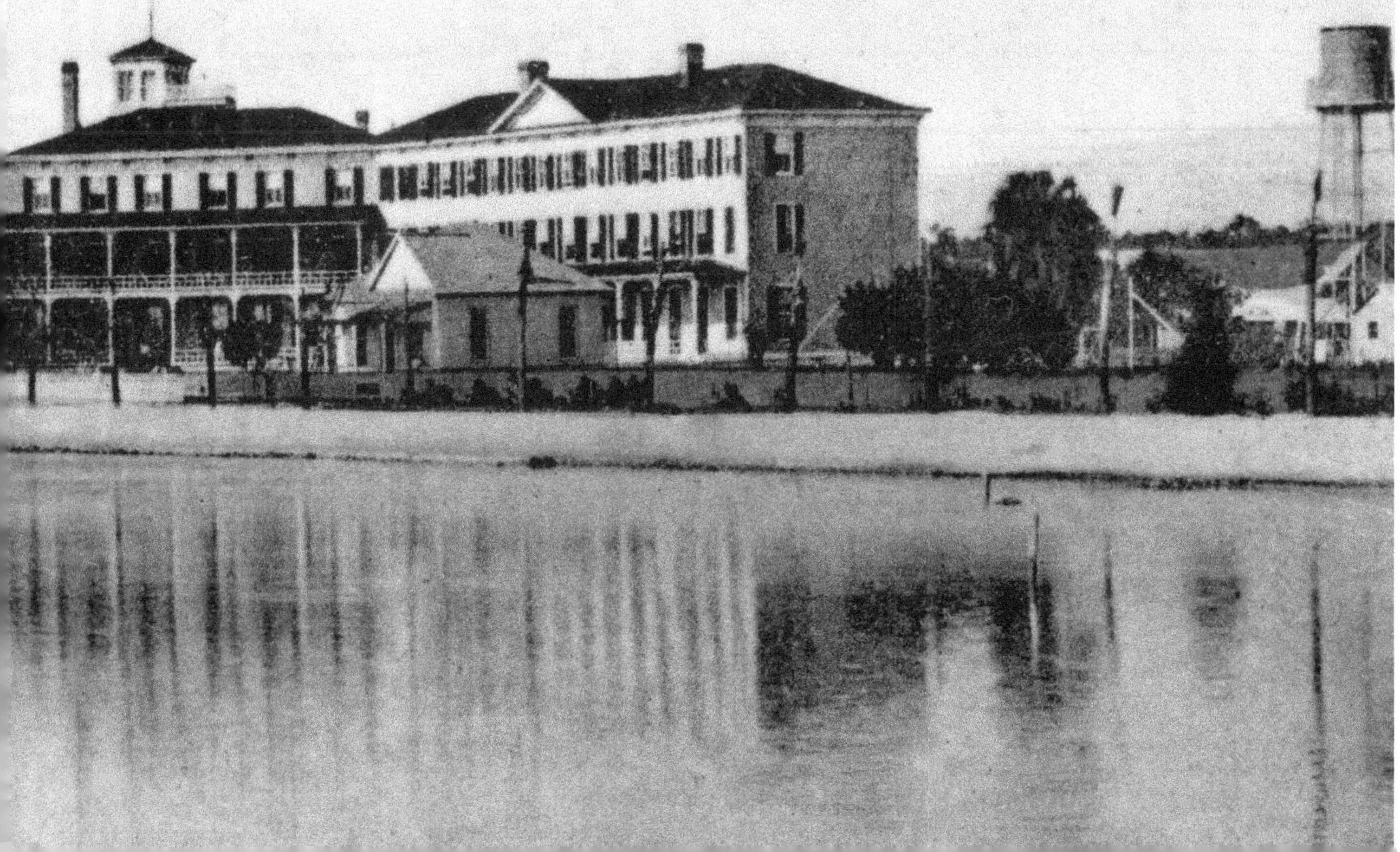

Turner Publishing Company
4507 Charlotte Avenue • Suite 100
Nashville, Tennessee 37209
(615) 255-2665

www.turnerpublishing.com

Historic Photos of Sarasota County

Library of Congress Control Number: 2008901710

ISBN-13: 978-1-59652-453-8
ISBN-13: 978-1-68442-026-1 (hc)

Printed in the United States of America

08 09 10 11 12 13 14—0 9 8 7 6 5 4 3 2 1

Contents

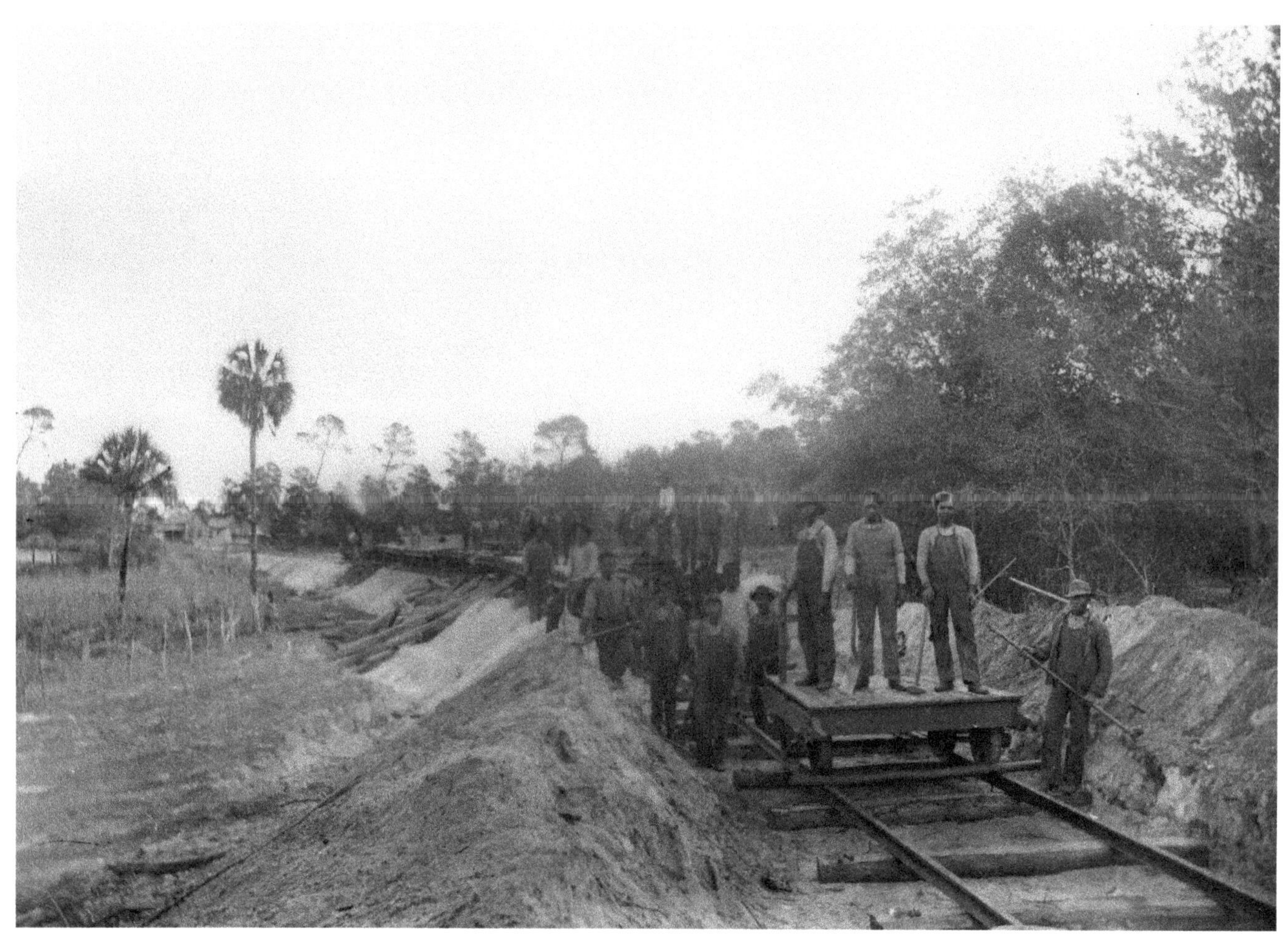

This crew is building the railroad between Sarasota and Palmetto Junction in 1903. The U.S. and West Indies Railroad and Steamship Company, soon to be absorbed by Seaboard Air Line Railway, carried people and freight. The first train on the U.S. and West Indies line, consisting of an engine, a Pullman car, and a baggage car, arrived from Bradenton in 1903, but was met by a small group of only fifty.

Acknowledgments

With the exception of cropping images where needed and touching up imperfections that have accrued over time, no other changes have been made to the photographs in this volume. The caliber and clarity of many photographs are limited by the technology of the day and the ability of the photographer at the time they were made.

This volume, *Historic Photos of Sarasota County,* is the result of the cooperation and efforts of many individuals, organizations, and corporations. It is with great thanks that we acknowledge the valuable contribution of the following for their generous support:

State Archives of Florida

Preface

Long before families and individuals started migrating to what is now Sarasota County from places such as Boston, Chicago, Scotland, and other European and American cities, the area along the gulf coast was inhabited by Native American tribes. Before history was recorded in written form, the area was frequented by Timucuans, Calusas, and Seminoles. They shared knowledge of the region with others, and eventually European explorers became interested in the riches which the area reputedly offered to anyone willing to conquer it.

One such would-be conquistador was Hernando de Soto, who arrived in 1539 from Havana. He may have stopped at Longboat Key before setting up a mainland camp near present-day Bradenton. After searching for gold and killing many natives, he and his expedition left the area by land to the north after finding none of the fabled treasures.

Maps of the area from the 1700s show its name with various spellings, each of the variations thought by some to be based on "sara-se-cota," an Indian word meaning an easily observed landfall. Another theory suggests the name comes from "sarao sota," a place of dancing. But by the late 1830s, the spellings of Zara Zote, Porte Sarasote, Sarazota, and Saraxota had more or less become standardized as Sarasota.

The region was not devoid of white men; prior to the arrival of the first official settler in 1842, there were Cuban and American fishermen in the area, but their ranchos and fish camps were only temporary.

William Henry Whitaker of Savannah, Georgia, arrived in the area in 1842, the first permanent settler of European descent. Whitaker lived for a time along the Manatee River, then built a log cabin on Yellow

Bluffs, an outcropping of yellow limestone near the intersection of Sarasota's present Twelfth Street and Tamiami Trail. He sold dried fish and roe to Cuban traders, and he started a cattle business in 1847.

Whitaker married Mary Jane Wyatt in 1851, and they raised eleven children. They received an Armed Occupation Act deed to 145 acres the year they married. That first log cabin of Whitaker's was burned down by Seminoles in 1856; a second was built that same year, but it, too, later burned, the cause unknown, to be followed by construction of a third. The Whitaker name remains as given to the Whitaker Bayou and the Whitaker Cemetery.

John G. and Eliza Webb arrived from Utica, New York, in 1867 and settled on another bluff overlooking the water. They lived in a log home with a palmetto-thatched roof located on a promontory now known as Spanish Point. Their home was south of the Whitaker settlement and evolved into the town of Osprey. That name was chosen by John Webb in 1884 when he needed a designation for his new post office.

Another early settlement along the coast was Horse and Chaise, so named because sailors attempting to locate it from the Gulf of Mexico were guided by a formation of trees resembling a horse and carriage. The settlement eventually took on the name Venice, which was suggested by pioneer Frank Higel, who noticed a similarity between the coastlines of Florida and Italy.

Each of the coastal communities began to grow, largely because of the promise contained in the Homestead Act of 1862. A settler had to move onto the land, make it his homestead, build a house, and till the soil. Five years later, he would receive a deed to his 160 acres of formerly federal land, or so it was thought.

—Steve Rajtar

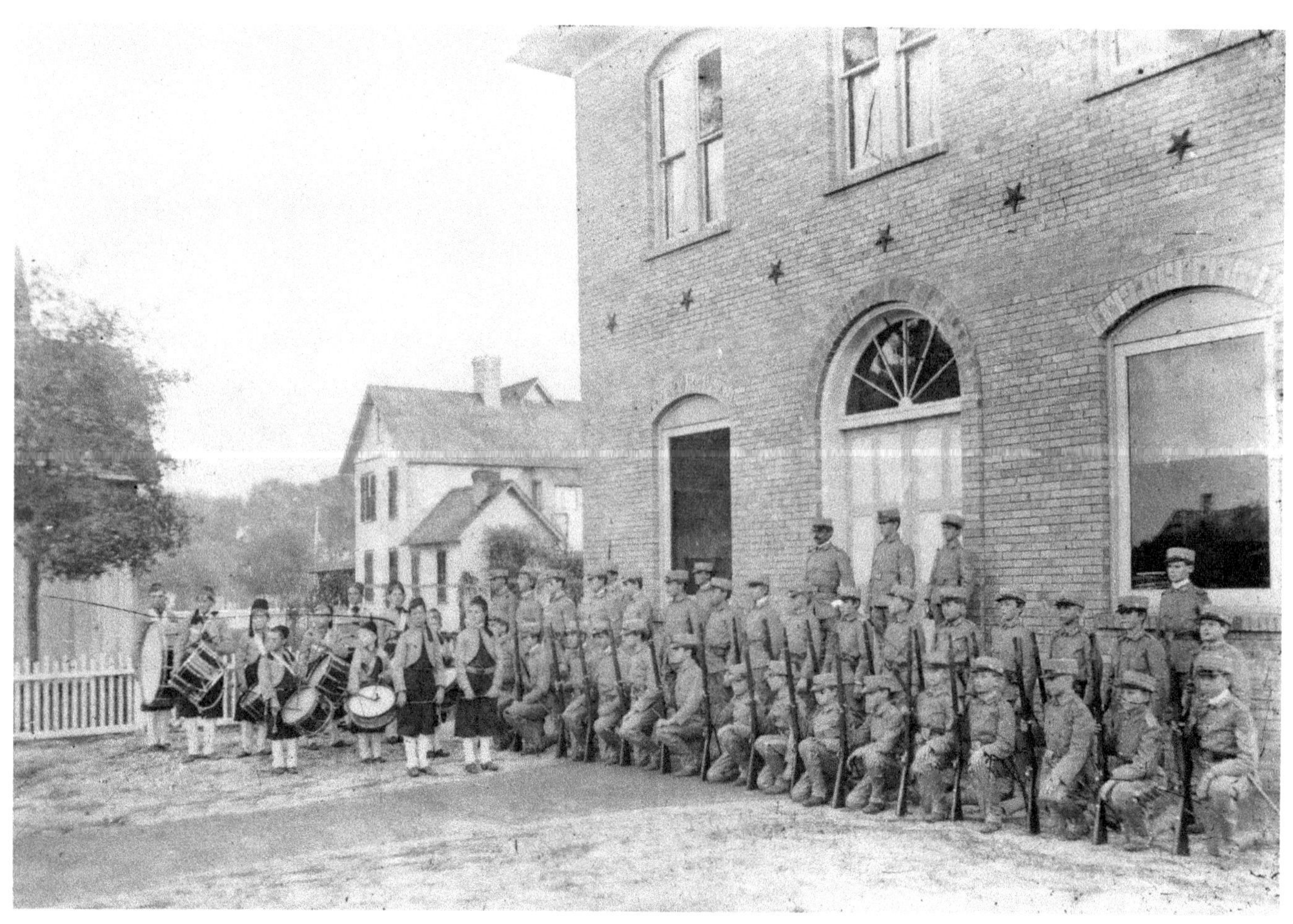

Military academy students and a drum corps are shown here in formation during the late 1880s in the Sarasota-Bradenton area. The local Scottish influence is reflected in the musicians' uniforms, which include kilts and Glengarry hats.

The Scottish Experiment

(1880–1899)

In the Sarasota region, the promise of Homestead Act land was dashed in 1881. Politicians pointed out that previous federal law granted the state title to all swamp and overflow lands, and they were successful in designating 22 million acres as swampland, including the Sarasota area. Suddenly, claims of homesteaders who had received federal deeds were invalidated, and the land passed into the hands of speculators. For a time, the influx of colonists halted.

Most of the land was conveyed by the state to three railroad companies and five other speculator firms, including a British firm called the Florida Mortgage and Investment Company, led by Sir John Gillespie. Stories in British newspapers touted Sarasota as a place where a man would not have to work very hard to make a living.

In 1885, a contingent of Scottish immigrants crossed the Atlantic from Glasgow and arrived in Sarasota. They had purchased town lots and 40-acre estates and expected to see completed, broad avenues, but found these existed only in the plans drawn up by the Florida Mortgage and Investment Company. The 60 families and others, who were called the Ormiston Colony, after Gillespie's hometown, were greeted by wilderness and a rare Florida snowfall.

One of the prominent families in the group was that of John B. and Jane Kerr Browning. Son Alex used his Scottish architectural training to design several Sarasota homes. Not every immigrant found Sarasota to his liking, however. Many headed back to Scotland or to other parts of the U.S. within a few months, leaving only the Brownings, two other families, and a few individuals. Yet despite the failure of the first attempt at settlement, others from Scotland continued to arrive.

Intending to fulfill its promise to build a town, the Florida Mortgage and Investment Company had its local manager, A. C. Acton, undertake the project. He had a wharf constructed at the foot of Main Street and cleared that road to Five Points, where a rooming house was built. Dr. Thomas Wallace, one of the few remaining original Scots, built a home and a clinic.

J. Hamilton Gillespie, Sir John's son, attempted to make the Sarasota experiment a success. He opened roads, built the DeSoto Hotel, set up a golf course, and constructed the area's first railroad. But he found he could not single-handedly produce a town that would attract many colonists. The real growth of what became Sarasota County would take place after others arrived from the Midwest and the Northeast. Nevertheless, the Scottish influence can be seen in the area to this day.

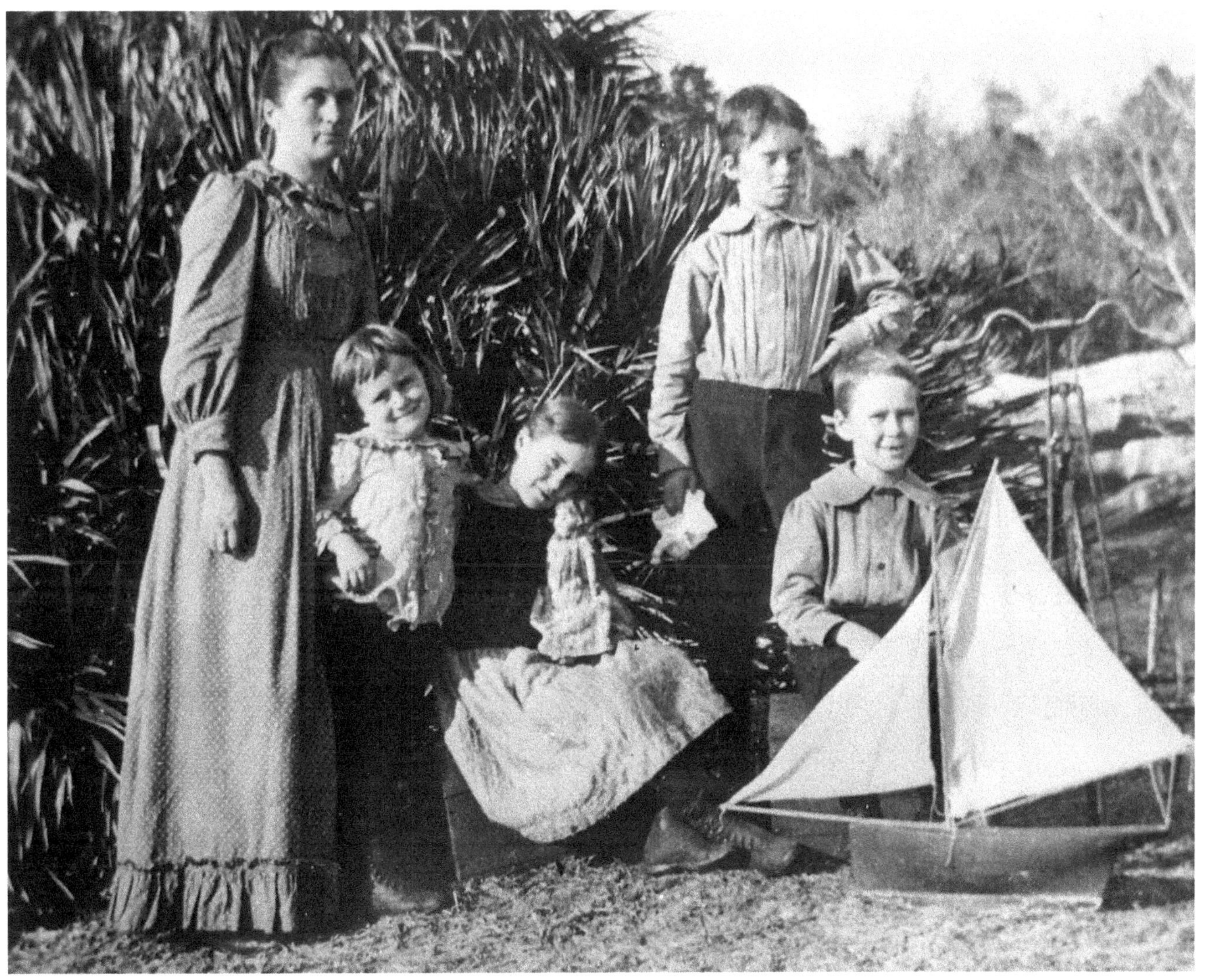

Nellie Abbe Whitaker poses in Sarasota in 1893 with her children Stuart Anstey, Grace Spencer, Harper Elliott, and Dwight Abbe. Nellie, the daughter of postmaster Charles Abbe, was married to Furman Chairs Whitaker, a prominent physician who built the sailboat model shown here. This photo was taken shortly before Stuart died at the age of five.

In 1885, Sarasota's First Street was rutted dirt with only a few wooden buildings. Looking westward, this is the section between Central Street and Pineapple Avenue, photographed by Felix Pinard.

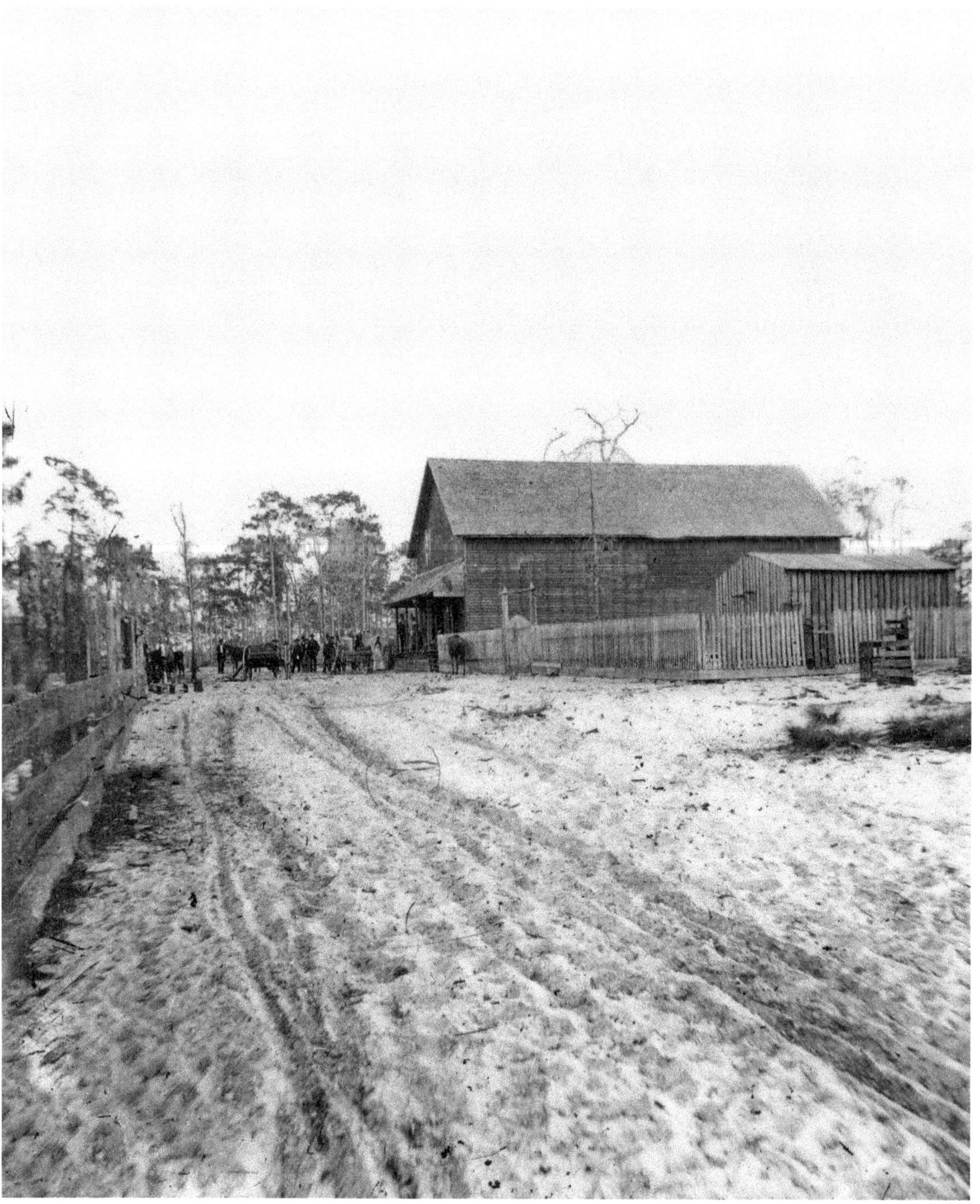

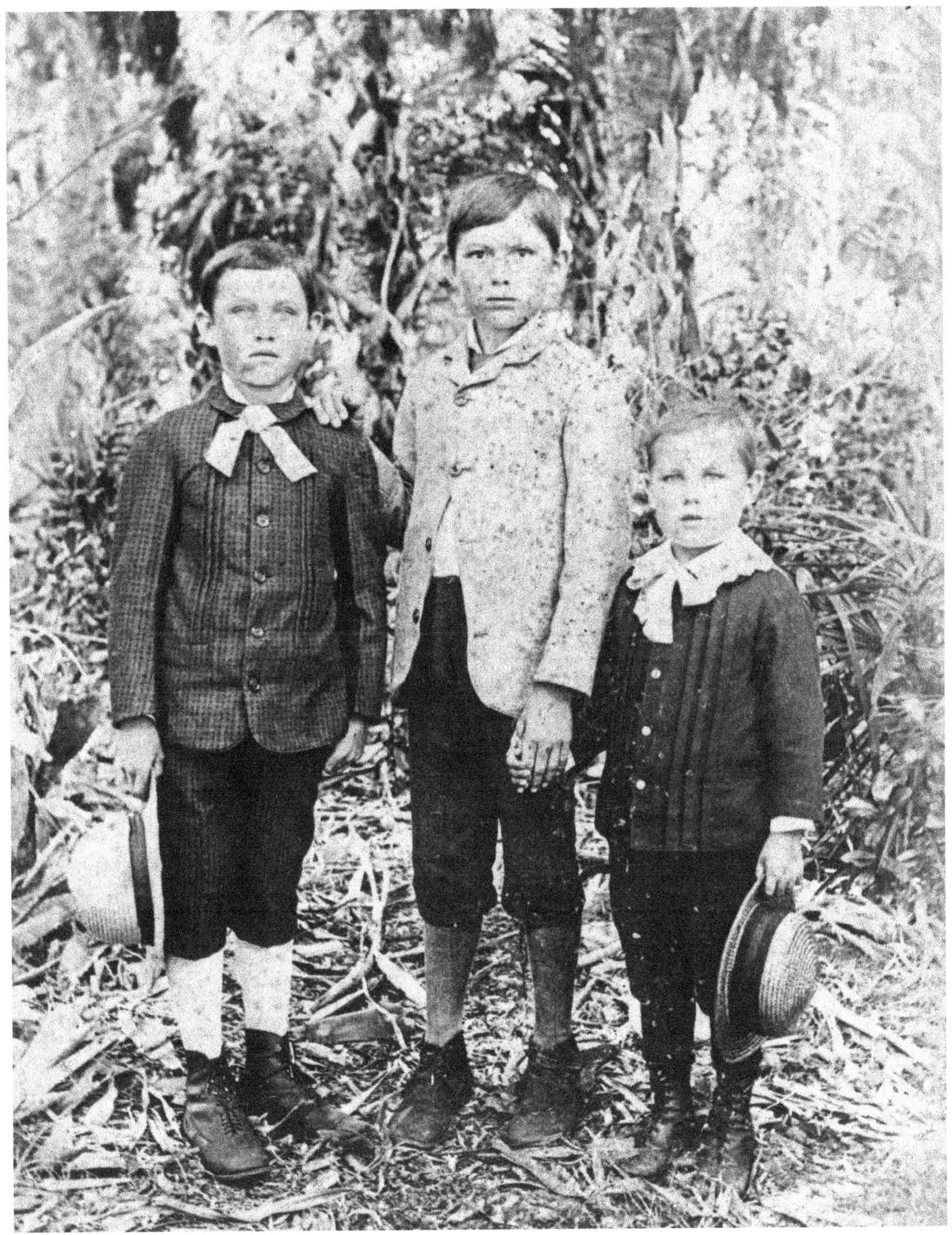

Near the end of the 1800s, the Sarasota area saw many families arrive to begin new lives. Unlike with earlier wilderness settlements, or even Sarasota in the years when attacks from Seminoles were feared, it wasn't just a matter of individuals arriving to make their fortunes. Here, brothers Walter, Jim, and Luther Manson pose for a portrait by their uncle, Felix Pinard.

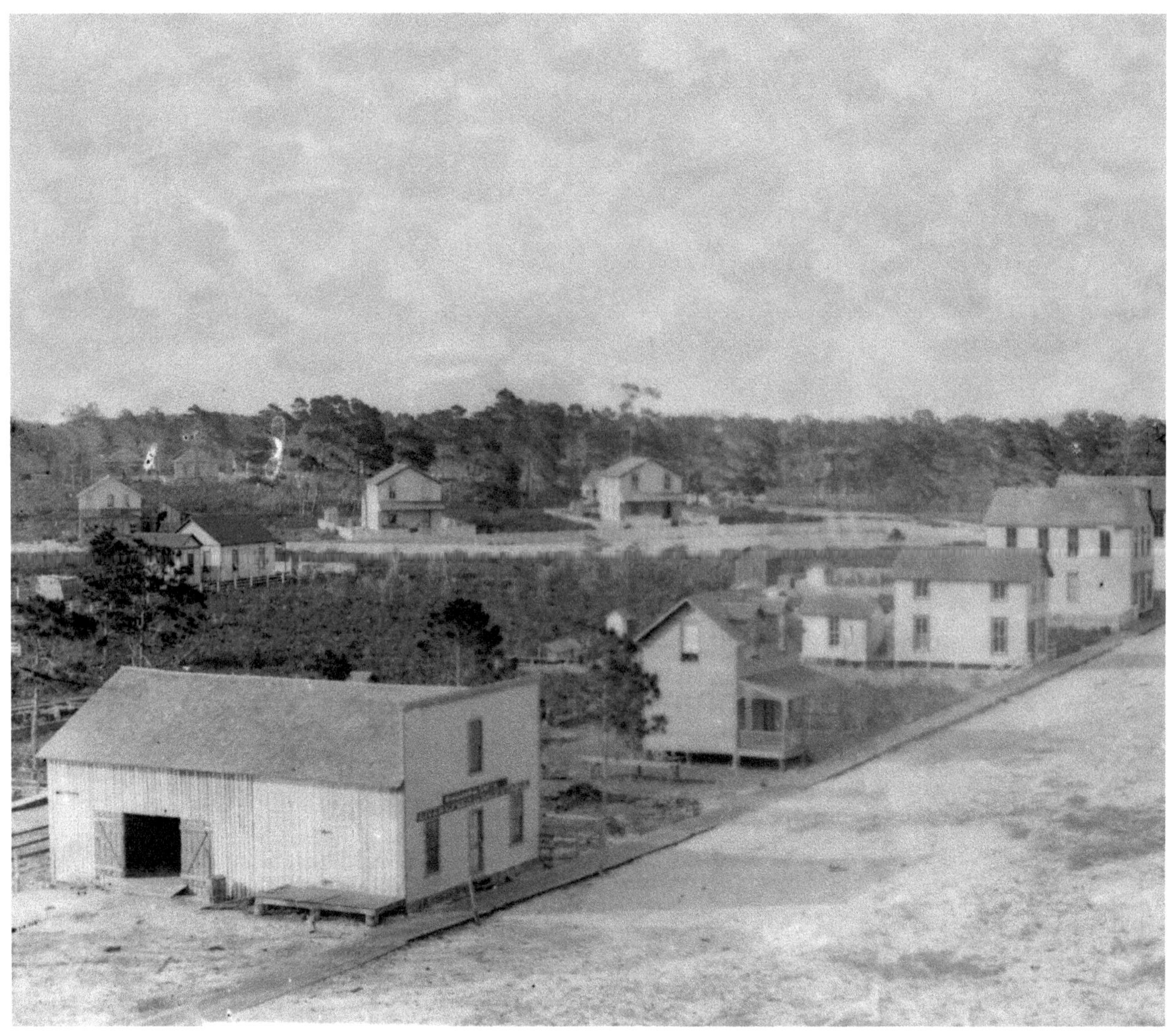

The tall DeSoto Hotel offered the best aerial view of Sarasota, including this one of lower Main Street. The hotel, built by Col. J. Hamilton Gillespie, opened on February 25, 1887, with thirty rooms, a dining room, and a large lobby. He intended it as a lodging for "those of wealth and influence," and it catered both to tourists and prospective investors.

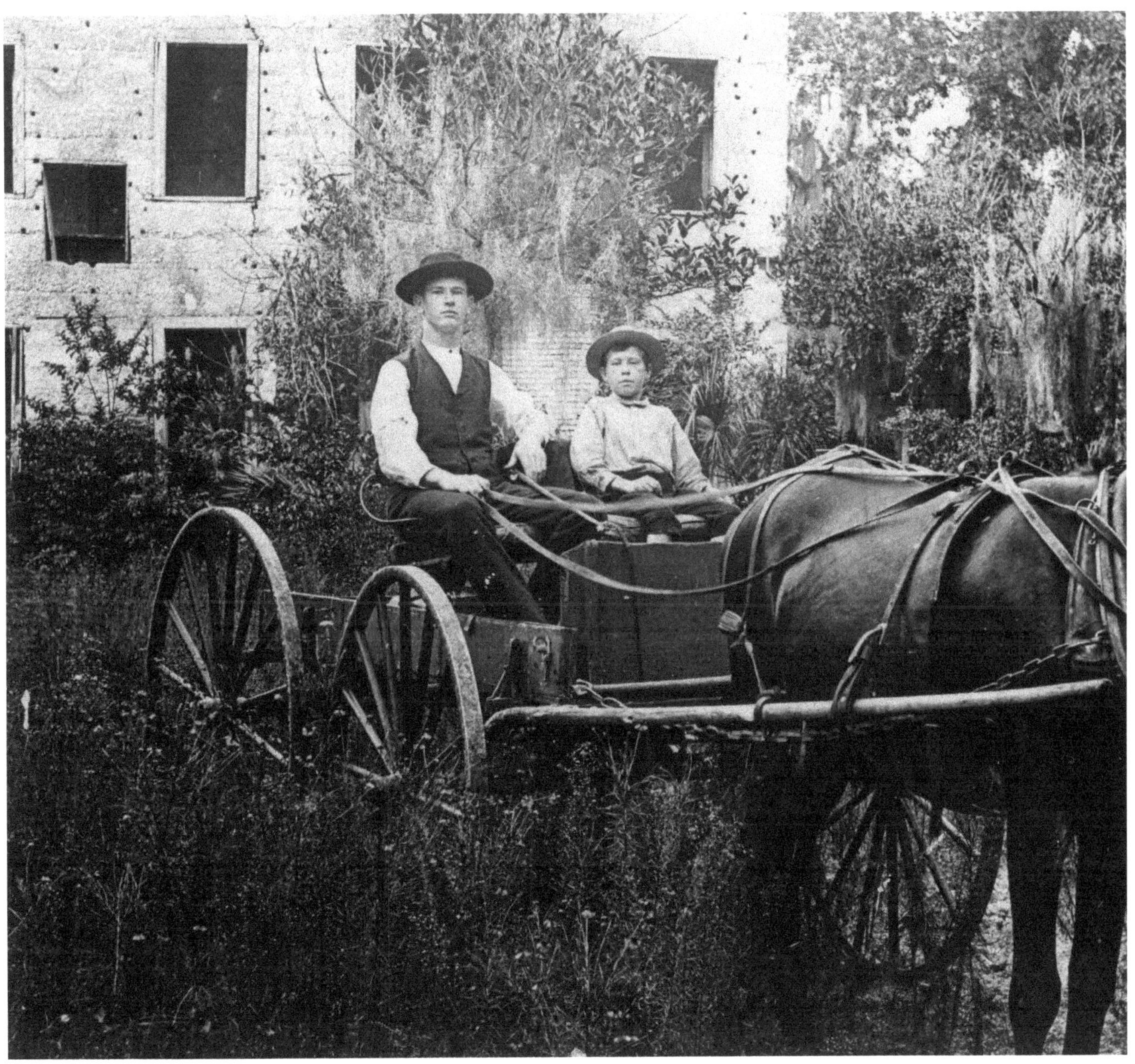

This photo emphasizes the difficulties of transportation in the early days. Notice how high on the wheels the weeds reach. For travel to other towns, passengers were much more likely to book passage on a steamboat than a wagon pulled through the wilderness. In the background are the ruins of the Braden house, which Indians burned in 1856.

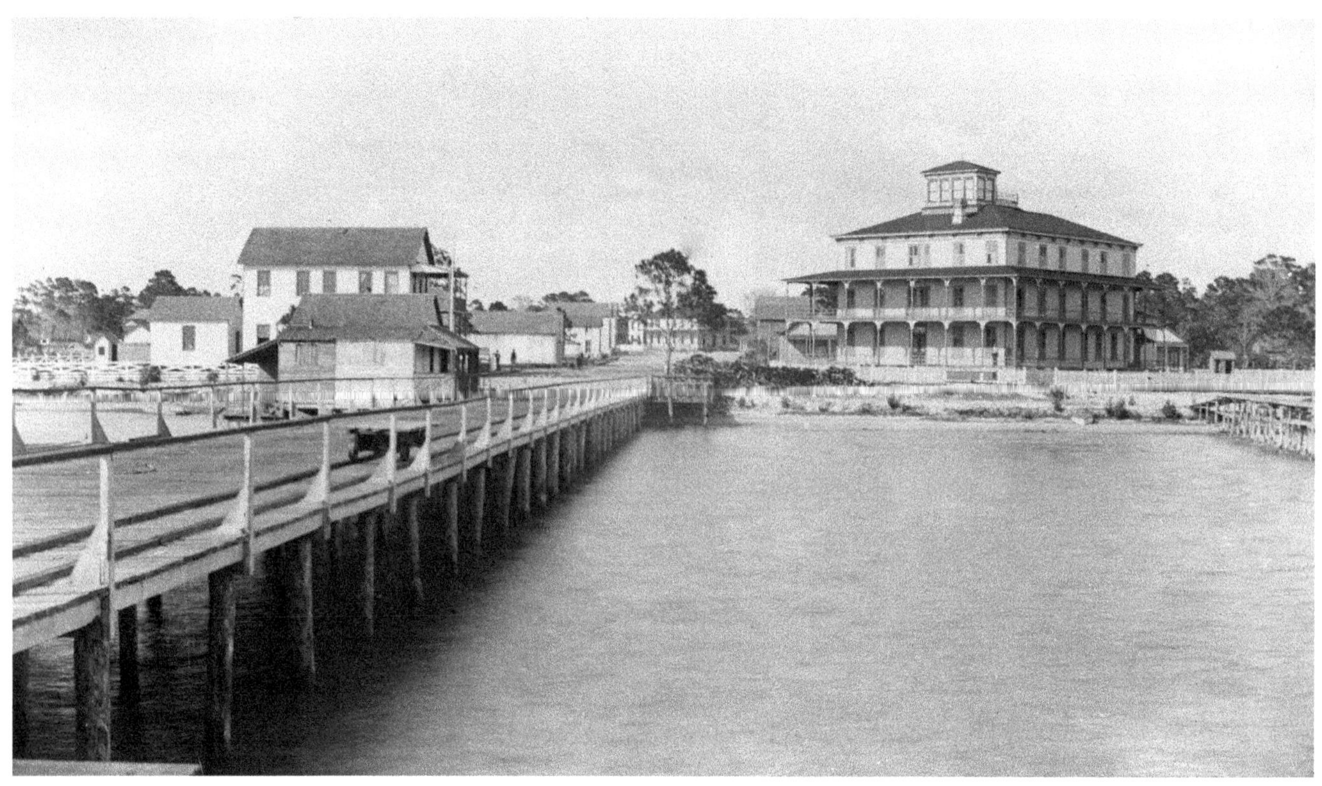

Looking toward downtown in 1888, the largest structure is the DeSoto Hotel. Businesses operating on the dock over the years included an oyster house opened by the Vincent brothers and by 1899 owned by Dave Broadway, who moved to the area in 1893. He later moved his business into a fifty-foot extension of the dock that included the Hover Arcade.

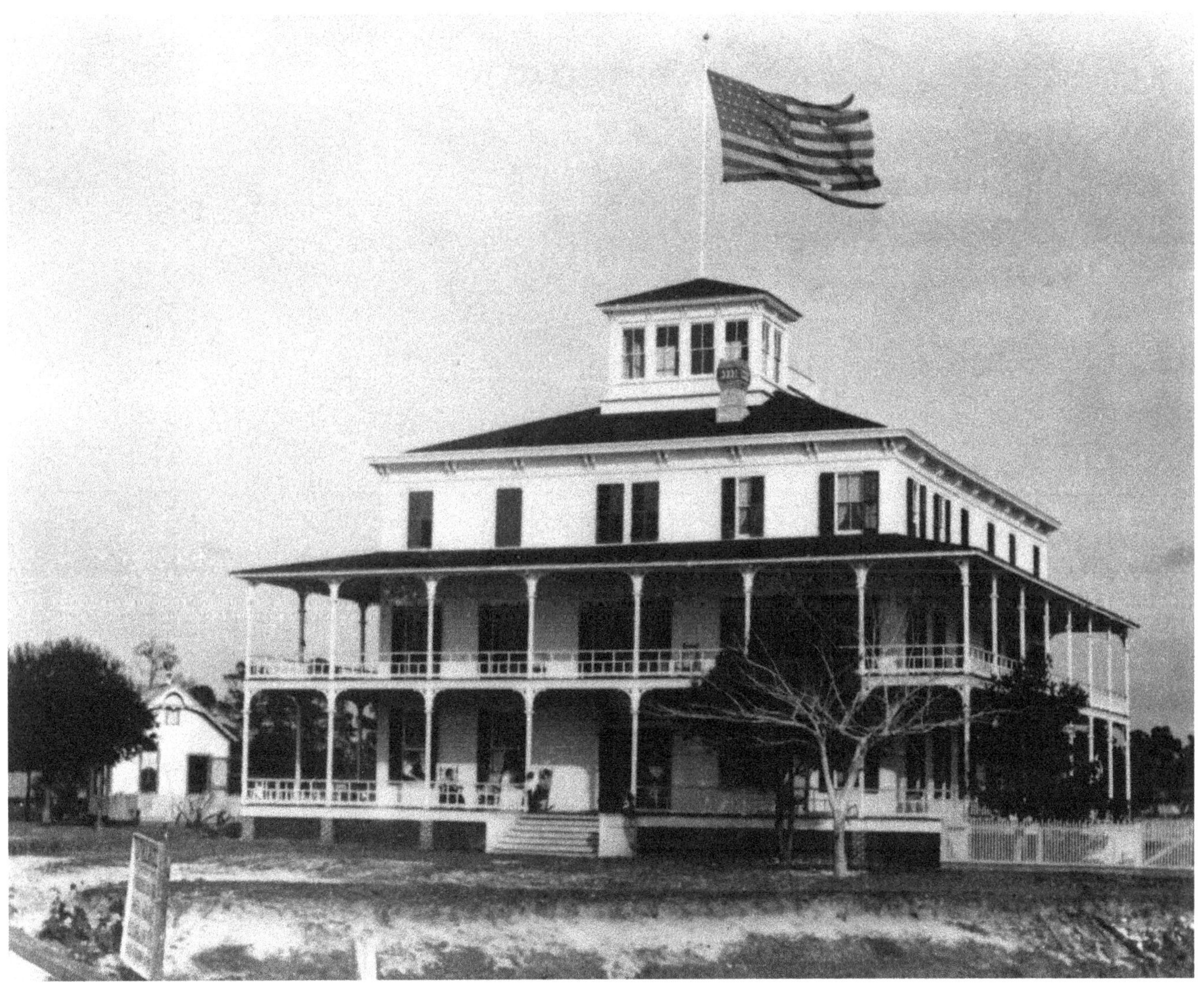

The DeSoto Hotel, owned for ten years by its builder, J. Hamilton Gillespie, sold for $1,500 in 1899 and for $4,500 in 1902, and was renamed the Belle Haven Inn. Unlike many hotels that only opened for the winter, the Belle Haven was open all year long. A room for $2.50 per day included a fireplace, croquet, tennis, sulfur baths, and rowboats.

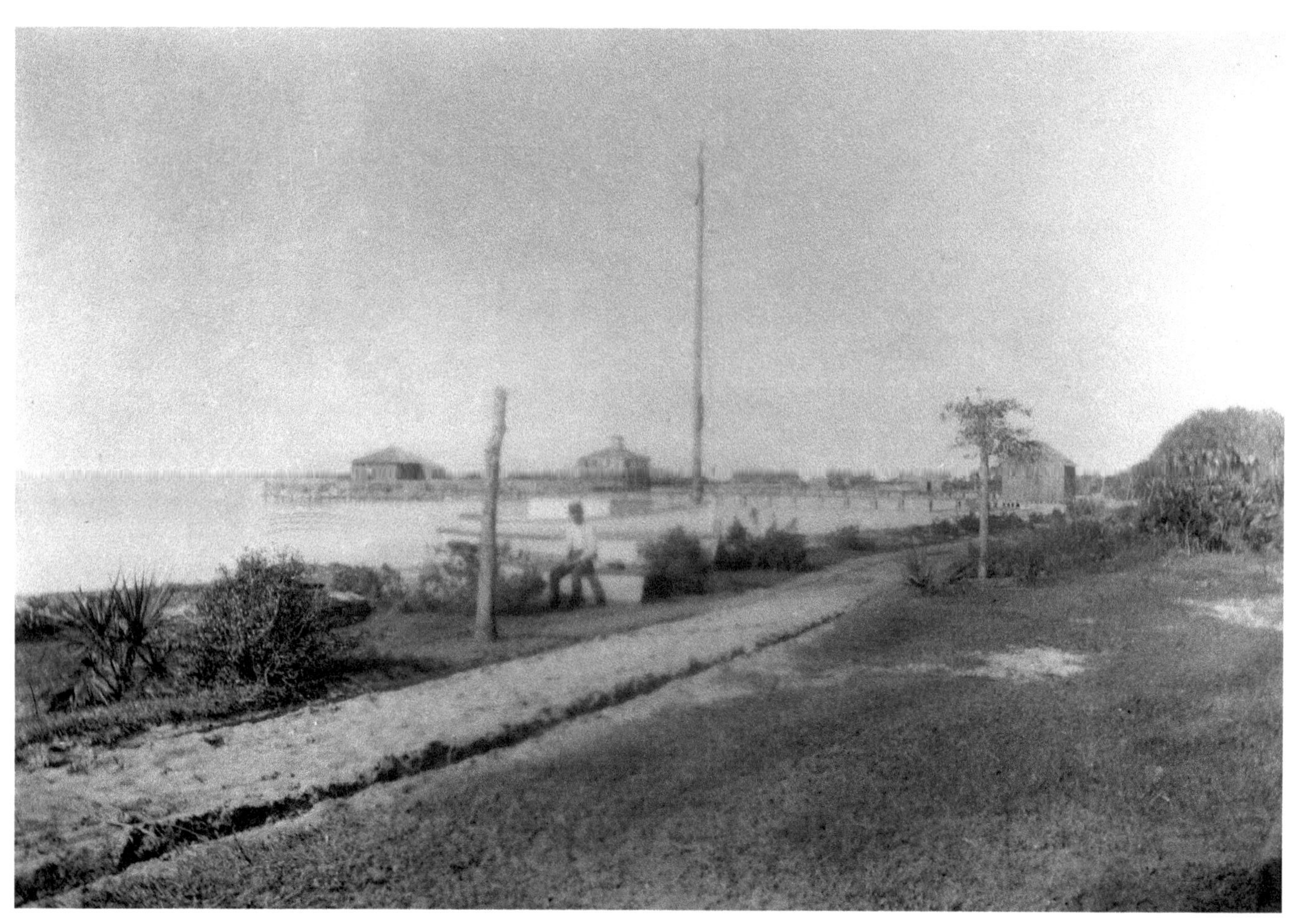

One of the early Sarasota neighborhoods was South Gulf Stream Avenue, shown here in 1894 near its intersection with Mound Street. Contractor Hugh Browning lived there and served on the city council. Other residents included Harry Higel, Louise Edmondson, John Iverson, A. E. Cummer, and Richard Jeffcoat, who is seated on a bench in the middle of this photo.

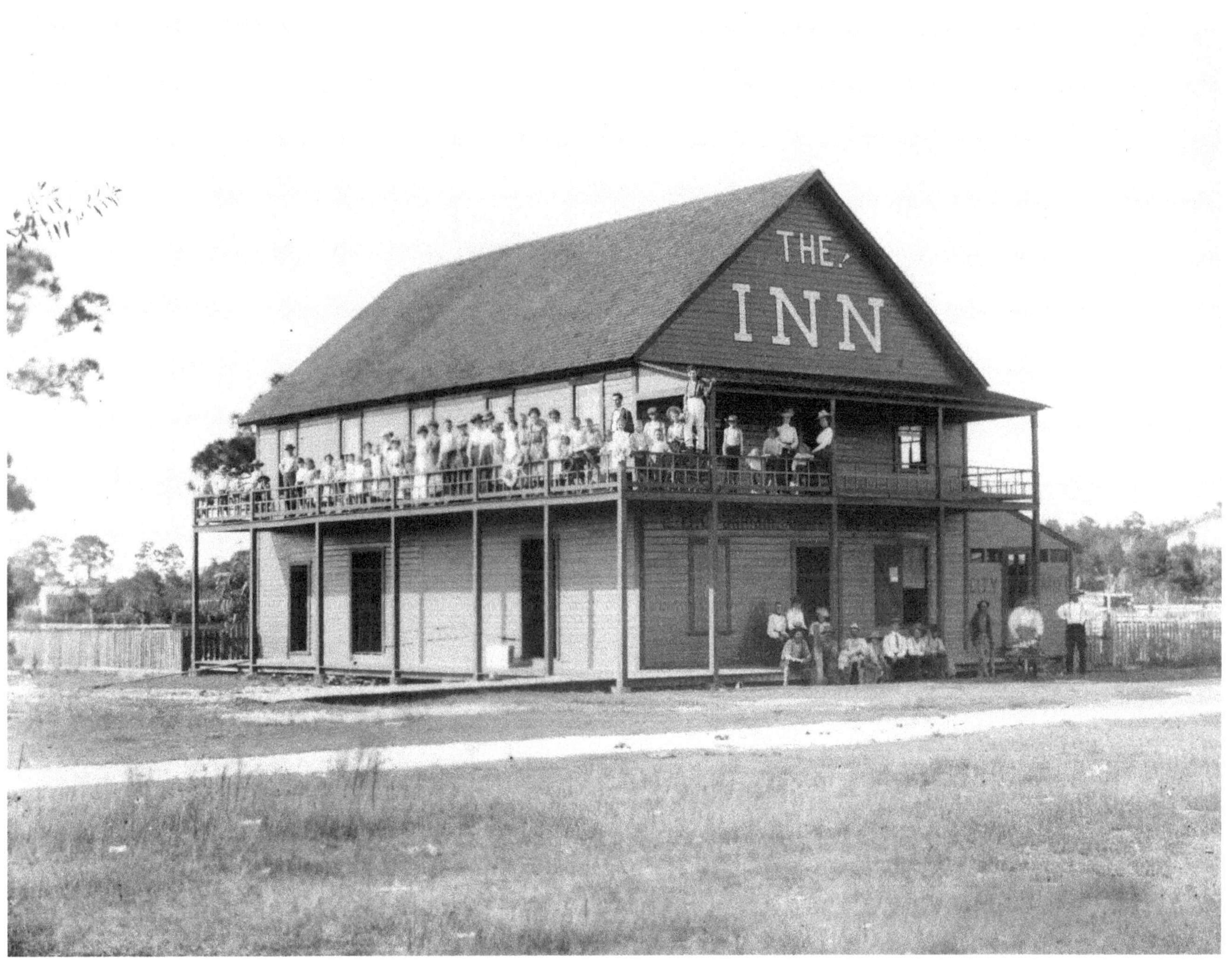

Sarasota hosted its first Baptist convention in 1894, and some of the attendees are shown here in front and along the balcony of the Inn. The building began as Whitaker and Smith's livery stable, then a pool room and a second story with nine bedrooms were added by proprietor Elijah Grantham. In the 1920s, the building was moved to a location on Fruitville Road, where it stood until 1994.

This house was photographed around 1899 by one of its residents, Felix Pinard of France, who took numerous other photos included in this collection. He was married to Helen Drew Pinard, and their children were Francis T. and Josephine. The house was located on Gulf Stream Avenue, which in the early days was close to the shore. Subsequent landfill has put some distance between the avenue and the water.

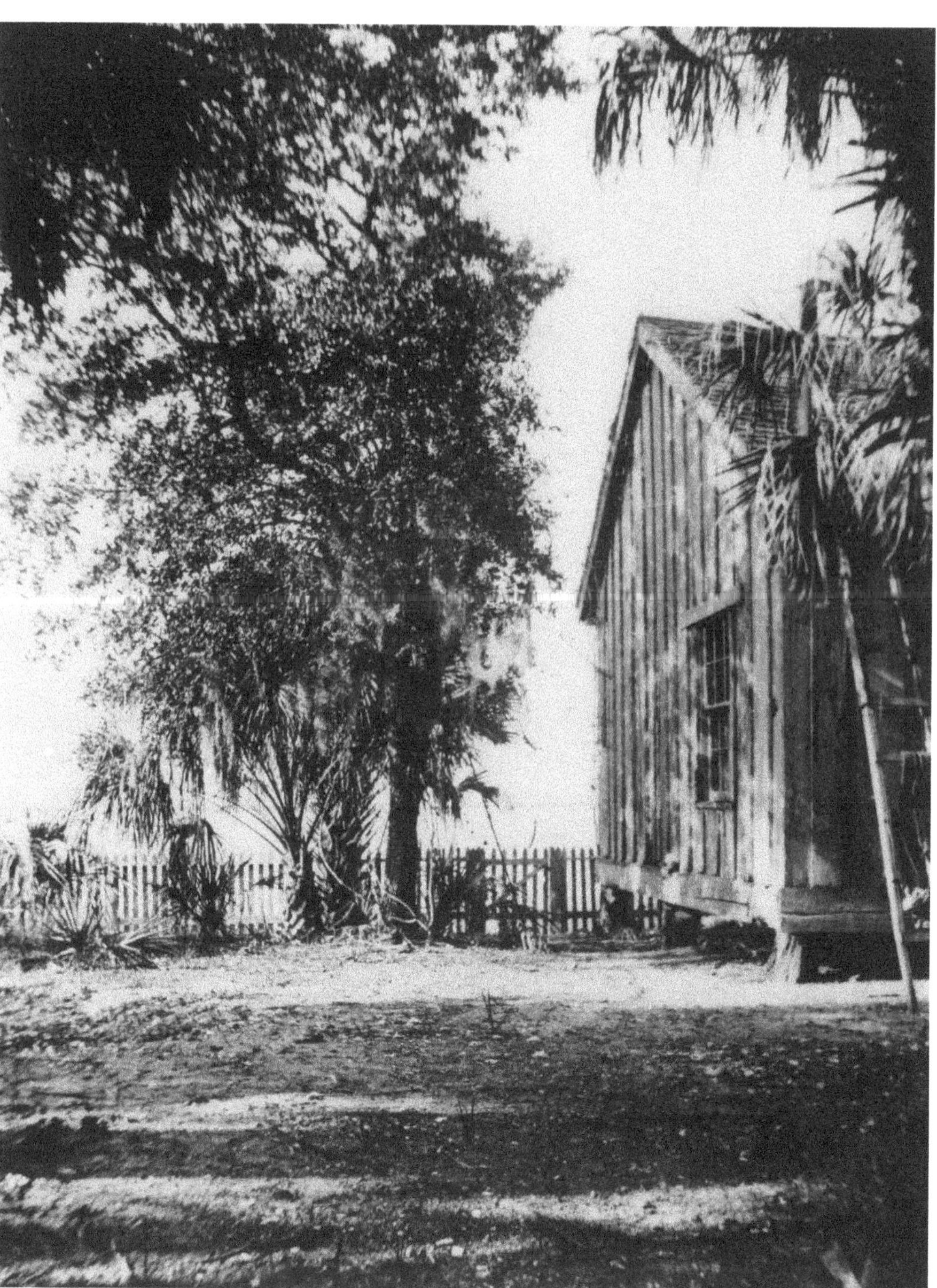

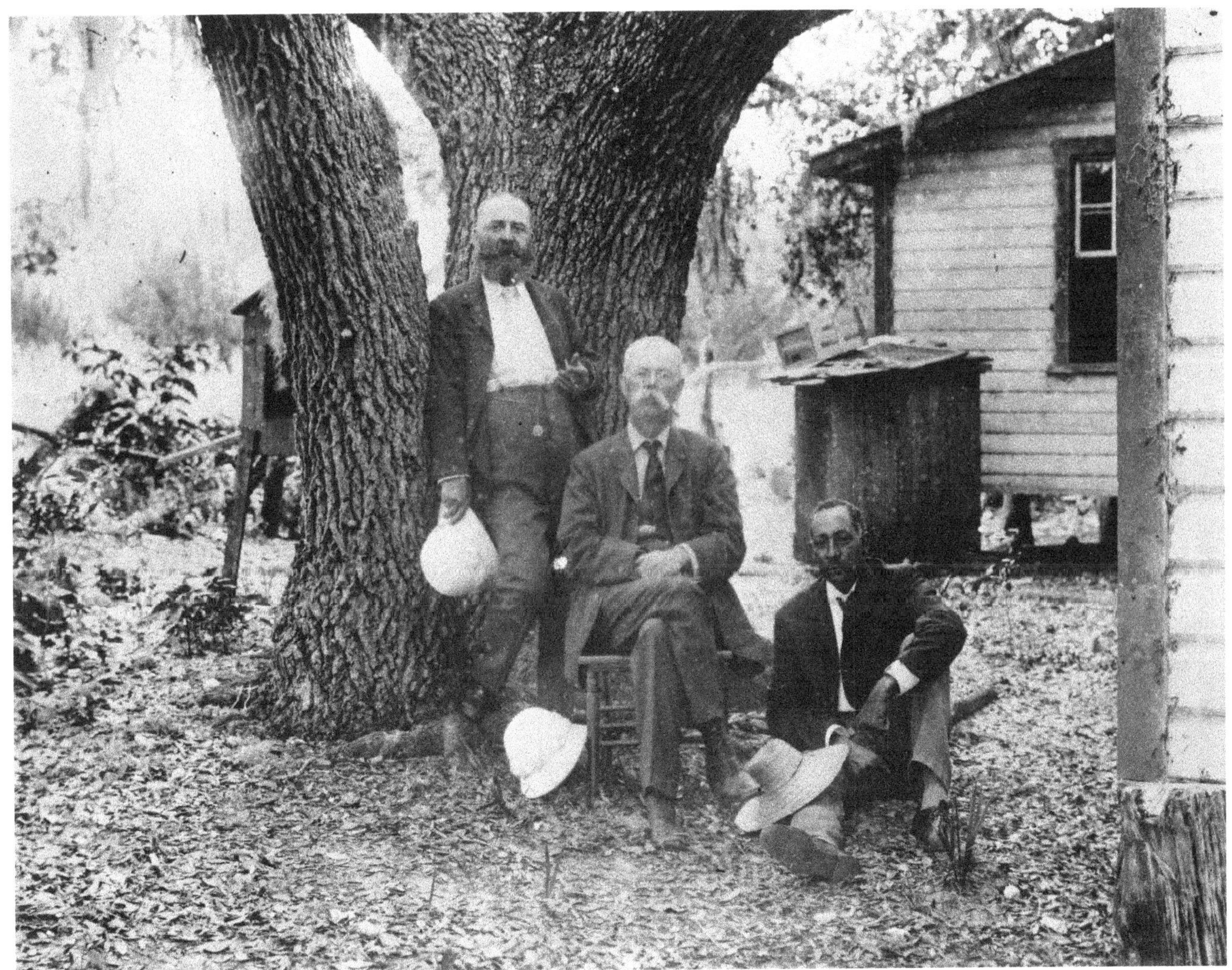

The Palms Hotel partially visible behind these three visitors resulted from a feud between J. Hamilton Gillespie, who owned the DeSoto Hotel, and Alfred and Annie Jones, who leased it. Gillespie's first wife, Blanche McDaniel, did not get along with the Joneses. The Joneses decided not to operate the DeSoto anymore, so they gave up their lease and sought another hotel to operate.

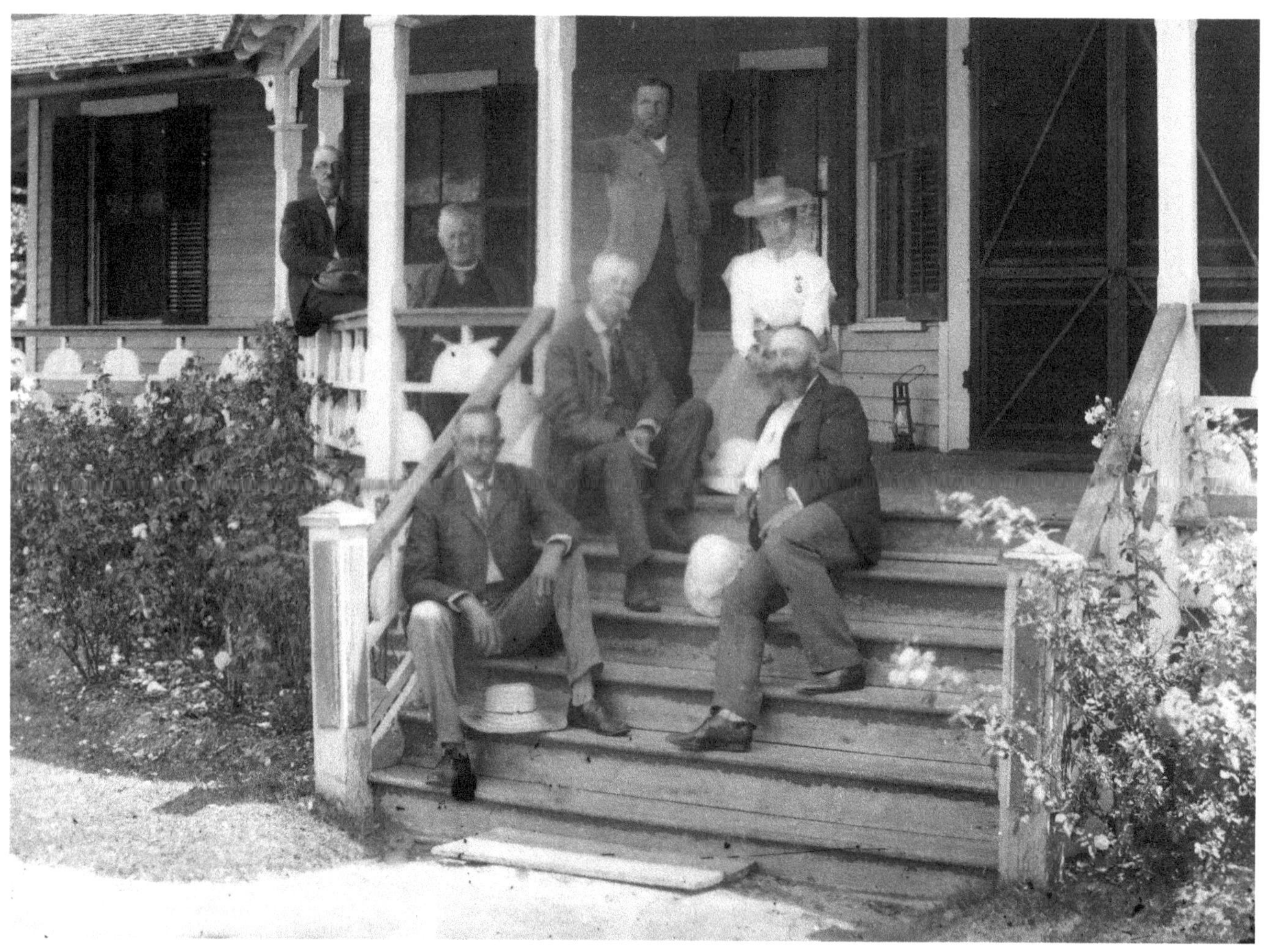

To provide Mr. and Mrs. Jones with a new hotel to run, sportsmen from New York and Chicago arrived during the late 1880s and built the large Tarpon Club on a portion of the former William Whitaker estate on Indian Beach. It was designed by Alex Browning, Sarasota's first architect. The building is shown here after it was renamed the Palms Hotel.

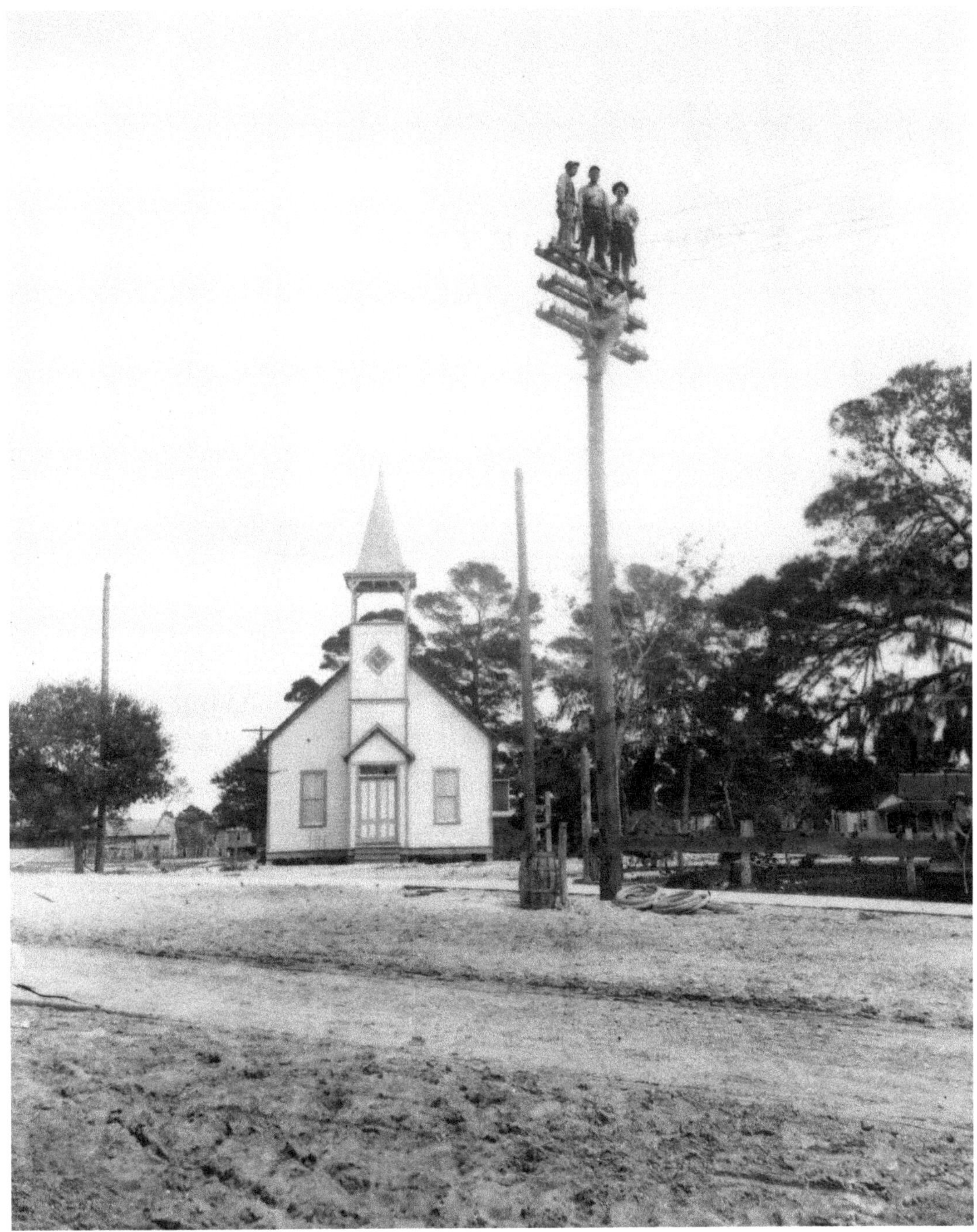

In front of the First Methodist Church, Peninsular Telephone Company men stand atop a pole, likely hamming it up on a break from working on the telephone line. The First Methodist Church organized in 1891 and purchased this building at Five Points for $40, then added the belfry and steeple. They later sold it and built a new sanctuary in 1914 across Pineapple Avenue.

High Society

(1900–1919)

Joseph H. Lord arrived in the area in 1889 to purchase land for the mining of phosphate. Over the next two decades, he acquired 100,000 acres stretching from Sarasota south to Venice, and east to the Myakka River. Originally from Boston, he was based in Chicago, so his Florida activities caught the attention of other Chicagoans, particularly one Bertha Honoré Palmer. The wealthy widow of Chicago developer Potter Palmer, she fell in love with the Sarasota area after reading an advertisement of Lord's in the *Chicago Sunday Tribune.* By 1911, she had bought thousands of Lord's acres, including the former Webb family homestead in Osprey and a mile and a half of beachfront property now forming a portion of Venice.

At the Oaks, her winter home along Little Sarasota Bay at 350-acre Osprey Point, now known as Spanish Point, Palmer laid out extensive gardens. She also acquired a 25,000-acre ranch in the eastern portion of the county. She called it Meadow Sweet Pastures, and it was later turned into Myakka River State Park.

The influence of Bertha Palmer is best evidenced by the relocation of the town of Venice. Before she arrived in the area, a coastal settlement had been known as Venice since the 1880s. Palmer envisioned a seaside town to the south, with a million-dollar hotel, and granted permission for the railroad to extend its tracks to land she owned near the proposed hotel site. But she wanted the railroad station and new post office to have the name of Venice. She succeeded in having the name moved, although it was claimed she obtained enough signatures on her petition only by including transients and disreputable persons. Residents of the former Venice had to choose a new name, and in 1917 they decided on Nokomis, for the grandmother of Hiawatha in a poem by Henry Wadsworth Longfellow.

Bertha Palmer's influence was felt long after her death in 1918. Newspapers had reported she thought Sarasota Bay more beautiful than the Bay of Naples, so others from Palmer's Chicago headed south to see. They brought money and formed an upper crust of local society, setting themselves apart from the fishermen and farmers who made up a large part of the population. The new arrivals included Stanley and Sarah Field (of the Marshall Field department store family), Edson Keith, and Homer Galpin, the chairman of the Republican Party in Cook County, Illinois. From other regions came oil tycoon William G. Selby and New York Central Railroad executive Ralph C. Caples—and circus magnate John Ringling.

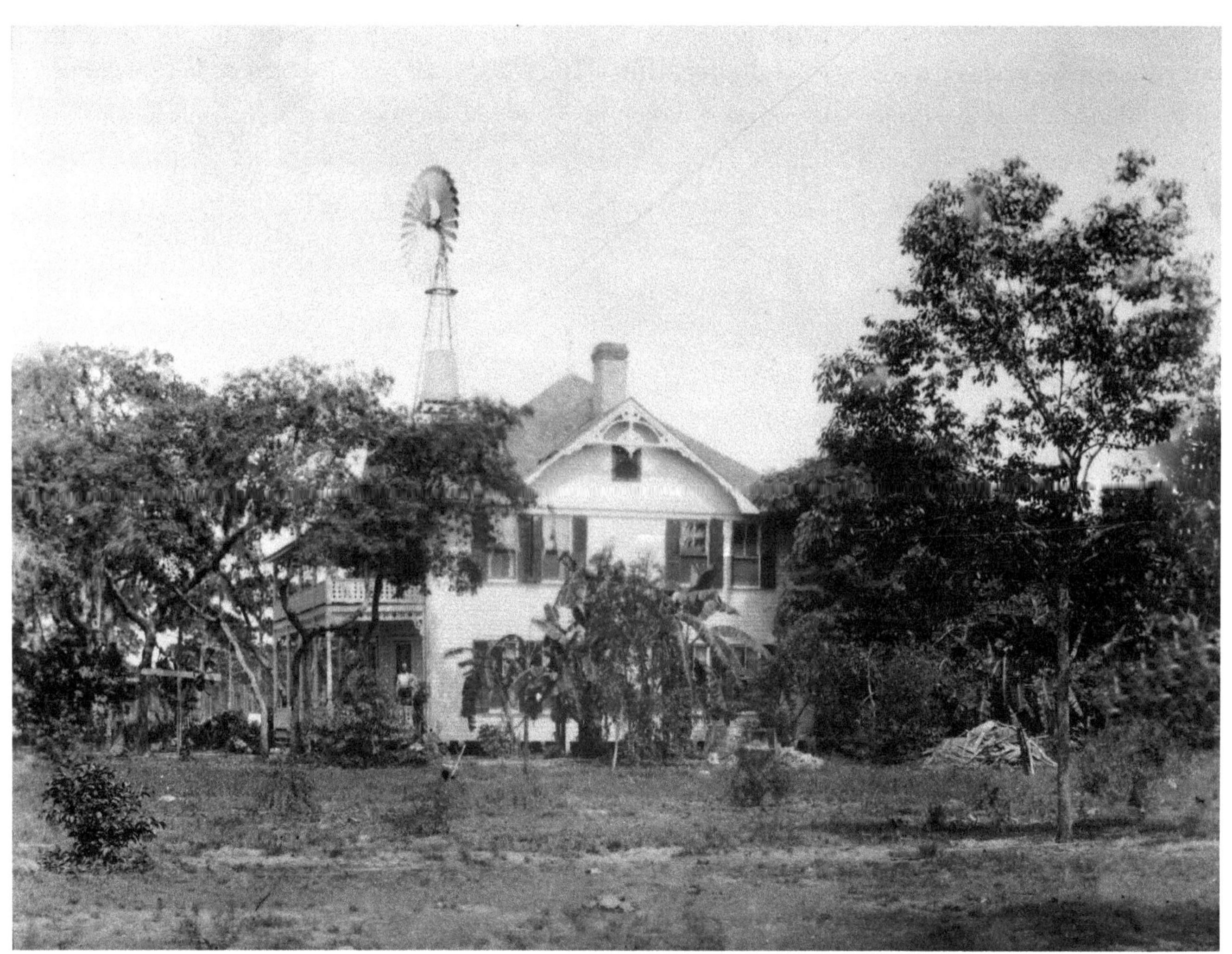

The Palms Hotel stood at Indian Beach, the site of an Indian village prior to the Seminole Wars. Some believe it was a landing site for Hernando de Soto during the 1500s. It attracted some of the richest settlers of Sarasota, including Colonel Charles N. Thompson, D. L. Wooster, and John and Charles Ringling. The hotel burned down in 1927.

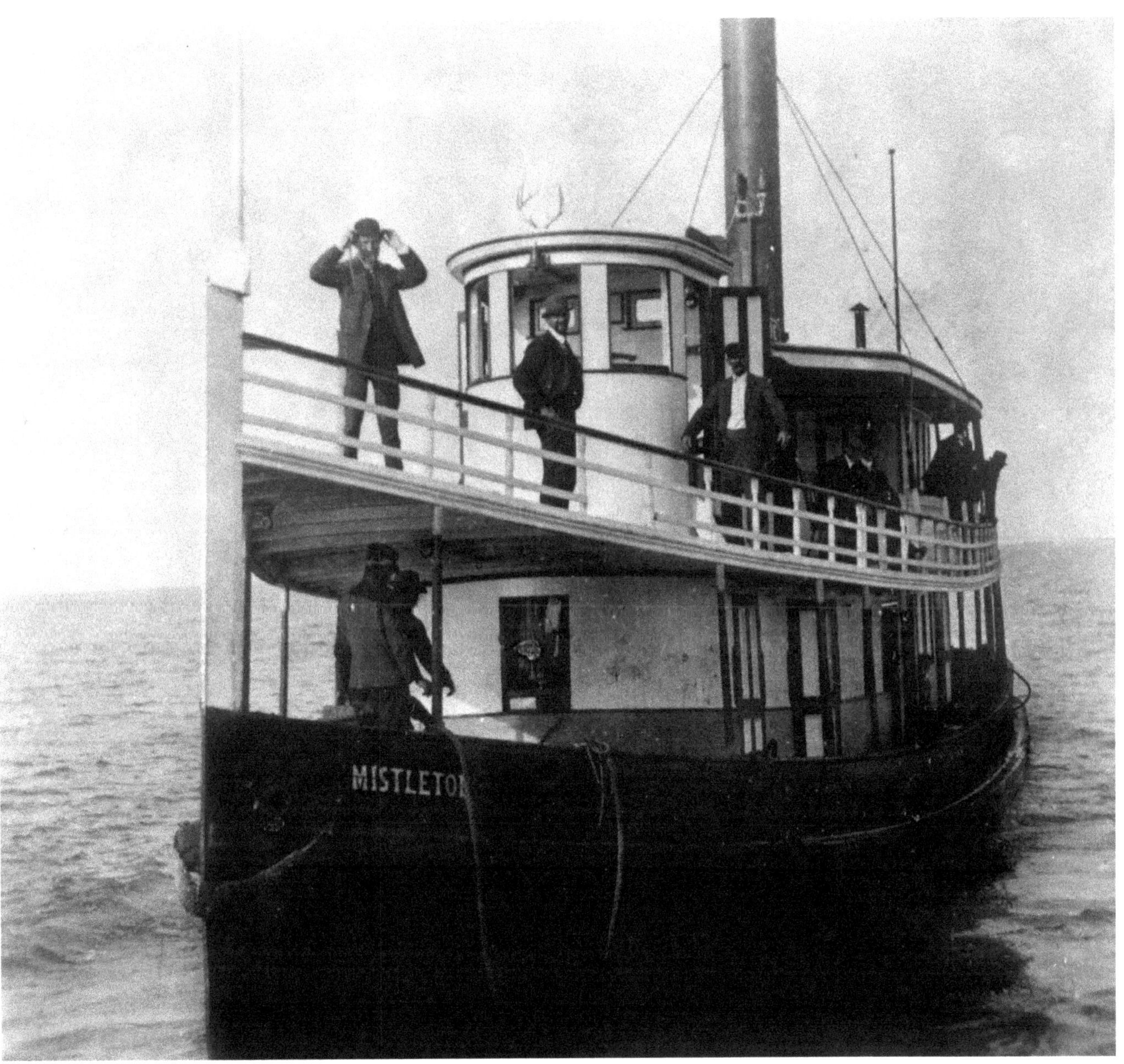

John Savarese's steamship *Mistletoe* began carrying passengers and freight to Tampa in 1895, powered by steam produced by burning pine logs. In the early days, this was the only way Sarasota obtained ice, which in turn enabled the fishing industry to thrive. The *Mistletoe* sank in 1910 in a hurricane. It was refloated, enlarged, and renamed the *City of Sarasota*.

Louis Roberts moved from Key West and settled on Siesta Key. An extension of his home there became the Roberts Hotel in 1906, famous for its views and clam chowder until it burned in 1919. Roberts operated the fishing boat shown here in Sarasota Bay, a popular place to land tarpon, with the Gillespie bathhouse seen in the background at the end of the pier.

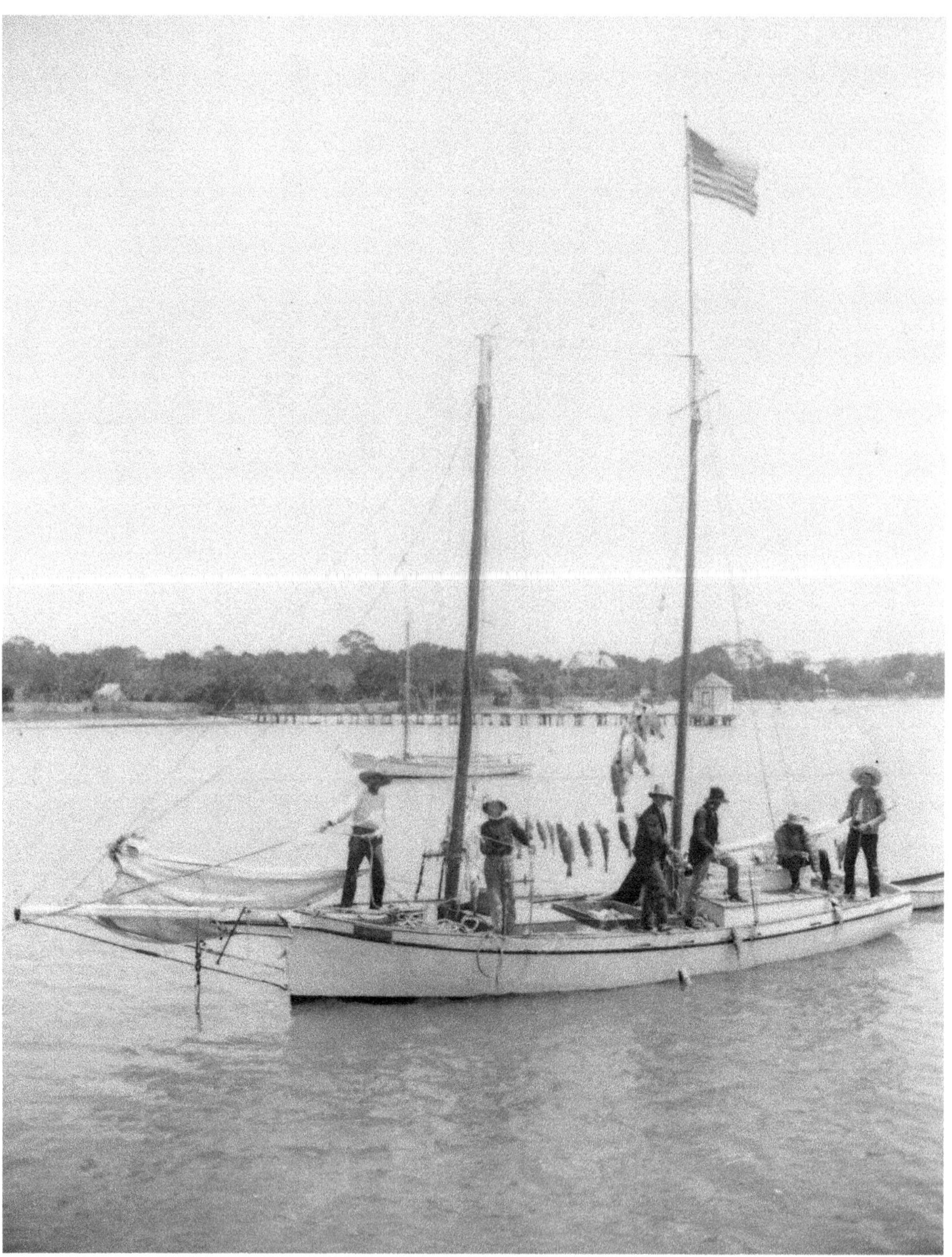

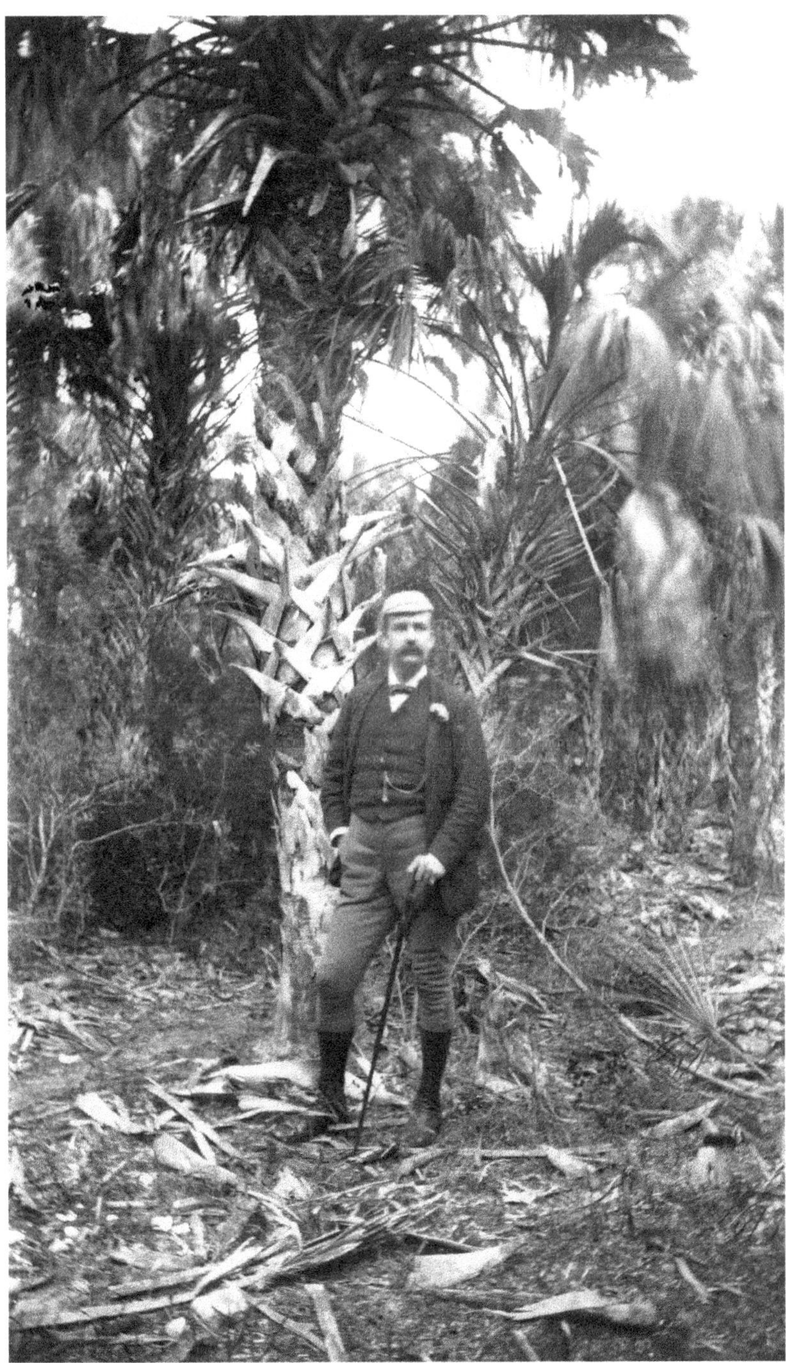

In May 1886, Colonel J. Hamilton Gillespie cleared the woods along Main Street and set out a long fairway for a golf course that some sources credit as having been the first in the United States. By 1905, the 110-acre tract included a full nine holes and a clubhouse. Nicknamed the Father of American Golf, Gillespie served as the first mayor of Sarasota and died in 1923 while playing golf on the course he created.

Seaboard Air Line Railway employees lay track at Sarasota's Sixth Street, while Frank Pinard, Frank Higel, Bone Hogan, and Bill Jeffcoat look on. In 1902, news that the railroad was coming motivated residents to incorporate the town. A rail line was laid to Venice in 1912, but it had little business and was closed in 1921.

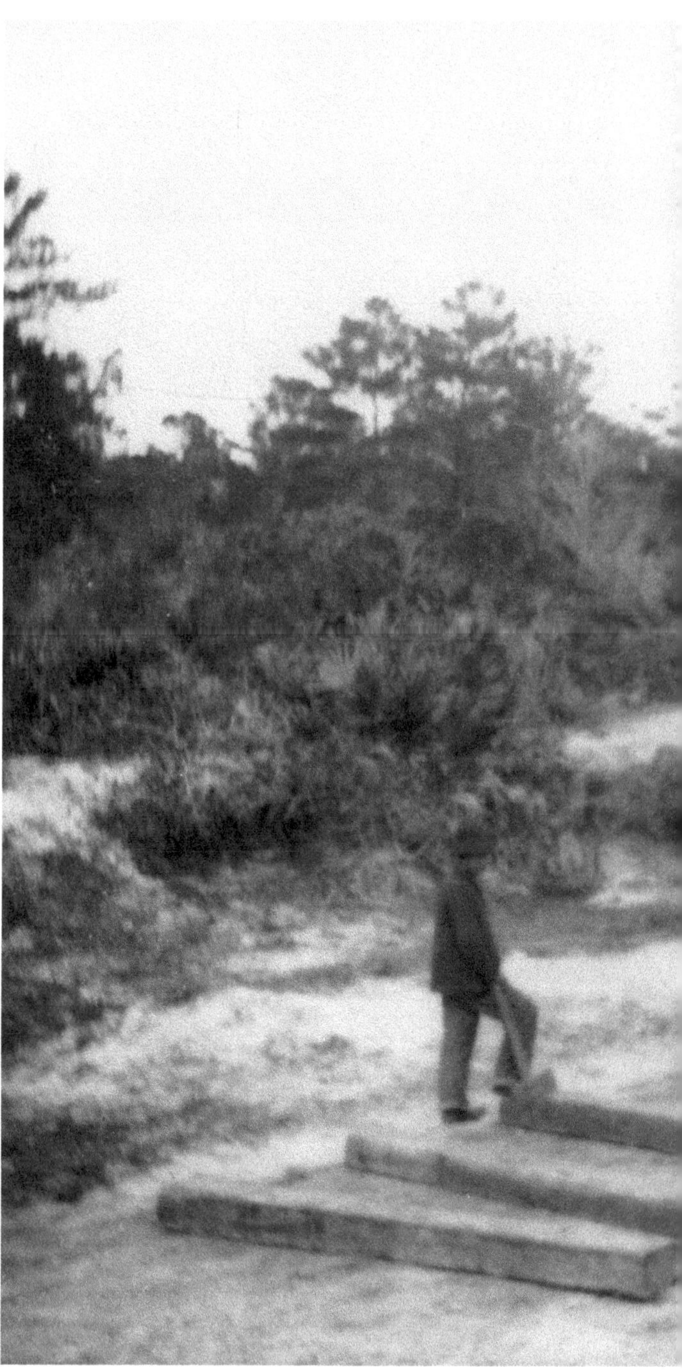

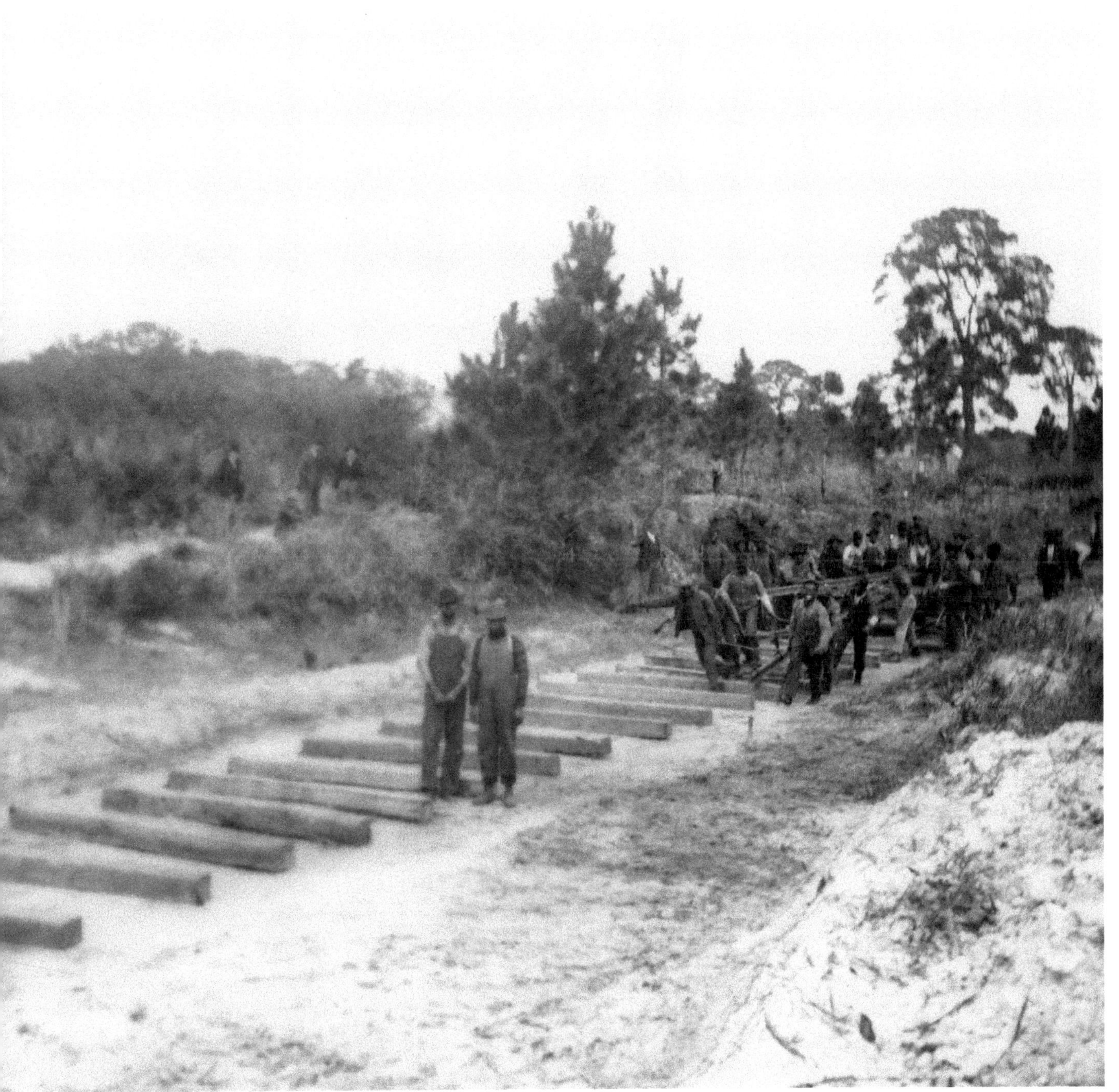

Dr. Leffinwell and Dr. Warren toast their successful day of fishing. Sarasota became known as a fishing village after the 1894-95 freezes decimated the citrus and vegetable crops. The fishing industry thrived in 1898, especially, when soldiers around Tampa needed fish to eat while waiting for deployment in the Spanish-American War.

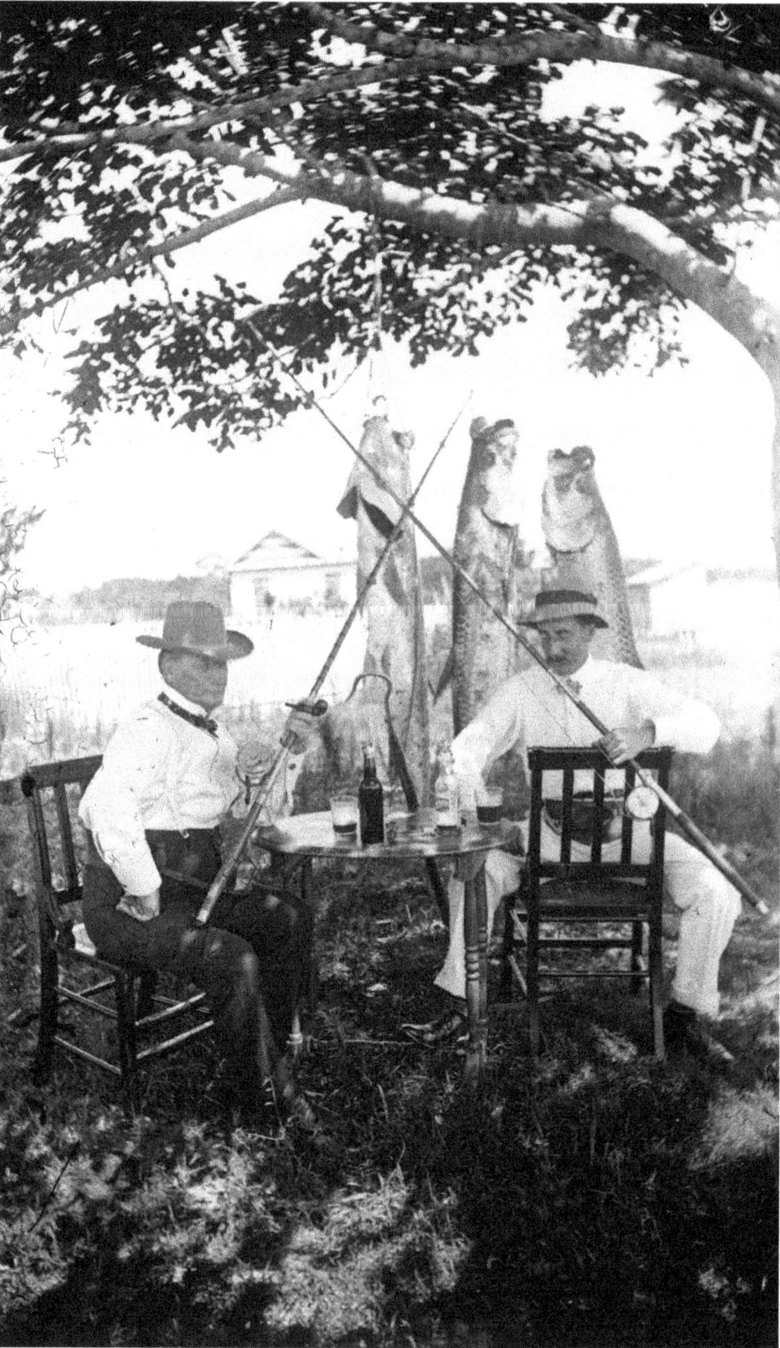

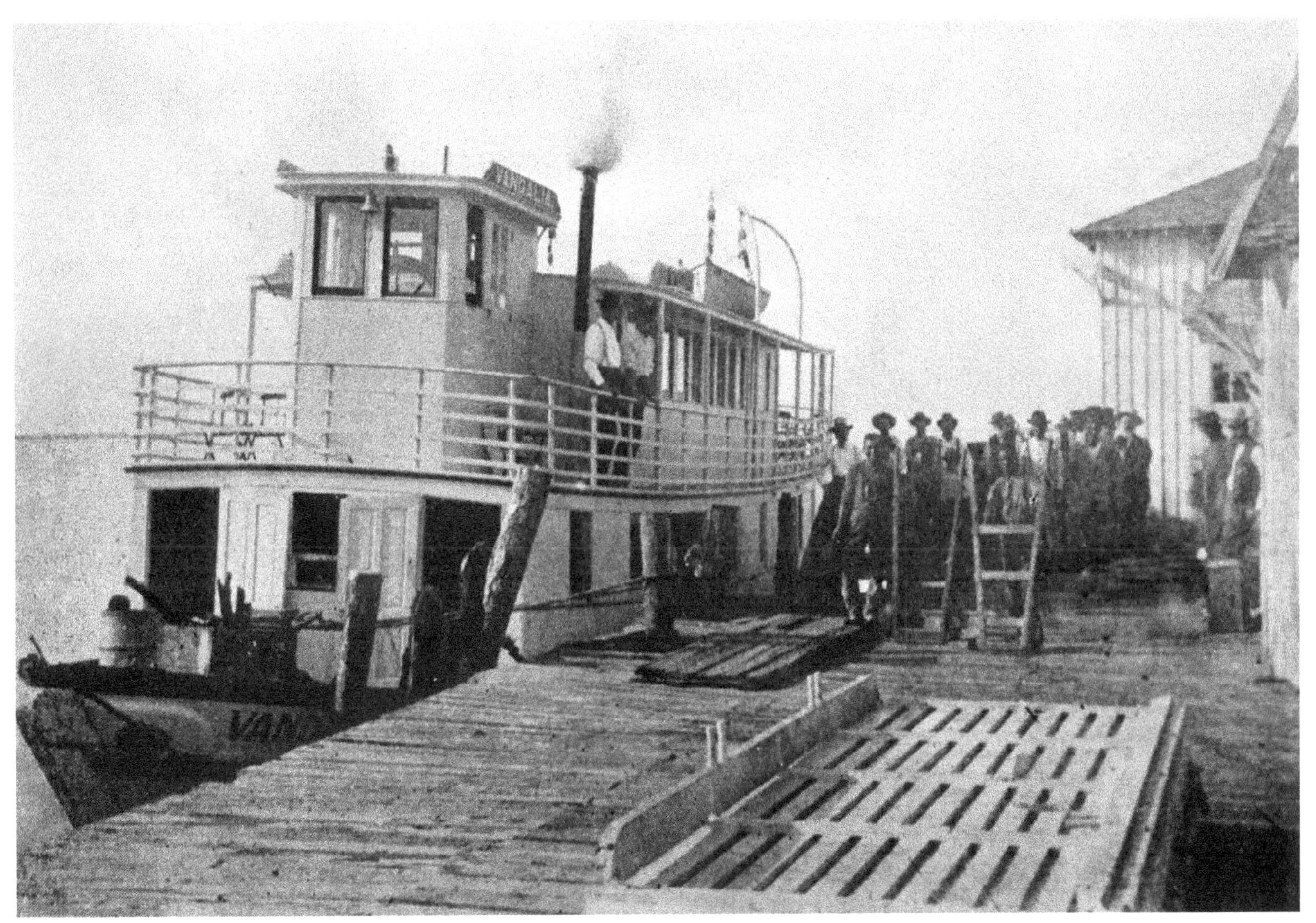

Fish dealer John Savarese owned the steamboat *Mistletoe* and made three runs a week between Tampa and Sarasota. In 1907, he experienced difficult economic times and ceased carrying freight and passengers. The route was continued by Harry Higel, who purchased the *Vandalia,* shown here, and made regular runs with passengers, fish, and ice.

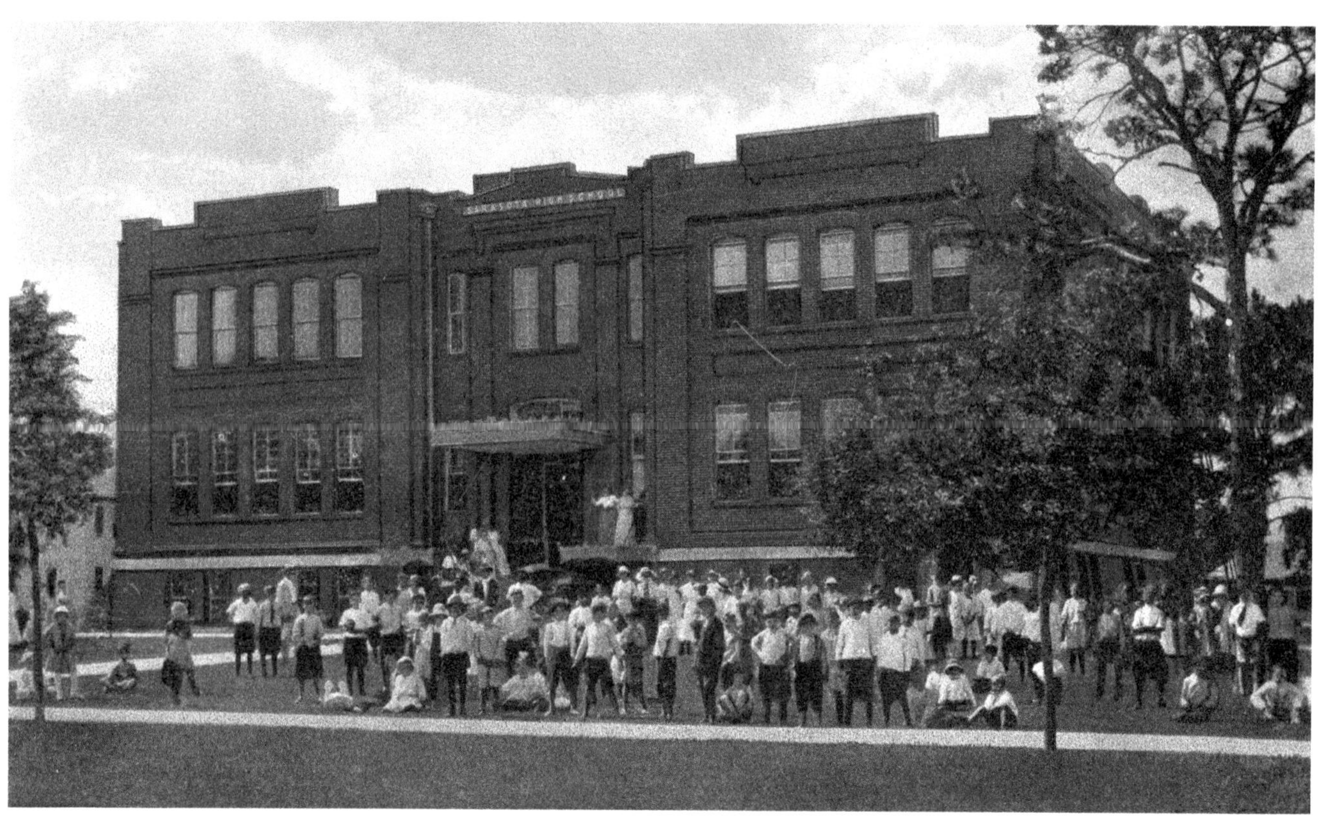

The first schoolhouse in Sarasota was built in 1904 on Main Street, across from the present-day site of the First Baptist Church. The brick school pictured here, Sarasota High School, built in 1913, had eleven classrooms and an auditorium. Town leaders predicted it would satisfy educational needs for a decade, but it opened with 350 students and was instantly overcrowded.

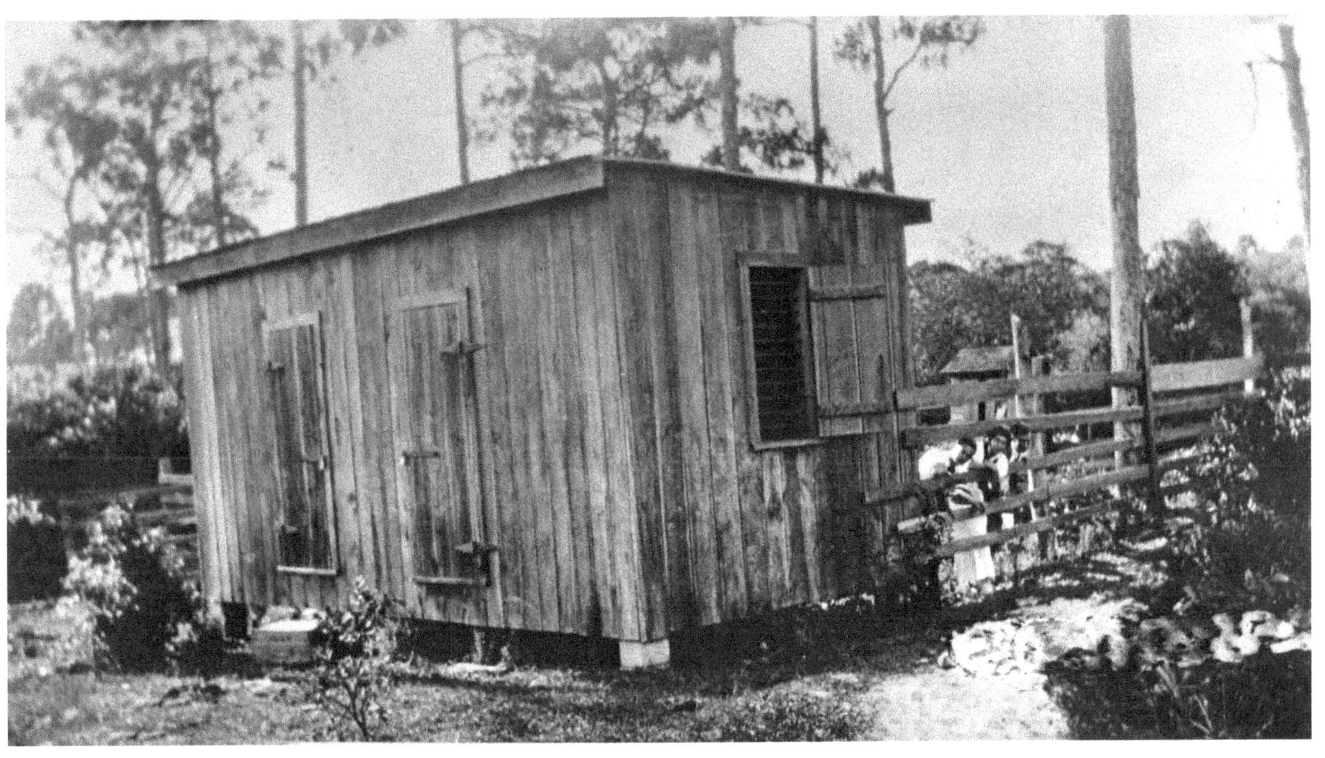

Photographed in 1911, this small wooden structure served as the Sarasota jail. It was located along Lemon Street, and its oppressively hot interior during the summertime may have been a deterrent for budding criminals. It was replaced by a larger and stronger structure made of concrete blocks.

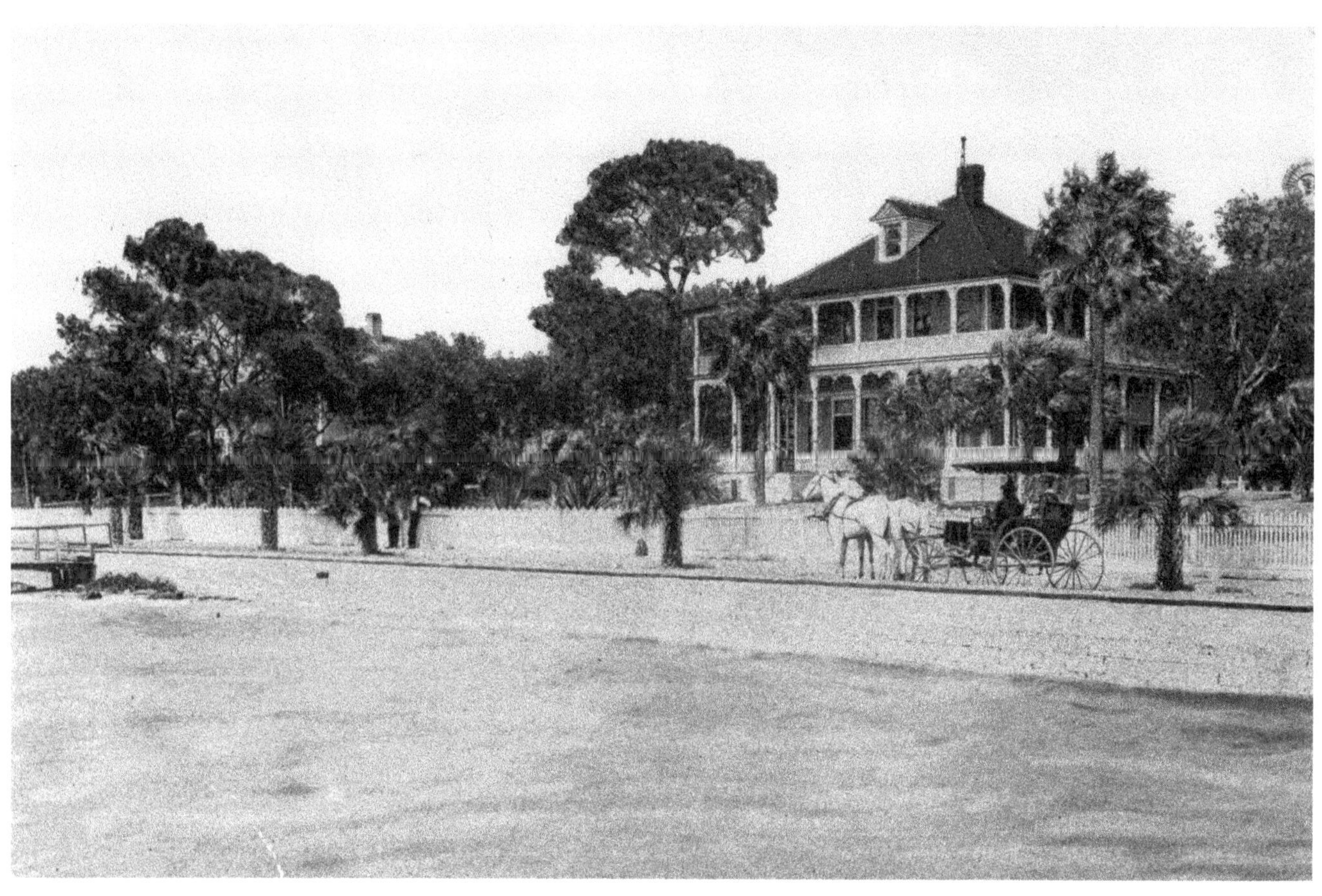

Horses pull a carriage past one of the stately homes on Bay Shore Drive, which hugged the shoreline, in 1913. As time went on, larger and more magnificent homes were constructed in this area. Bay Shore Drive's residents included railroad executive Ralph Caples, circus man John Ringling, and Charles Thompson, who had managed Buffalo Bill's Wild West Show.

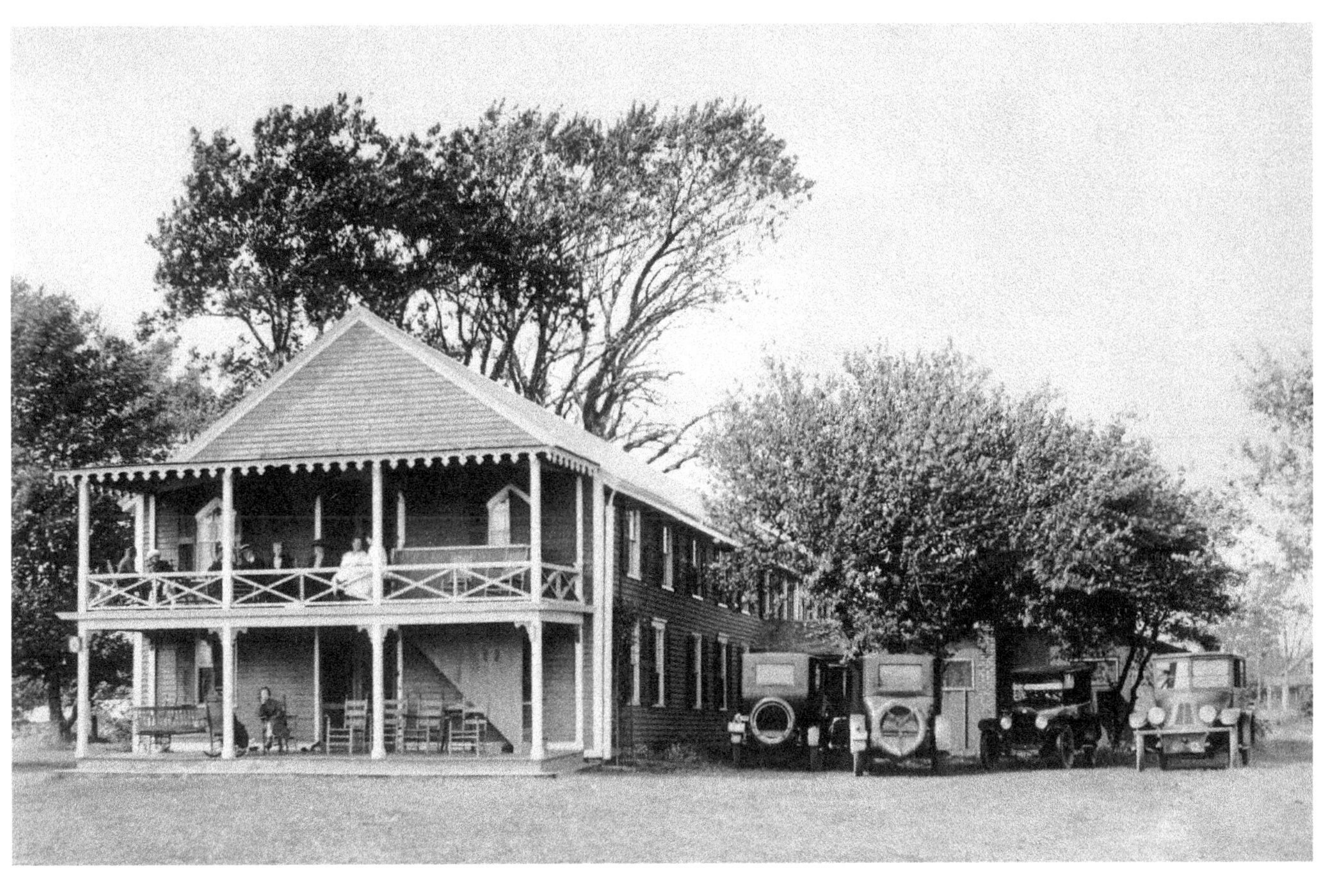

Early Sarasota had several hotels, like this one, that catered to tourists. One was the Higelhurst Hotel, a two-story building on the shore served by the boat *Siesta,* which took visitors to Siesta Key. The Higelhurst burned down in 1917. Another was J. B. Chapline's Bay View Hotel, at the corner of Main Street and Palm Avenue, which burned on November 5, 1908.

This early machine shop was located on Longboat Key, to the northwest of downtown Sarasota and partly in Manatee County. The area today is known more for its beautiful beaches and resorts than for its industrial activities.

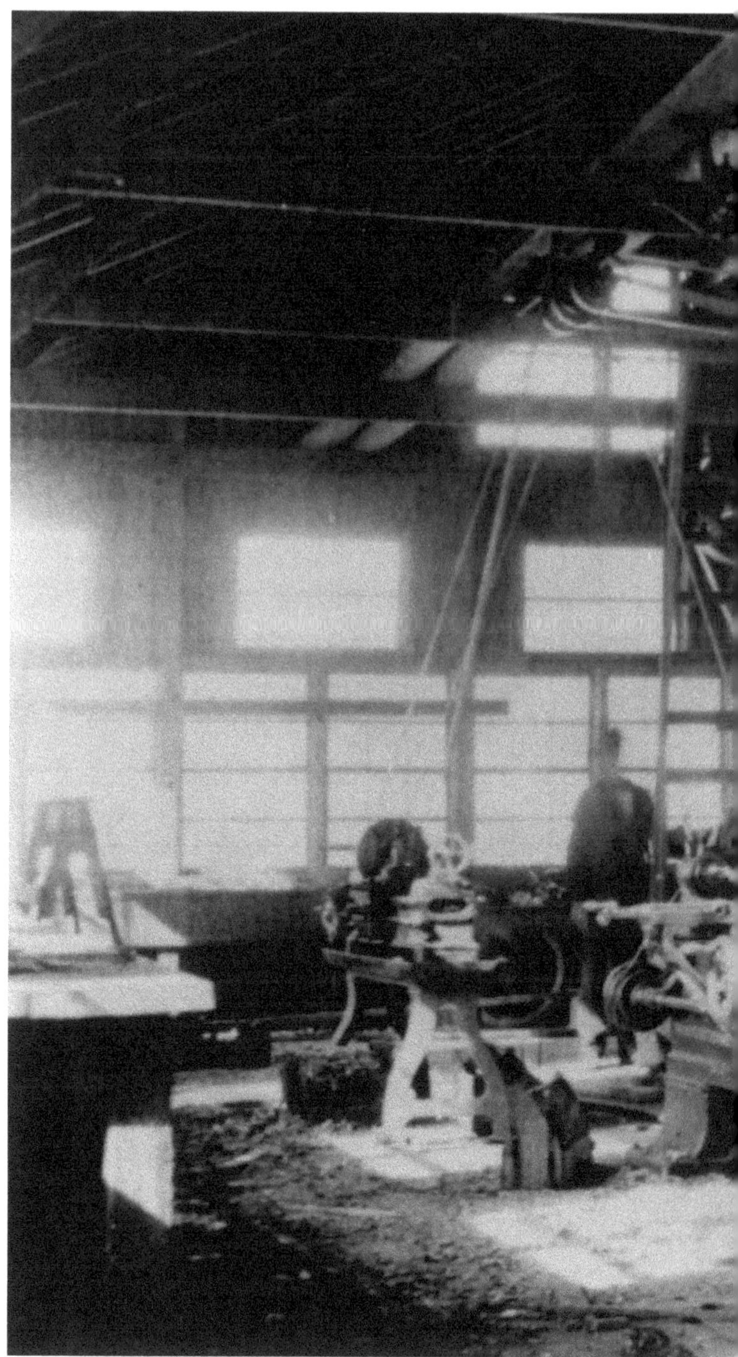

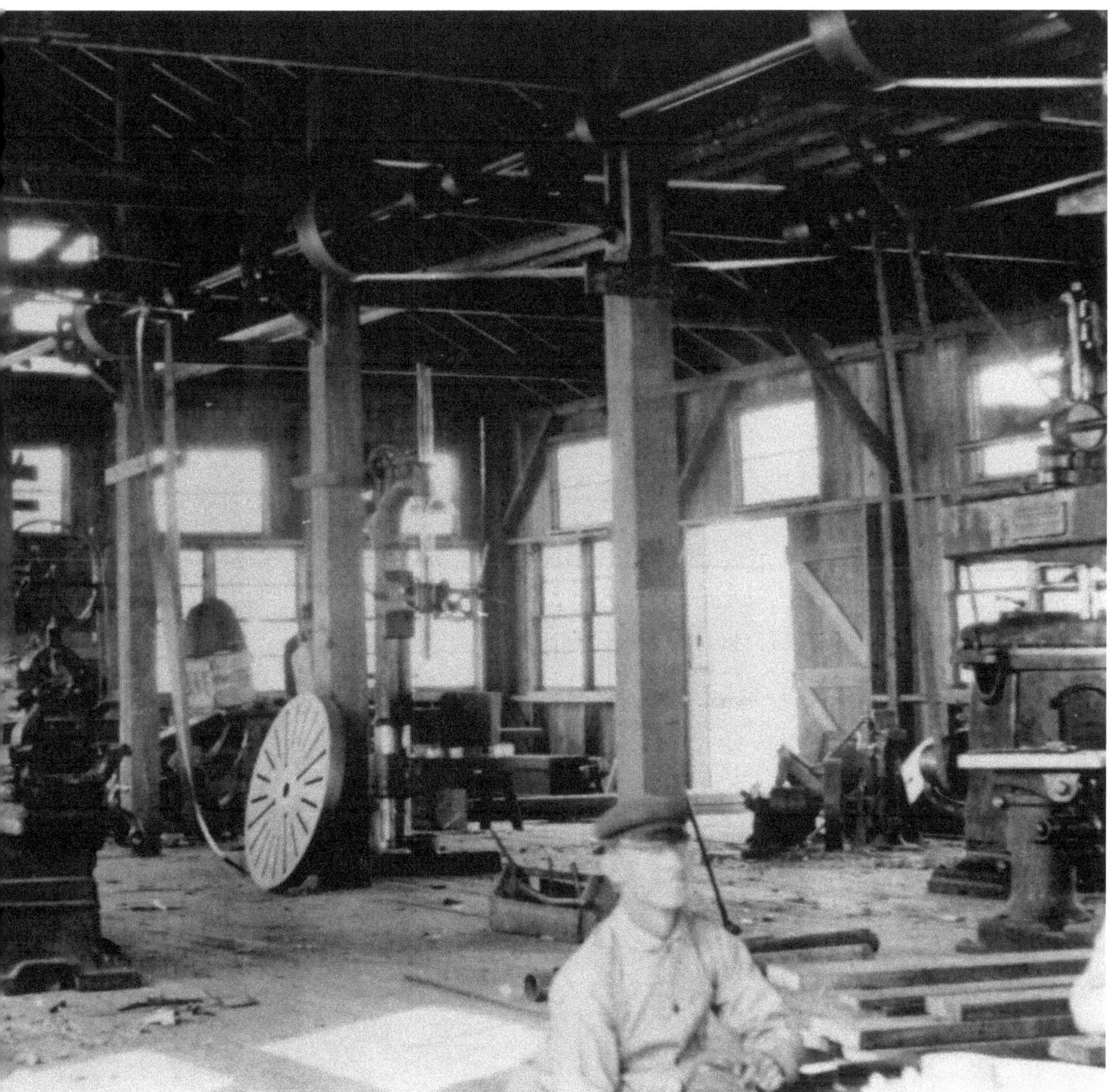

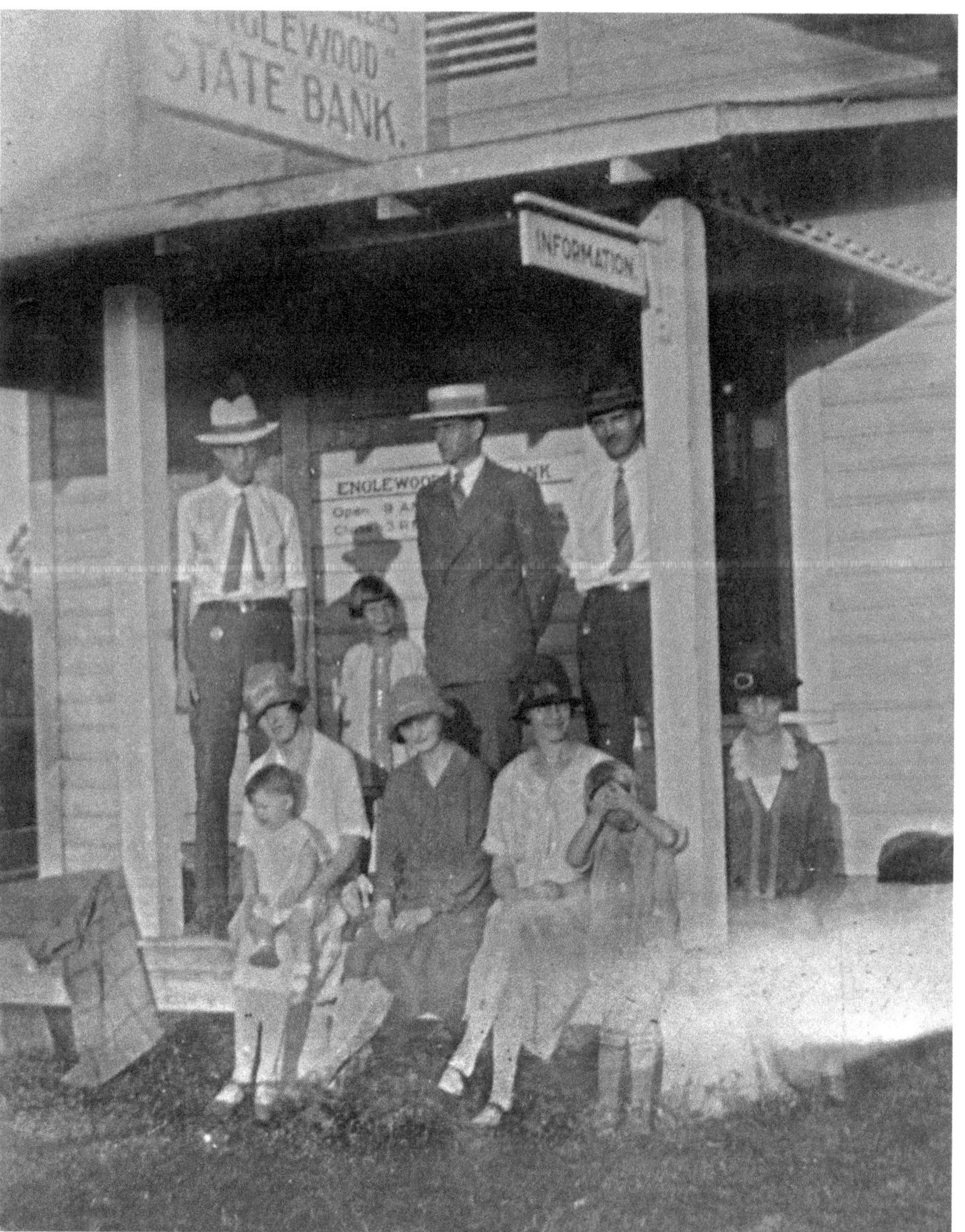

Founded by Herbert N. Nichols of Chicago in 1896 and named for a Chicago suburb, Englewood sits at the southernmost point of the county. The building shown here functioned as the temporary home of the Englewood State Bank, some time after the turn of the century. Served by the Englewood Inn from 1897 until 1910, many tourists visited the area.

The Circus Man Comes to Town

(1920–1929)

John and Mable Ringling visited Sarasota for the first time in 1911; they later returned to spend time with Ralph and Ellen Caples and neighbors Charles and Mary Louise Thompson. In 1912, the Ringlings purchased the Thompson house, Palms Elysian, to serve as temporary lodging while they built the winter home of their dreams. Later that year, Charles and Edith Ringling, John's brother and sister-in-law, built a vacation mansion on adjoining property. John's main home and the front office for the Ringling Brothers and Barnum and Bailey Circus remained in New York City.

During World War I, Ringling turned his attention to Sarasota and its development. Over the next decade, he acquired land on Longboat Key, Bird Key, Shell Beach, Lido Beach, and elsewhere. His development efforts helped create a postwar economic boom. Sarasota became a destination for those looking for jobs and potential investment. During the mid-1920s, the Brotherhood of Locomotive Engineers purchased 30,000 acres south of Sarasota, including the village of Venice begun by Bertha Palmer. The union hired New York architects to lay out a town that would include a business district, hotels, a bank, and a theater, and turned the area into the town of Venice.

Another Ringling contribution to last was the development of Bird Key, accessible because he built the first causeway connecting it to the mainland. He partnered with Owen Burns of Maryland, who had already begun projects in downtown Sarasota following his purchase of three-fourths of the city from the Florida Mortgage and Investment Company. Ringling and Burns created an upscale shopping district on the island and named it St. Armands, after an early homesteader who served as an engineer on the first locomotive arriving in Sarasota.

Near the end of the 1920s, Ringling began the construction of an art museum to hold his collection. The Ringling home, which he named Cà d'Zan, was filled with Venetian art and was used for entertaining such friends as the governor of Florida and the inventor Thomas Edison. Ringling was a busy man, however, and it has been estimated that he spent only about 90 days in his Sarasota home during the seven years he owned it. Nevertheless, his influence on the growth of Sarasota and the entire county was enormous, through his transformation of the city into a cultural center, his impact on its real estate development, and his making Sarasota the winter headquarters of the Ringling circus.

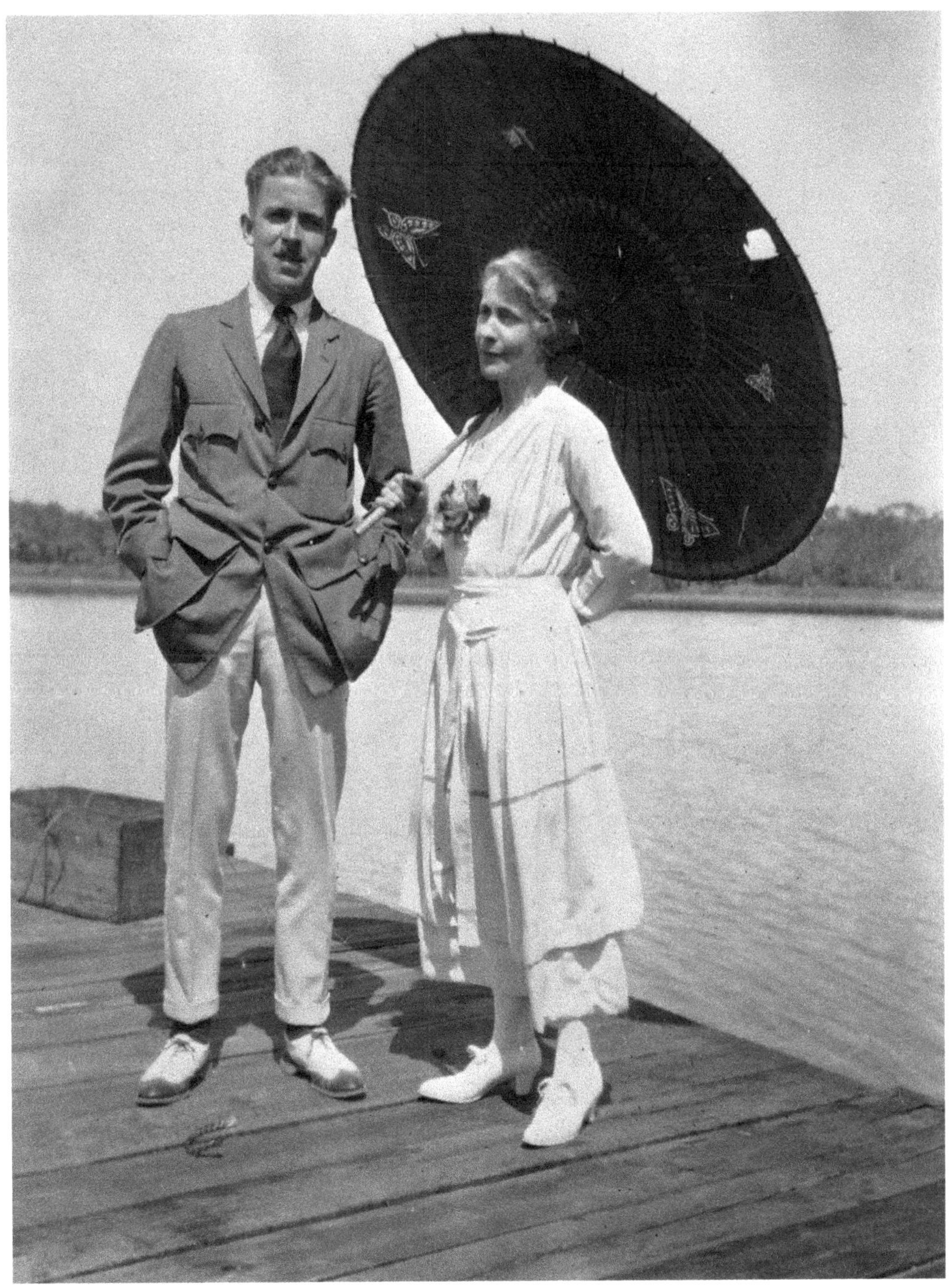

By 1860, Edson Keith, Sr., was heavily involved in a family company that grew to be Chicago's leading wholesale millinery house. He also was active in real estate development through Edson Keith & Co., starting in the 1880s. One of his sons, Edson Jr., shown here in 1920 with his wife, settled in Sarasota.

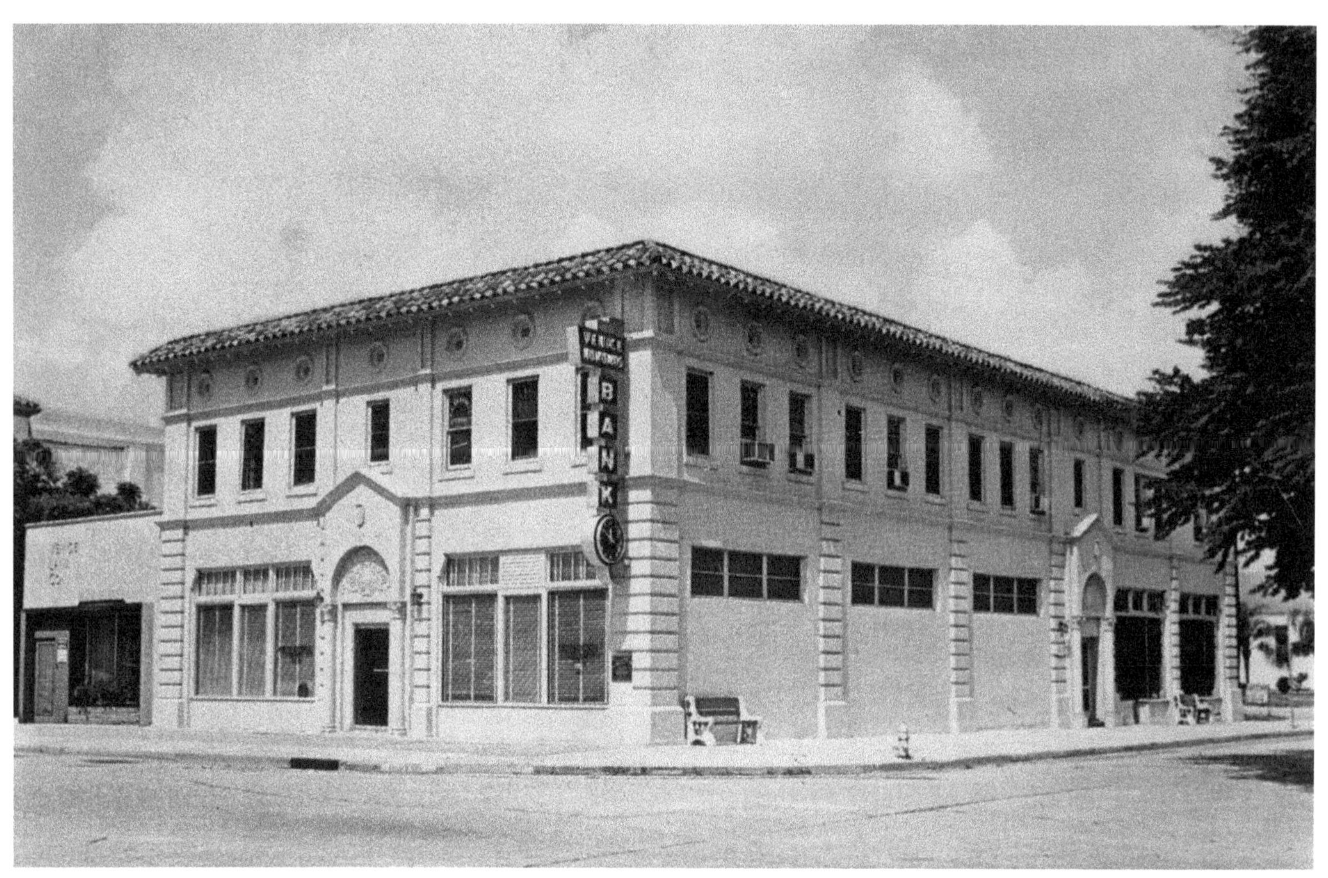

The area which became Venice and Nokomis was first settled by Jesse Knight, who arrived in 1868. The two towns were split at the request of Bertha Palmer, with Roberts Bay dividing them. The Venice-Nokomis Bank shown here was founded in 1925 by Fred H. Albee, who also started the Venice-Nokomis Chamber of Commerce.

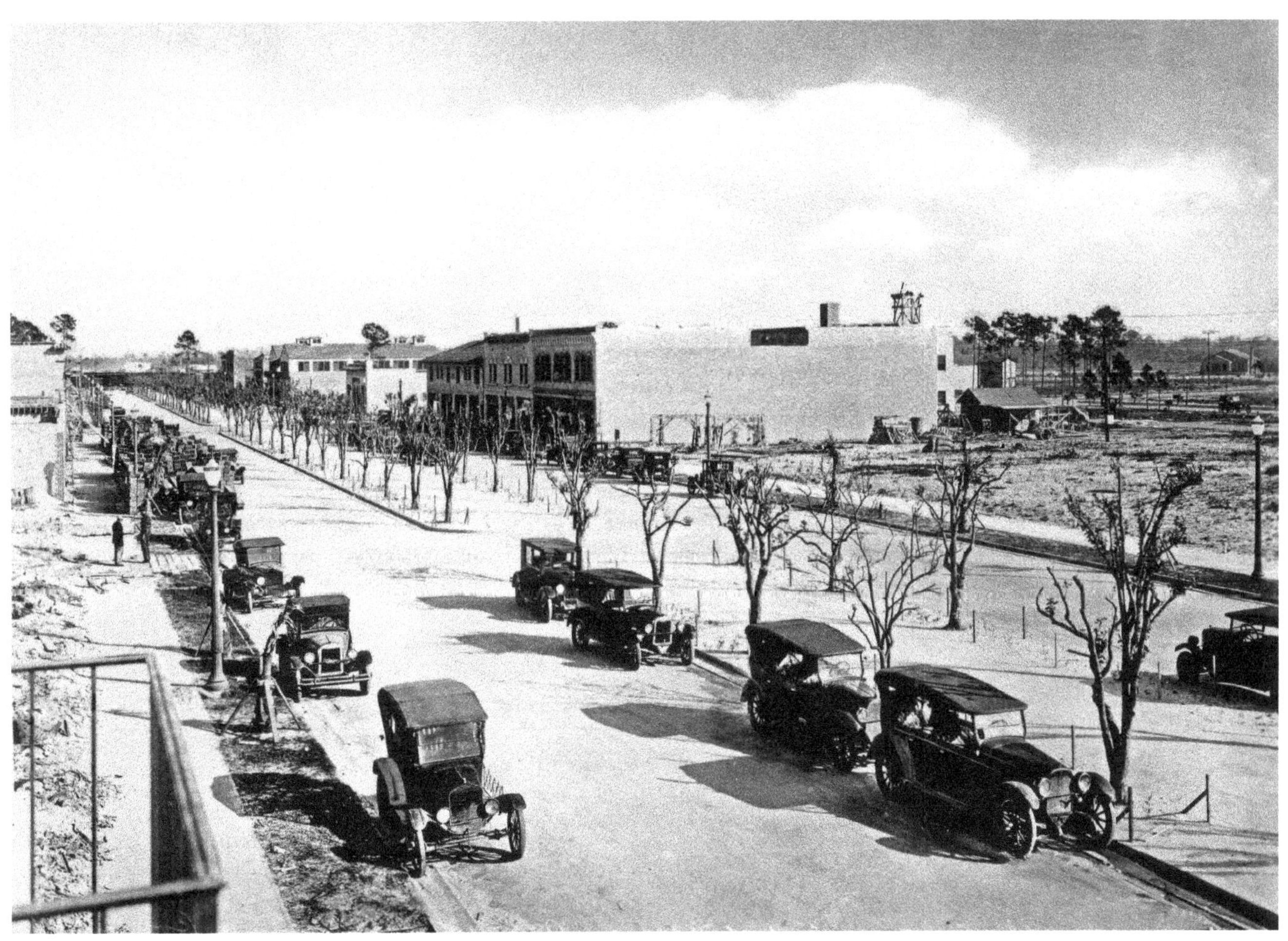

Dr. Fred H. Albee commissioned urban planner John Nolen to design the city of Venice, but before construction began, Albee sold the land to a labor union. The New York firm of Walker and Gillette revised Nolen's plans. Nassau Street was the first thoroughfare to open, on June 10, 1926. Not long afterward, Venice Avenue, shown here, was paved.

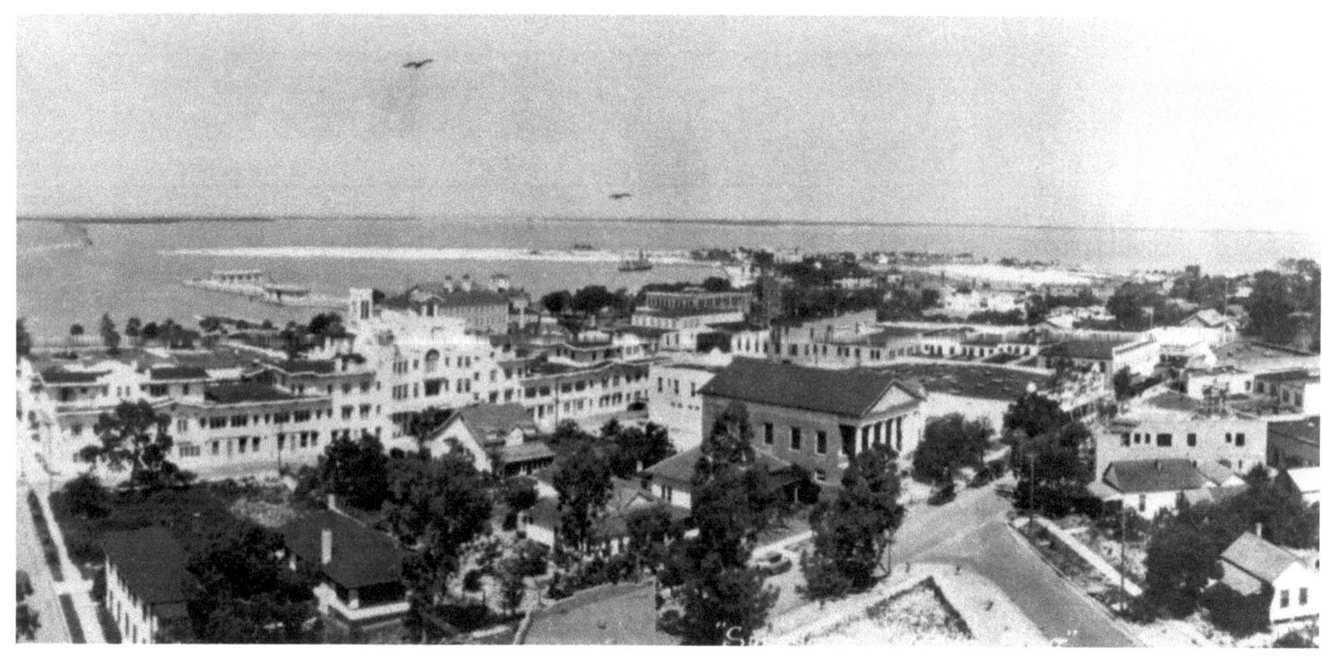

Andrew McAnsh built a hotel, auditorium, and apartment complex in exchange for free water and electricity, and a decade of no property taxes. Work on the apartments began in 1922 and was completed 60 days later, then he started on the auditorium and the Mira Mar Hotel, the four-story white building just to the left of center in this 1924 Sarasota view.

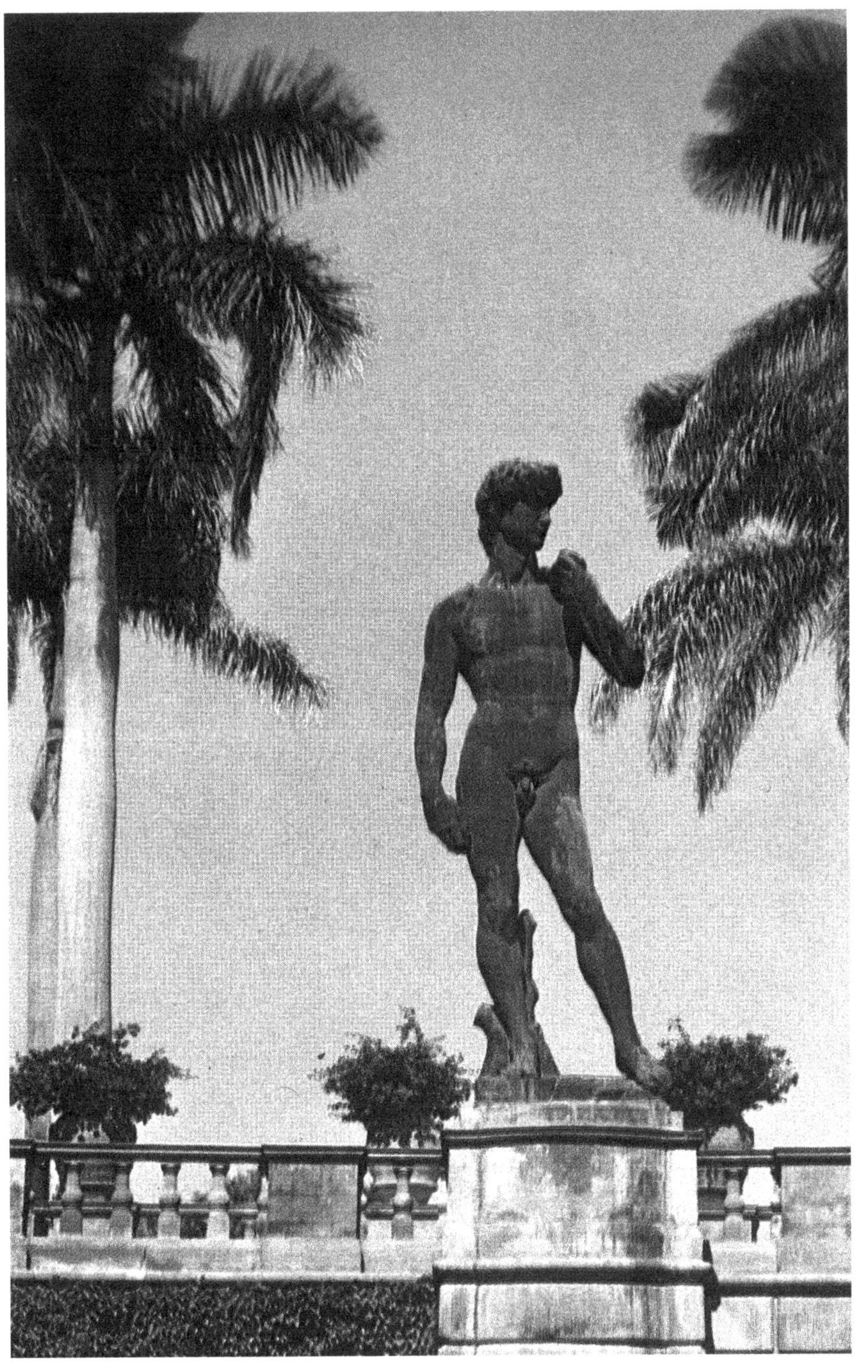

This full-size, bronze replica of Michelangelo's *David* commands a view of the beautifully landscaped courtyard of the Ringling Museum of Art. It is the best-known piece in the collection and, at a height of 16 feet, one of the largest. It was cast at the Chiurazzi foundry in Naples using forms which had produced other copies in 1874.

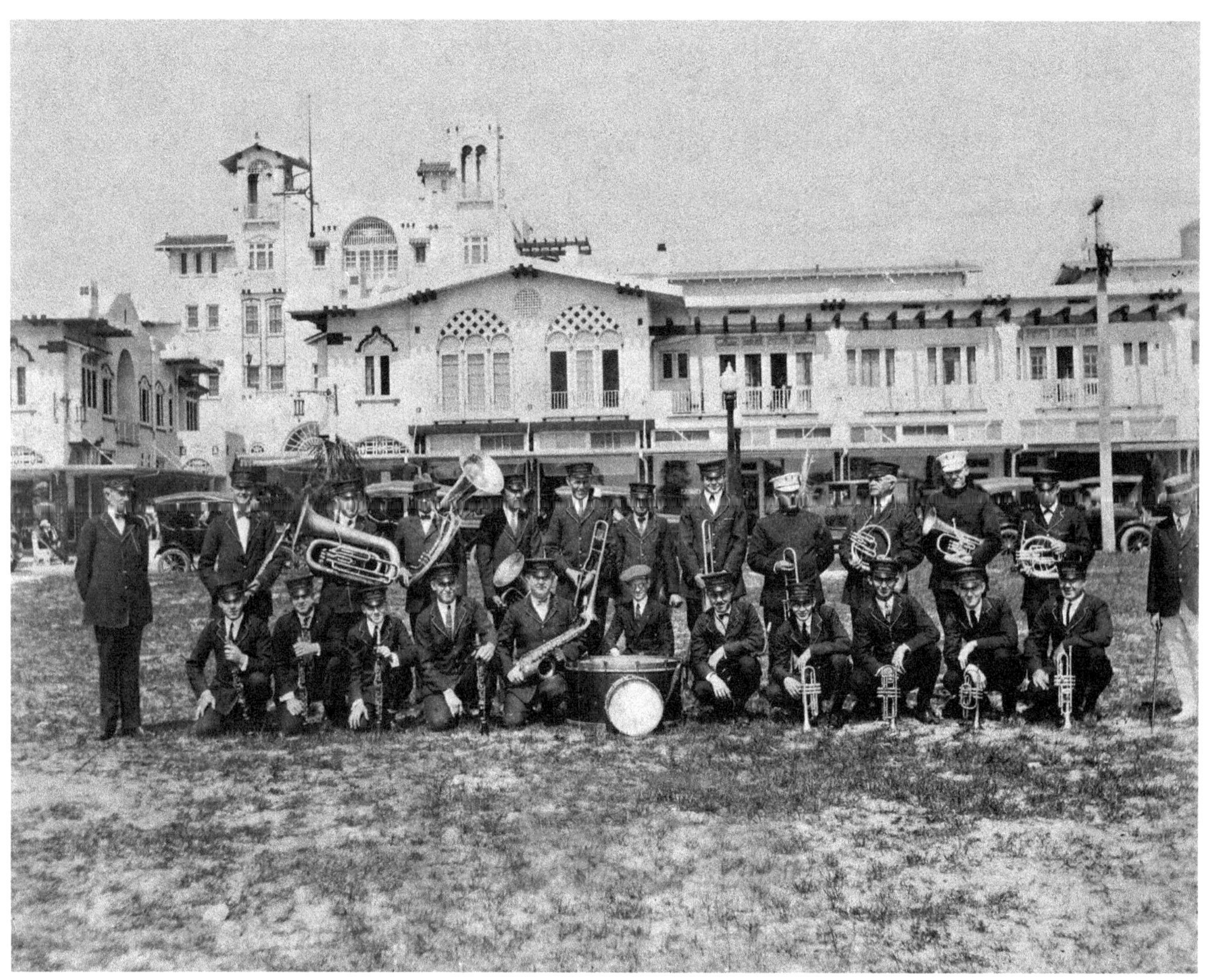

This is the Kiwanis Band in 1924, just two years after the local Kiwanis chapter was founded with 68 members. The band was composed of members from Sarasota and Manatee counties. Until 1921, Sarasota County was part of the large Manatee County, with Bradenton as its county seat.

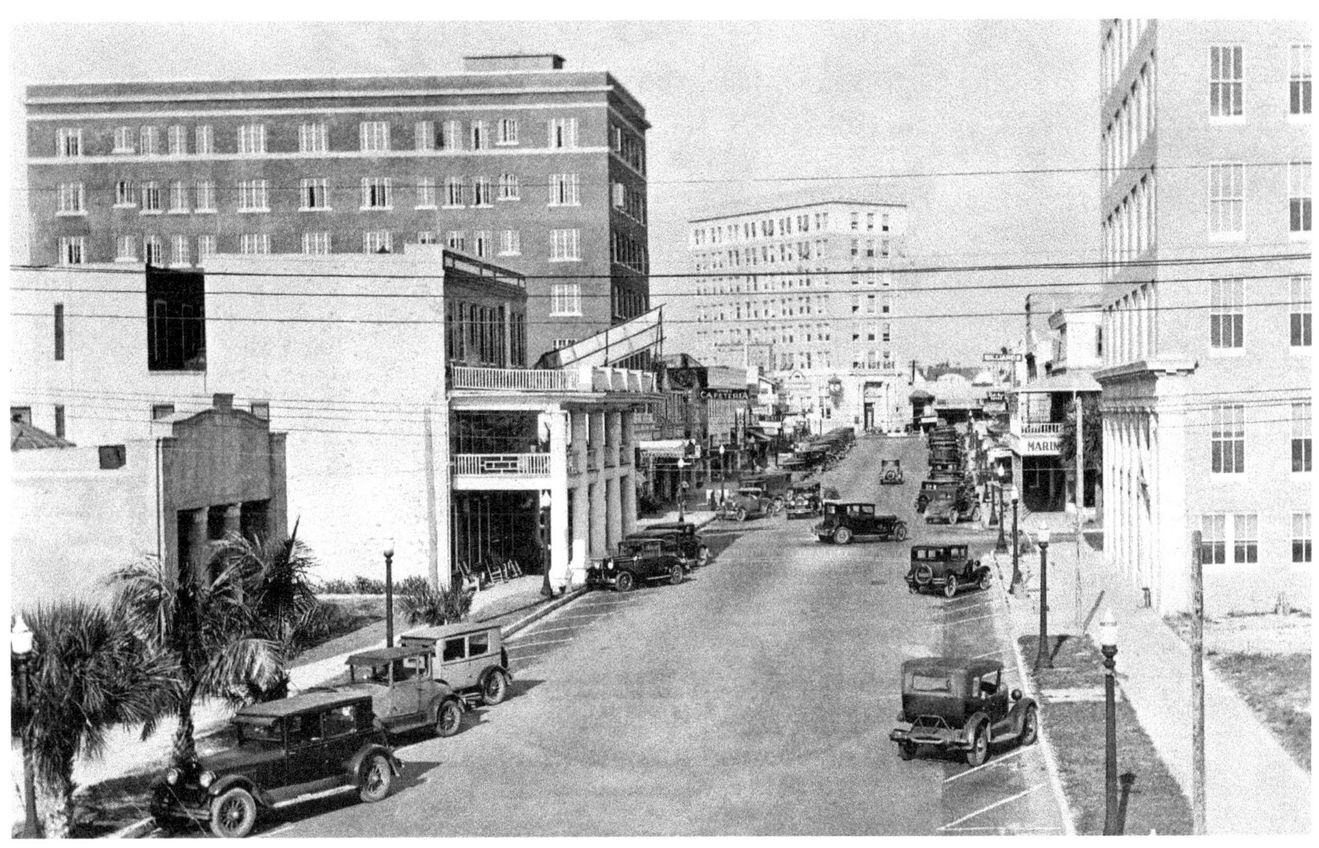

In this view looking east on Main Street toward Five Points during the 1920s, the building on the left with the white columns is the Watrous Hotel, later renamed the Colonial Hotel. It housed part of the New York Giants baseball team when the Giants began holding spring training in Sarasota in 1924. The hotel was torn down in 1962.

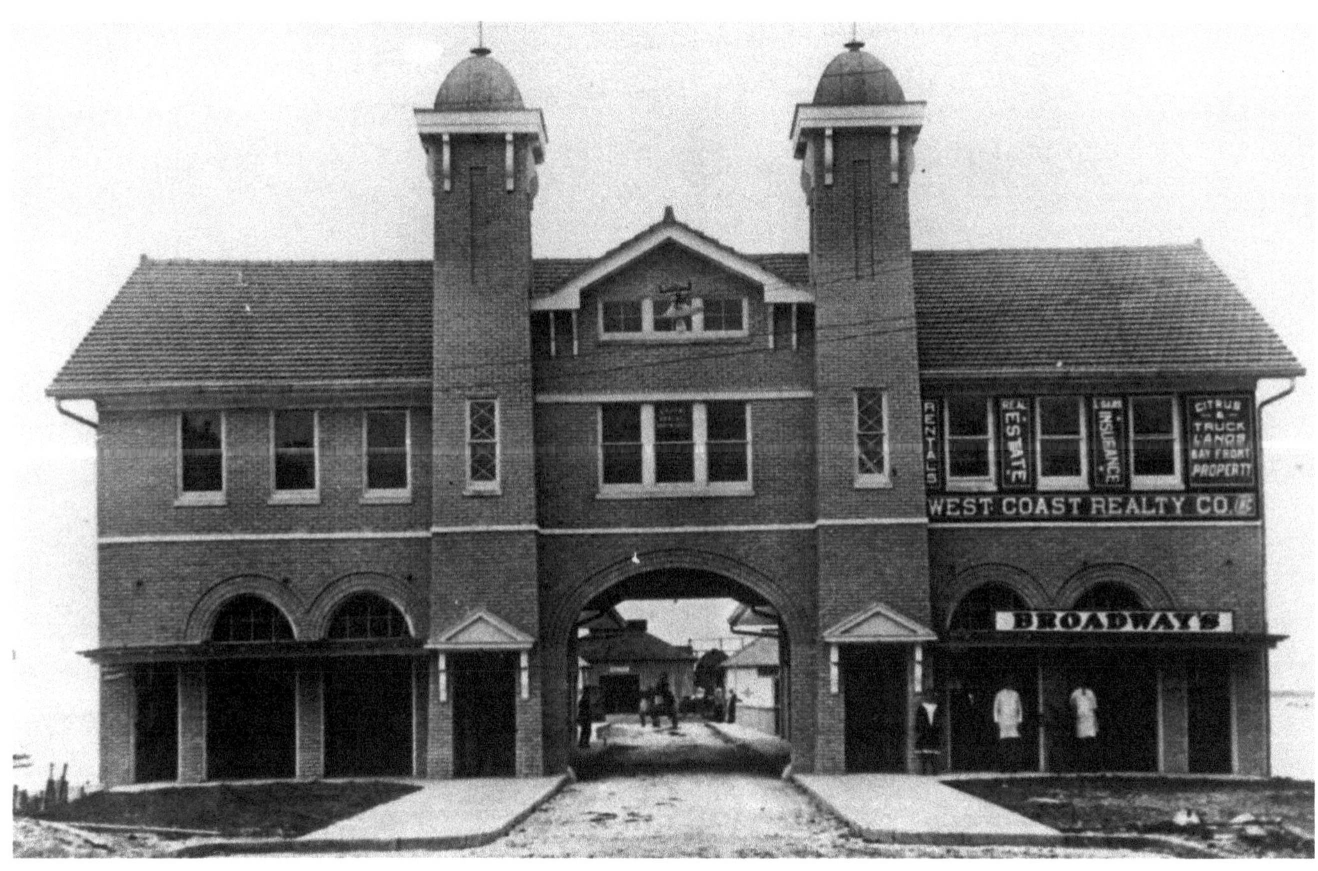

W. E., J.O., and Frank B. Hover purchased the pier from Harry Higel, extended it, and in 1913 built the archway and building shown here. The Arcade Building included Dave Broadway's restaurant, an ice cream parlor, and a movie theater. In 1917, the city bought the building, which became Sarasota City Hall. It was torn down in September of 1967.

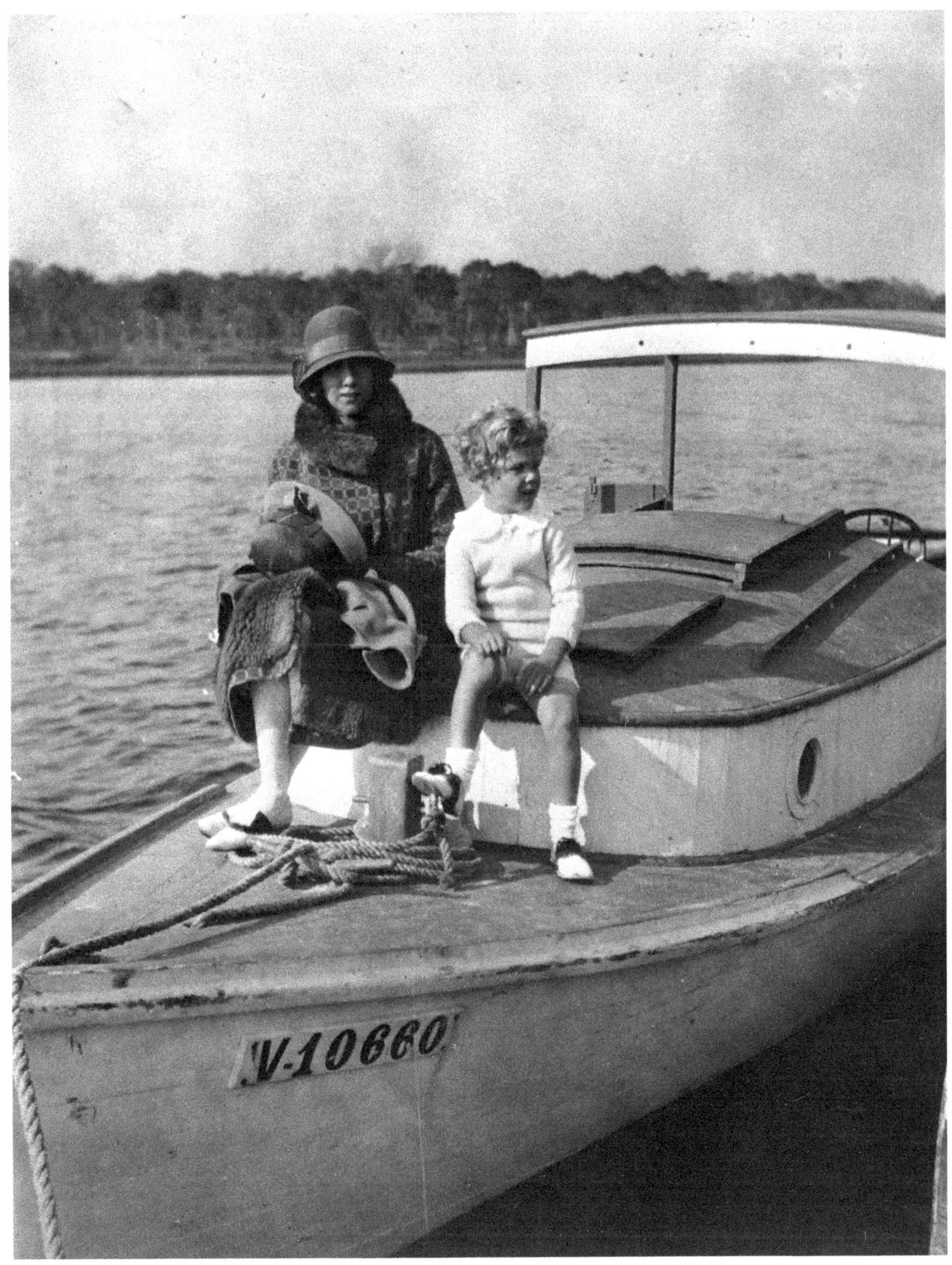

Edson Keith, Jr., active in the Chicago businesses started by his father and uncles, chose to move to Sarasota. He sold his interest in Edson Keith & Co. in 1901 but retained his position with the hat company, which continued to operate in Chicago and Milwaukee through the 1920s. Edson Jr.'s wife, Nettie, is seen here with their son Frederick.

In 1916, the Keiths built an Italian Renaissance–style home on 60 acres along Phillippi Creek, based on the design of Otis and Clark of Chicago. Despite living in Florida year-round, Edson Jr. remained active in the family business, which sold hats and gloves to Marshall Field and other stores. Here, son Jimmy Keith plays with his mechanical dog.

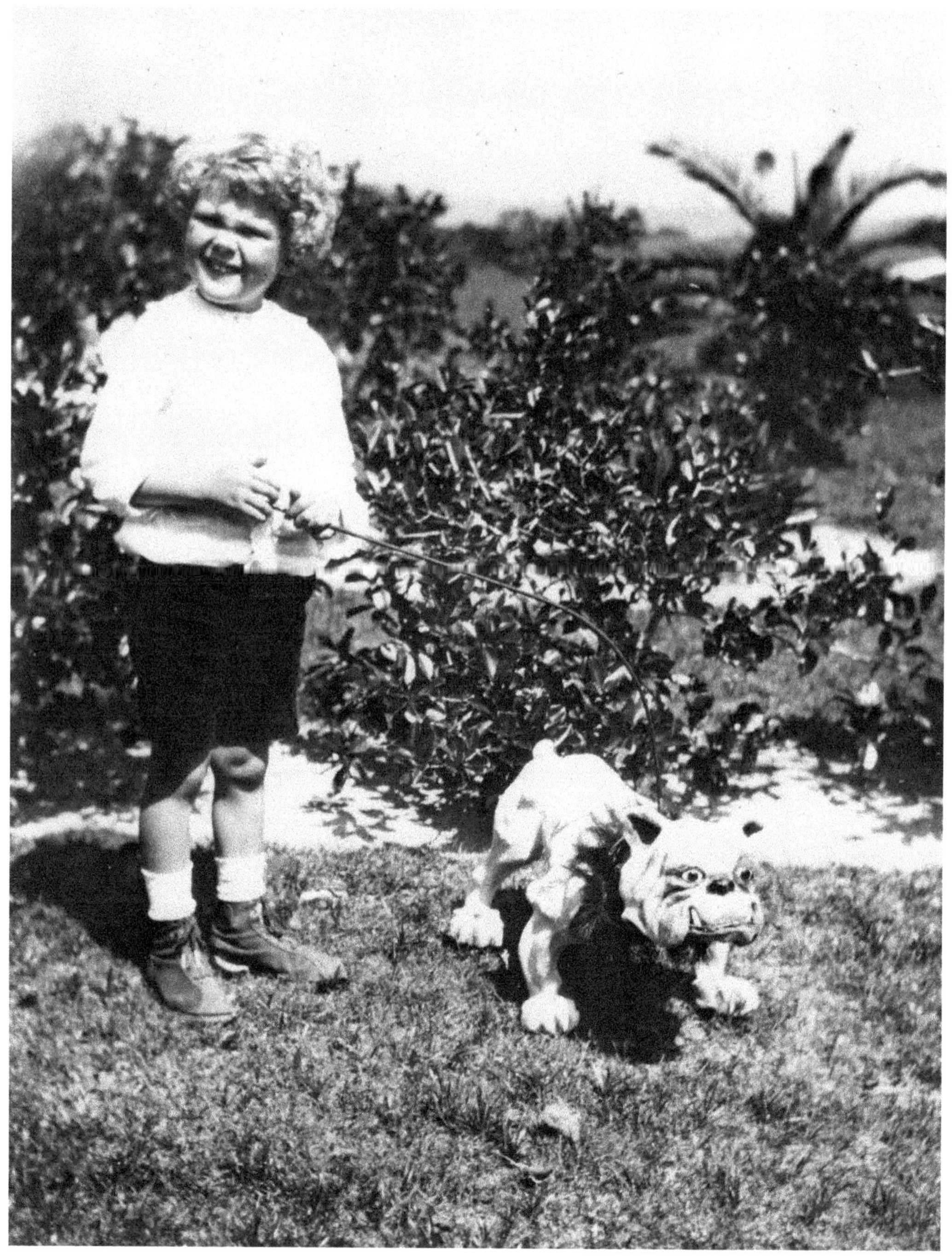

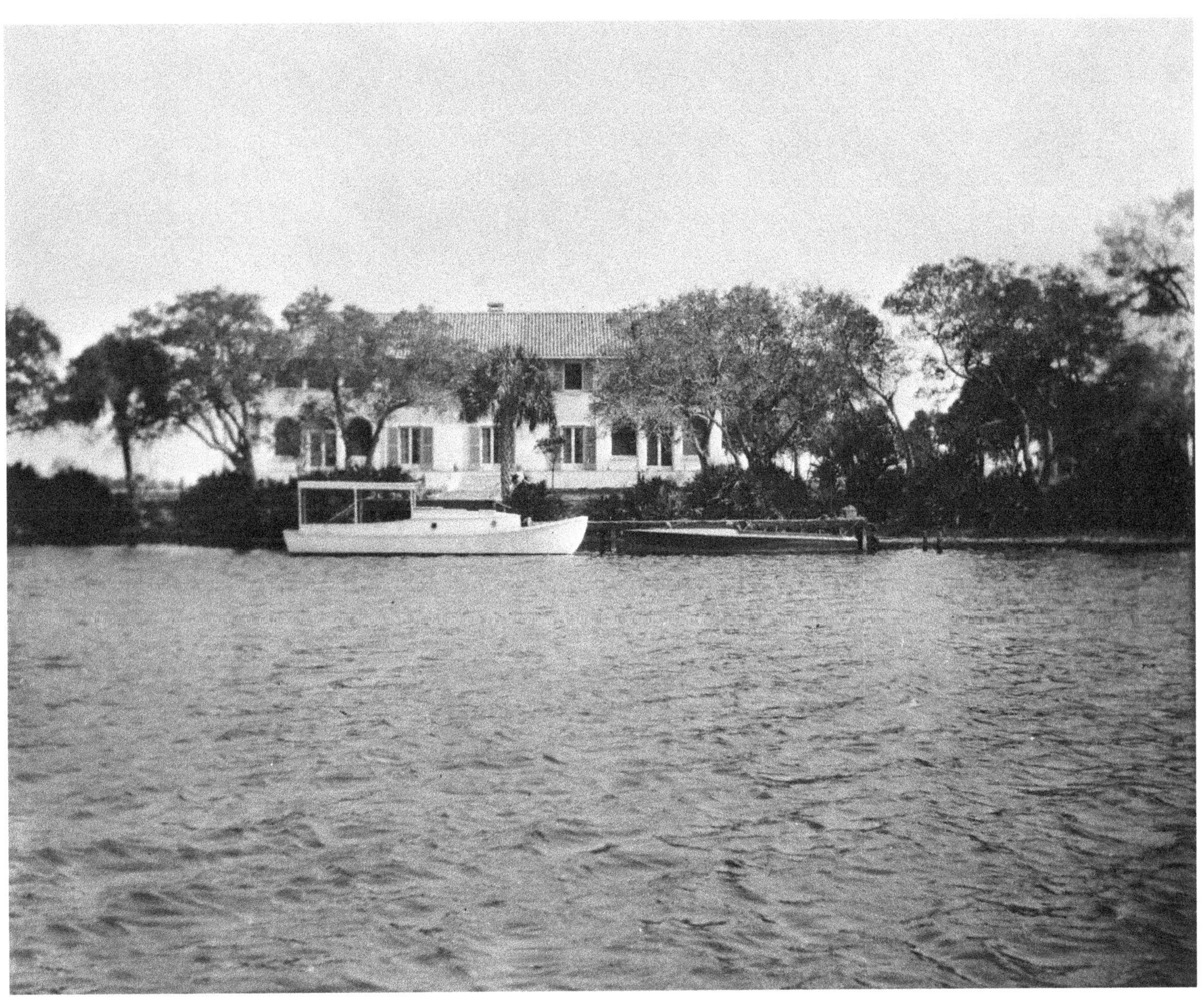

This is a 1925 view across Phillippi Creek toward Immokalee, the home of Edson Keith, Jr., and his family, now called the Phillippi Mansion. The creek was named for Phillippi Bermudez, who in 1842 lived on a rancho where Cherokee Park is now located. Bermudez applied for a deed under the Armed Occupation Act, but his claim was denied.

The Keith property was operated as a farm, complete with animals, citrus groves, and vegetable gardens. After Edson Jr.'s death in 1939, the property was purchased by Mae Hansen, then in 1986 the county purchased it for $5.2 million. Today, Phillippi Estate Park, including the Keith Mansion, is used for special events. In the mid-1920s, the Keith family also had their own bathhouse, called "the shack."

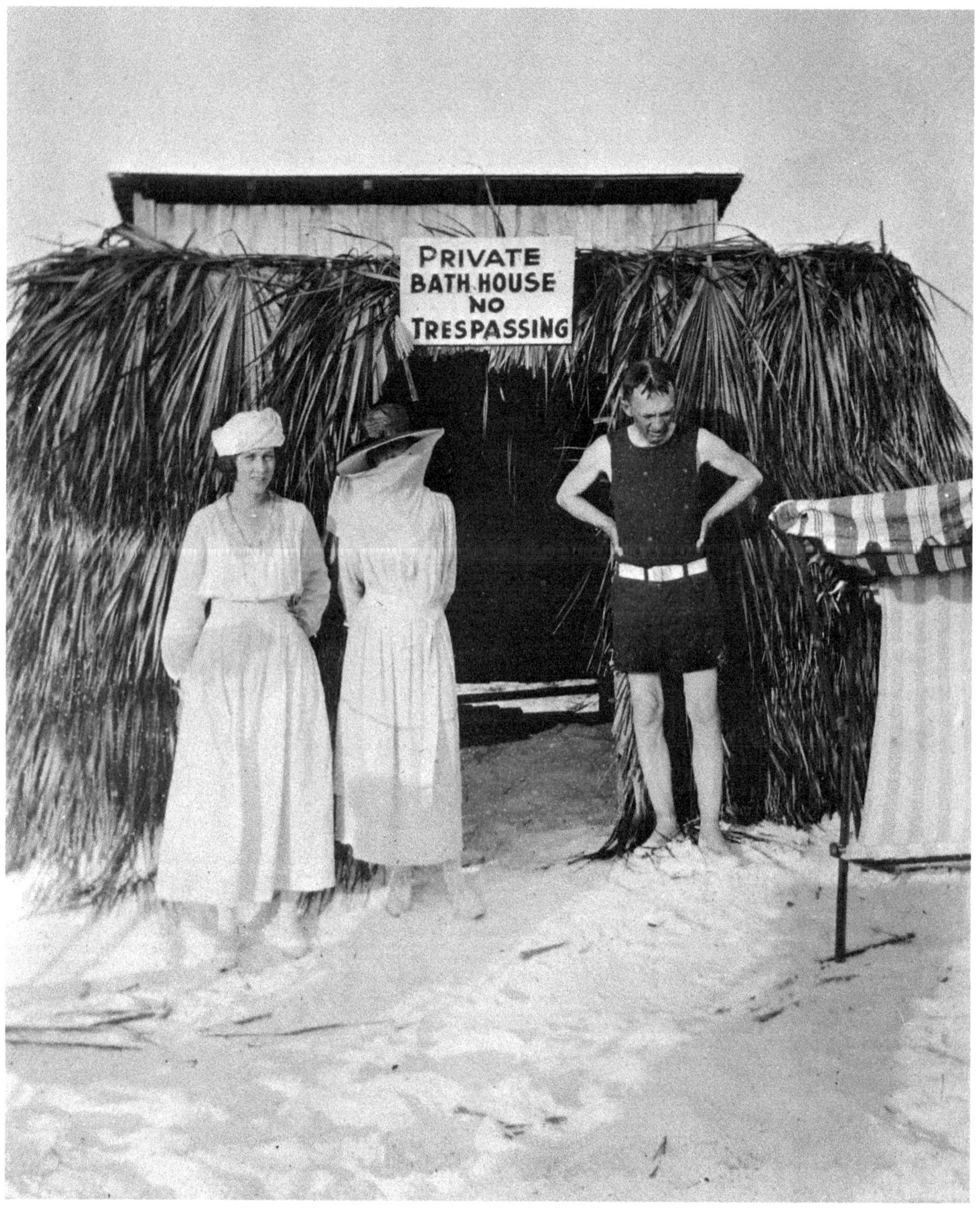

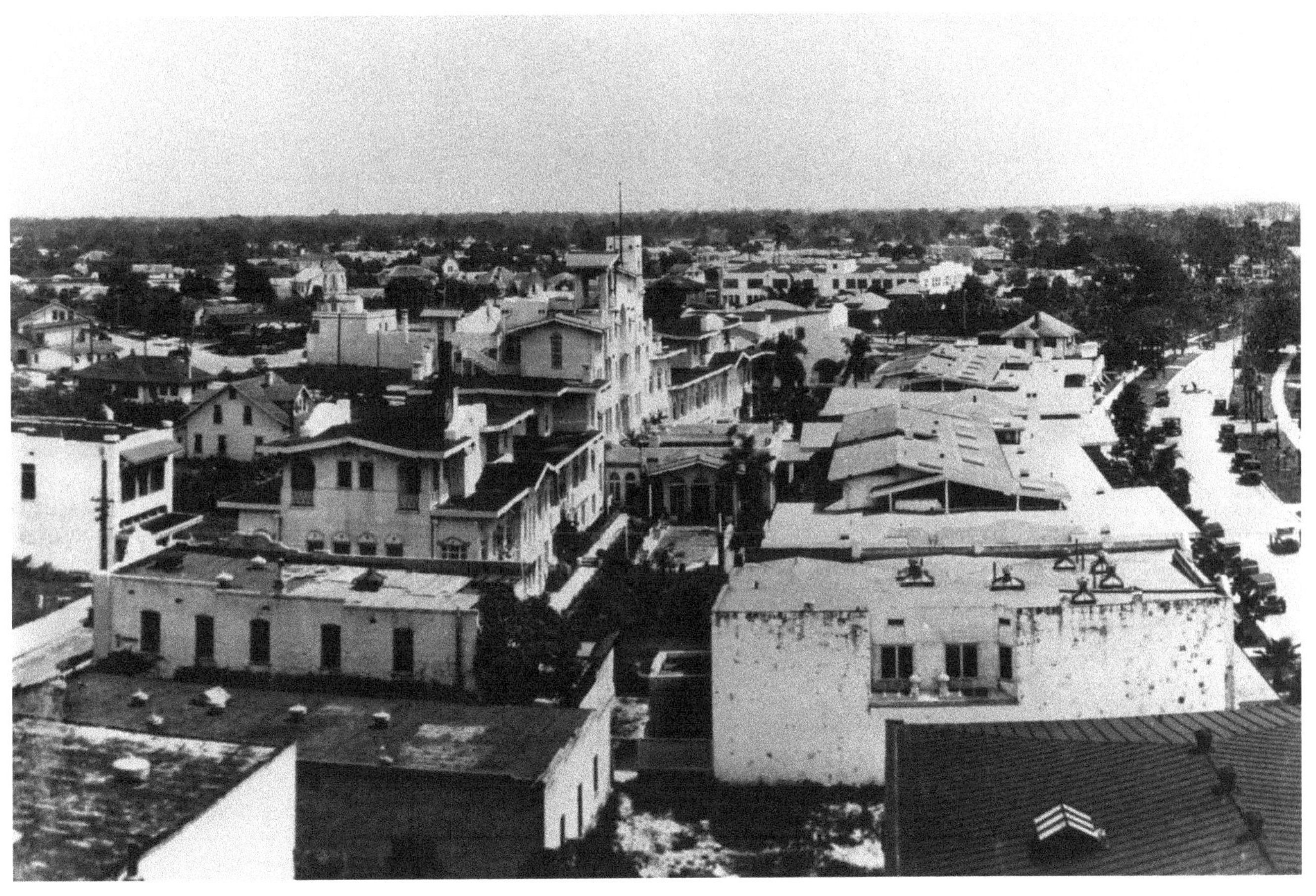

Chicago businessman Andrew McAnsh built the Mira Mar Apartments, at right, in 1922, and the Mira Mar Hotel, the tall building at center, the following year. The hotel was intended for those with money who chose to leave their homes in the cold North during the winter to take advantage of the warm Florida climate. The hotel was located at 37-67 South Palm Avenue.

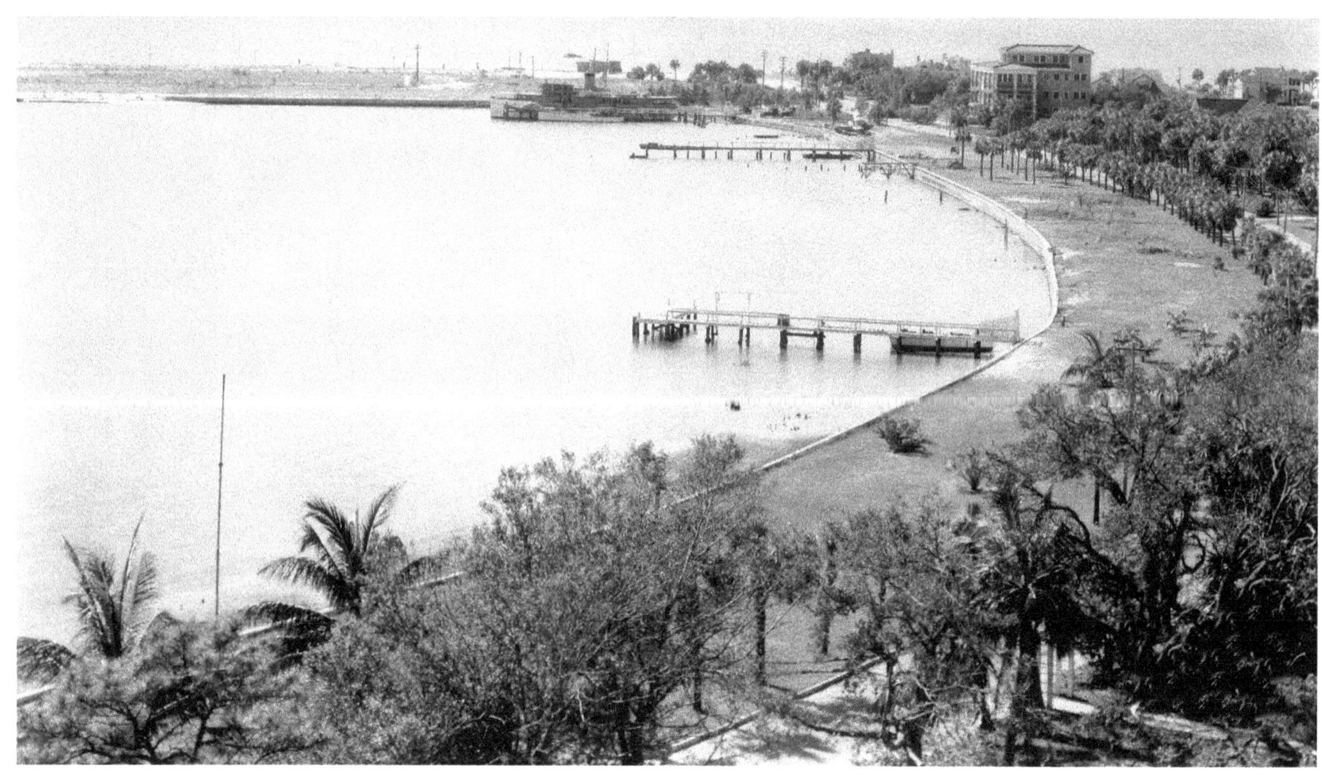

The tall building almost on the horizon is the former Sarasota Yacht and Automobile Club, built in 1913 on North Gulf Stream Avenue. It took over from the Sarasota Yacht Club that Harry Higel built on Siesta Key, too far away to become popular. This building was remodeled in 1923 by Mable Ringling and converted into the Sunset Apartments.

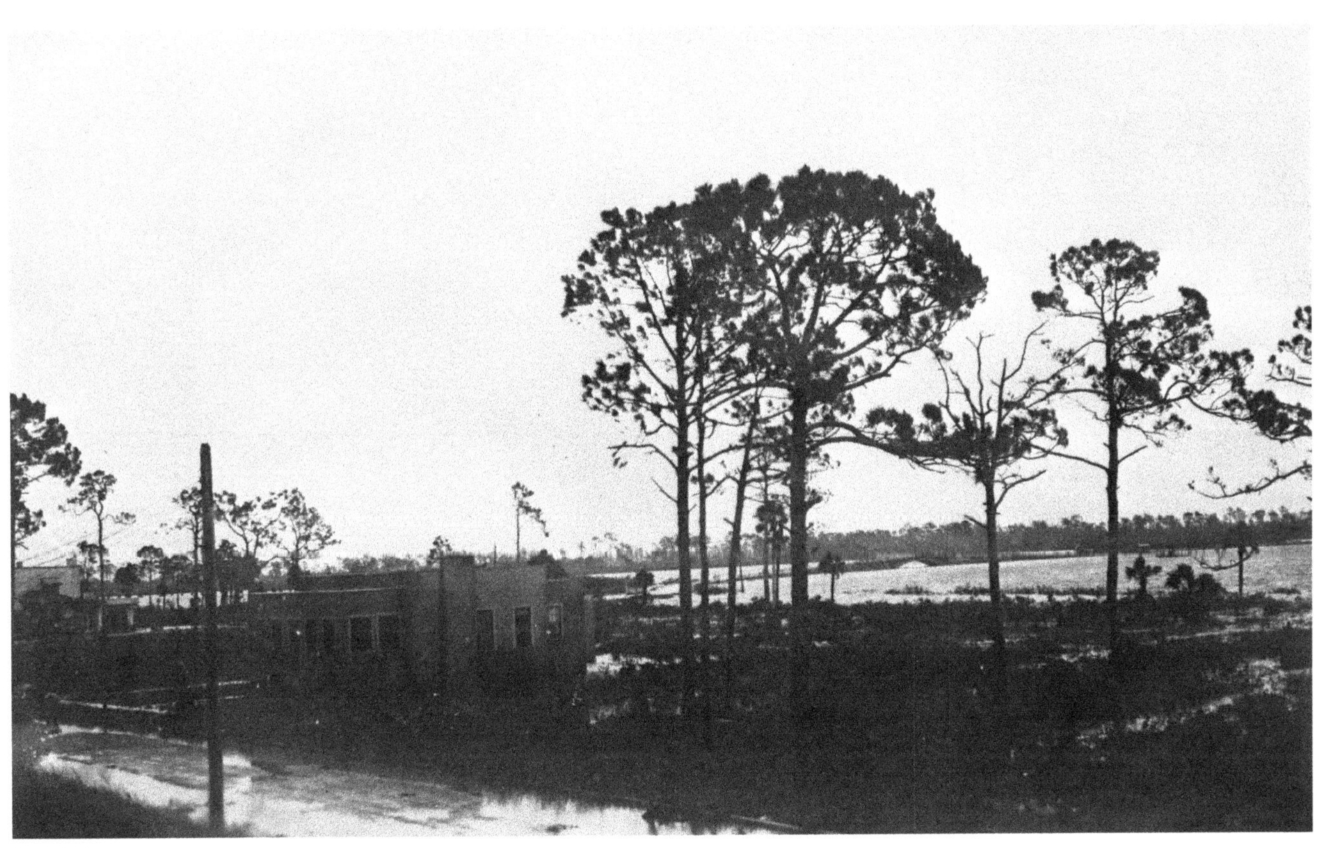

It wasn't until 1953 that hurricanes were given human names. Older storms are referred to by the years they struck, such as the 1926 hurricane, which killed hundreds. That storm hit the state on September 18 and damaged Miami, Fort Lauderdale, Moore Haven, and other communities in the southern part of the state, and caused the flooding seen here in Nokomis.

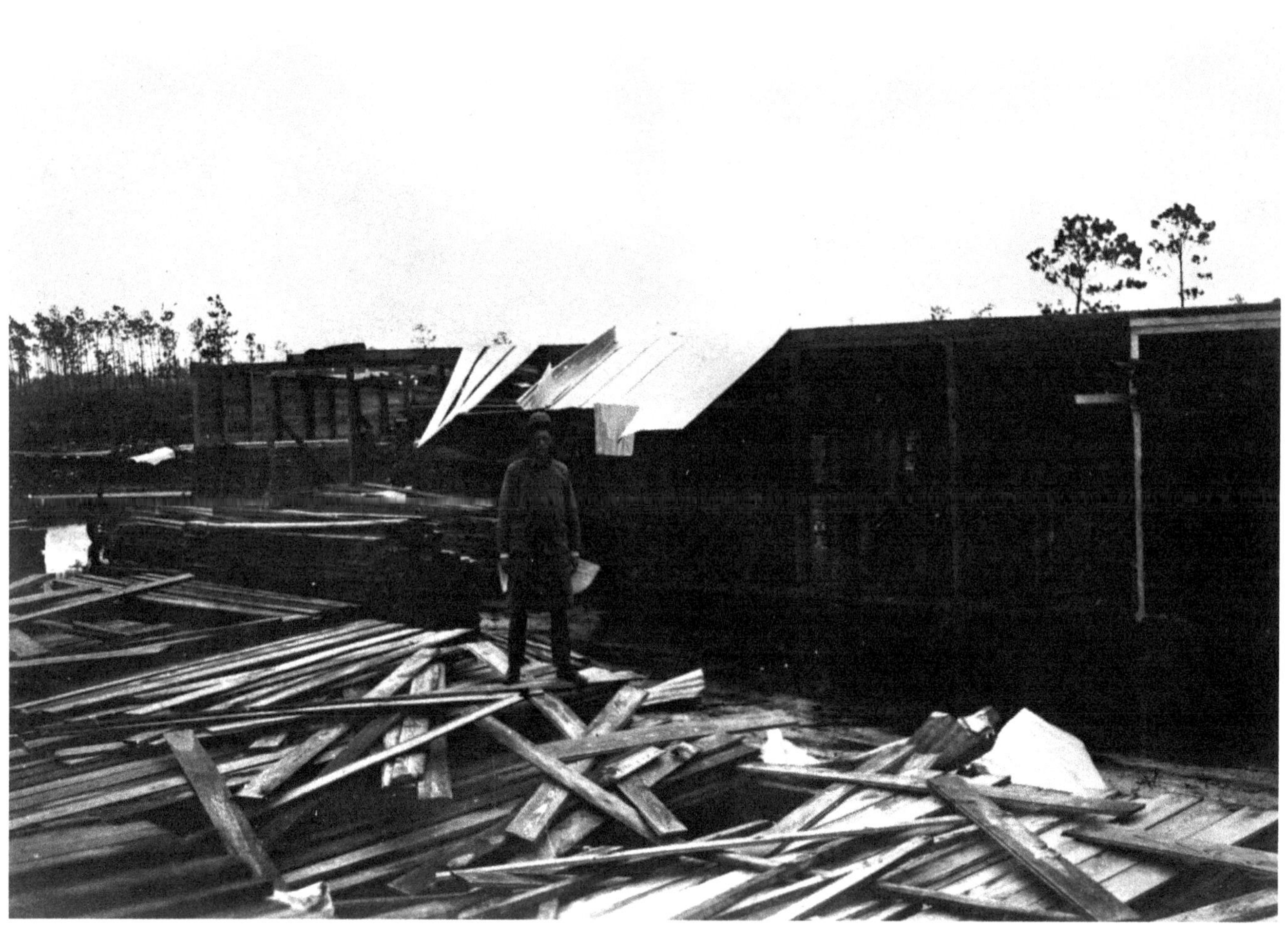

As can be seen from this view of the destruction, Nokomis was hit hard by the 1926 hurricane, which produced the sixth-lowest pressure ever recorded for a Florida storm. The 1903 sanctuary of the Methodist Church was completely destroyed, and the cast-iron bell was one of the only items that could be saved. The bell was loaned to another Methodist Church while a new sanctuary could be built.

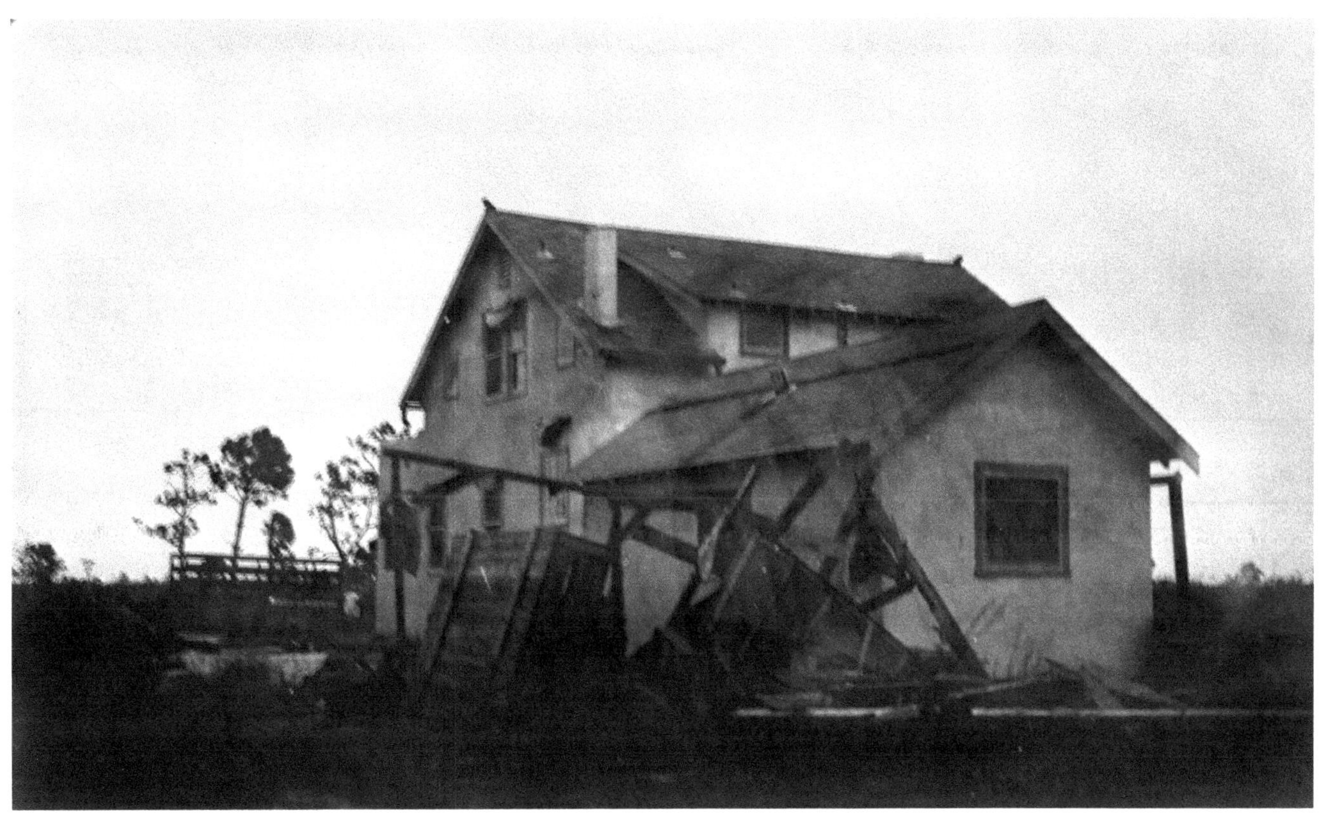

The 1926 hurricane hit the Florida peninsula at Coral Gables and passed through Dade and Broward Counties, also damaging coastal communities along the Gulf of Mexico. This Nokomis home felt the wrath of the storm, which effectively stopped the 1920s South Florida building boom and sent the economy downward.

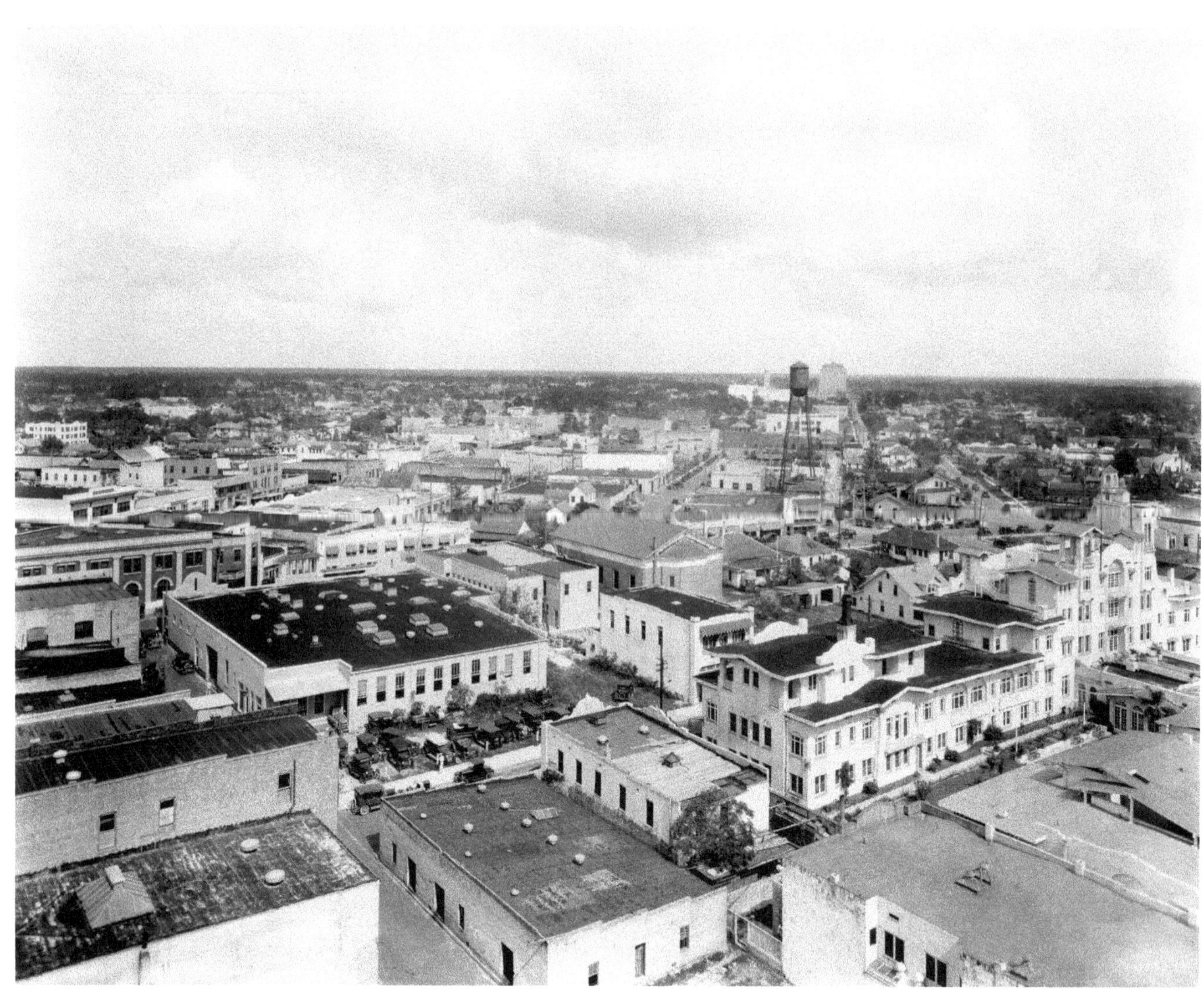

The building just above center in this 1926 photo by the Burgert Brothers studio is the Methodist Episcopal Church, South. The brick sanctuary with peaked roof was erected on Sarasota's Pineapple Avenue in 1914 at a cost of $10,000. It was replaced by the present, modern sanctuary on the same lot in 1955.

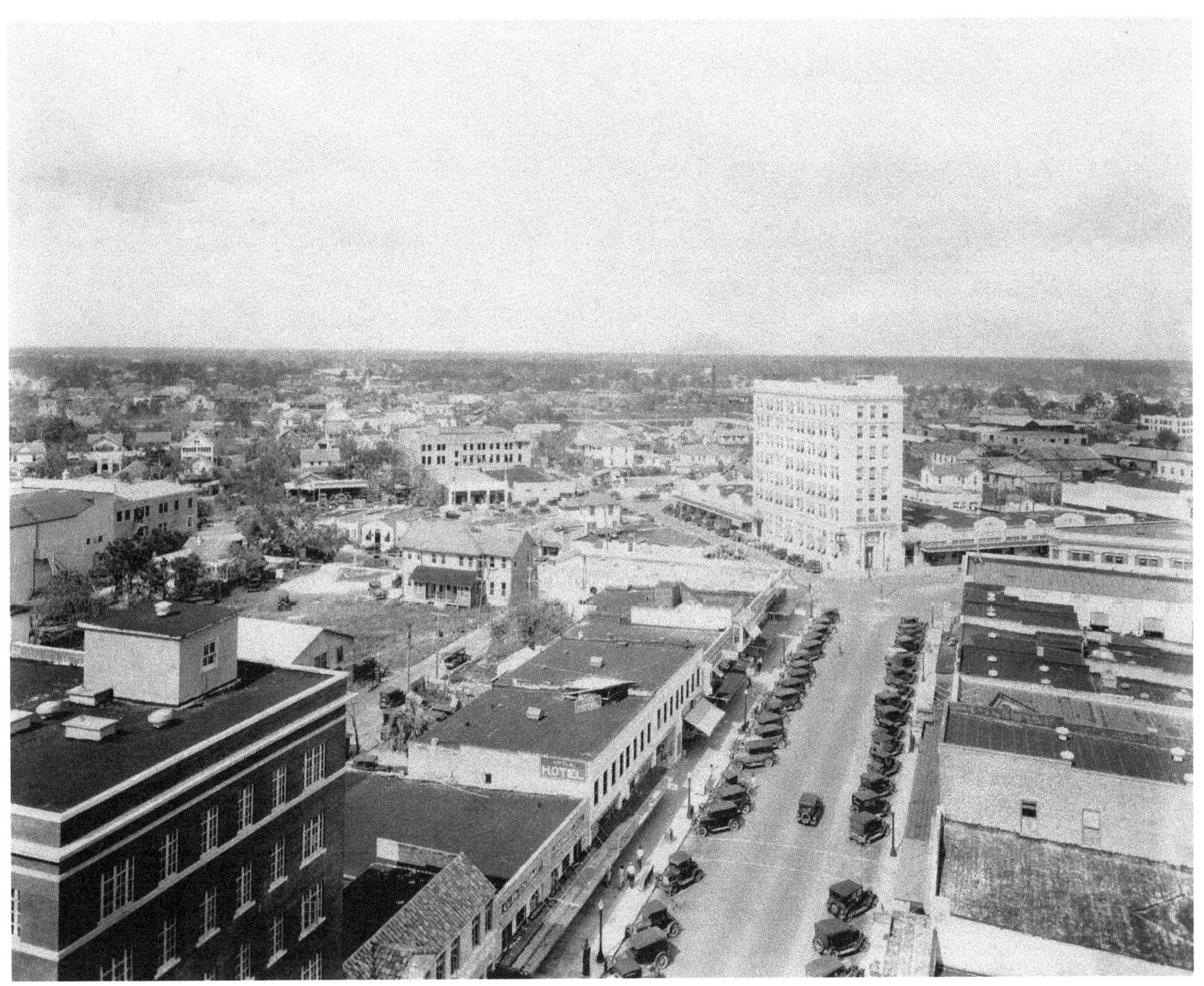

A center of activity from the earliest days of Sarasota is Five Points, the intersection of Main Street, Pineapple Avenue, and Central Avenue. In this 1926 view east, Five Points is the area just beyond the rows of parked cars. The tall white building across the intersection replaced a hotel-boardinghouse constructed in 1885 by the Scottish colonists.

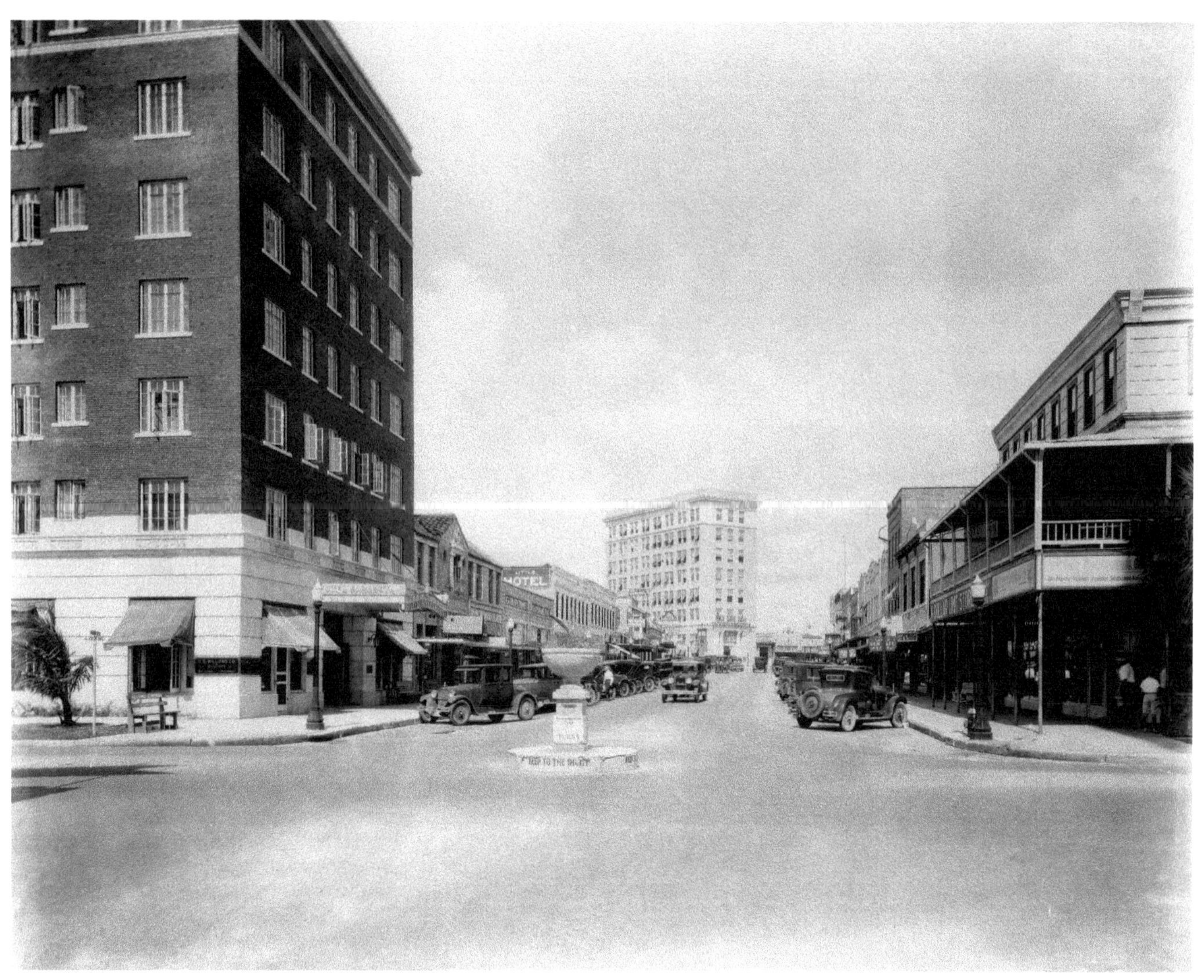

Designed by M. Leo Elliott and erected by Joseph H. Lord of Boston, the First Bank and Trust Building, at center, featured steam heat, a drinking fountain on each floor, and the city's first electric hydraulic passenger elevator. The tall building on the left is Sarasota's first skyscraper, the Sarasota Hotel.

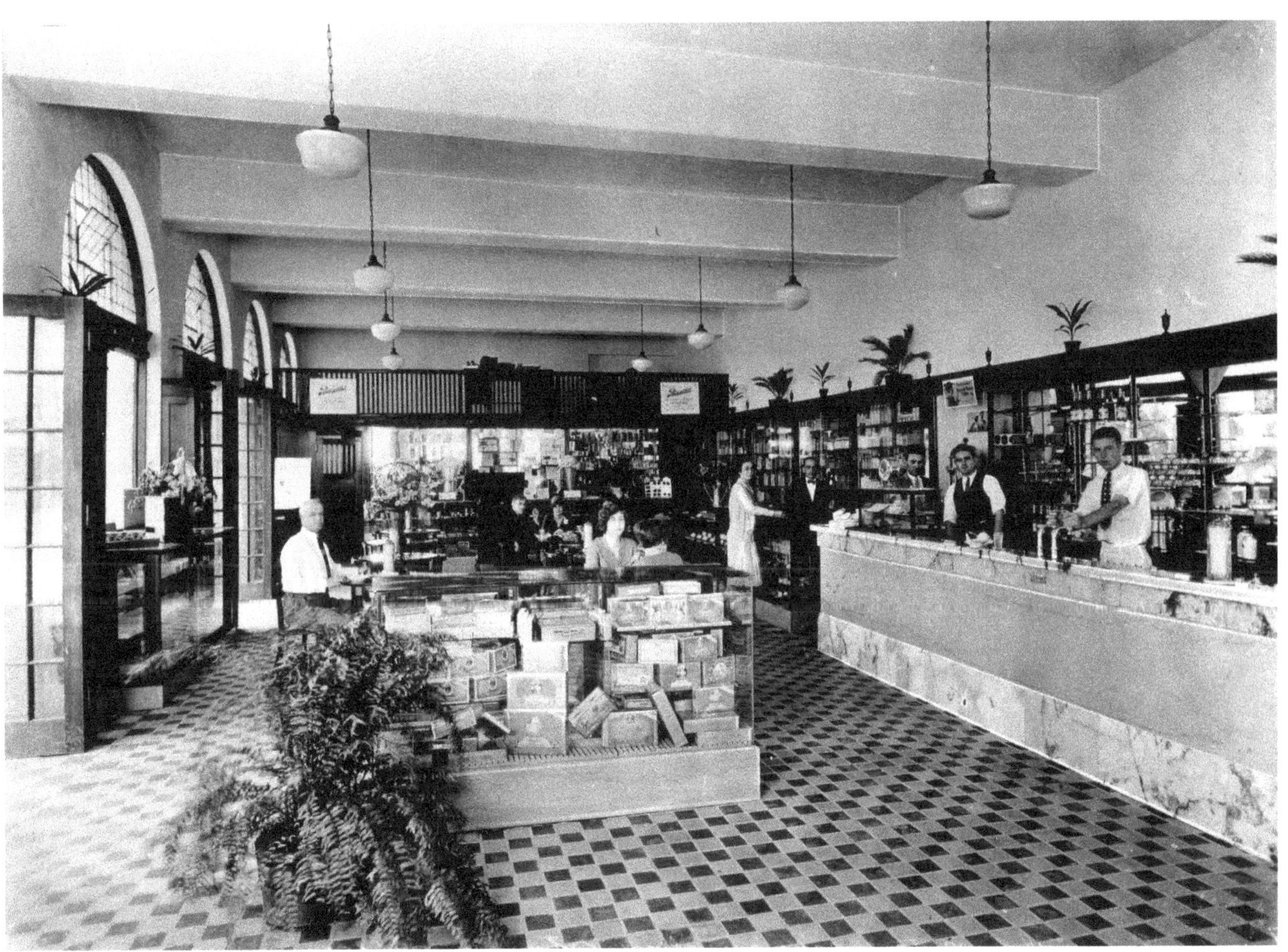

In keeping with the theme of a high-class city, the Venice shopping area catered to the well-to-do, who perhaps patronized this fine Venice store of the 1920s. Although Bertha Palmer was no longer around, those from her social class—including several prominent families from her Chicago—made up a significant portion of the city's population.

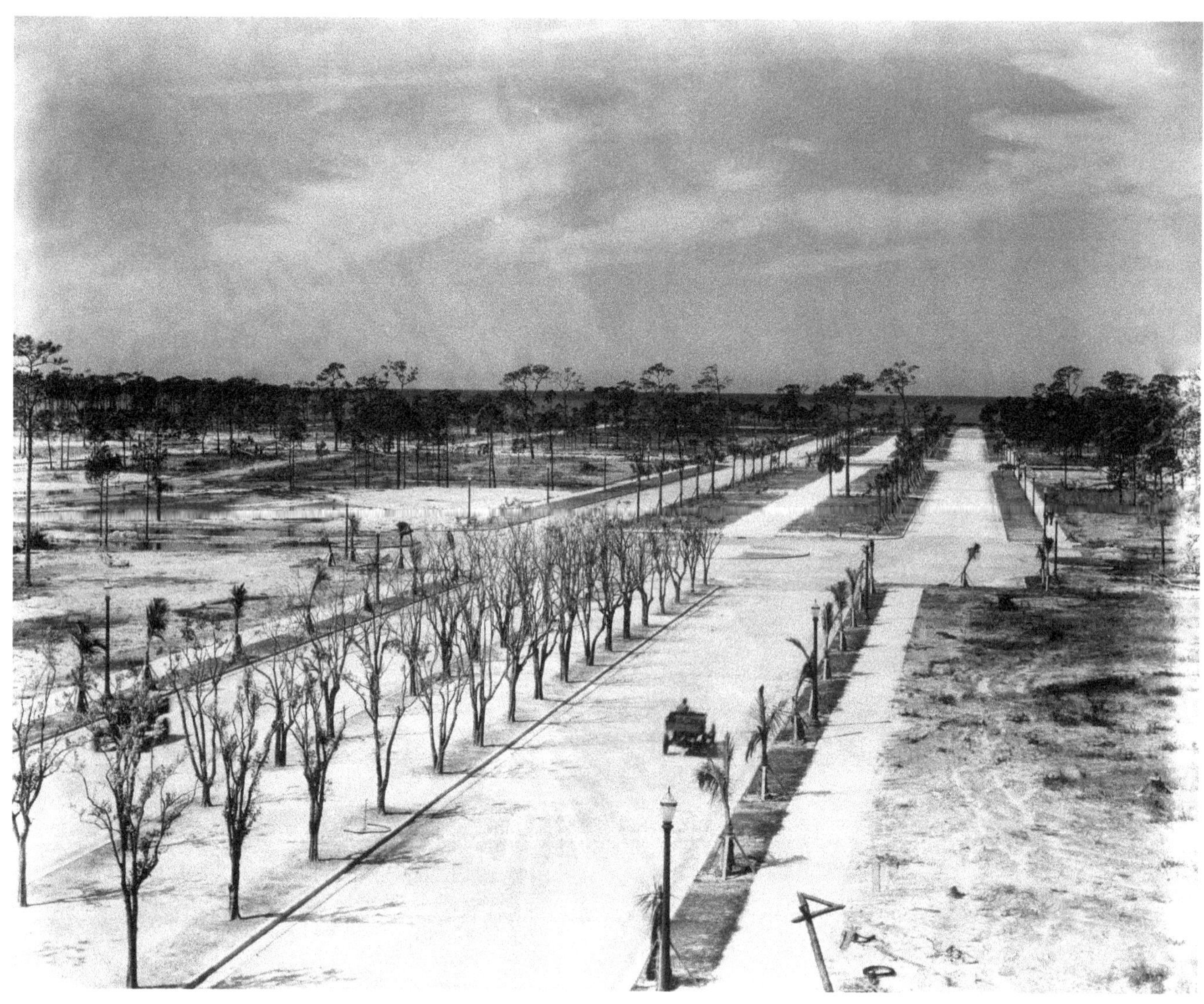

In 1918, the town of Woodmere was founded about five miles south of Venice. Its main activity was lumbering, and the town was abandoned by 1930 because of fire and a lack of local lumber. Much of the lumber cut or processed at Herman Kluge's Woodmere Lumber Mill wound up in the construction of Venice, shown here in 1926 in its early stage.

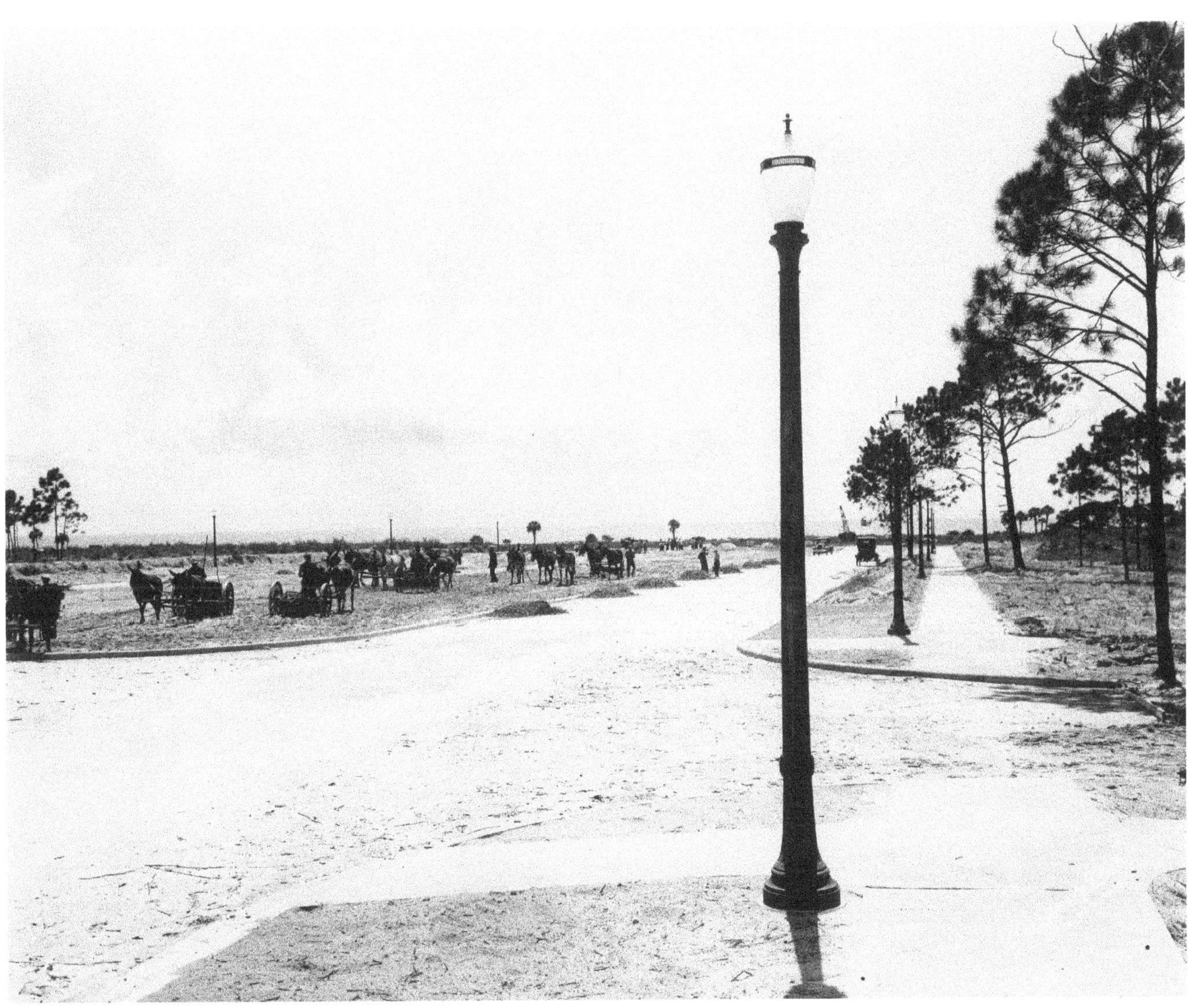

In 1925, the Brotherhood of Locomotive Engineers was one of the country's richest labor unions. The beaches, climate, and railroad potential convinced the union that $40 million was a good price to pay for land on which a model city could be constructed. The following year, the construction workers shown here and many others were hard at work building Venice.

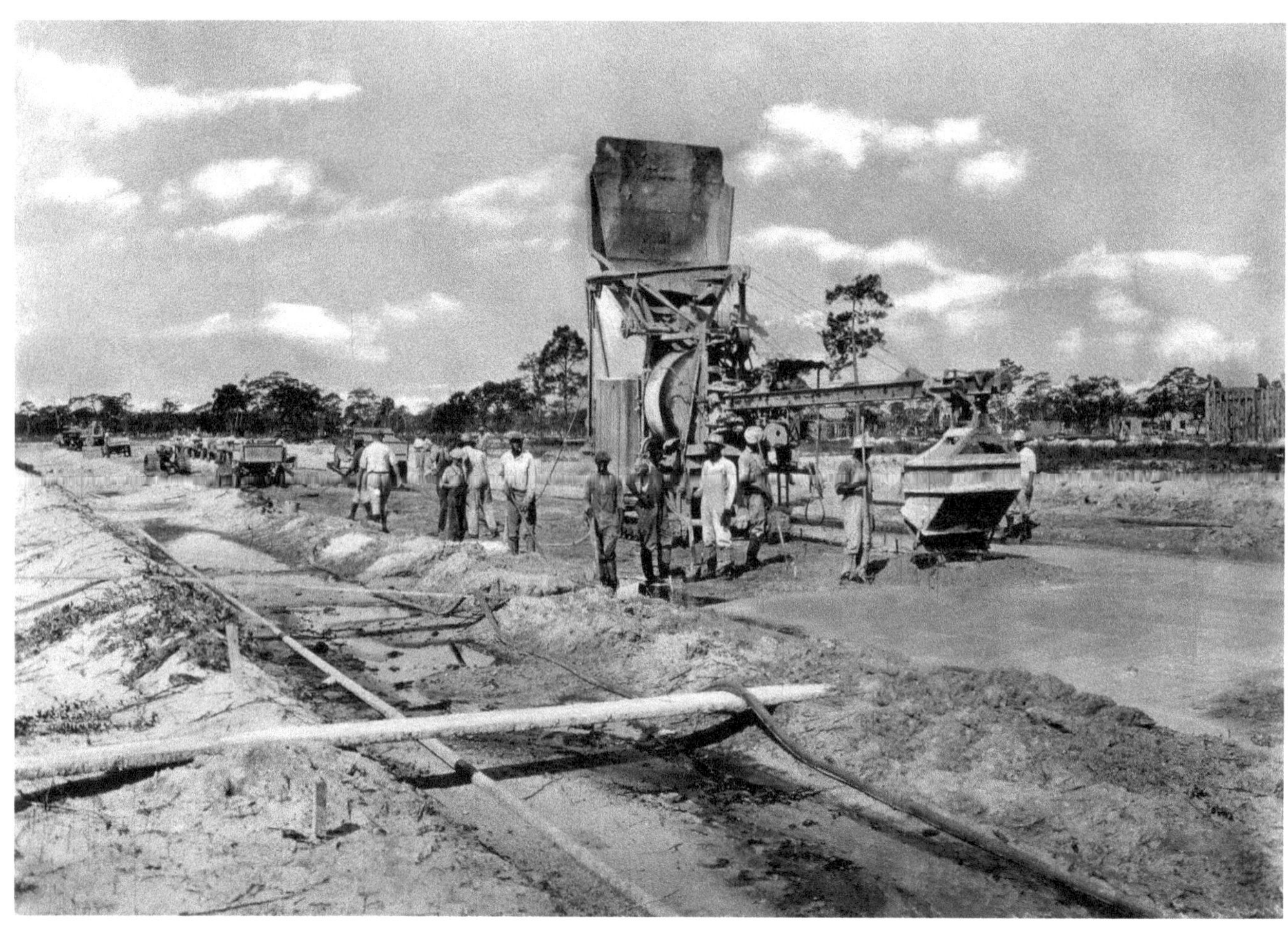

In 1914, Venice residents lobbied for better roads, with the result that nine-foot-wide roads were built connecting Venice with Sarasota, Osprey, and Eagle Point. After World War I, the asphalt continued to Englewood. For city streets, six-inch-thick concrete was the material of choice, and in this 1920s photo, workers can be seen constructing a Venice street.

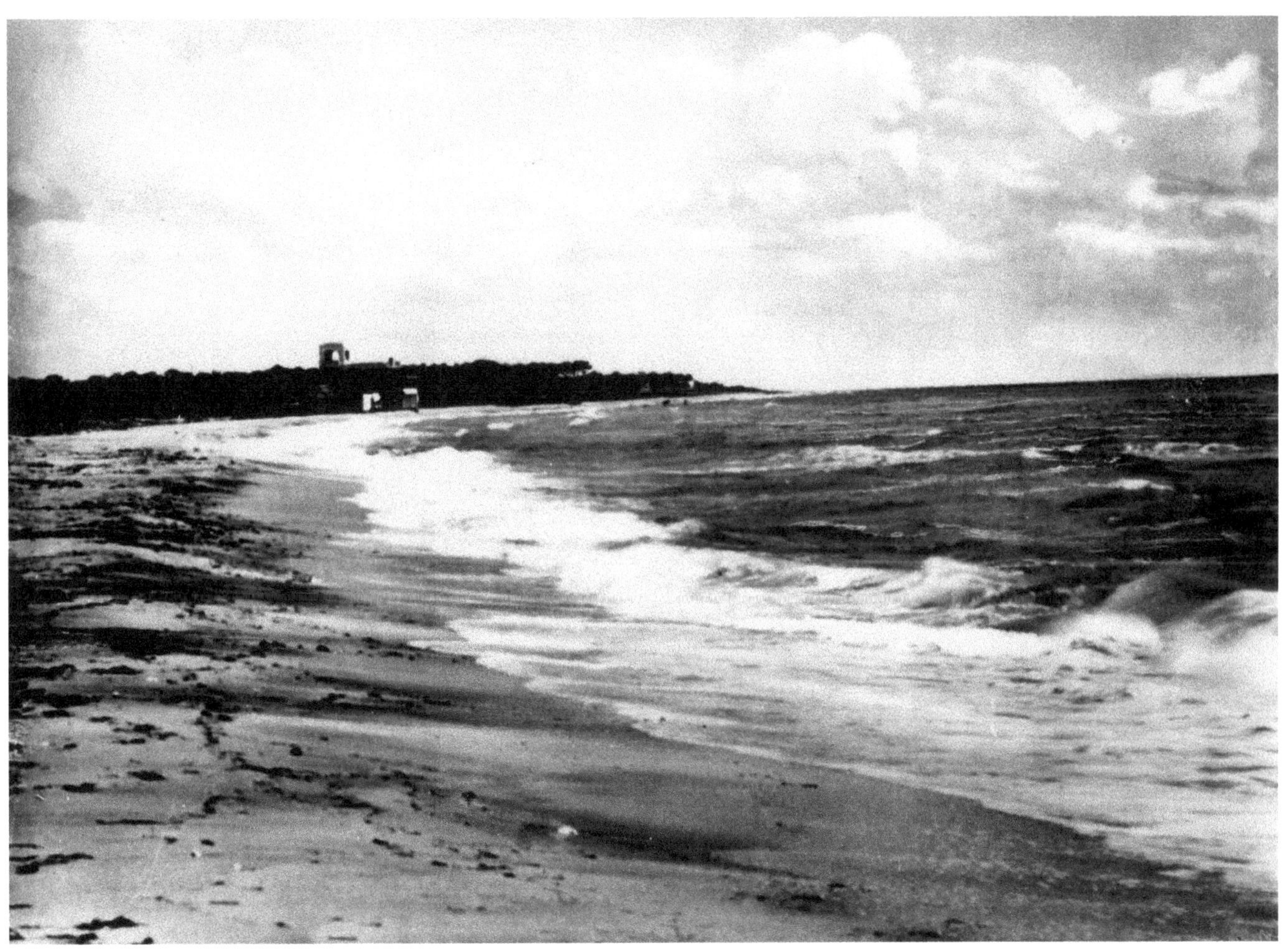

Both Fred H. Albee and the Brotherhood of Locomotive Engineers desired a port to rival Port Tampa, but it turned out that Venice's bays were too shallow. It was impracticable to dredge them to the depth necessary to make Venice a major commercial port. Instead, the developers of the city relied on views such as this to entice visitors and purchasers.

In the 1920s, these people drank tea on the beach in the little shelter known as the Oasis. The decade ended badly for Venice, starting with the hurricane of 1926 and continuing with the economic downturn that followed shortly thereafter. Those misfortunes, along with the stock market crash, nearly turned Venice into a ghost town. Even the arrival of the Tamiami Trail highway in 1928 helped little.

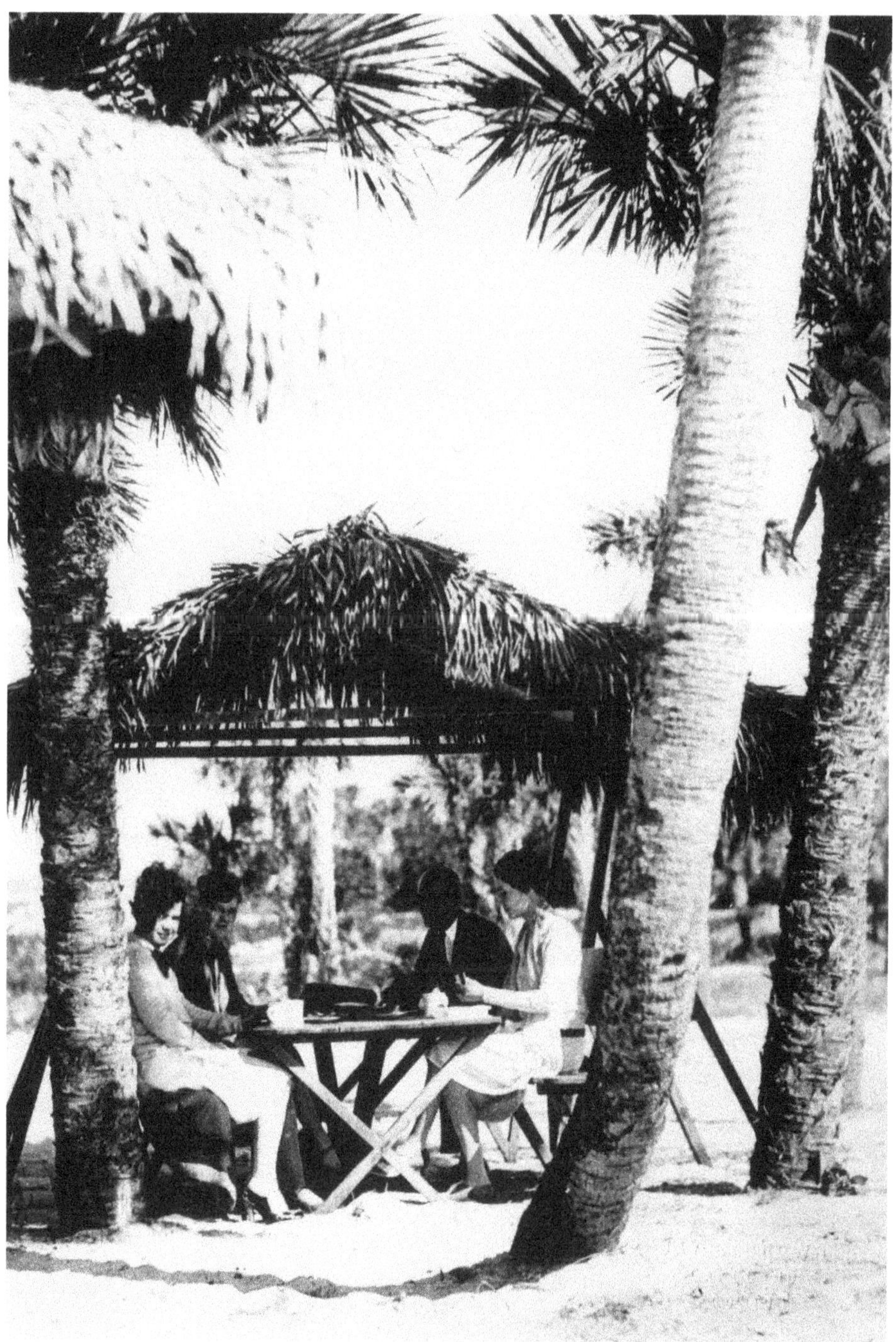

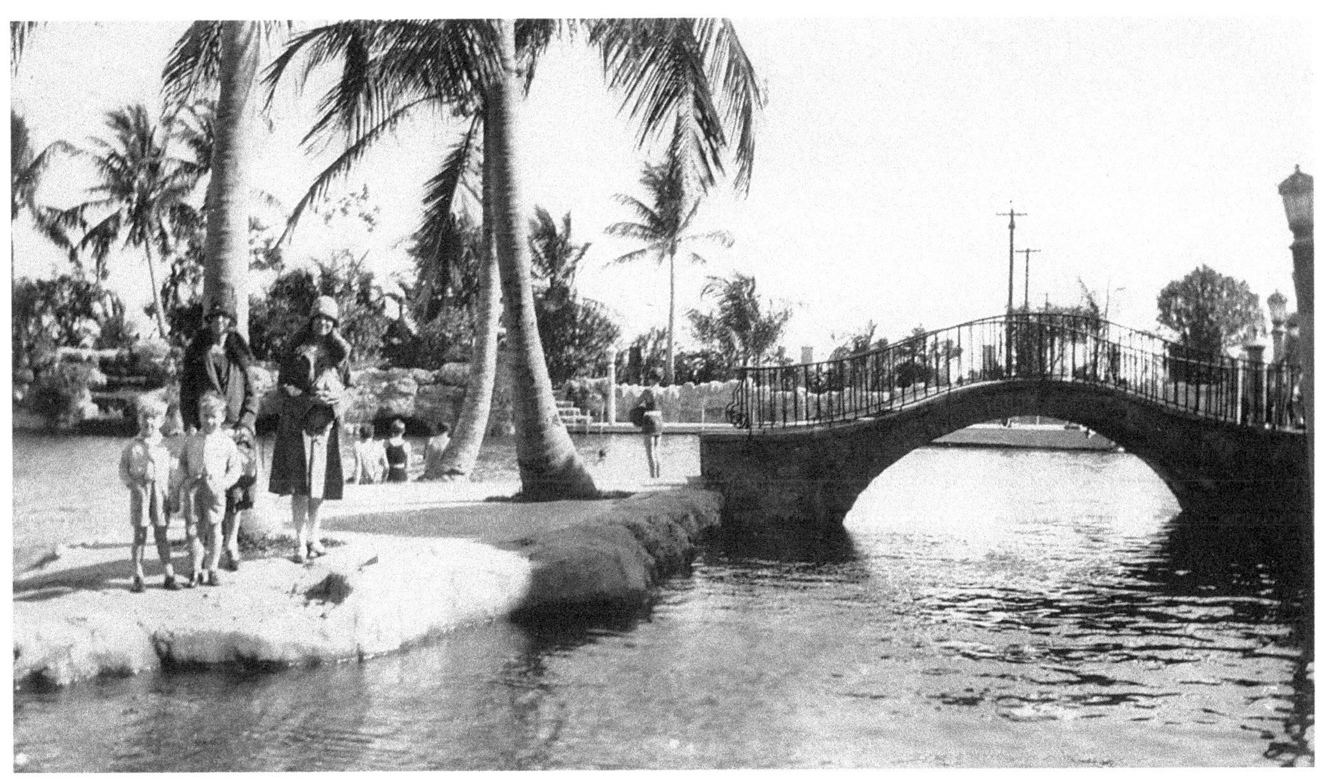

The proposed plan for Venice included beautiful landscaping as well as elaborate, Italian Renaissance–style architecture. Here, in 1926, Lillian, Charles, and Bob Bloyd, with Florence Mayfield, visit a portion of the city resembling the canals and bridges of Venice, Italy.

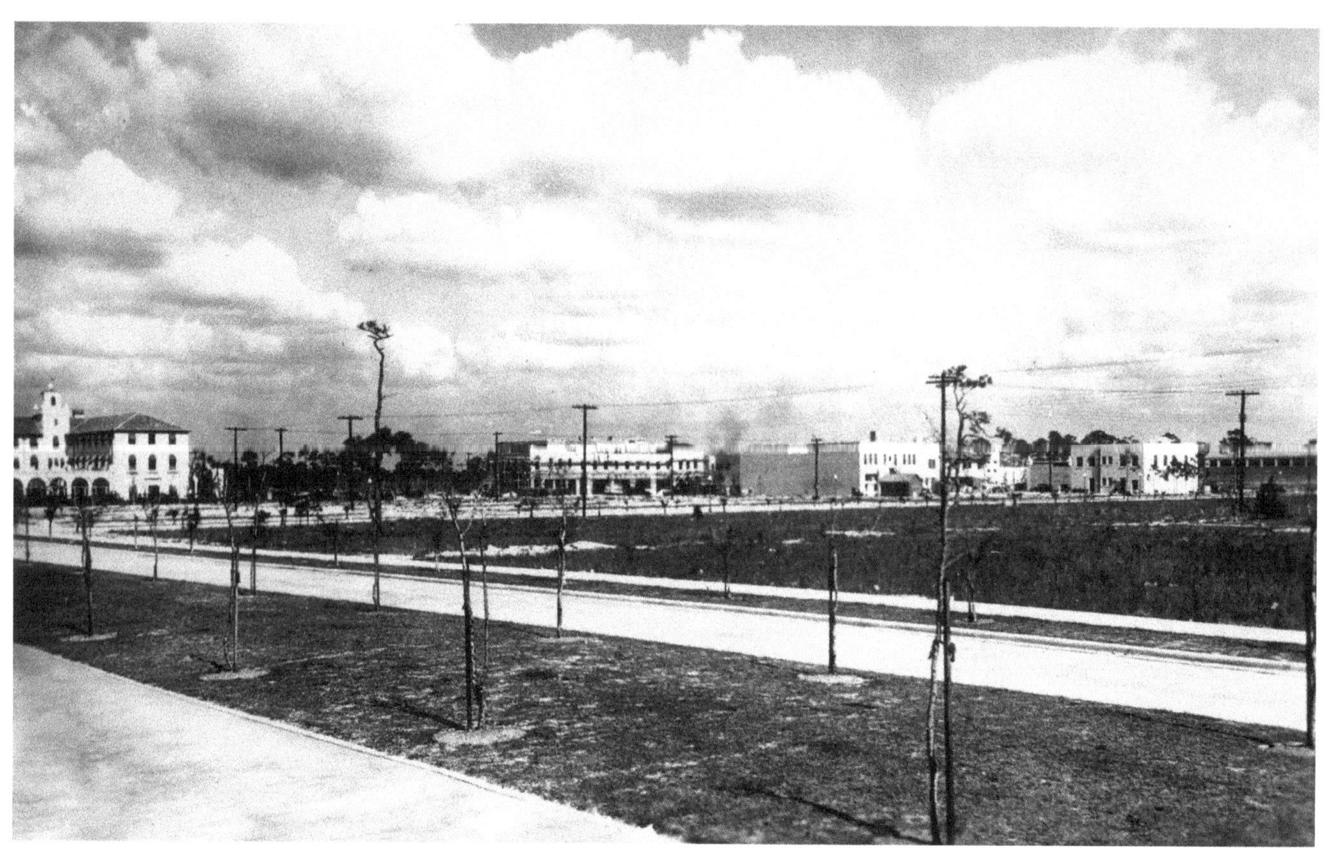

Even from a distance, the buildings going up in the 1920s Venice business district are obviously Northern Italian Renaissance in style. Such appearance had been mandated in the plans drawn up by John Nolen, and by Bertha Palmer herself. The building on the left is the Park View Hotel, later torn down to make room for the post office.

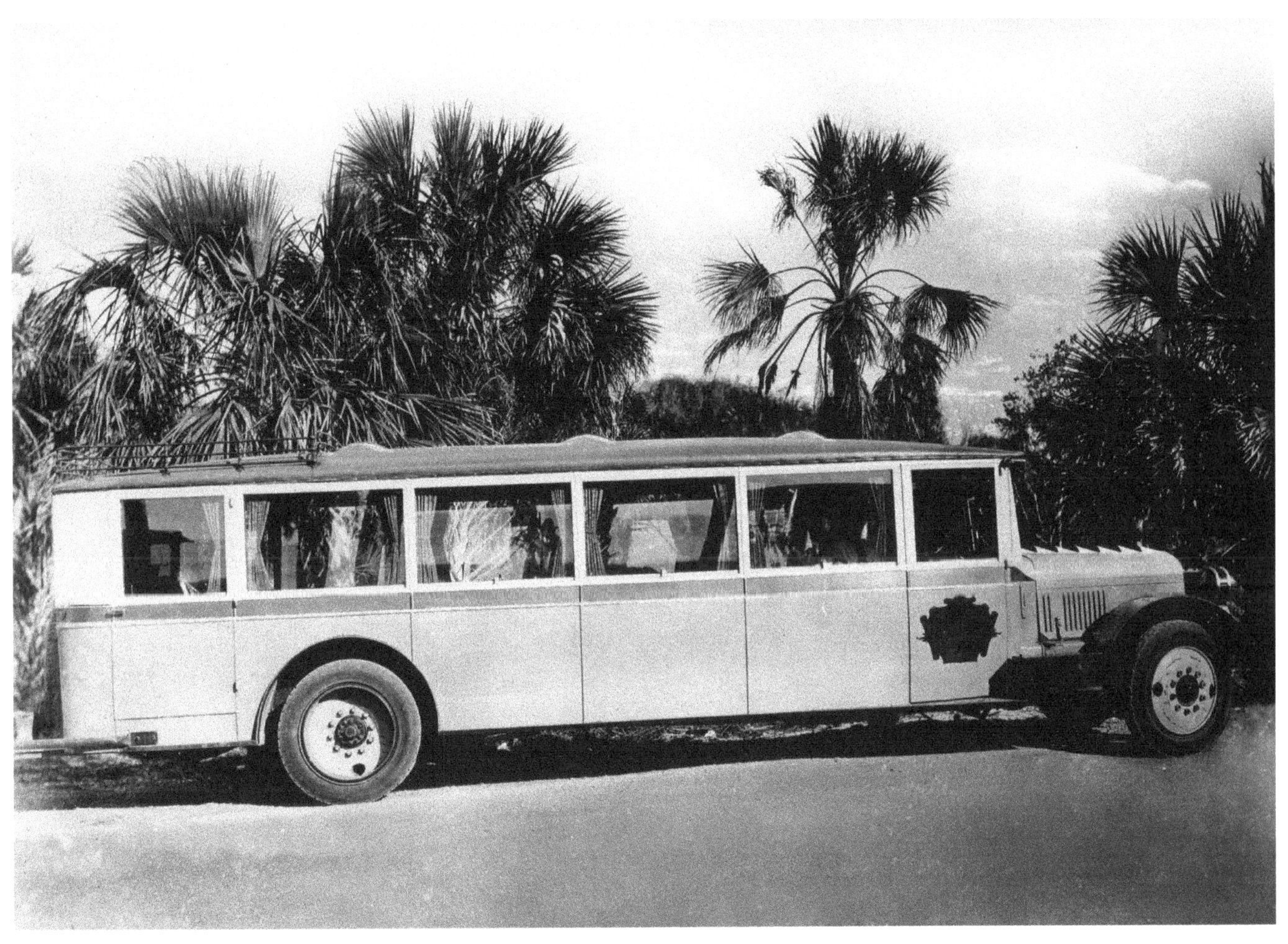

The BLE Corporation not only developed the city of Venice and supervised its construction, but also advertised lots for sale in Florida and elsewhere. Prospective purchasers were treated to tours of the area on "Venice deluxe coaches" such as the one shown here. They were not air-conditioned, but instead had shades that could be pulled over the windows.

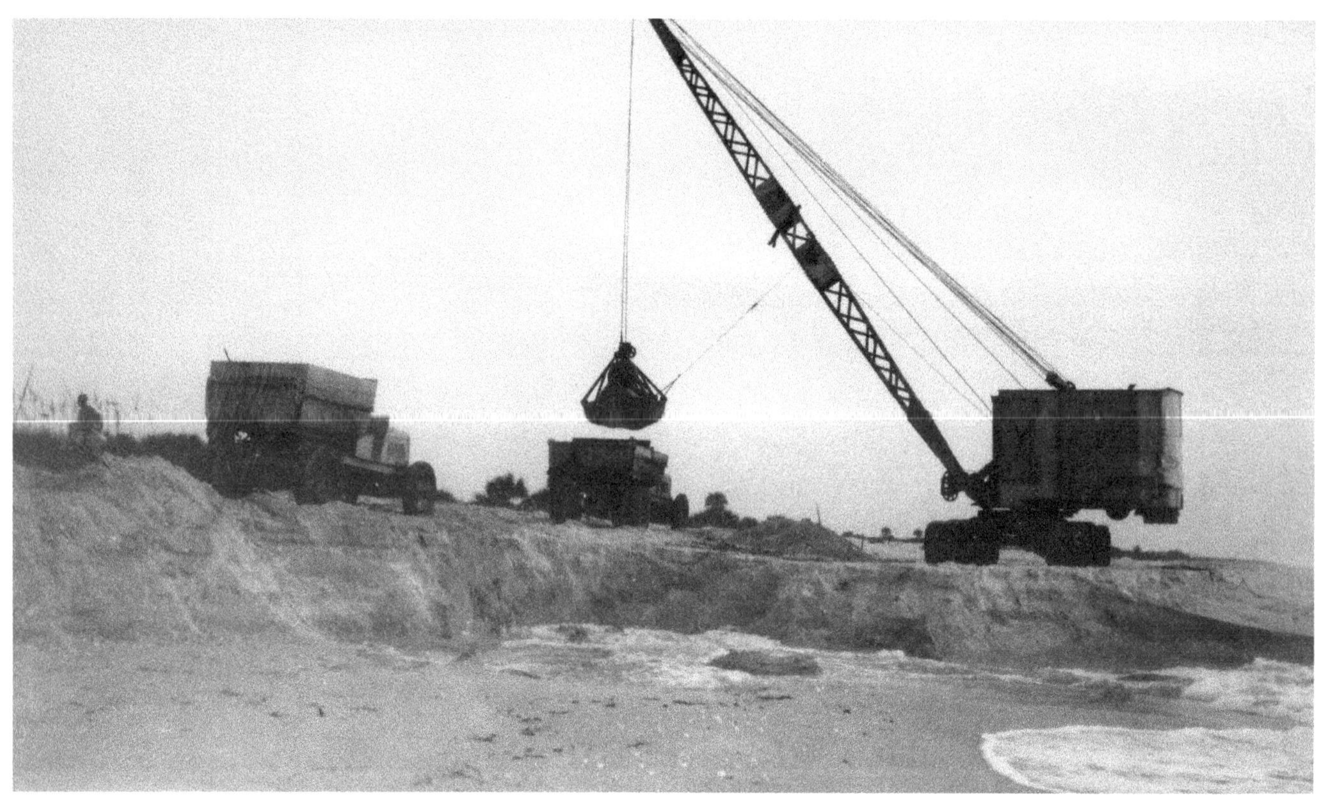

The mainland is protected from the waves of the Gulf of Mexico by a string of barrier islands occasionally requiring the replenishment of sand, as shown here. One called Chaise's Key was renamed Casey Key, for John Casey, in 1856. When this photo of it was taken in 1927, that same island was called Treasure Island to entice visitors.

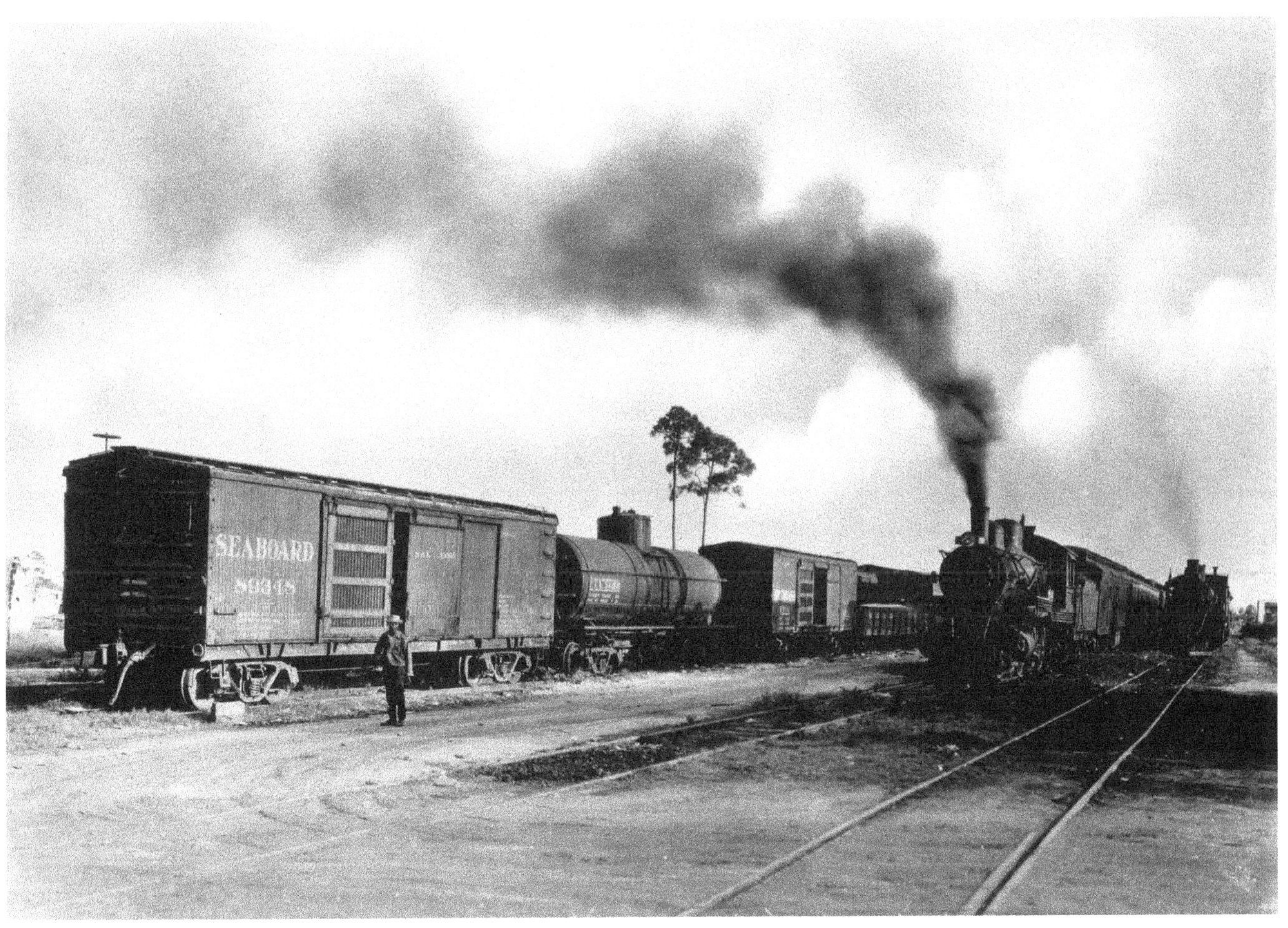

In the 1910s, Bertha Palmer acquired a great deal of land south of Roberts Bay, while the Venice post office and railroad station were located north of the bay. Palmer built a railroad depot on her land and wanted that location to be called Venice, so the name was moved south, and the community previously known as Venice was renamed Nokomis. The trains shown here sit on Palmer's former land.

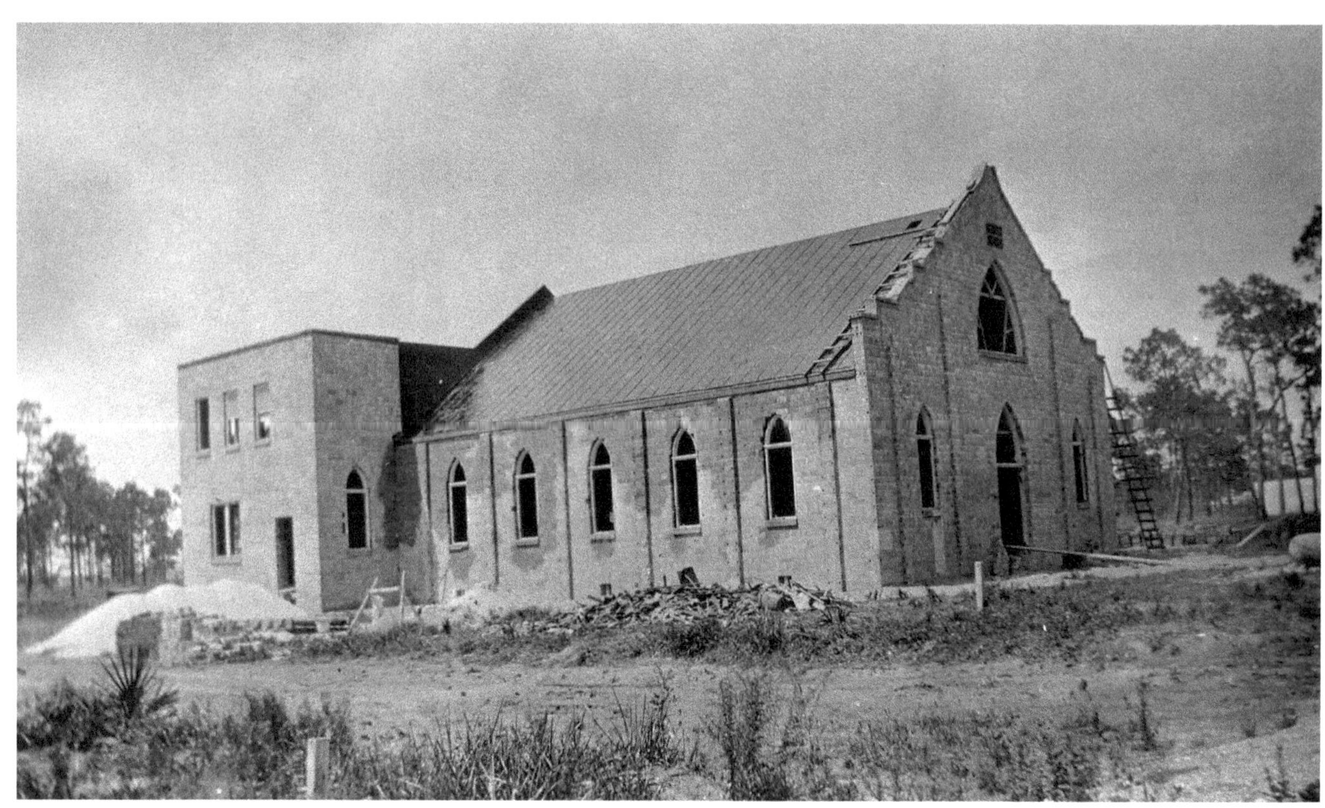

The Venice-Nokomis United Methodist Church was founded by 1860s settler Jesse Knight. After holding services on the Knight property, the congregation built its first sanctuary in 1903. The 1926 hurricane necessitated rebuilding, but because of economic problems, the building shown here lacked flooring and plaster on the walls until 1942.

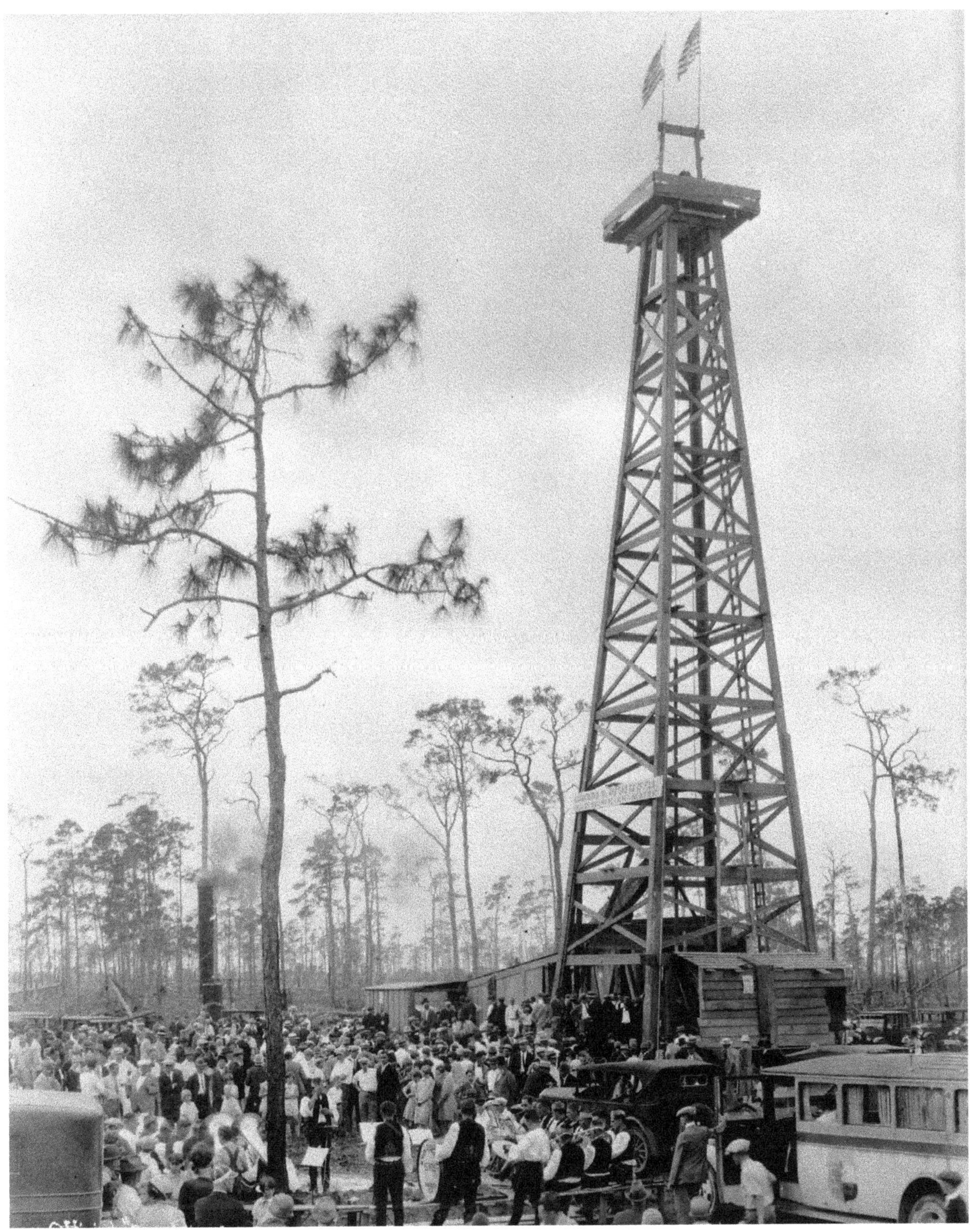

Entrepreneurs looked for sources of wealth other than land for development. In March 1927, John Ringling's Associated Oil & Gas Company began drilling for oil in the southern part of Sarasota County. Shown here is the official start of drilling of the first well, with the locally popular Czecho-Slovakian Band performing for the crowd.

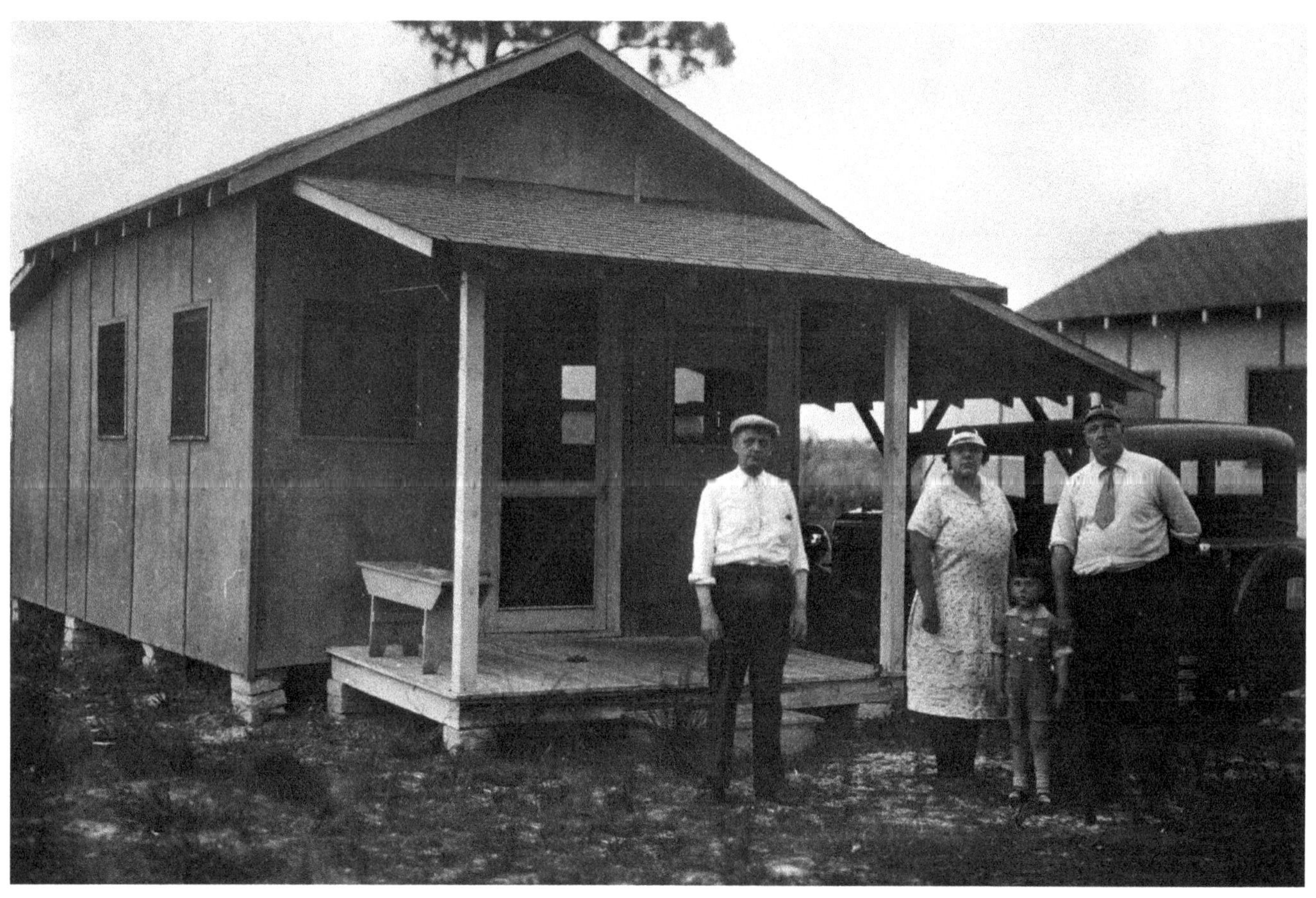

A fraternal organization for autocampers, the Tin Can Tourists of the World organized in Tampa in 1919 and thereafter held two meetings each year. One was held in Michigan, and the other alternated among Sarasota and other Florida cities. Families from northern states would drive to the Sunshine State to sleep in tents, cars, travel trailers, or simple structures such as the one shown here in 1929.

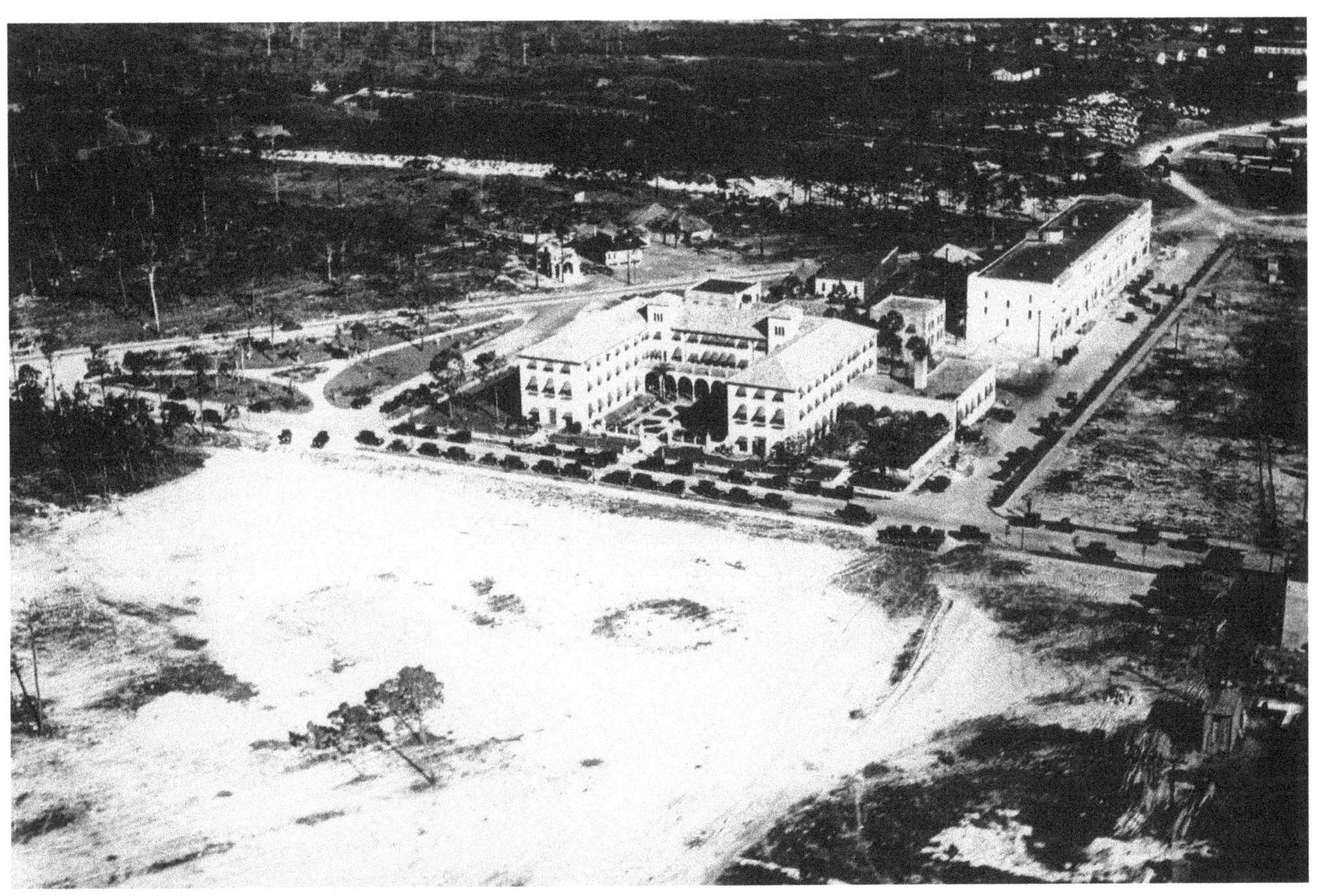

The Venice Hotel was one of the first built for the Brotherhood of Locomotive Engineers, beginning in January 1926. Its plans were also used for the Park View Hotel, known as one of the area's most elegant. After the Venice Hotel later served as the winter home of the Kentucky Military Institute, it was refurbished as the Park Place retirement home.

Tourists and the War Years

(1930–1949)

The 1930s began with the opening of the John and Mable Ringling Museum, showcasing an impressive collection of art previously unseen in the region. However, John Ringling was hurt financially by the Great Depression, and hurt even more by the death of his wife, Mable, just as the museum was being completed. He never recovered from either, and a decade after his death in 1936, his mansion, art collection, and museum became the property of the state.

Despite the difficult economic times, Sarasota County continued to draw tourists during the 1930s, many of them arriving by auto on the Tamiami Trail, so named because it was the first road to connect Tampa and Miami.

Federal relief funds were used on several local construction projects, including the refurbishing of the bridge to the keys that had been built by John Ringling. Roads, parks, and public buildings were also constructed in the 1930s. Probably the best-known of the era's projects was the Lido Beach Casino, which helped draw visitors to the beaches of the barrier islands.

During this period, the area continued to grow, albeit at a slower pace than before. In 1933, Venice welcomed the opening of the Florida Medical Center, which included a medical school and drew patients from around the world. It was turned into a military hospital during World War II. Another military connection was formed in the early 1930s when the Kentucky Military Institute, which had its main campus in Kentucky, opened its winter home in Venice, filling a pair of hotels that had been wanting for visitors.

At the outbreak of World War II, several Florida cities became military training centers, including two in Sarasota County. The Venice Army Air Base opened in 1941 at what later became the municipal airport. Sarasota Army Air Field was created to train bomber pilots but wound up with fighter pilots instead.

While the presence of soldiers, sailors, and pilots during the war helped bolster the local economy, the bases also had a more long-lasting effect. Following the war's end, many who trained at the bases returned to Florida to settle down. After their time in Florida and their service overseas, it often took just one cold winter back home to convince them that Florida was the place to live.

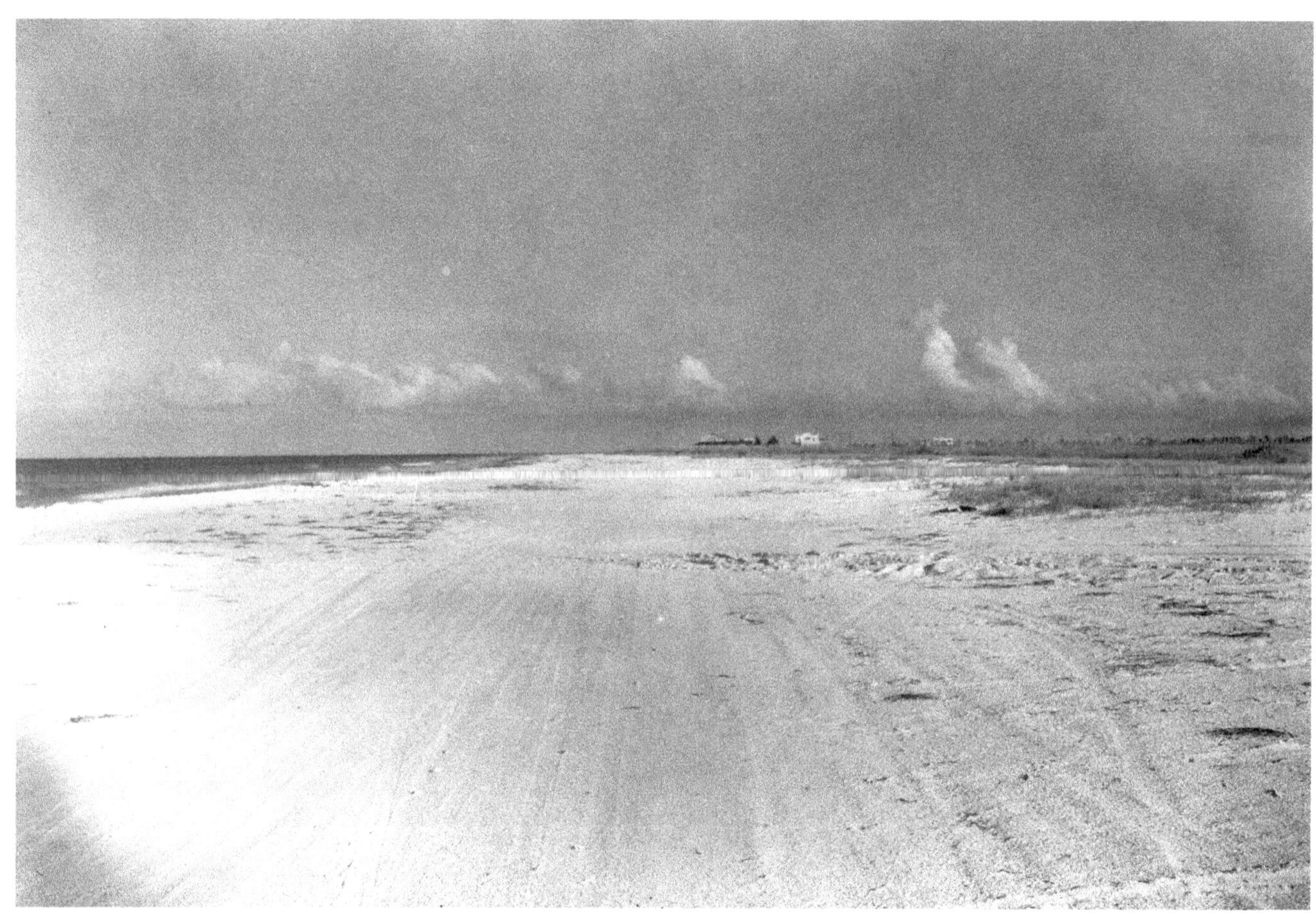

This is a 1930 view of the empty Sarasota Beach, looking northward. In prehistoric times, natives made use of the gulf coast beaches, but it is believed they were only drawn to the beaches during the summer rainy season, when breezes would keep the mosquitoes away, and when sea turtles and their eggs were plentiful as food sources.

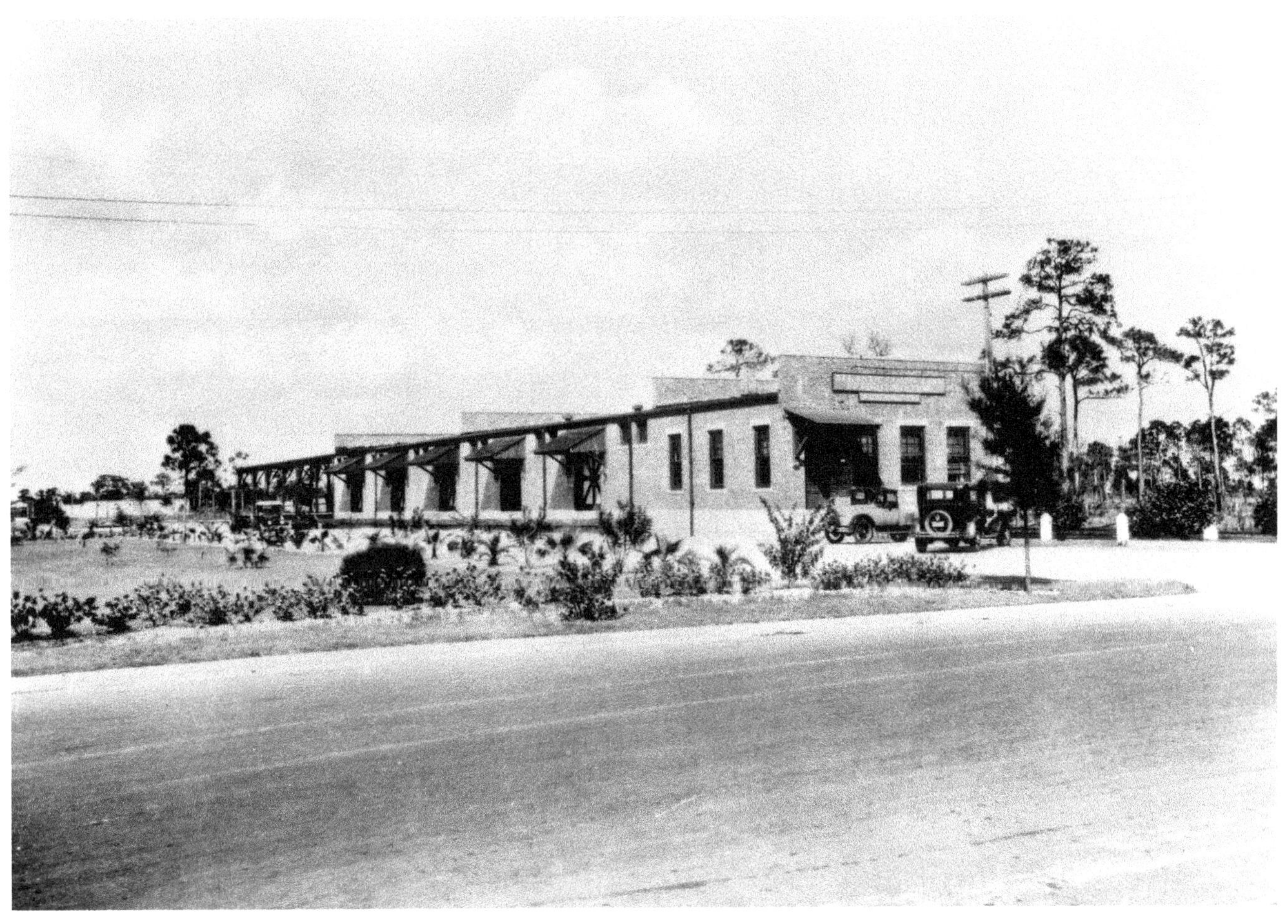

Sarasota's first railroad station opened in 1903, thirteen years after the first tracks were laid. Trains consisting of an engine and two cars began running in 1892, on the line nicknamed the "Slow and Wobbly," and stopped in 1895. The Atlantic Coast Line started carrying passengers to Bradenton in 1924 and used this station, pictured in 1930, for freight.

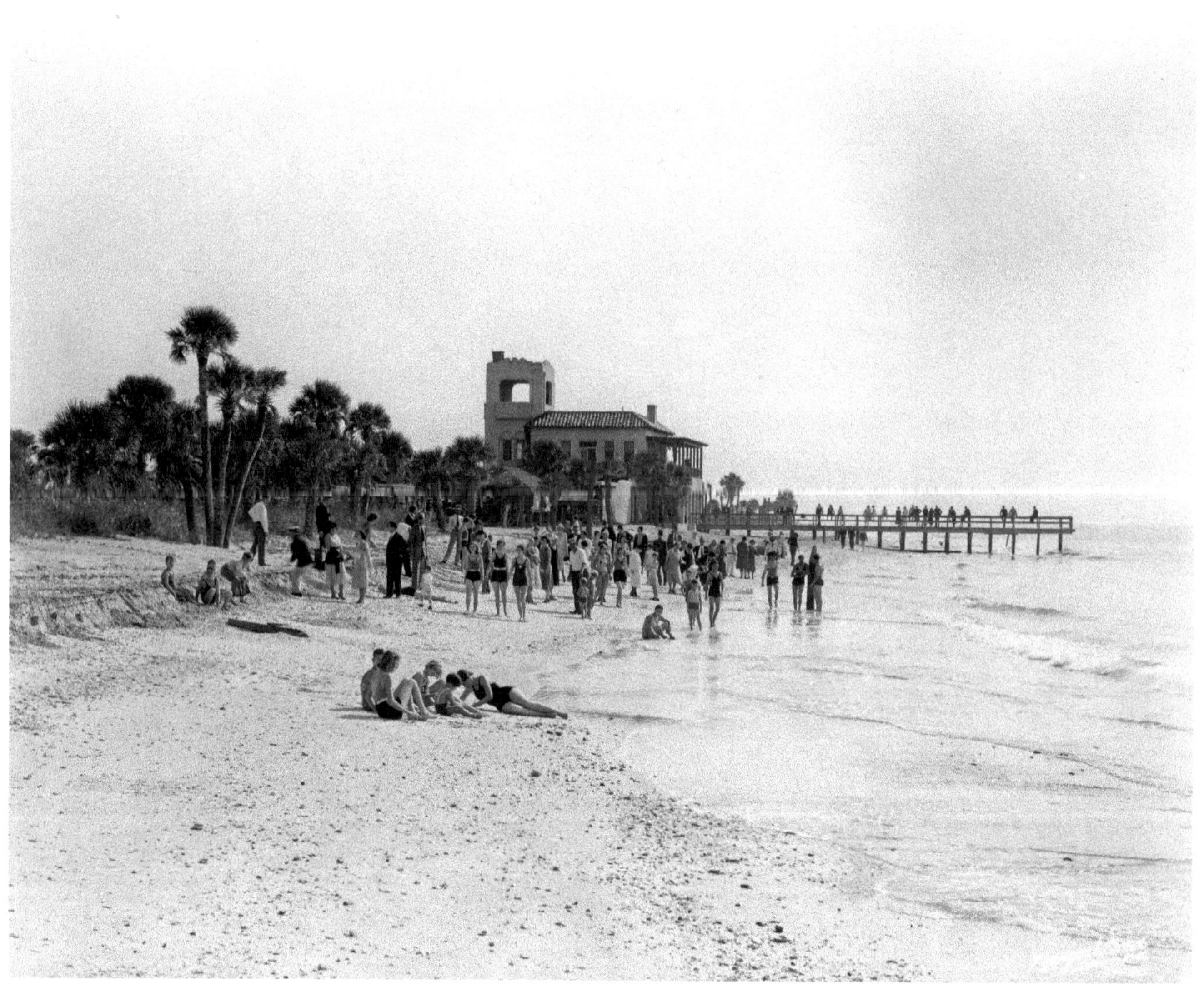

The tall building dominating the beach at Venice in November 1931 is the elaborate casino built by the Brotherhood of Locomotive Engineers. A small pavilion behind it was used for community gatherings ranging from church services to picnics.

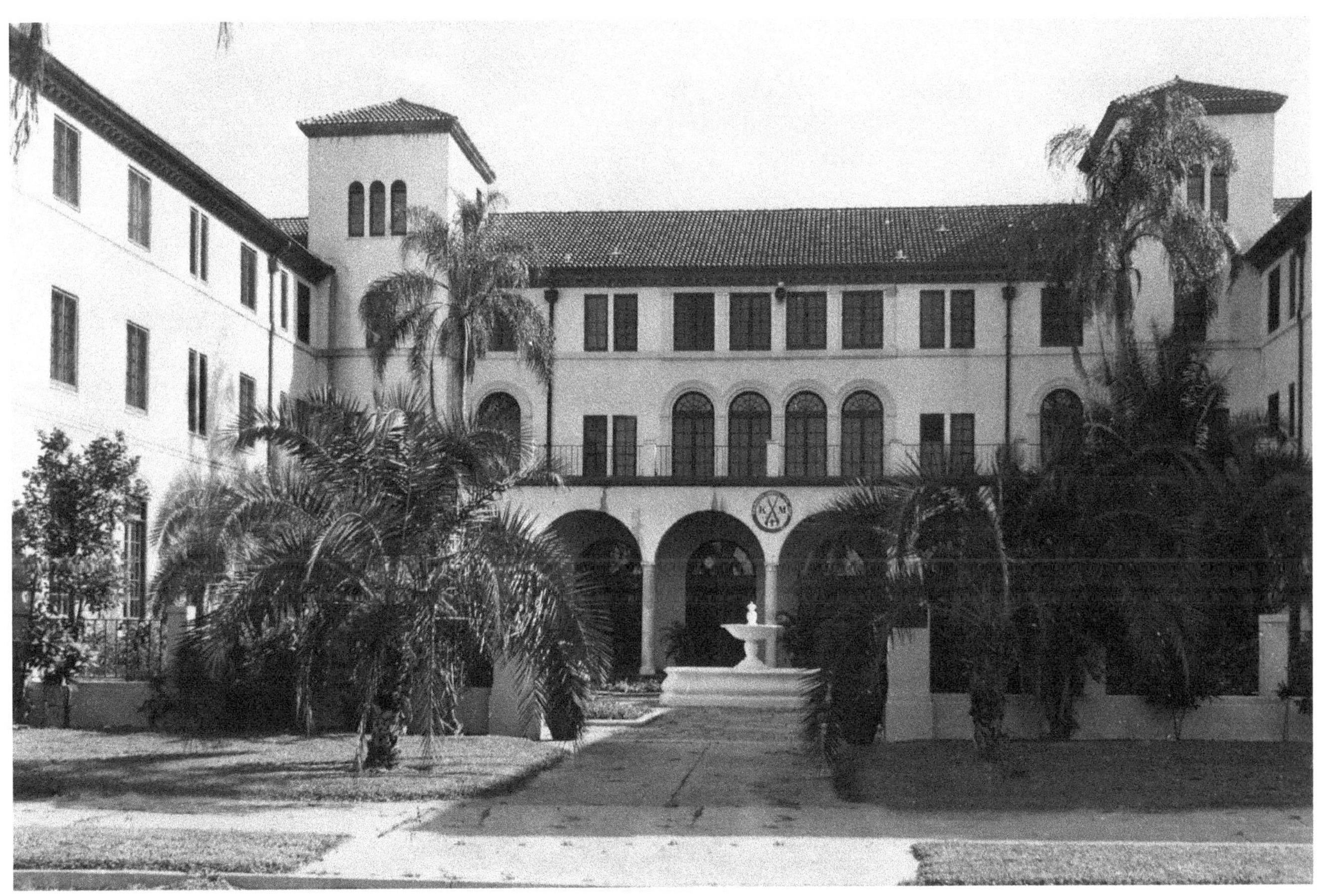

The Kentucky Military Institute was founded in 1845. Its 1894 headmaster believed that outdoor recreation in Florida would be of benefit, so the school opened winter quarters in Eau Gallie. In 1932, it moved to Venice and acquired the San Marco and Venice Hotels, the latter pictured here while it was occupied by military students. The Kentucky Military Institute left Venice in 1970.

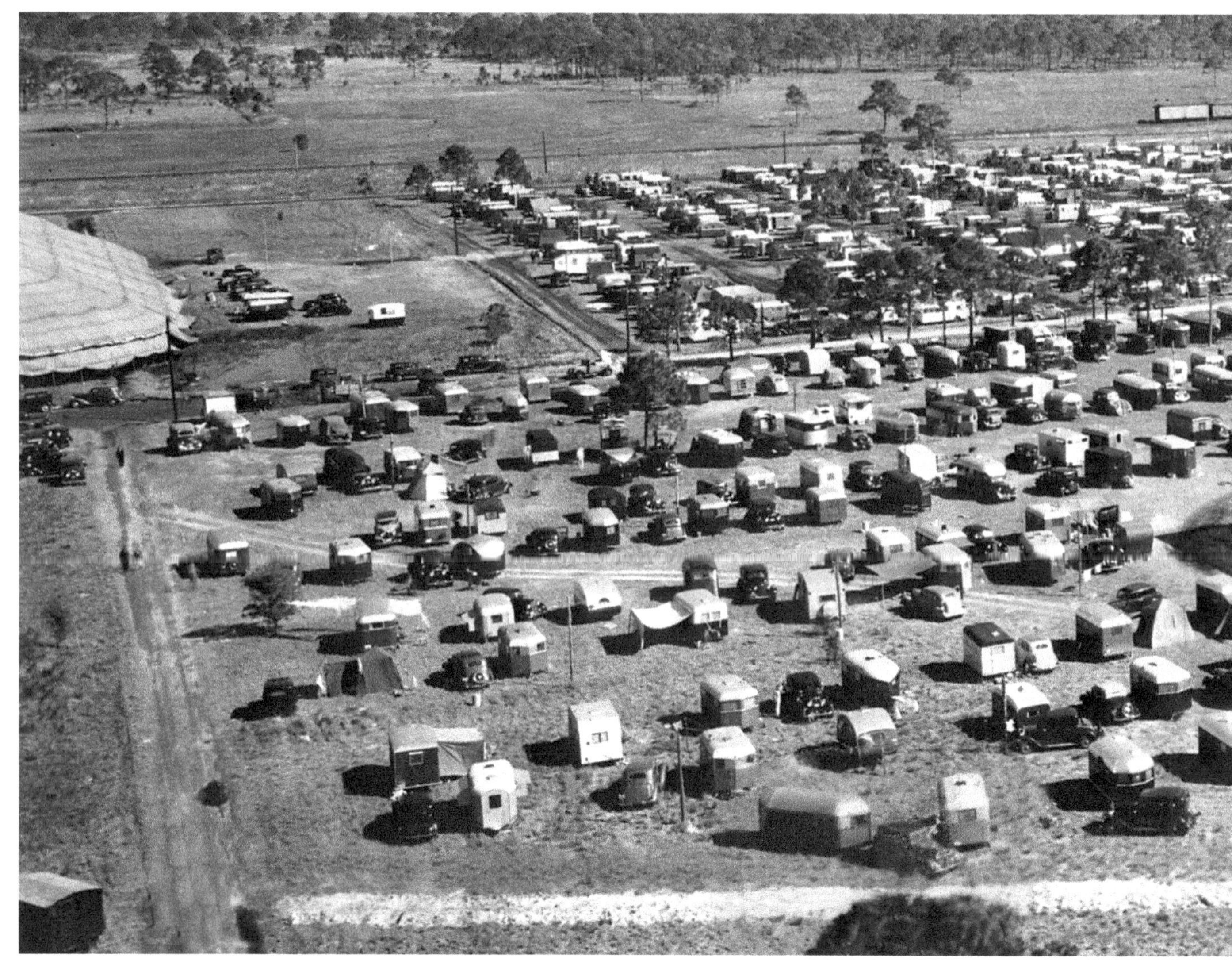

At various times from 1924 until 1988, this ballpark hosted spring training for three baseball teams: the Boston Red Sox, the Chicago White Sox, and the New York Giants. Named for Calvin and Martha Payne, who sold the 60 acres to the city, the park was also the site of the 1936 Tin Can Tourist convention shown here. In 1980, the baseball diamond was replaced with tennis courts and running trails.

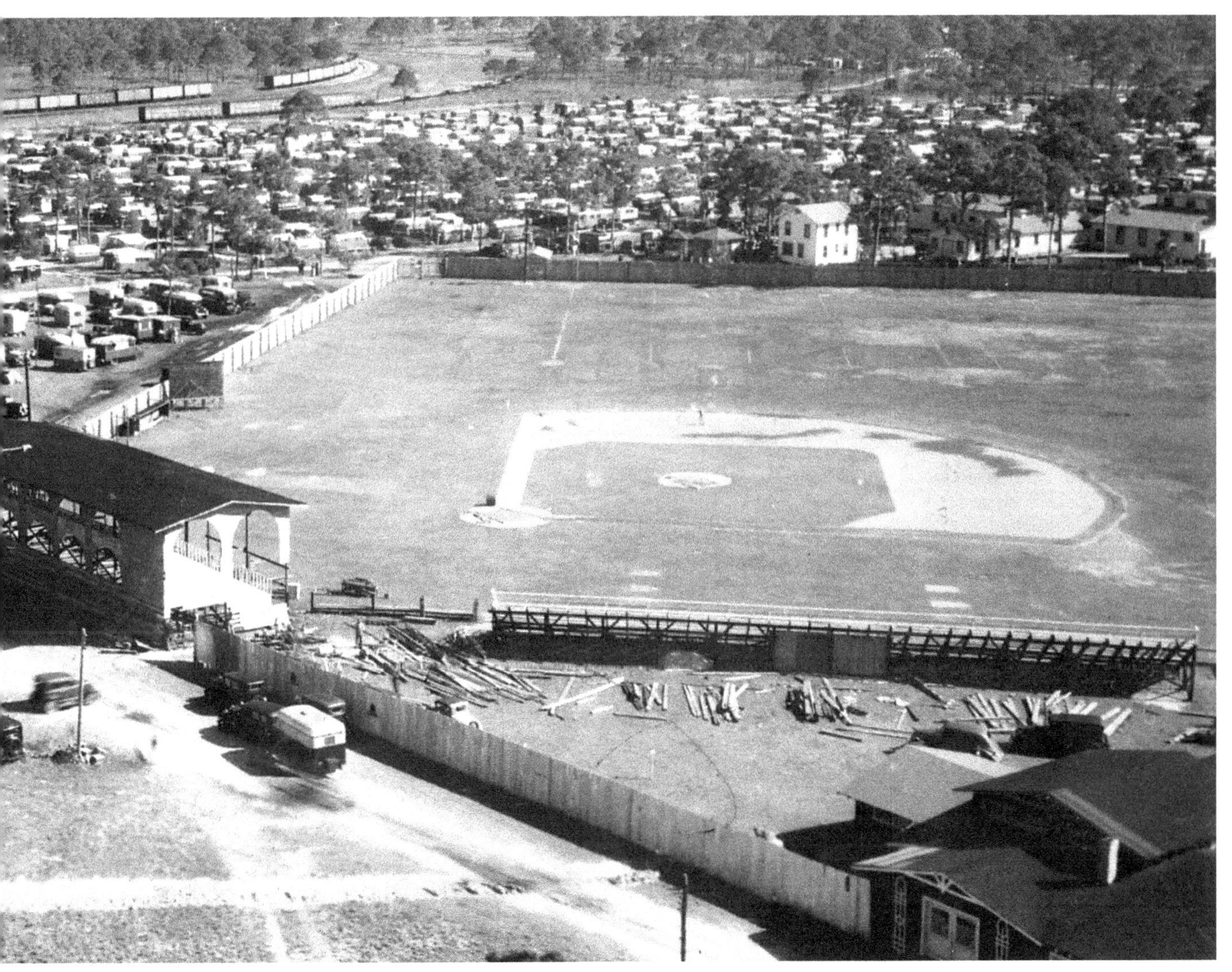

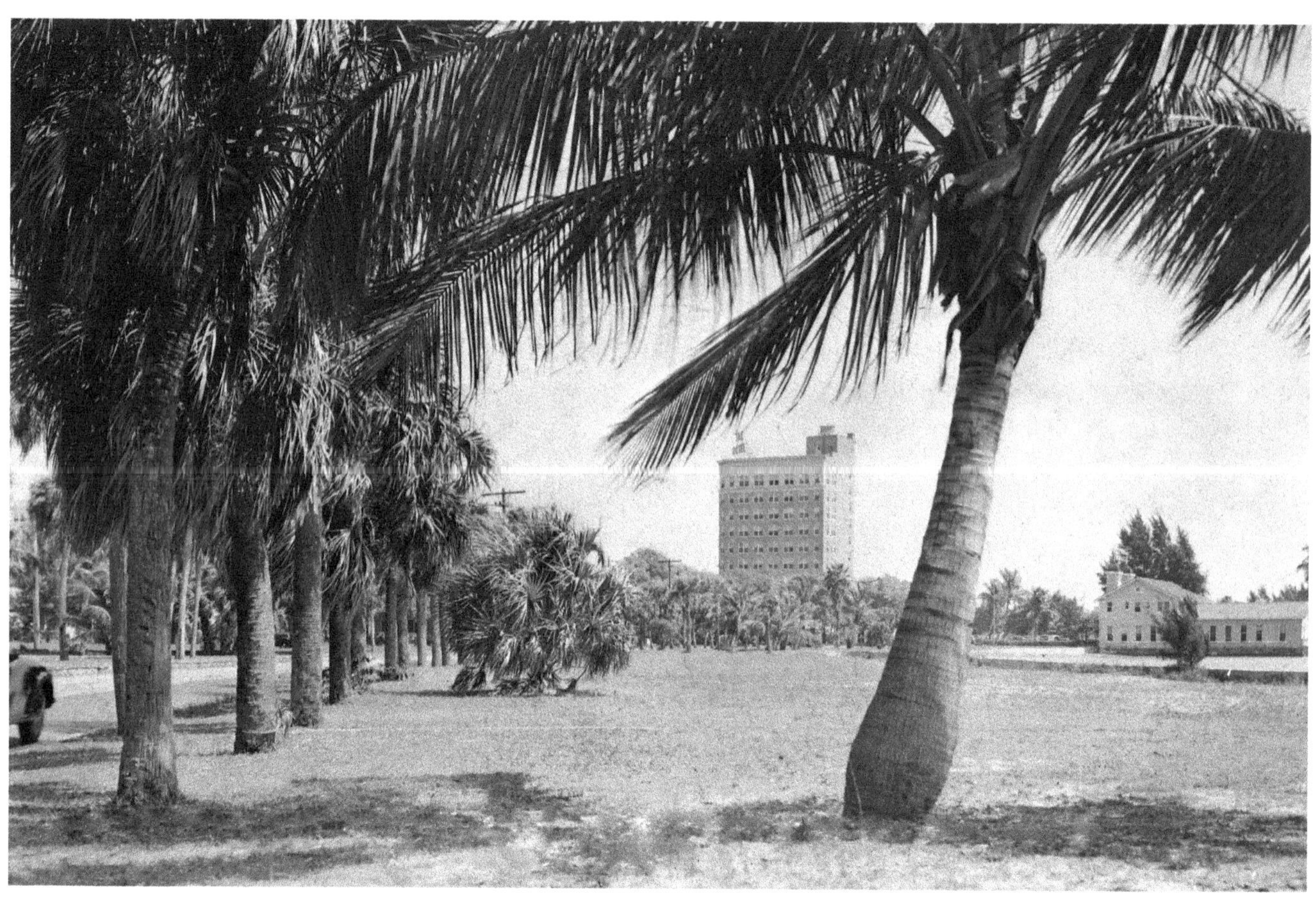

American National Bank was built on the former site of the Belle Haven Inn in 1926. In 1928, the bank closed and depositors received less than 19 cents for each dollar they had on account. It stood vacant until 1937, when it became the Orange Blossom Hotel shown here. In 1967, the building was converted to the Orange Blossom Club Apartments.

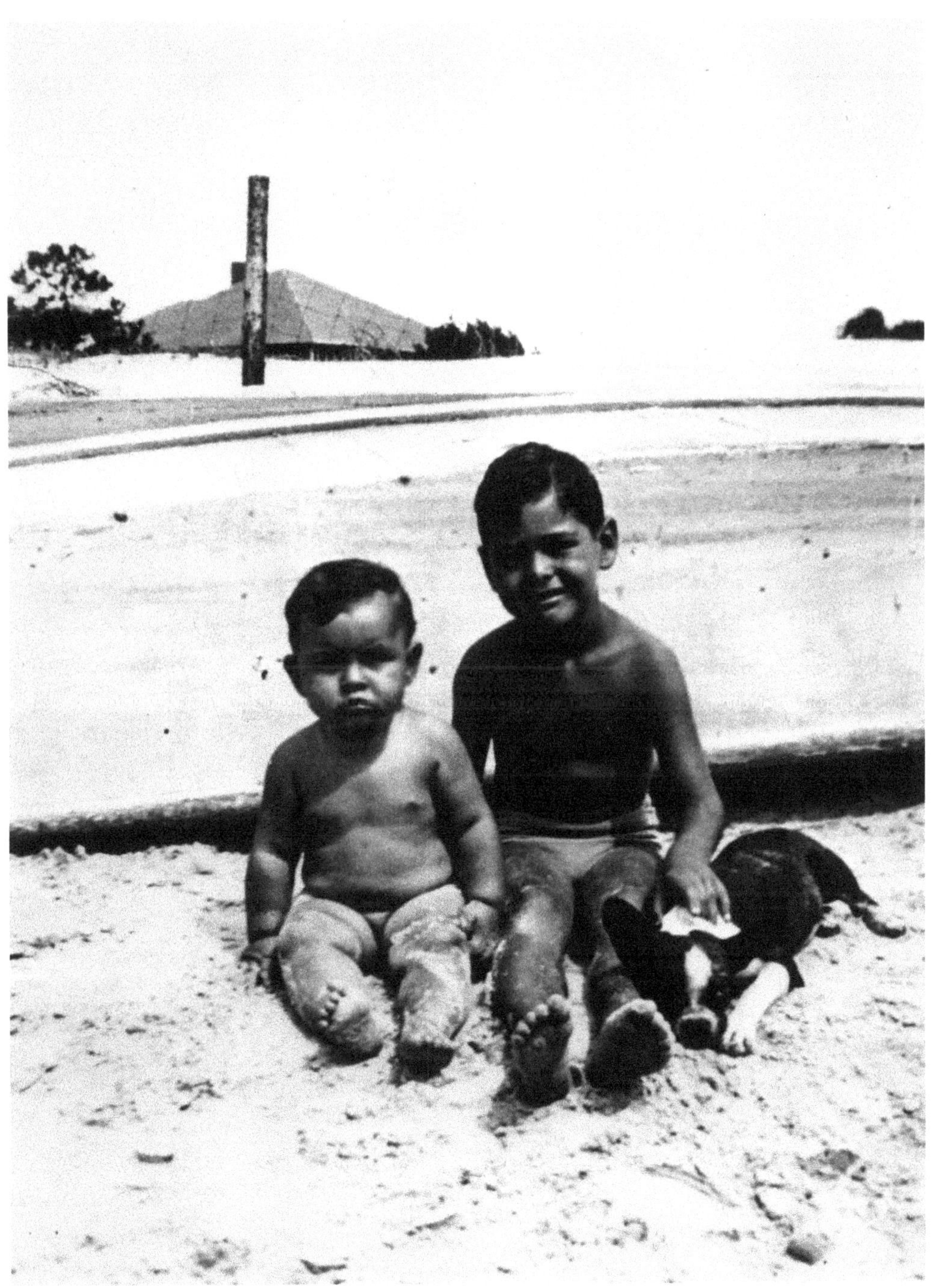

Alex and Bob Rosin and their dog, Bobo, enjoy Sarasota Beach in 1939. Even during the Great Depression, the area's beaches attracted not only visitors, but those desiring to settle somewhere with a view of the Gulf of Mexico. Despite the major damage inflicted by hurricanes in 1921 and 1926, coastal construction continued, and still goes on today.

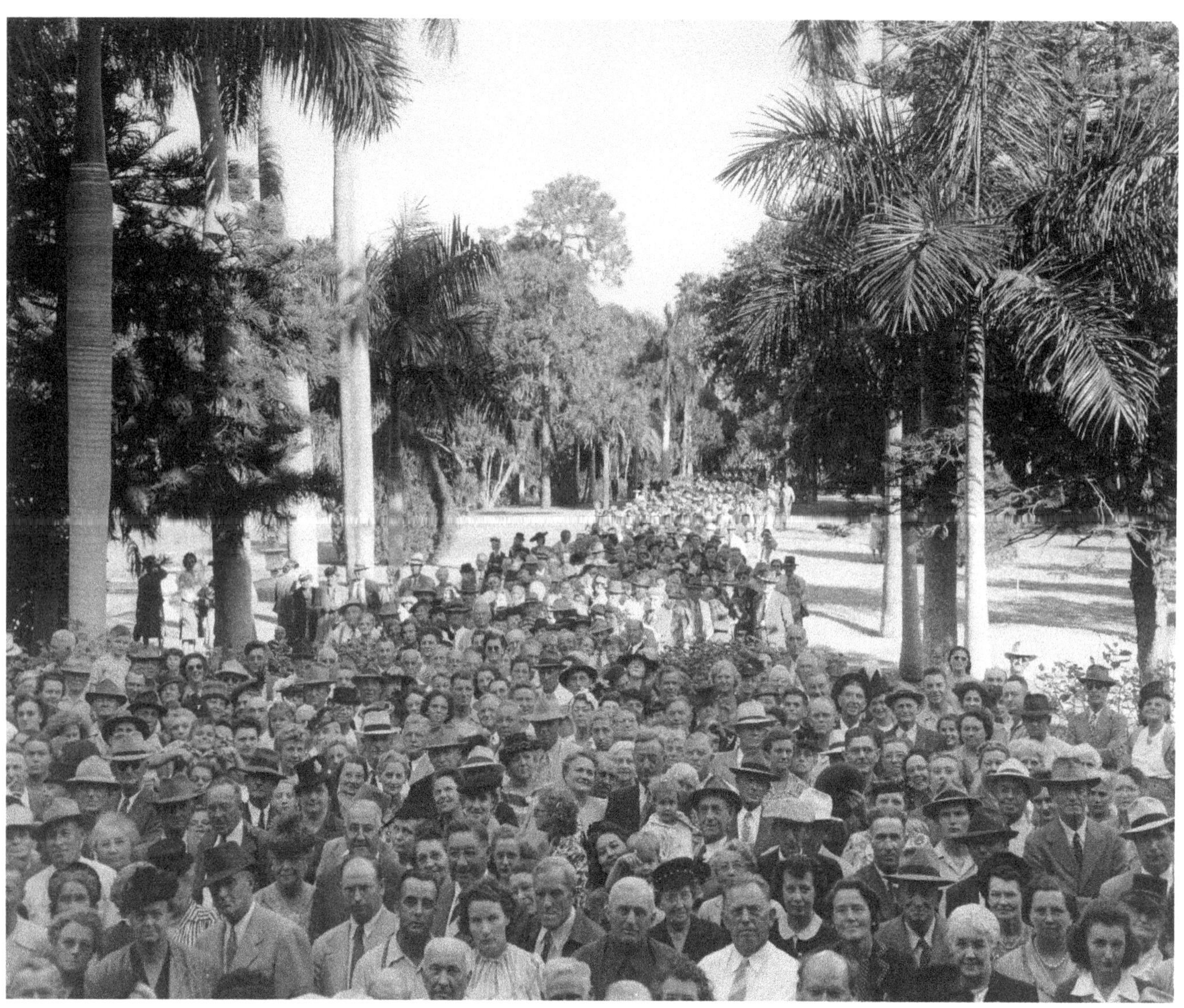

The John and Mable Ringling Museum of Art opened in 1931, two years after Mable's death. The Ringling fortune became entangled in a legal mess which wasn't sorted out until a decade after John's 1936 death. In 1946, the museum and the Ringling home were acquired by the state and drew crowds such as this one to view the impressive collection.

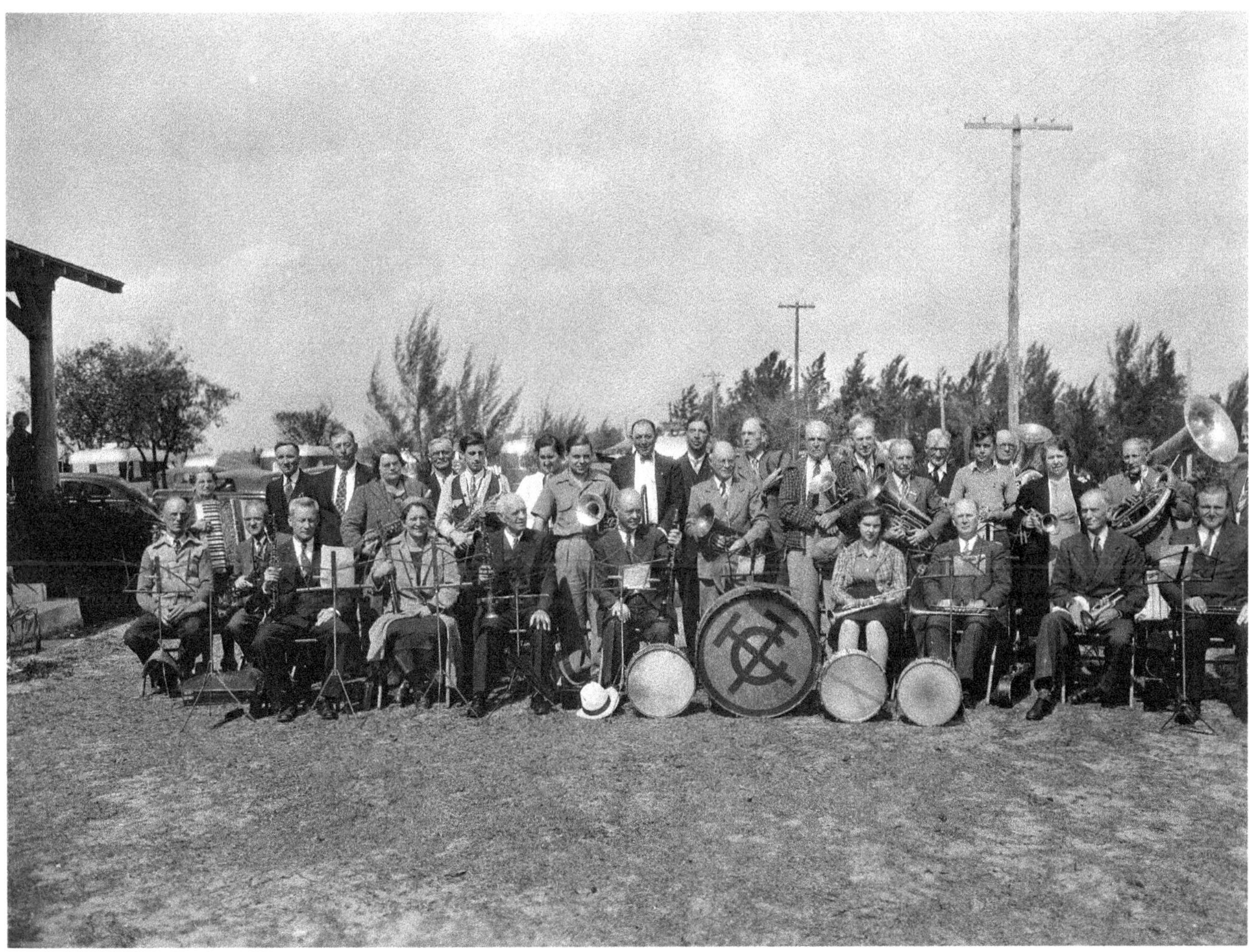

Tin Can Tourists formed their own social clubs, including the band seen here in the early 1940s, which was about the time of the third wave of tourists. The first wave, in the 1910s, had mostly used tents. The second, in the 1920s, had house trailers or stayed in converted homes. The third spurred the growth of motels, which initially were little more than small cabins with kitchenettes.

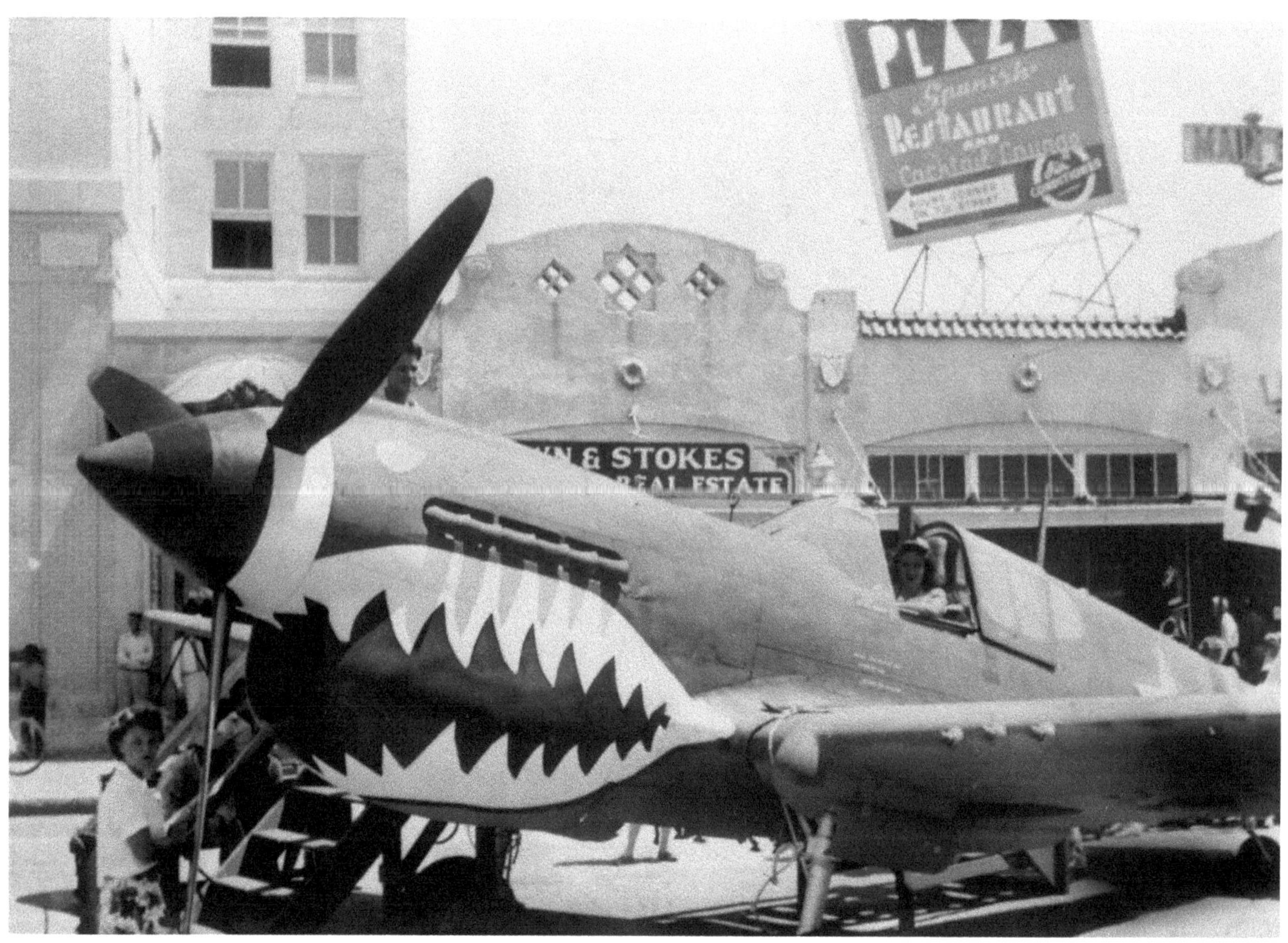

In 1942, the airport was made into the Sarasota Army Air Field, a bomber training base. The 97th Bombardment Group was moved there, but the planes were too heavy. To avoid runway damage, the base was converted into a facility for training fighter pilots. Jean Marani bought a war bond so she could have her picture taken in this P-40 Flying Tiger.

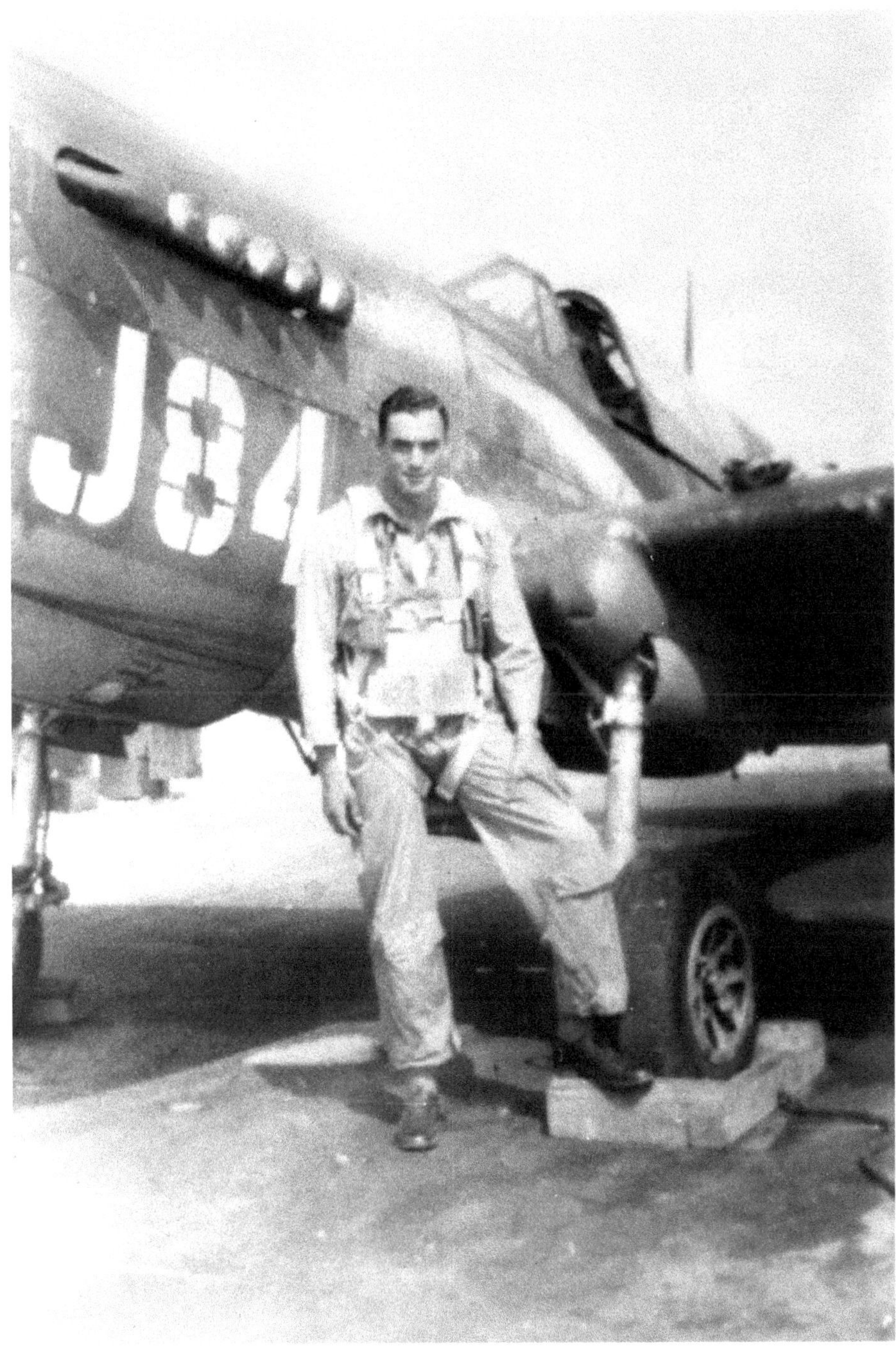

To supplement the training at nearby Sarasota Army Air Field, the Venice Air Base also began training pilots in 1943. Lieutenant Jerry Jacobs is shown here at fighter pilot school. He would later be shot down over Germany and spend nine months in a POW camp. Others trained in Venice included military patients recuperating at the army hospital who received instruction in fighting fires.

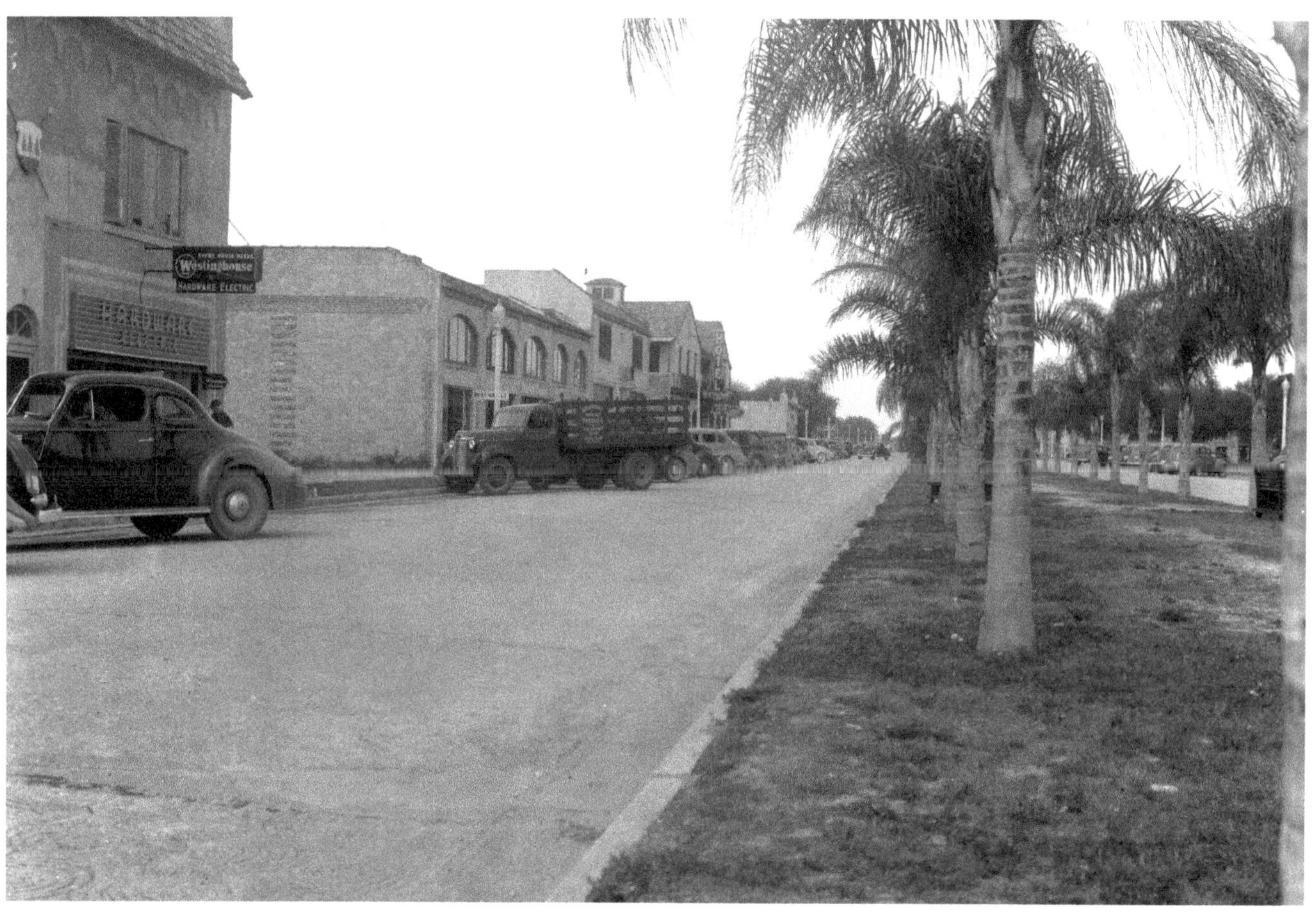

When John Nolen planned Venice, he felt it was an opportunity to balance trade, tourism, and agriculture. Farmland was to be developed along with downtown businesses and residences. The original plan also included a segregated Harlem Village for black residents. By the time this photo was taken in 1945, the Nolen plan had been abandoned.

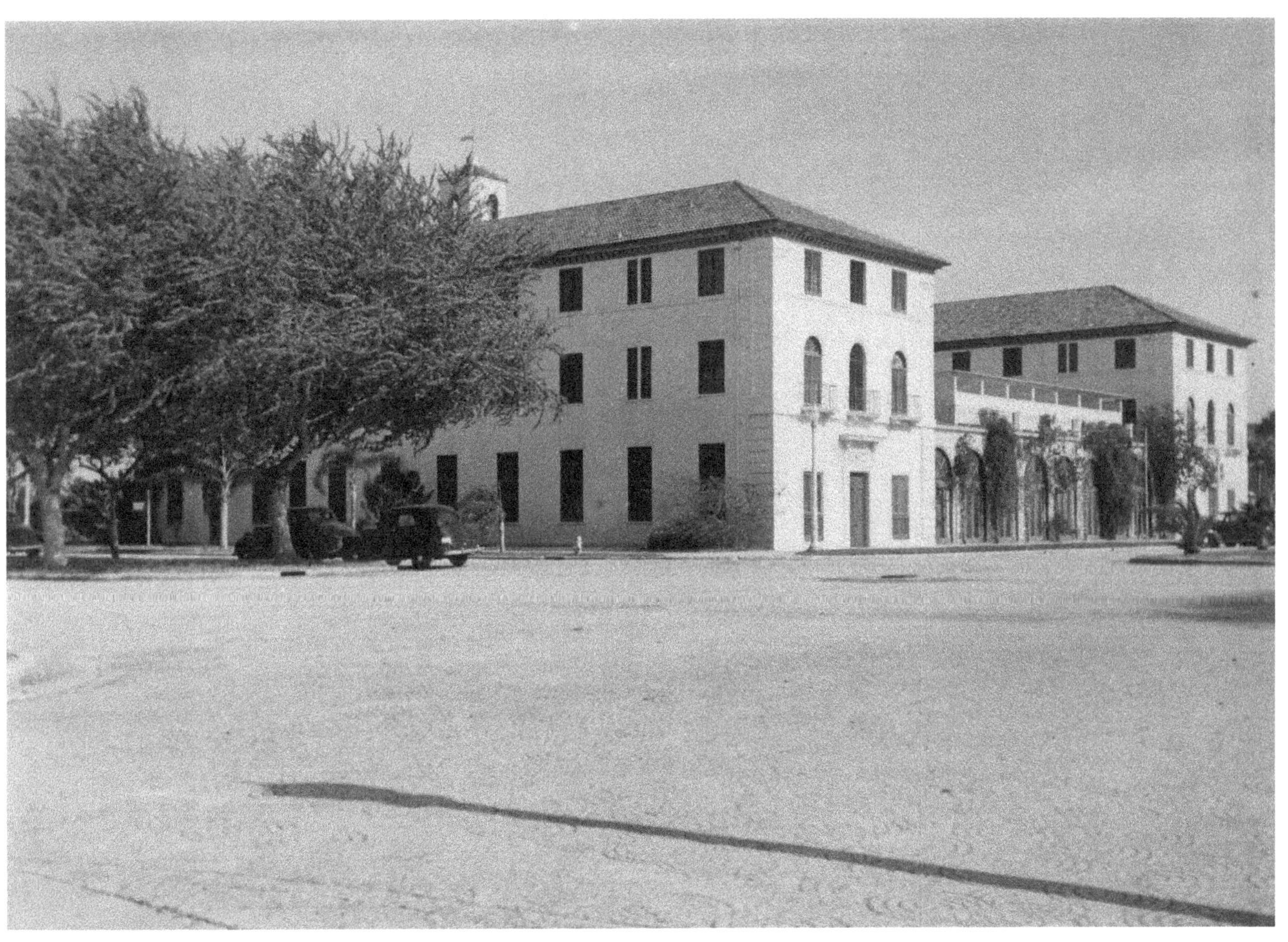

New York bone specialist Fred Albee arrived in Venice in 1916 and bought considerable acreage from Bertha Palmer, which he later sold to the Brotherhood of Locomotive Engineers. In 1933, believing that Venice was at the center of a belt of rare and healthful actinic rays, Albee opened this Florida Medical Center in what had been the Park View Hotel.

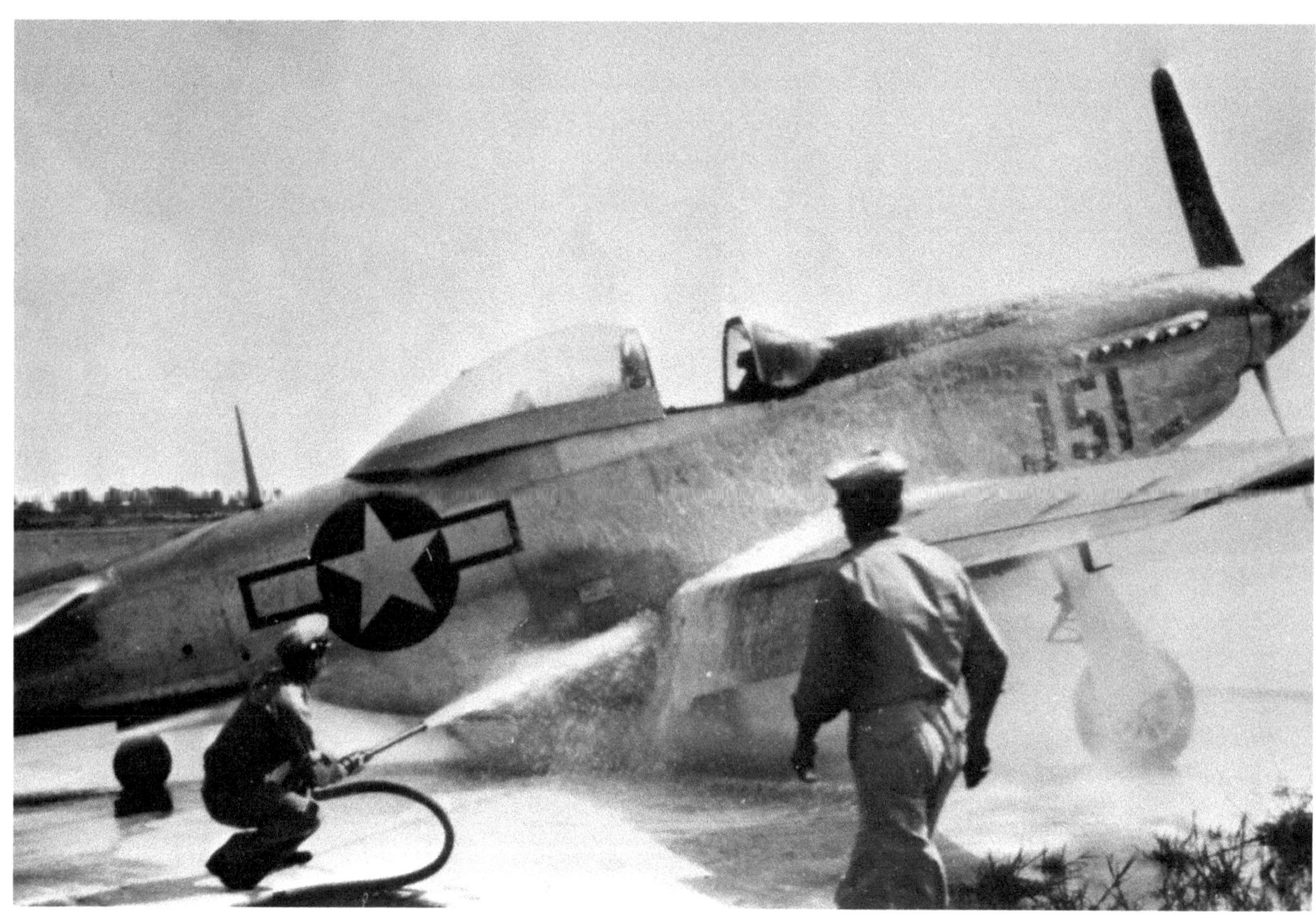

During World War II, one of the target ranges for Army Air Corps pilots in training was on the central section of Longboat Key. Flying their planes in just above the waters of Sarasota Bay, they would shoot at silhouettes of German tanks and armored personnel carriers to simulate what they would experience when they were deployed to North Africa. Here, a fire is being put out on a P-51 Mustang at the Sarasota field.

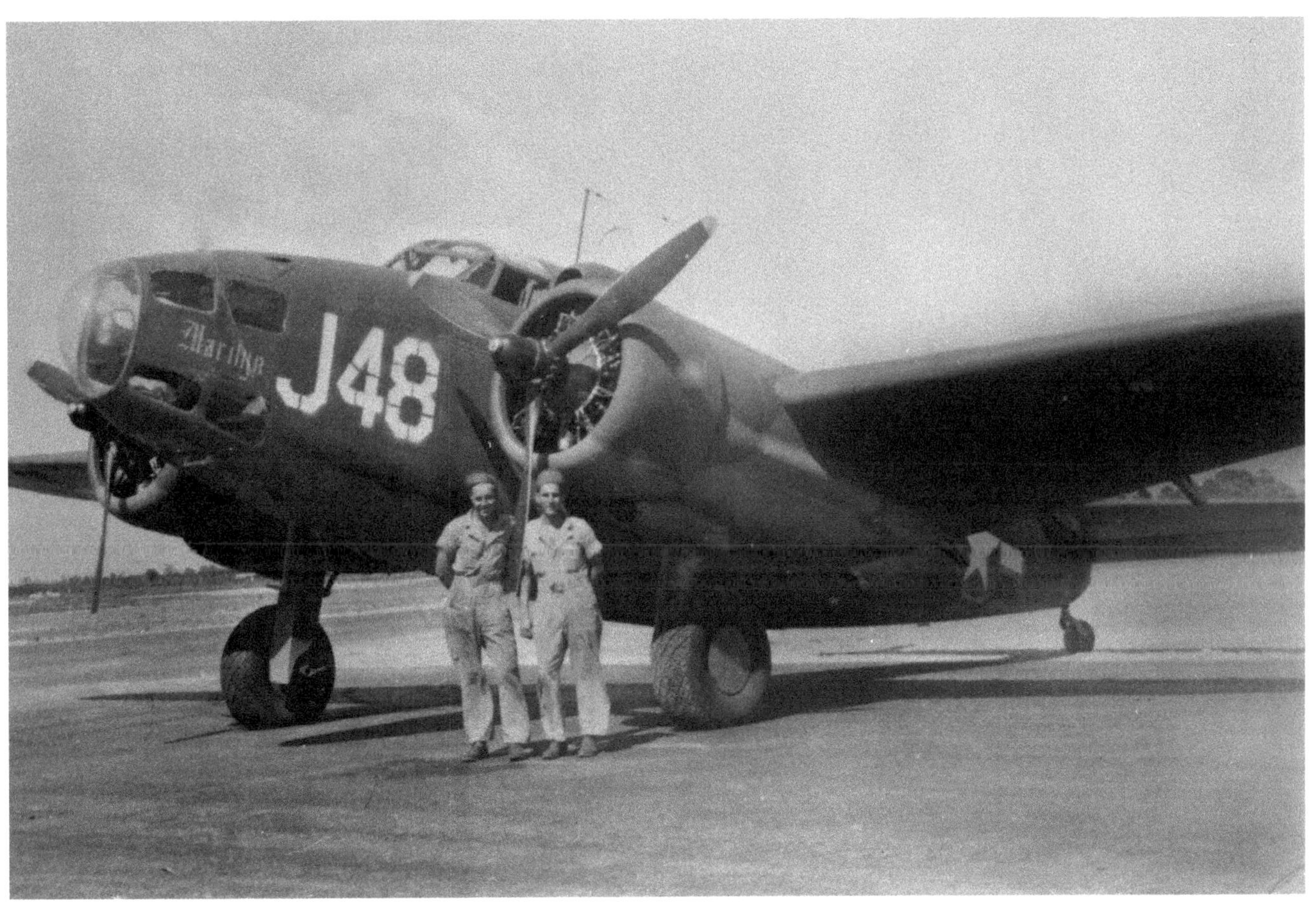

Photographed near the end of the war, this A-29 Hudson is a Lockheed bomber of a type often used to destroy submarines. It was stationed at the Sarasota Army Air Field, which, along with the Venice Army Base, was deactivated in 1946. Sarasota's airport, built in 1940 as a Works Progress Administration project, became the civilian Sarasota-Bradenton Airport.

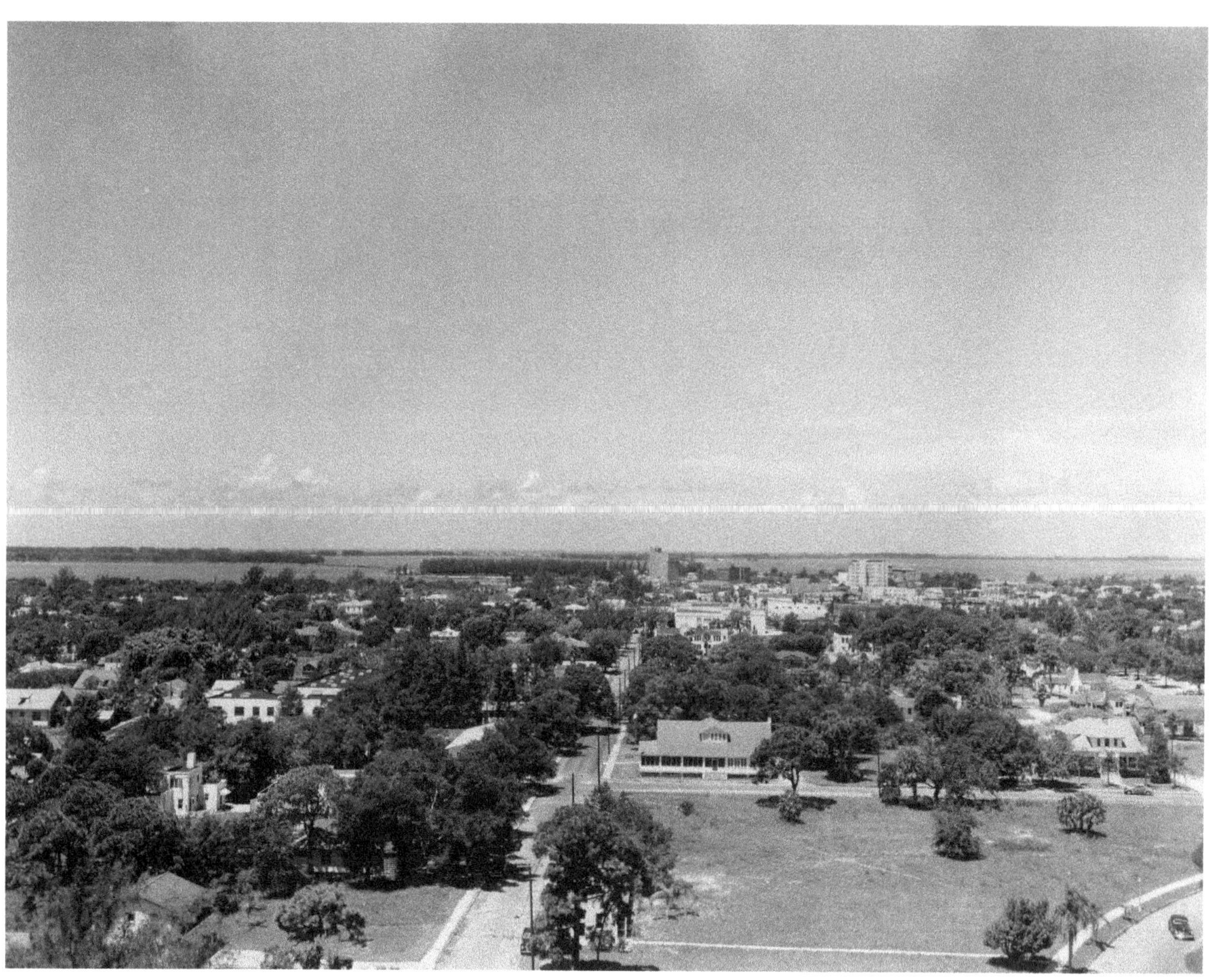

In 1946, one of the best views of Sarasota was from the roof of the ten-story Terrace Hotel. It was built by Charles Ringling in 1925 on the site of the first tee of Gillespie's golf course, and was later renamed as the Sarasota Motor Hotel. In 1972, it was converted into administrative office space and renamed the Sarasota County Terrace Building.

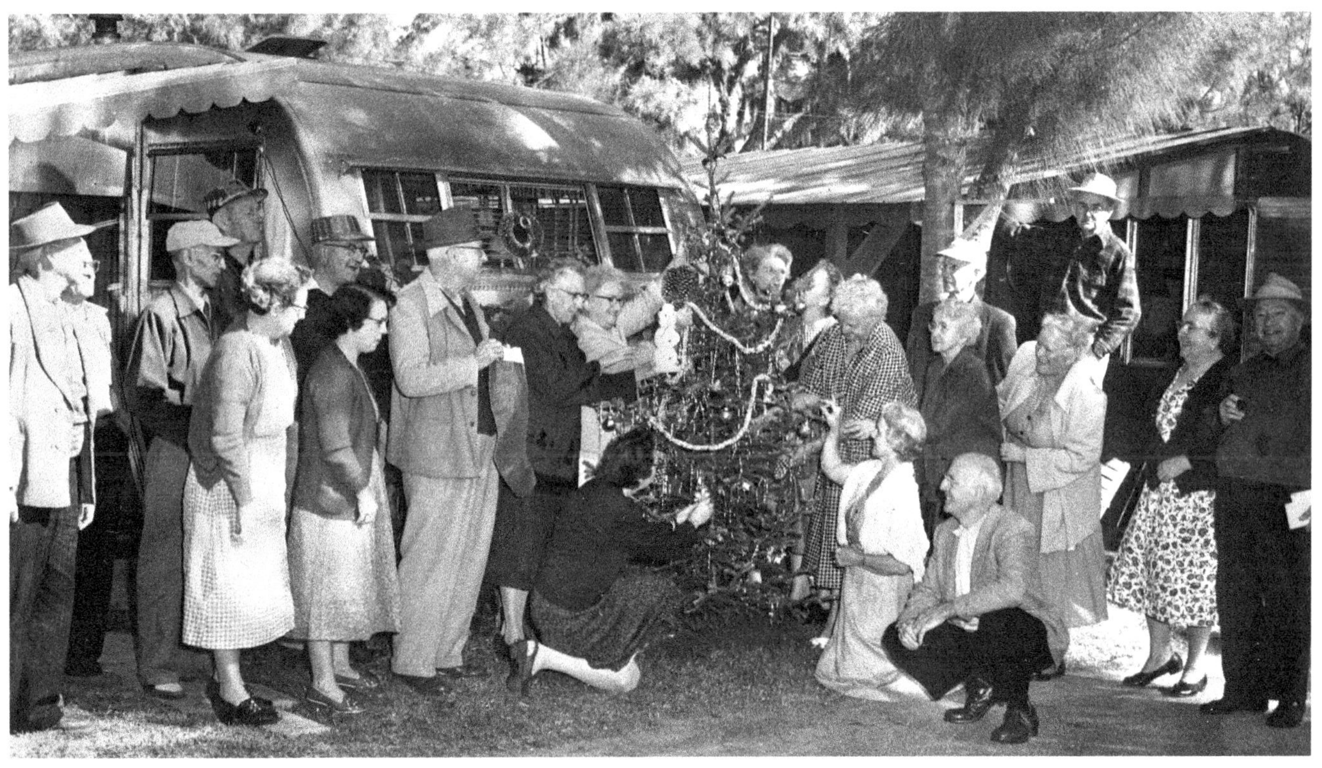

A group of elderly men and women decorate a Christmas tree in a Sarasota city park in 1946. They are likely Tin Can Tourists, among the many from all over the country who would stay in parks in a variety of travel trailers and recreational vehicles.

This tarpon was caught during a fishing tournament sponsored by the Sarasota County Anglers' Club, formed in 1930. The club's first president was Powell Crosley Jr., owner of Cincinnati radio station WLW. As John Ringling's guest in 1929, he caught his first tarpon and so loved the experience and the city that he built a mansion in Sarasota.

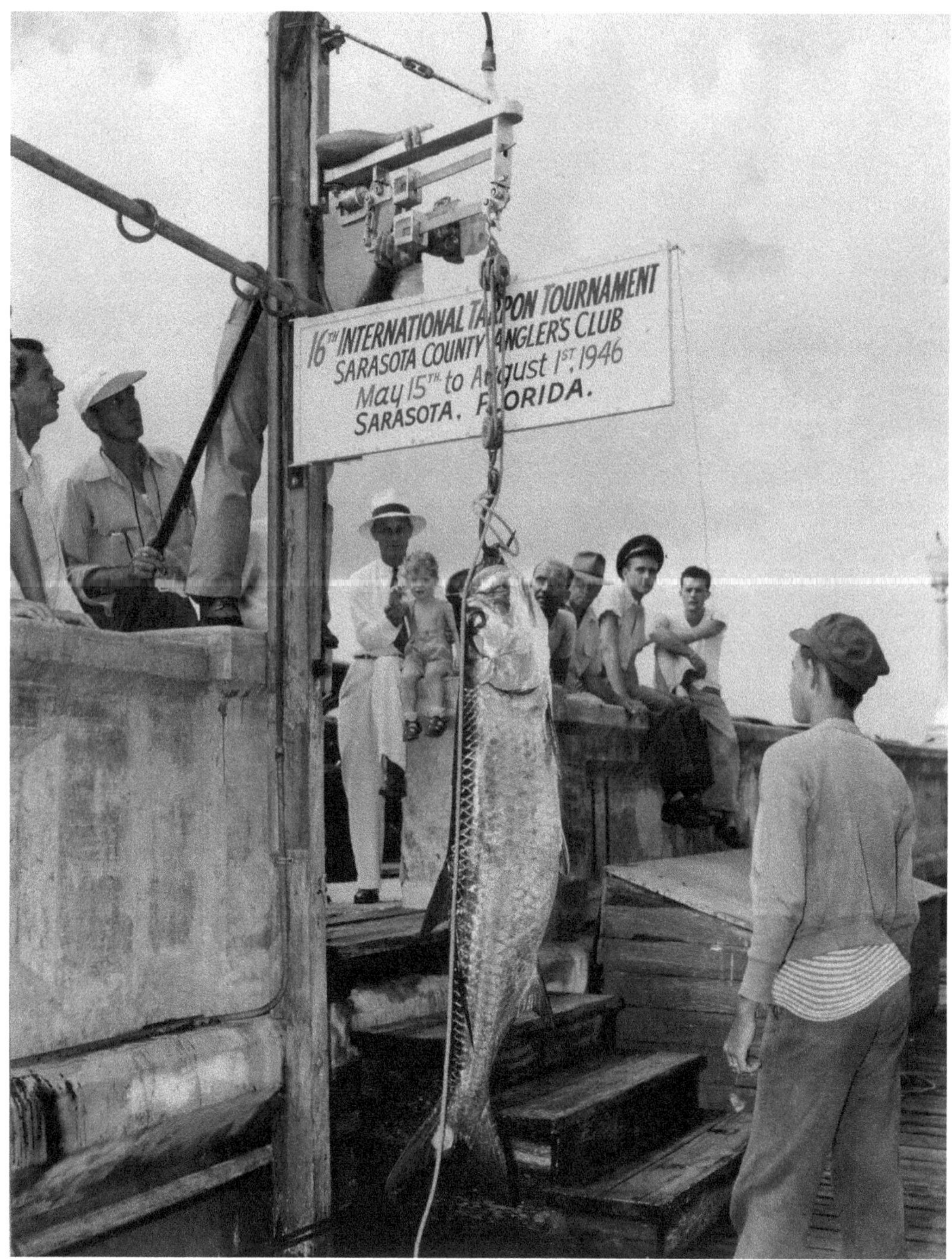

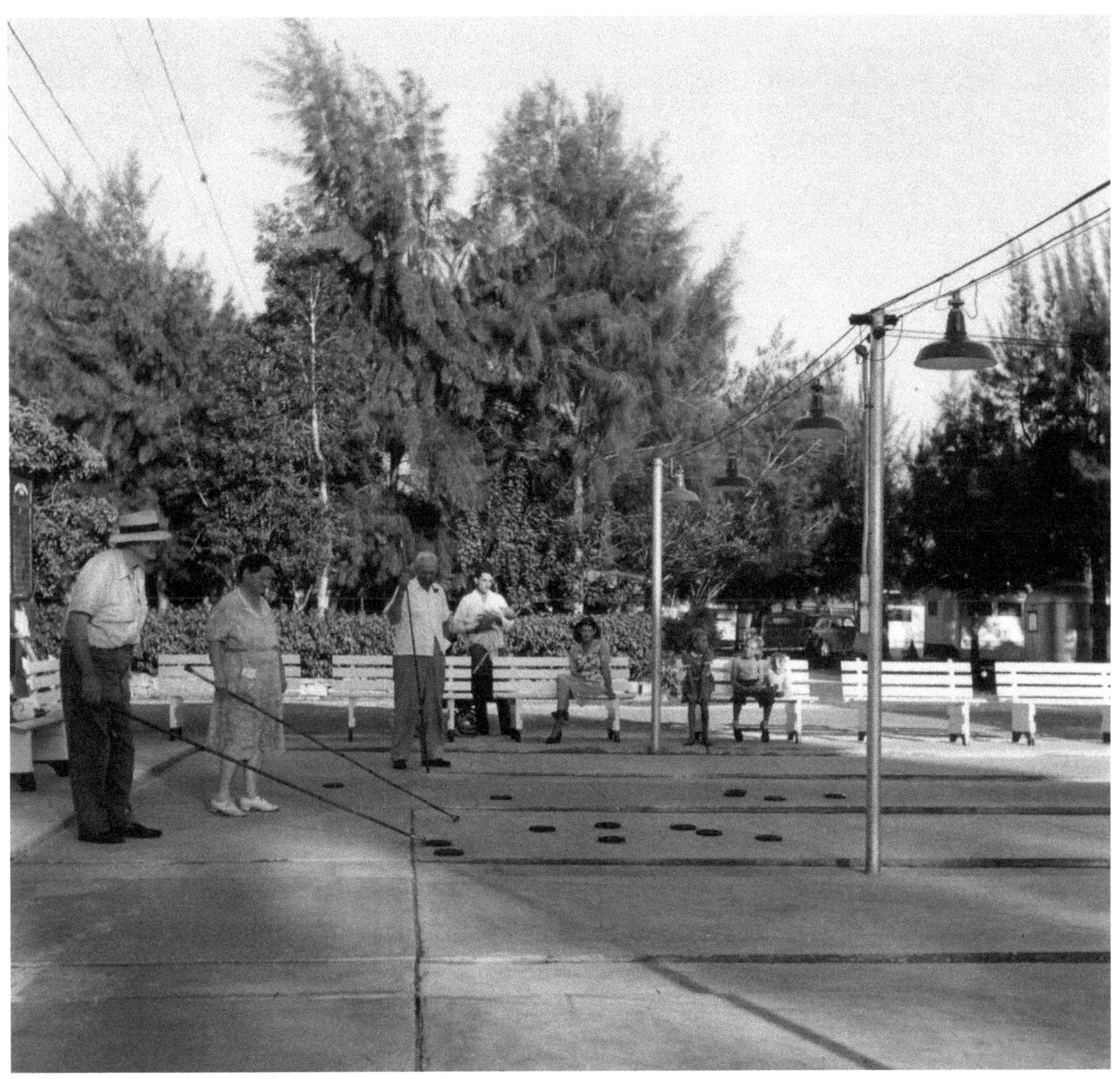

The Venice Shuffleboard Club was founded in 1938 and is still going strong. Shown here in 1946 is a trailer park in Sarasota with its own shuffleboard courts.

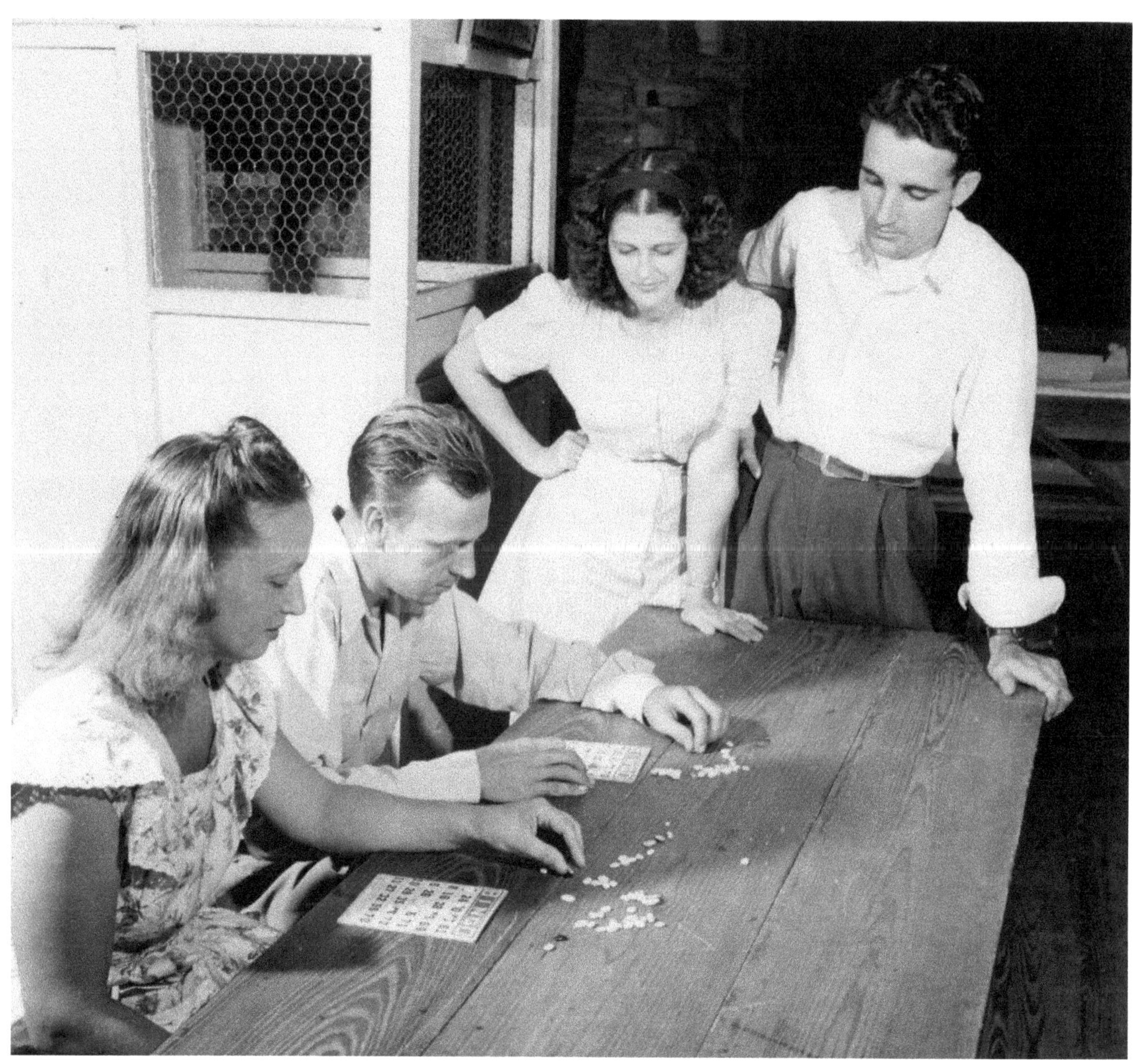

Another popular pastime at area trailer parks was bingo. Unlike at modern bingo parlors, where crowds play with multiple paper "cards" and vie for large jackpots, these trailer park guests are playing the game with a single card each and disc markers to cover the called numbers.

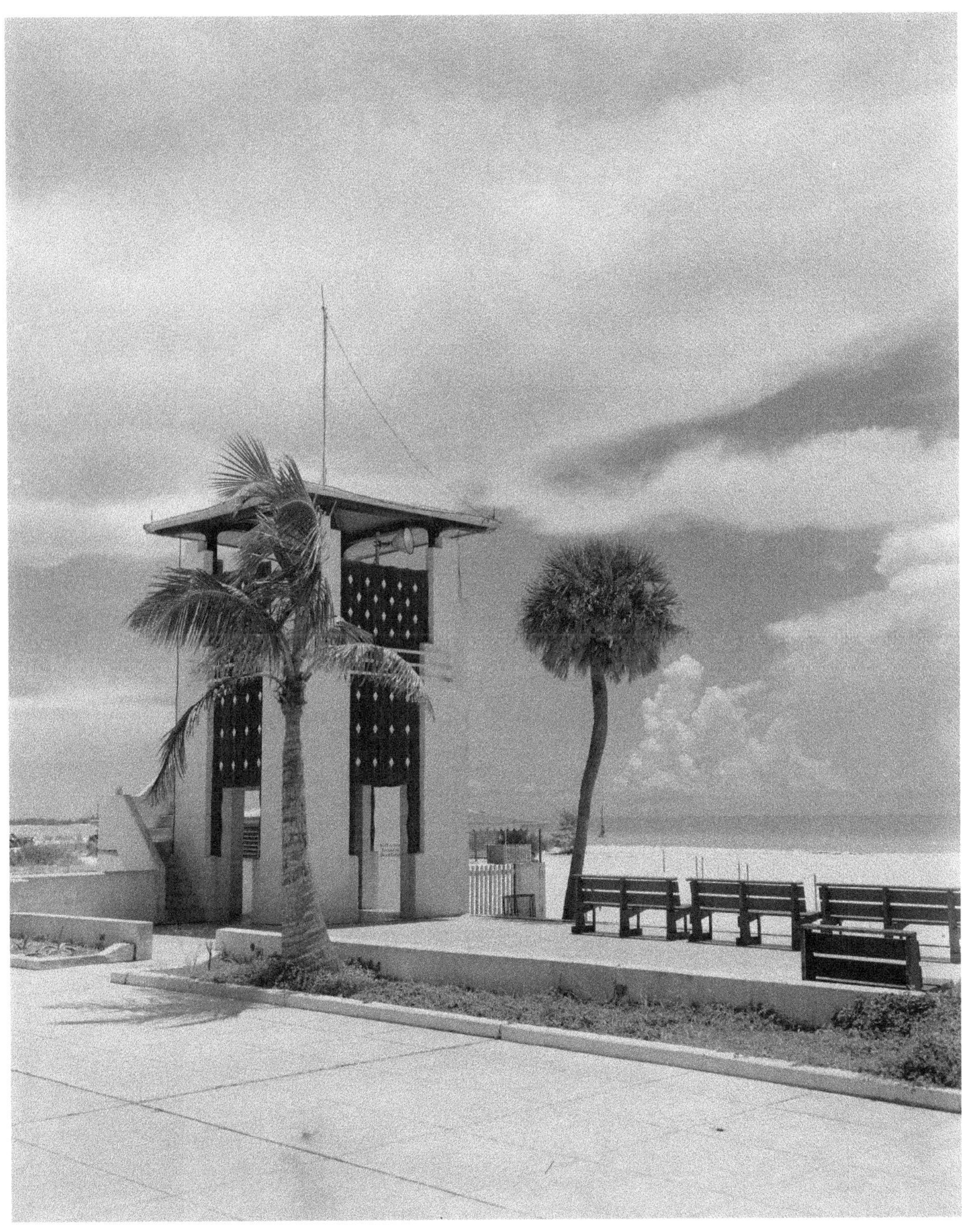

As the coast became settled by those who saw opportunities for development, visits to beaches such as this would usually end with visitors heading back to lodgings on the mainland. But with widespread use of air conditioning, beachside hotels and homes became much more comfortable and popular. Vacationers and residents began to stay longer.

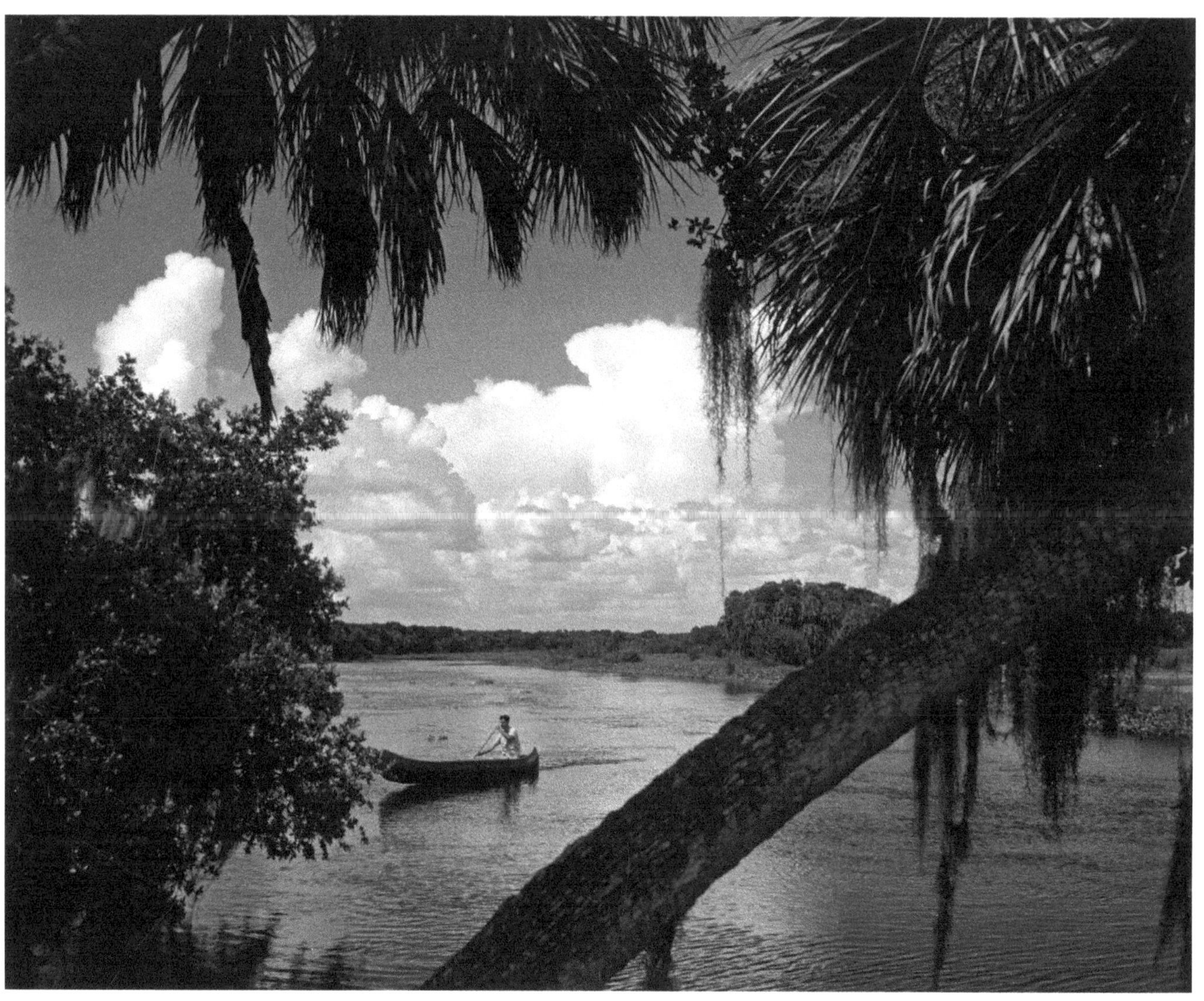

This is the Myakka River, which flows through the huge Myakka River State Park, as it appeared in 1947. Realtor A. B. Edwards, mayor of Sarasota in 1914-16 and 1919-21, was instrumental in convincing the state to acquire the land to be set aside as a natural area. By 1934, the state had already acquired more than 6,000 acres through foreclosure, but needed more.

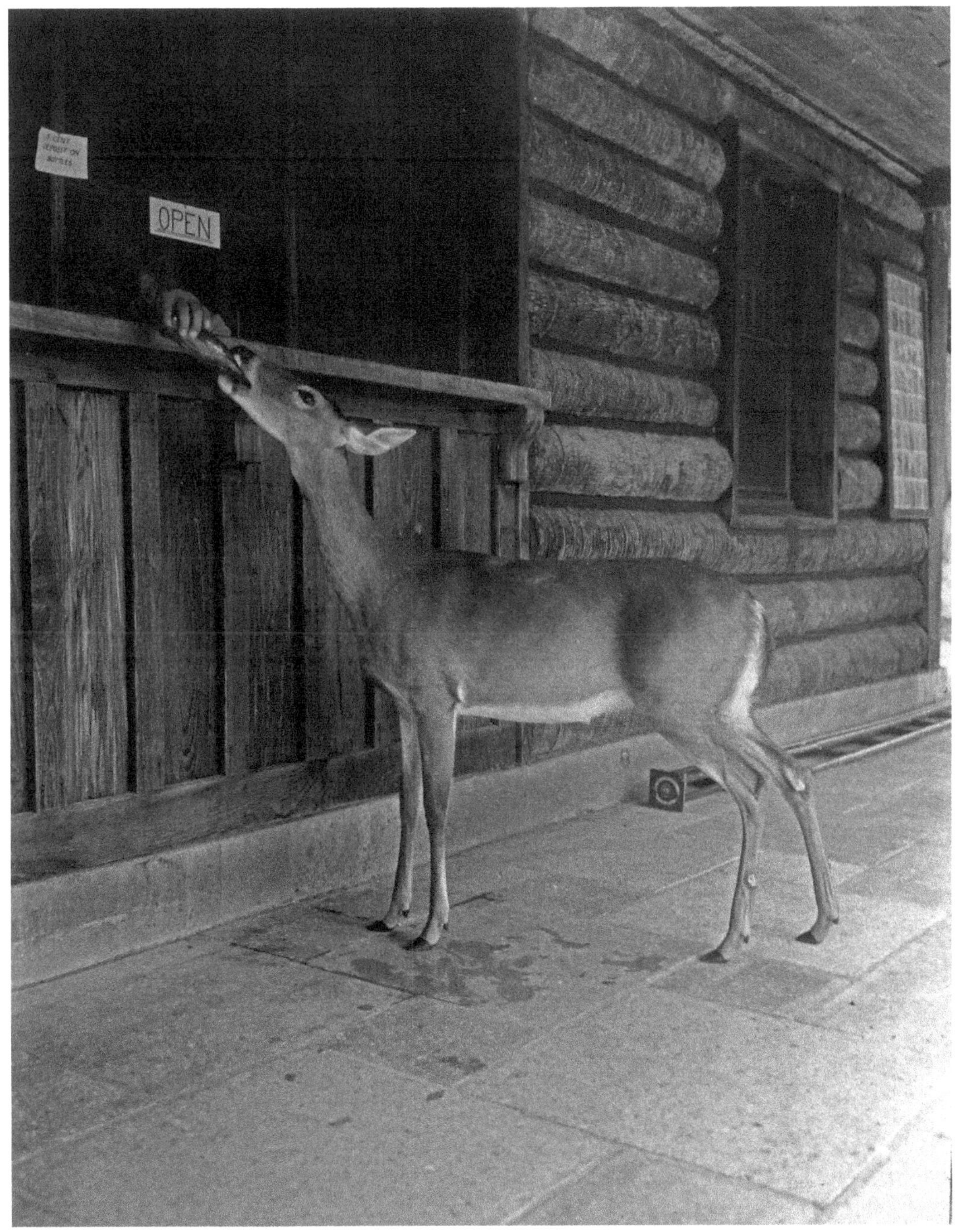

To expand Myakka River State Park, Florida purchased over 17,000 acres of Bertha Palmer's Meadow Sweet Pastures. Her descendants donated 1,900 acres to complete the park. Here, Baby Snooks, a young deer that was raised on a bottle and appeared in the 1947 movie *The Yearling,* drinks Coca-Cola from the hand of a park employee.

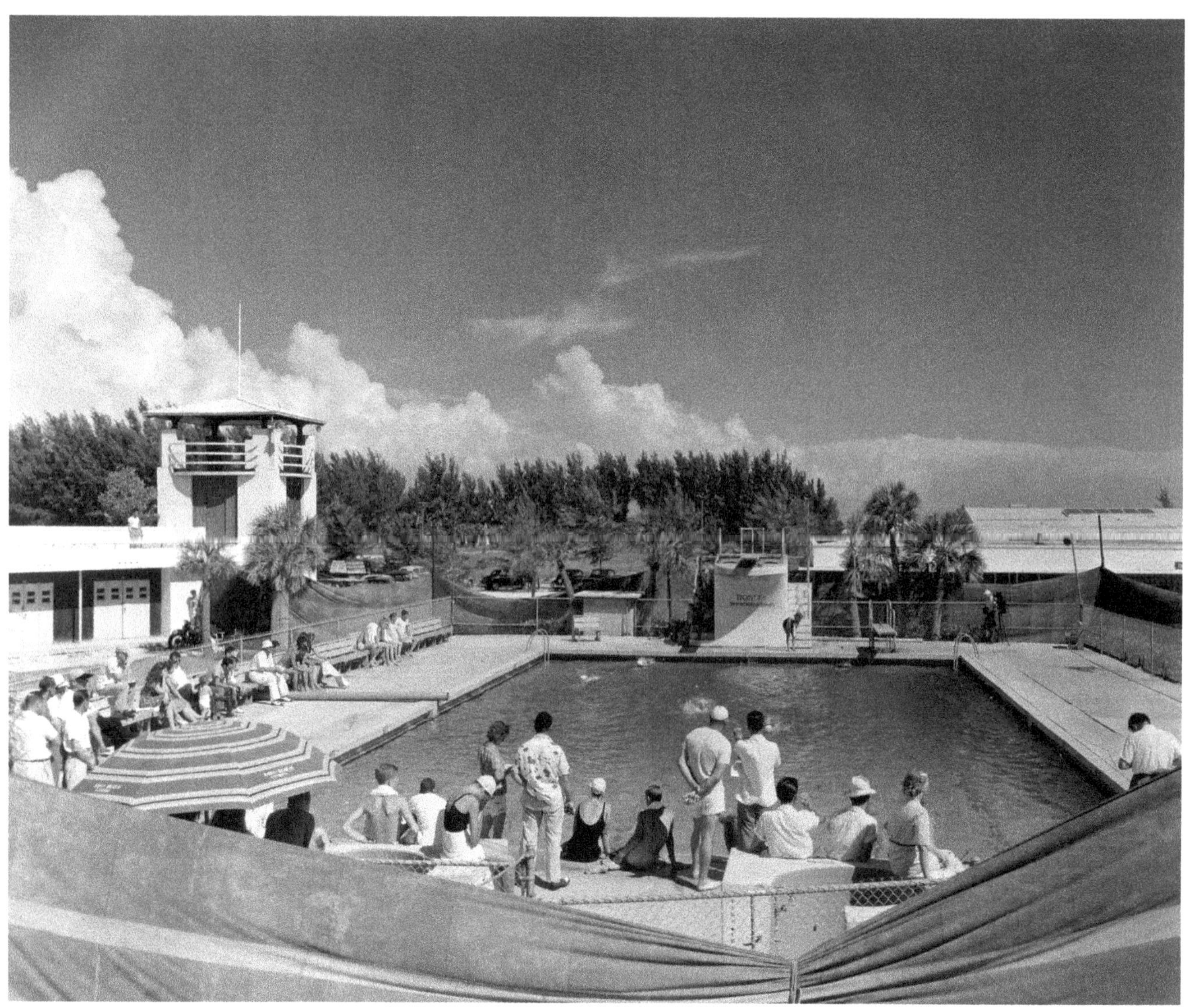

People watch the action in the water while sitting poolside on Lido Beach in 1947. In the early days, Lido Beach was part of a string of islands separated by channels that were often reconfigured by currents and storms. In the early 1920s, the islands were purchased by John Ringling, who spearheaded a monumental development project that involved moving millions of cubic feet of sand to reshape the islands.

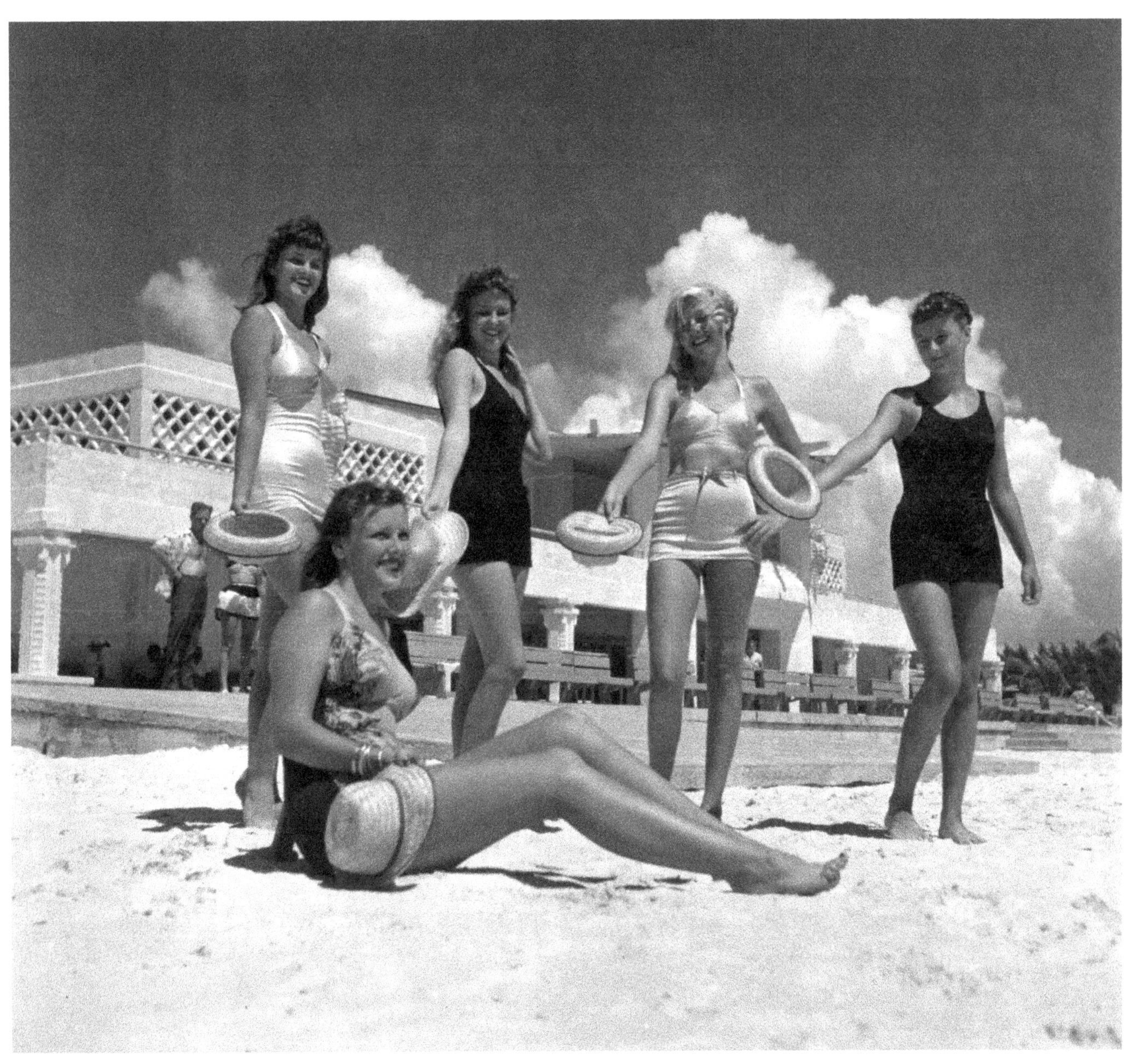

Joyce Davenport, Mary Davison, Dot Nelson, and Charlene Hornor stand behind Jean Forhan, with the Lido Beach Casino behind all of them. The casino's decoration scheme featured precast concrete seahorses, and visitors who opted not to go into the gulf waters could swim in the Olympic-size swimming pool surrounded by restaurants and lounges.

Hollywood star Esther Williams enjoys the sun in 1947 on Lido Beach, where filming took place for *On an Island with You,* co-starring Williams and Peter Lawford. Some of the scenes were shot at the casino. It was one of three MGM movies Williams made in Florida.

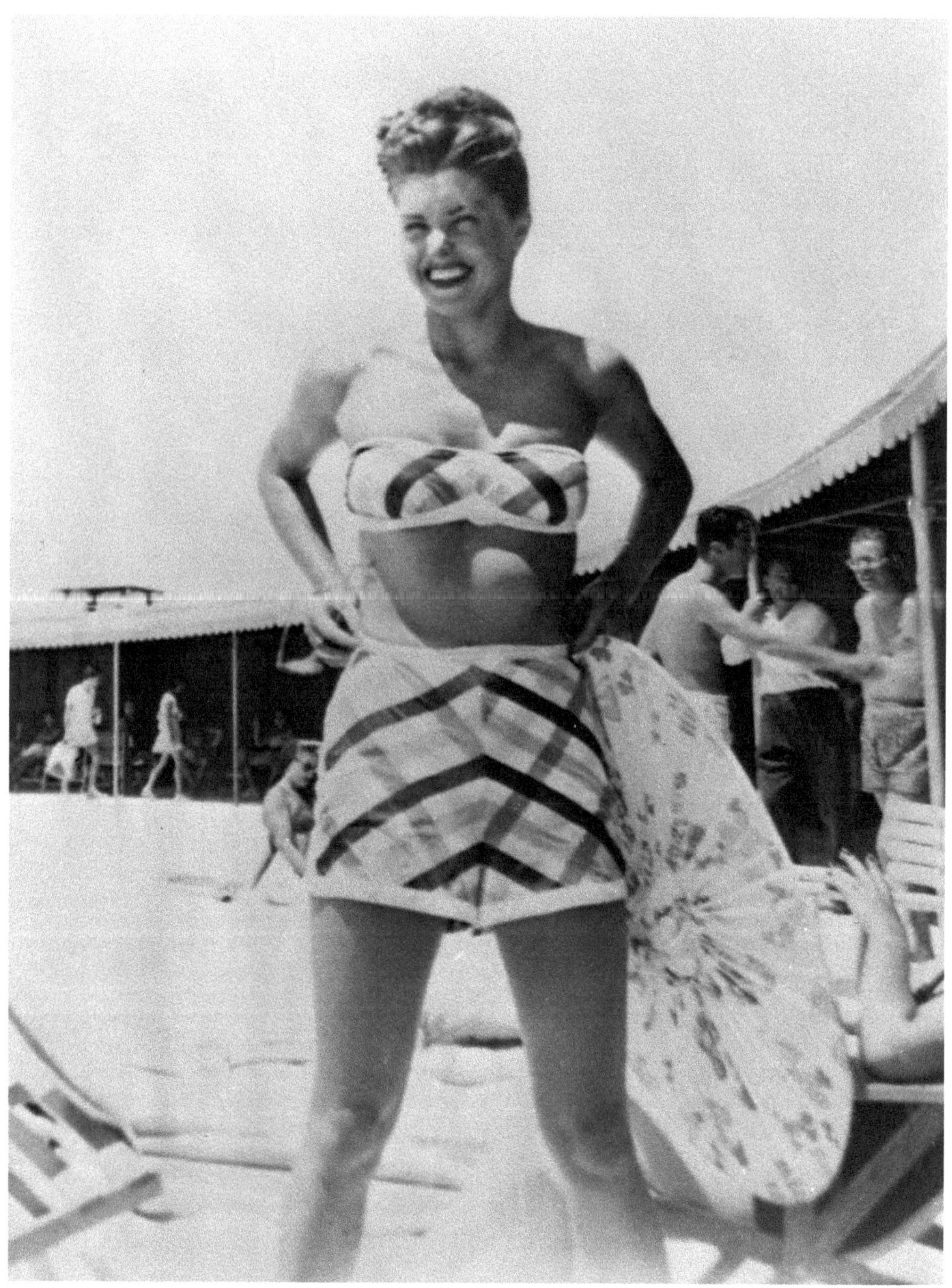

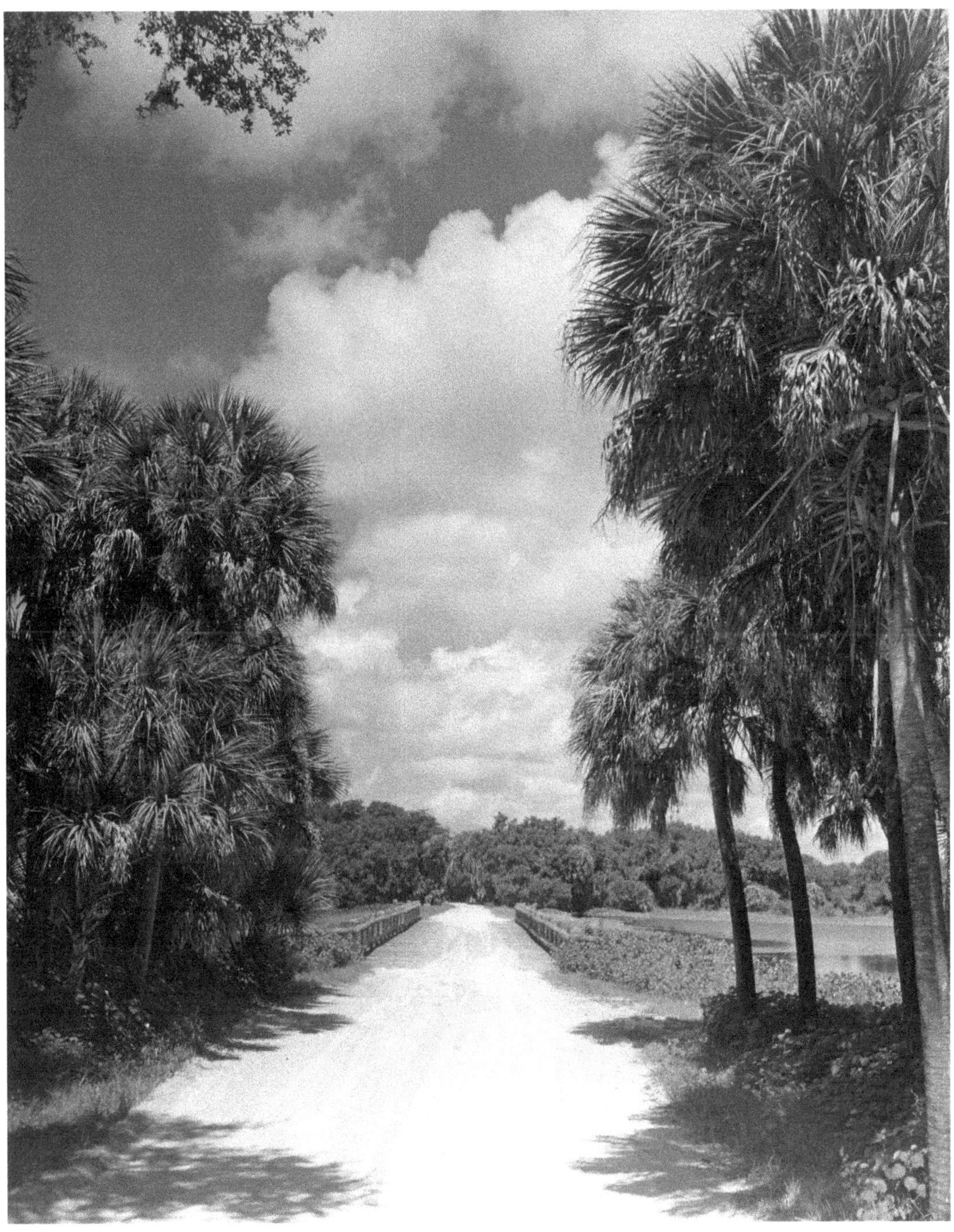

During the 1930s, the Civilian Conservation Corps built roads, cabins, and bridges such as the one pictured here in 1947. Local materials were used to blend in with the natural environment. Palmetto logs formed walls of buildings, stone from Manatee County was used for fireplaces, and roofs were topped with cypress shingles.

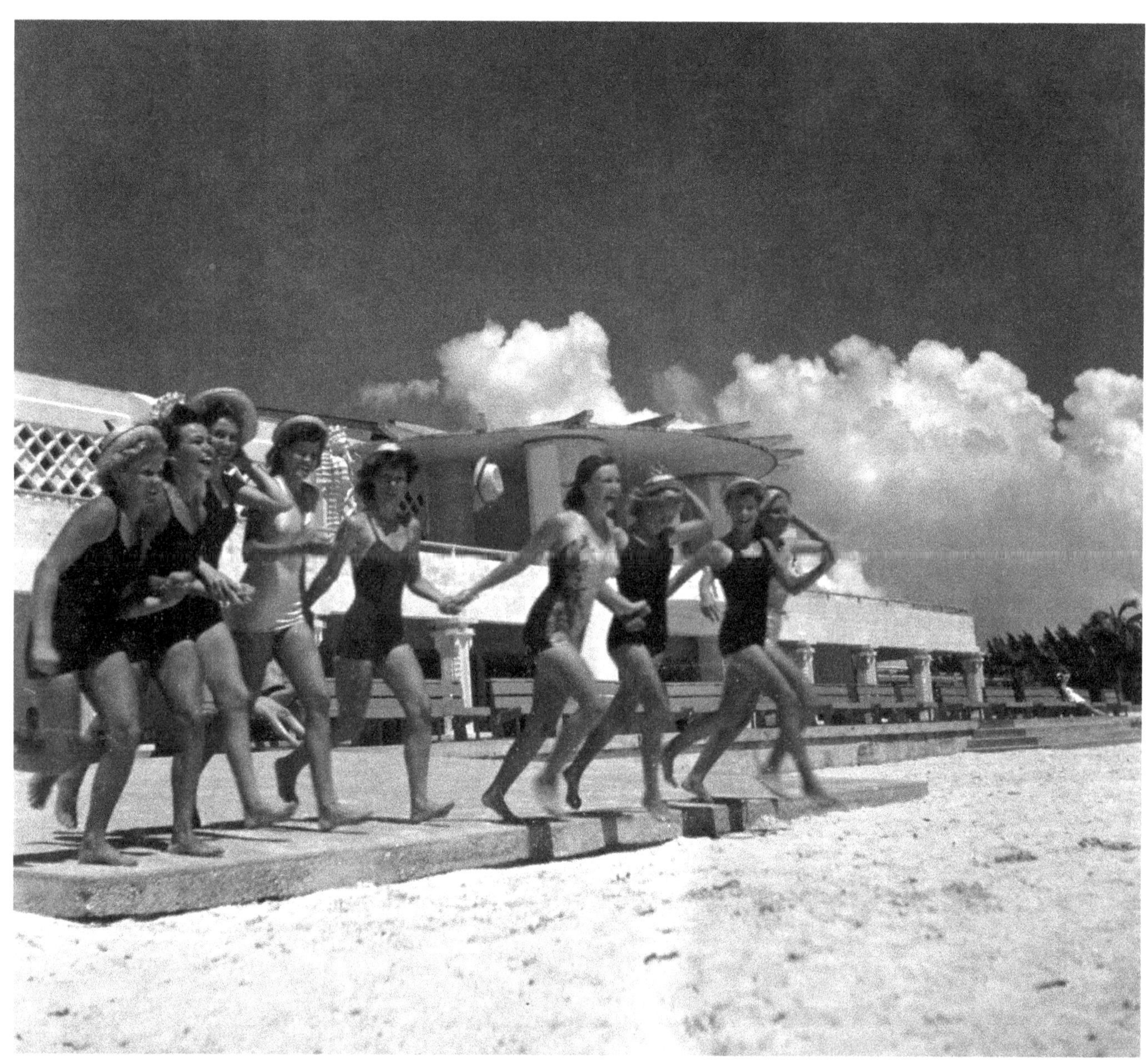

A Fort Lauderdale swim team runs on Lido Beach in 1947. John Ringling's interest in Italian culture led him to name the beach "Lido," which is Italian for "beach." Although he was well into development of the northern portion of the island at the time, the economic downturn of 1926 led to his abandonment of plans for the southern part.

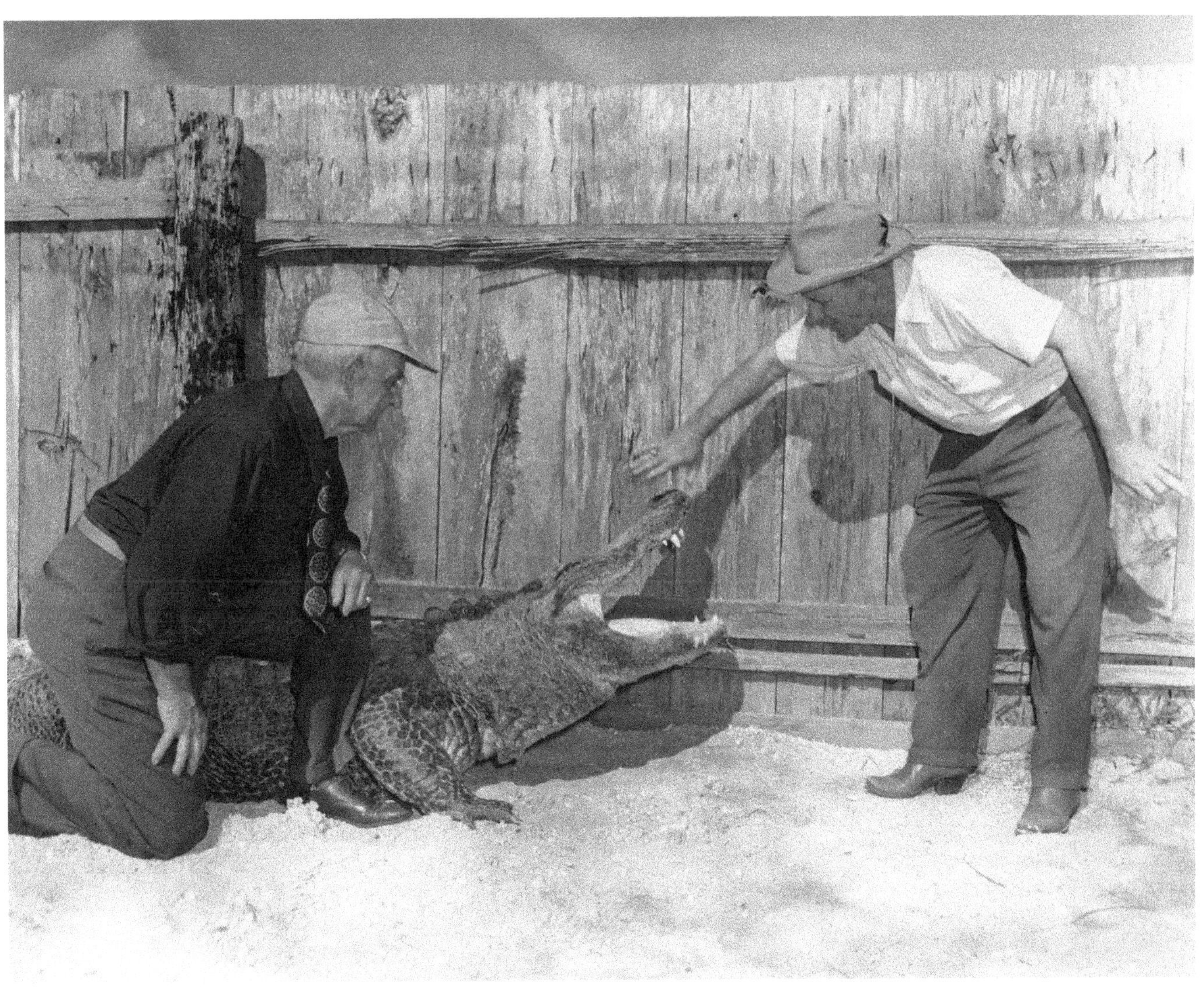

Opening around 1935, the Sarasota Reptile Farm and Zoo attracted tourists with its alligators, snakes, monkeys, and birds. Located along Fruitville Road, it was owned by Texas Jim Mitchell, so it was also called Jim's Alligator Farm. Mitchell, right, is shown here in the alligator pit with a park visitor in 1948. The park closed in 1965.

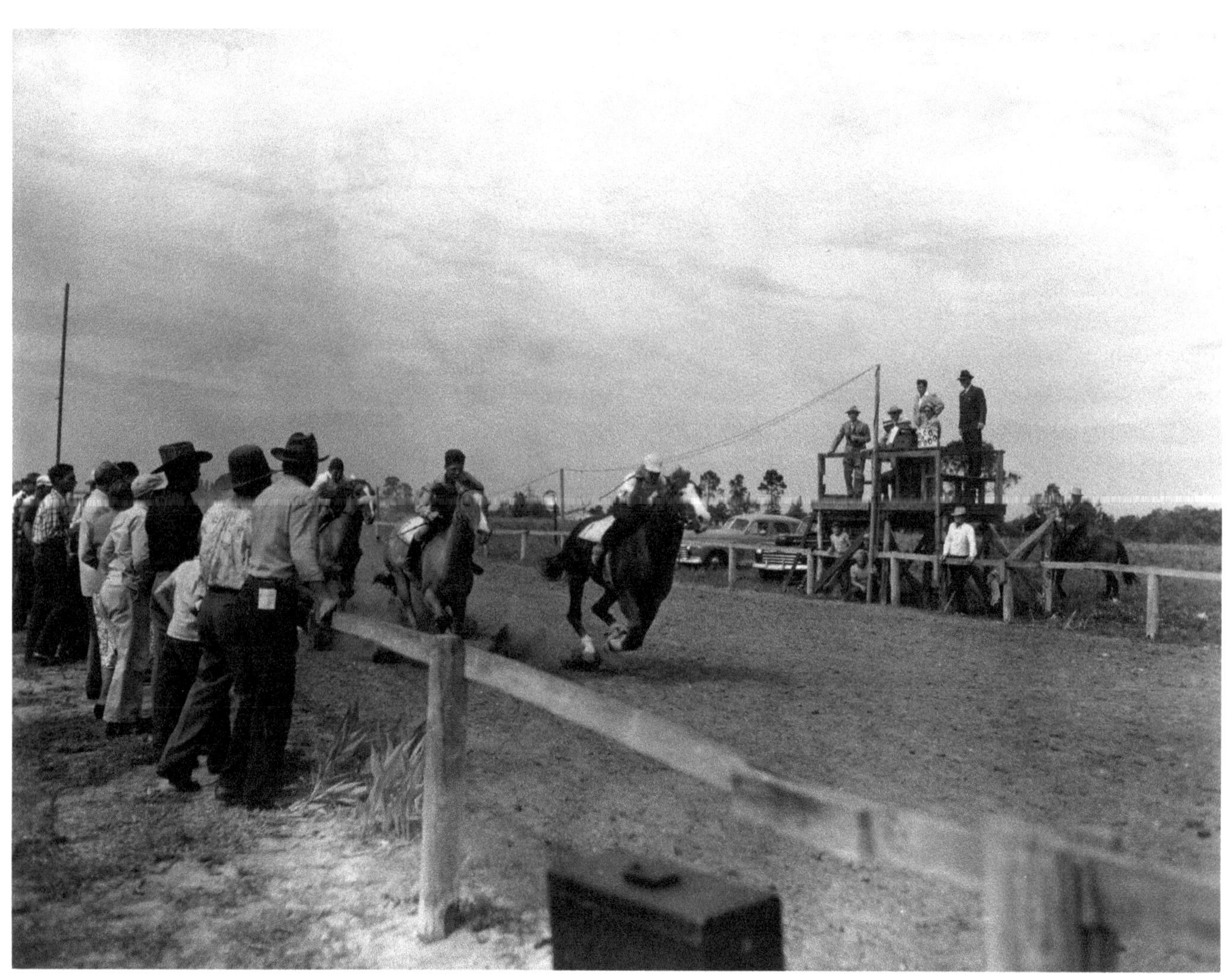

The first Sarasota County Fair opened in 1925 and featured horse racing, airplane stunts, a rodeo show, parades, and exhibits. In 1927, the site was conveyed to John Ringling for his circus. The fair was held at temporary sites until 1948, the year this photo of a horse race was taken, when it moved to a permanent site provided by the county.

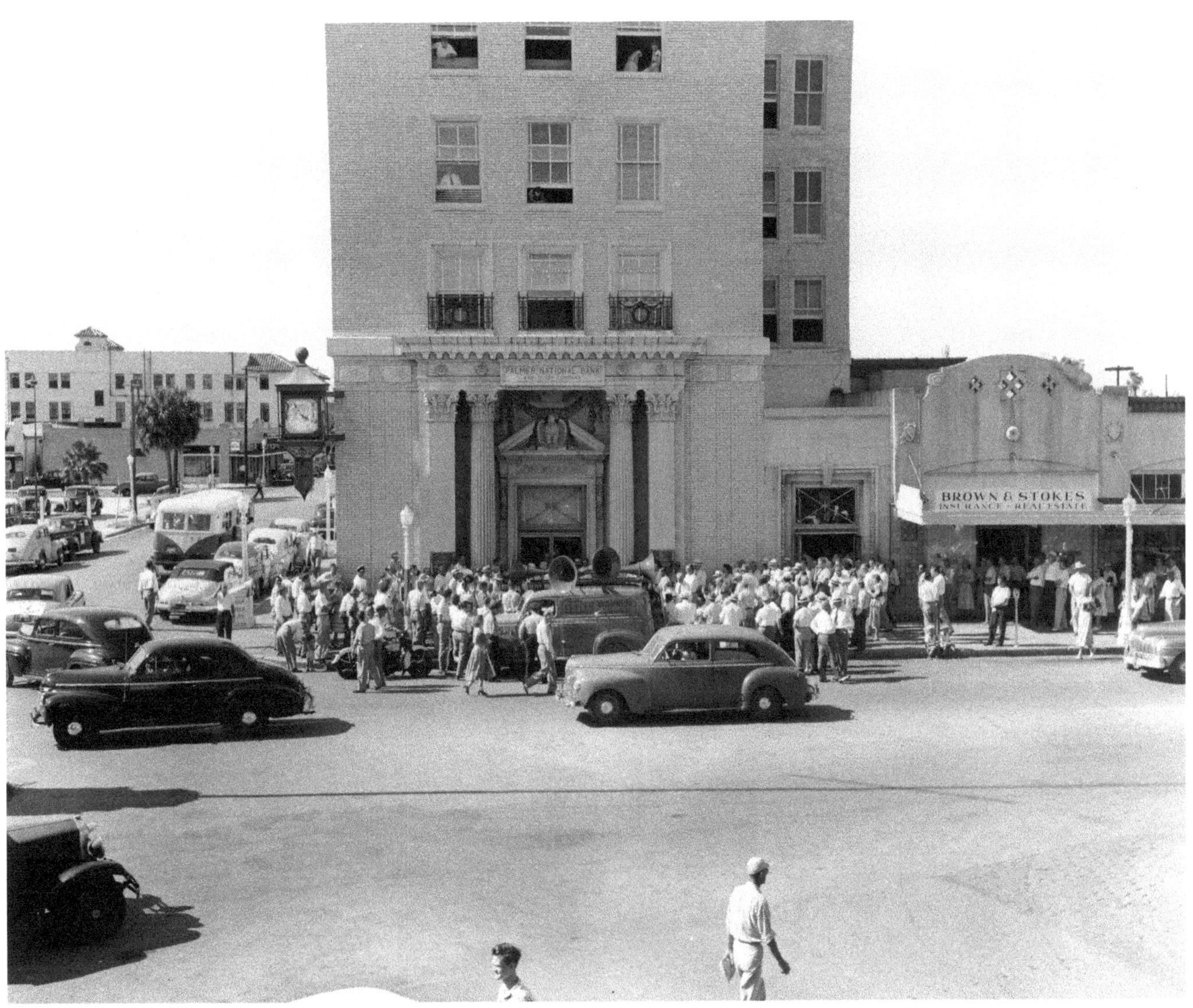

This truck in front of the Palmer National Bank in 1948 drove through the city to announce where and when gubernatorial candidate Fuller Warren would address the public. He won the election and was instrumental in establishing the state's turnpike system; he also supported reforestation, and developed quality control programs for citrus fruit.

In the 1930s, Sarasota realized that its financial well-being was becoming dependant upon tourists, especially those who fled cold winters to enjoy the beaches. At the urging of the Chamber of Commerce, a municipal bathing beach was established, and the Lido Beach Casino opened in 1940. It immediately began attracting tourists and locals alike.

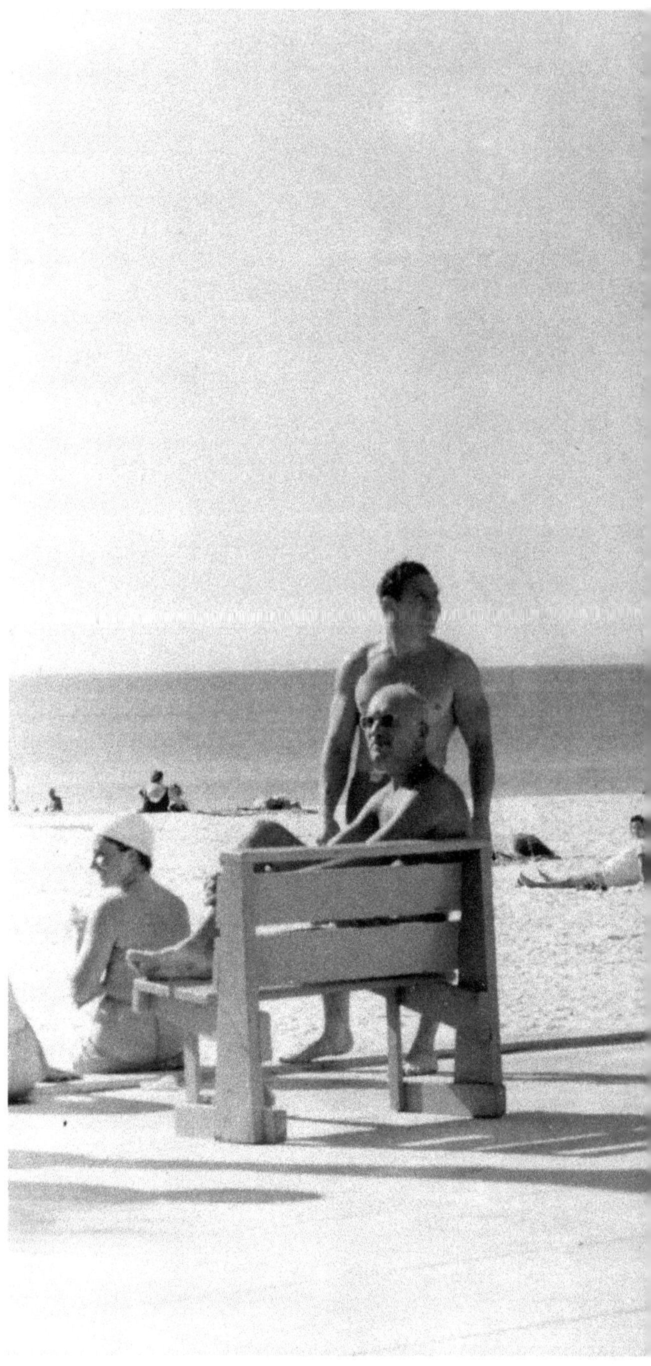

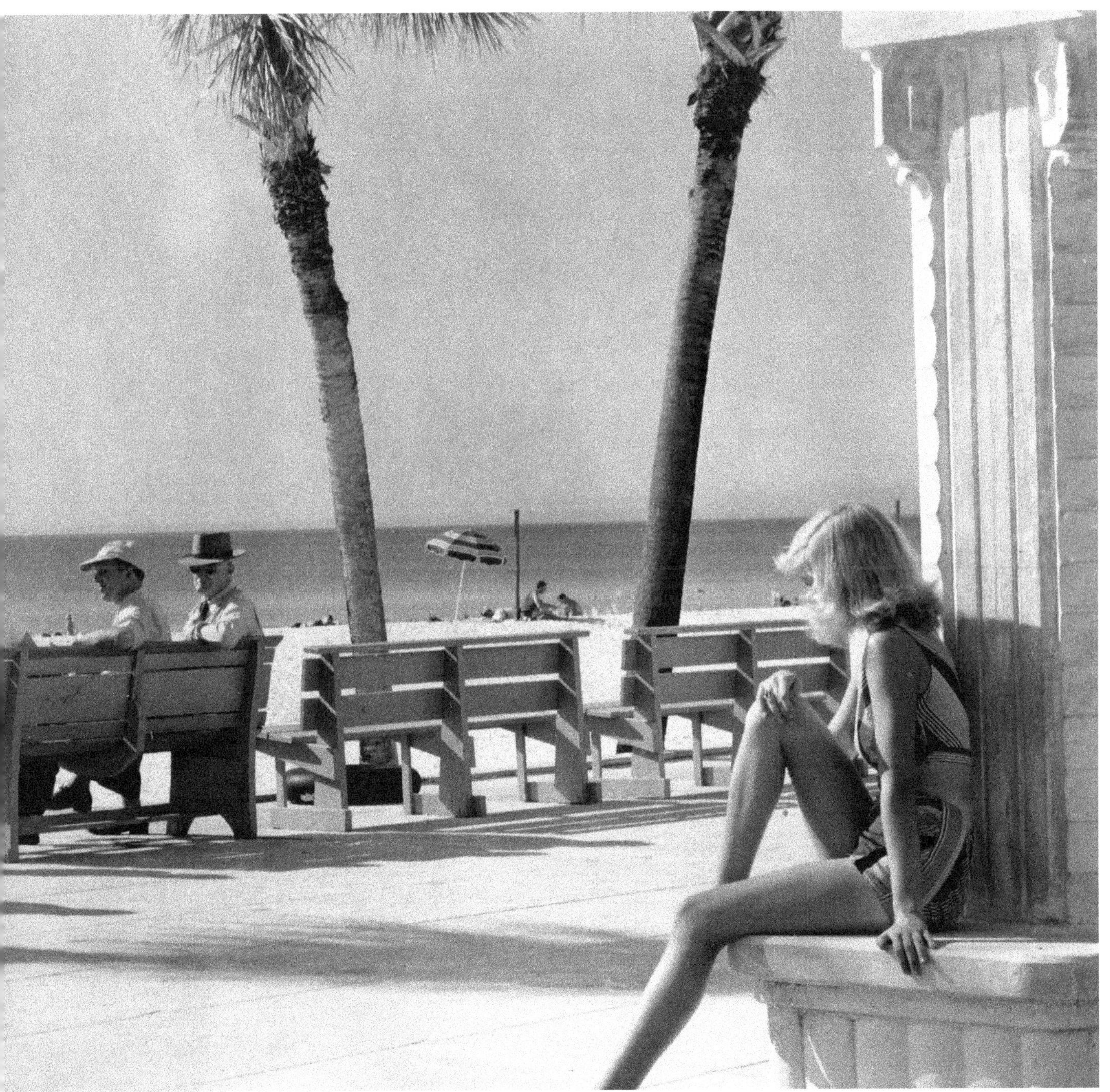

The Hover Arcade was built by Dr. W. E. Hover and his brothers, who sold it to the city in 1917 for $40,000. In the late 1960s, after long service as Sarasota City Hall, the building was replaced by benches and a water fountain. A new city hall designed by Jack West was built at another location in 1967. Also shown is the municipal pier built by bond issue proceeds which came from John Ringling.

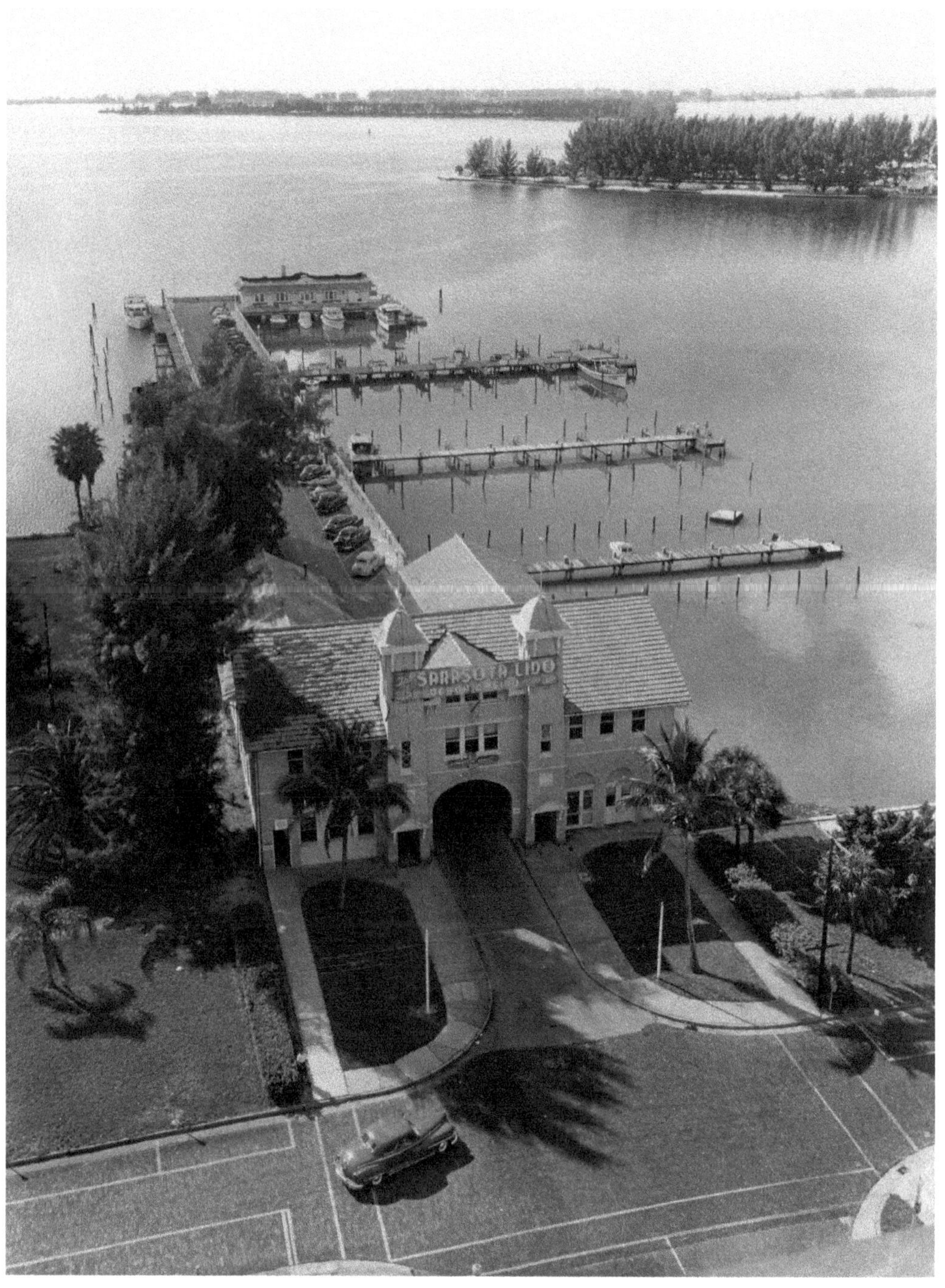

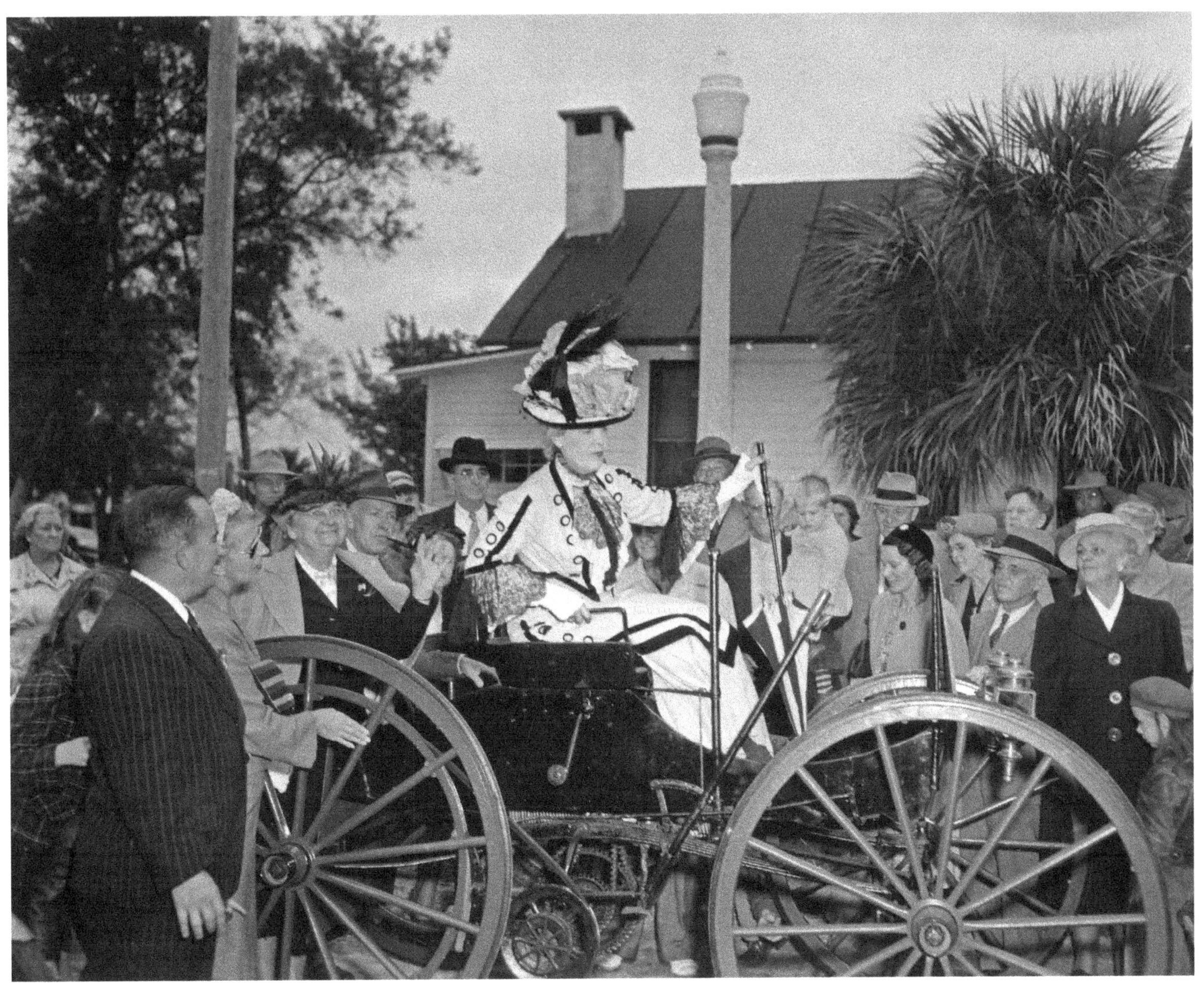

One of the most popular entries in the Gay Nineties festival of 1948 was this automobile of Mrs. Charles Bell of Sarasota. The Haynes two-cylinder runabout was built in Indiana by Elwood Haynes in 1894 and was believed to be the oldest automobile in Sarasota County.

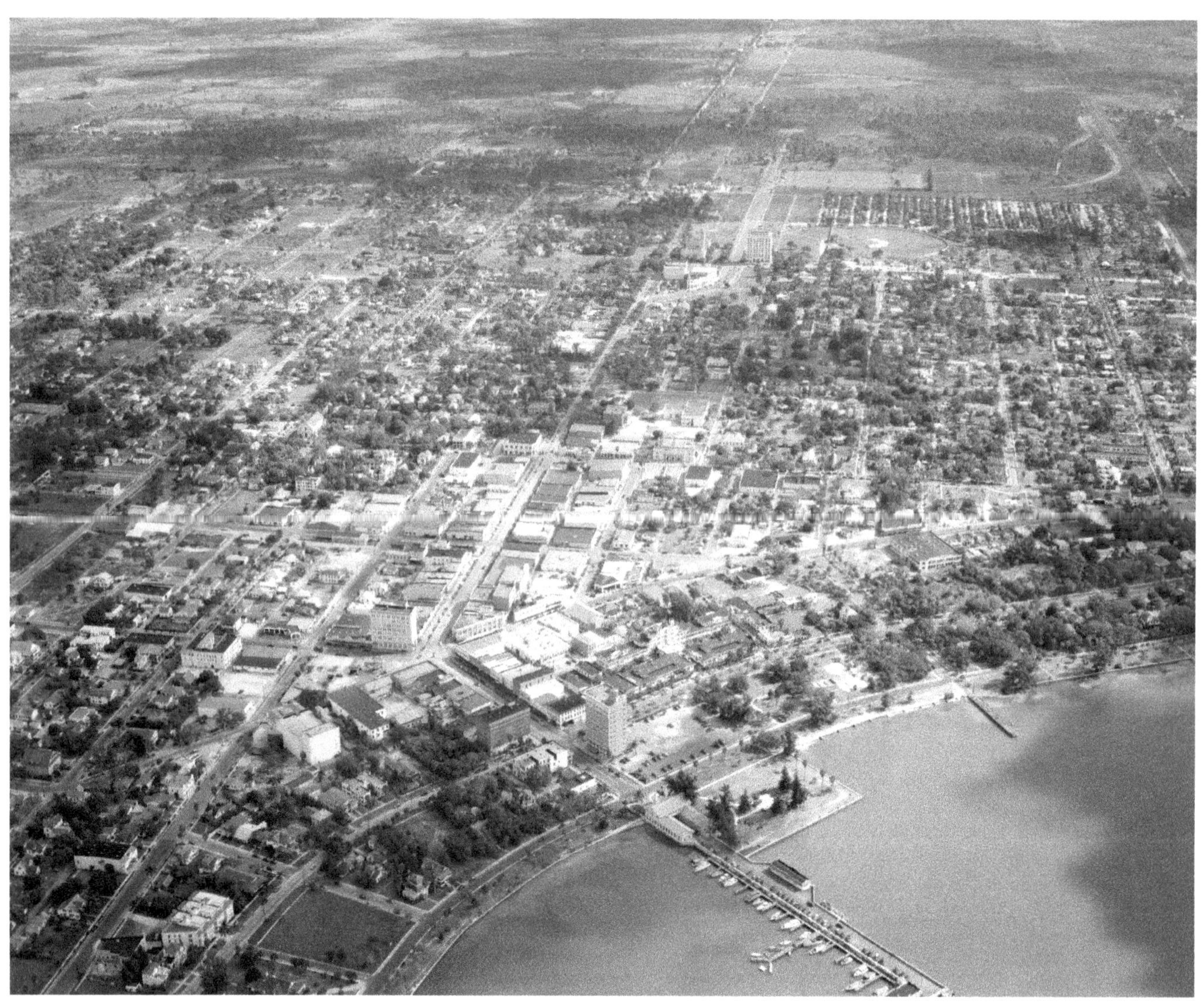

This late 1940s view of Sarasota was captured by Sherman M. Fairchild, a pioneer in aerial photography. Although some cameras could take pictures from above, shutter speeds were so slow that, even with the relatively slow early airplanes, images were blurred. Fairchild developed a camera with a shutter within its lens, allowing for faster speeds and clearer images.

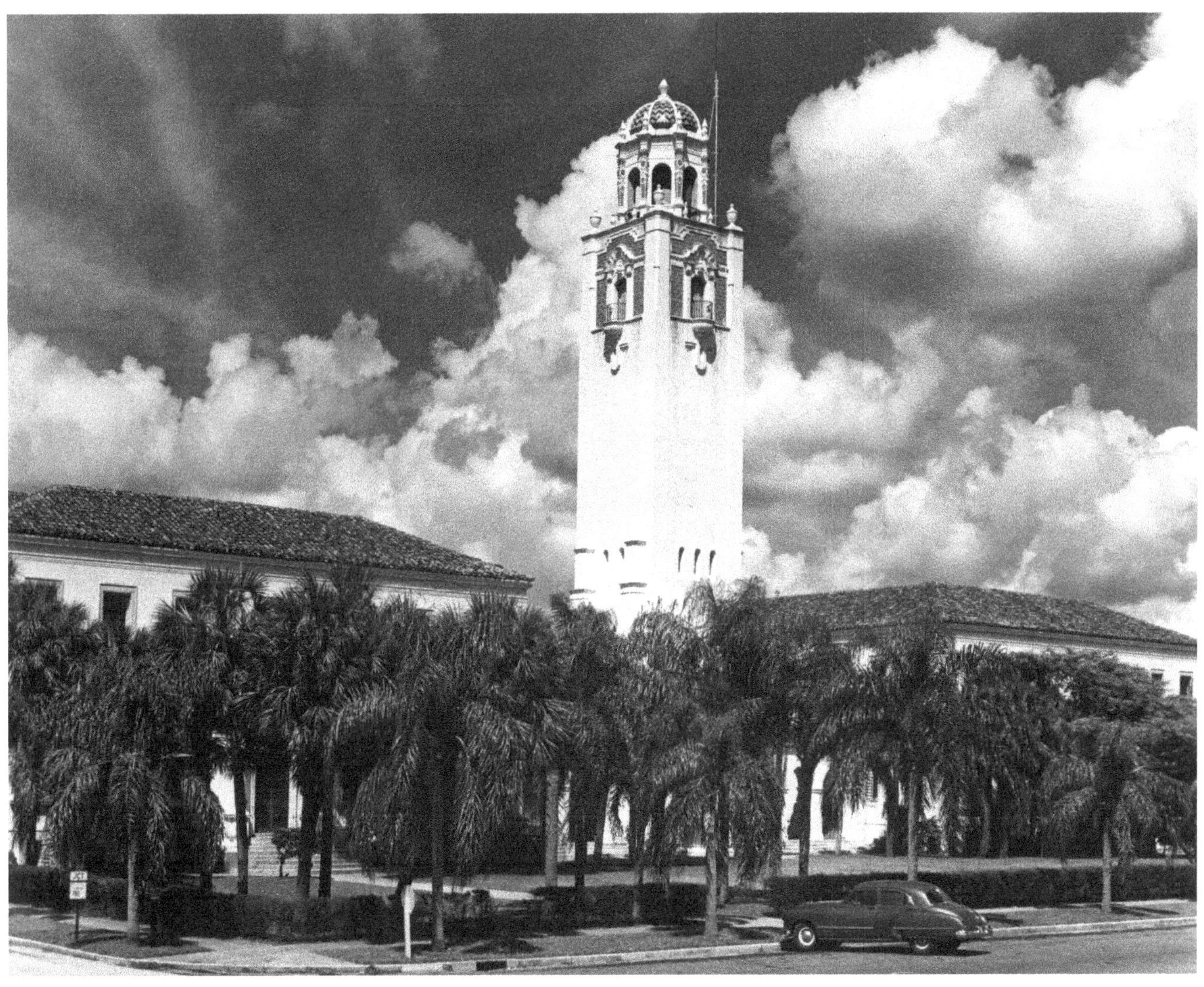

Sarasota County was formed from a portion of Manatee County in 1921, and Sarasota was named the county seat. Dwight James Baum was hired to design a courthouse to replace a temporary one housed in the Arcade Building. Seen here in 1949, the Sarasota County Courthouse, with its distinctive central tower, opened in 1927.

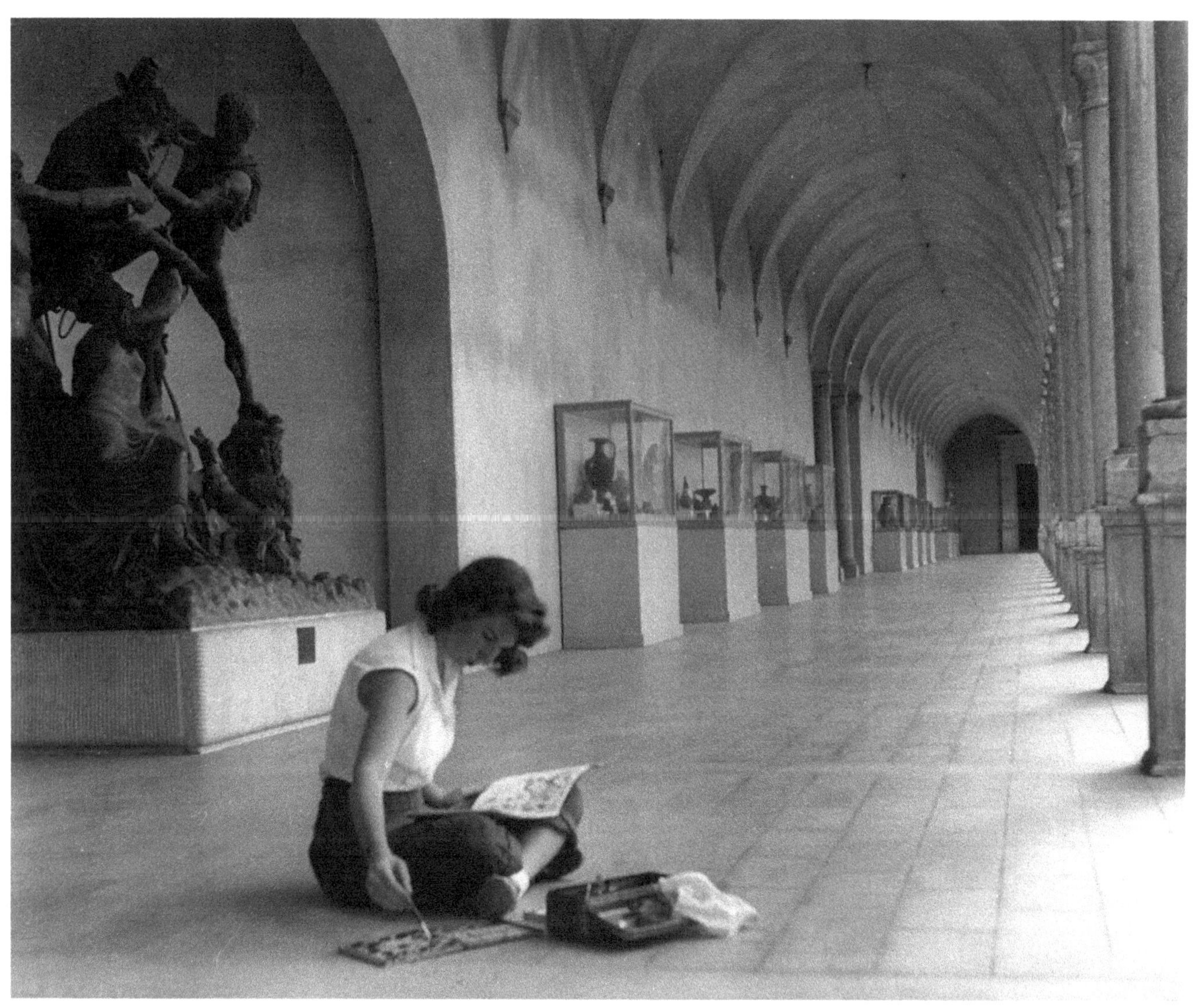

A ready draw for art students, among other visitors, the Ringling Museum has a long, vaulted lobby connecting two parallel galleries, which form the sides of a landscaped sculpture courtyard. At the far end, an elevated marble bridge overlooks a pool and raised terrace. In 1980, the Florida legislature designated the Ringling as the official art museum of the state.

The Greatest Show on Earth

(1950–1959)

The brothers Al, Alf T., Otto, Charles, and John Ringling began their entertainment careers in 1882 by forming a tiny variety show in Baraboo, Wisconsin. In 1884, the show evolved into a small circus, which in turn grew with the addition of several performing acts. By 1887, it bore the cumbersome name of Ringling Brothers United Monster Shows, Great Double Circus, Royal European Menagerie, Museum, Caravan and Congress of Trained Animals.

The Ringlings went on the road in 1889 and competed with more well-established circuses, including that of P. T. Barnum and James Bailey. After Bailey died in 1906, the Ringlings purchased the Barnum and Bailey circus, consolidating it into their main circus in 1918. In 1927, a year after Charles Ringling's death left John as the only surviving brother, the circus's winter home was moved from Bridgeport, Connecticut, to Sarasota's former fairgrounds. The circus, known as the "Greatest Show on Earth," continues today, long after the 1936 death of John Ringling.

The presence of the circus in Sarasota, and later in Venice, created jobs and also brought winter tourists eager to watch the spectacular acts preparing for each upcoming tour season. When Hollywood director Cecil B. DeMille filmed *The Greatest Show on Earth* in Sarasota, the "Circus Capital of the World," the movie added money to the city's coffers and helped publicize Sarasota and its relationship with the circus.

The area's circus reputation was also enhanced by Sarasota High School. Beginning in 1949 and expanding through the 1950s, the school's "Greatest Little Show on Earth" brought attention to a program in which school athletes learned from professional circus performers. The youth program continues, no longer limited to those of high school age, and keeps Sarasota's circus connection alive, despite the departure of John Ringling's company.

In 1959, the circus announced its plans to move its winter headquarters from Sarasota to Venice. That move greatly enhanced the economy of Venice and drew to it a larger share of the county's tourists. Opened in Sarasota in 1956, the Circus Hall of Fame would also eventually leave, but with a clown college, a circus museum, and a circus motif found throughout the area, the circus theme is still alive.

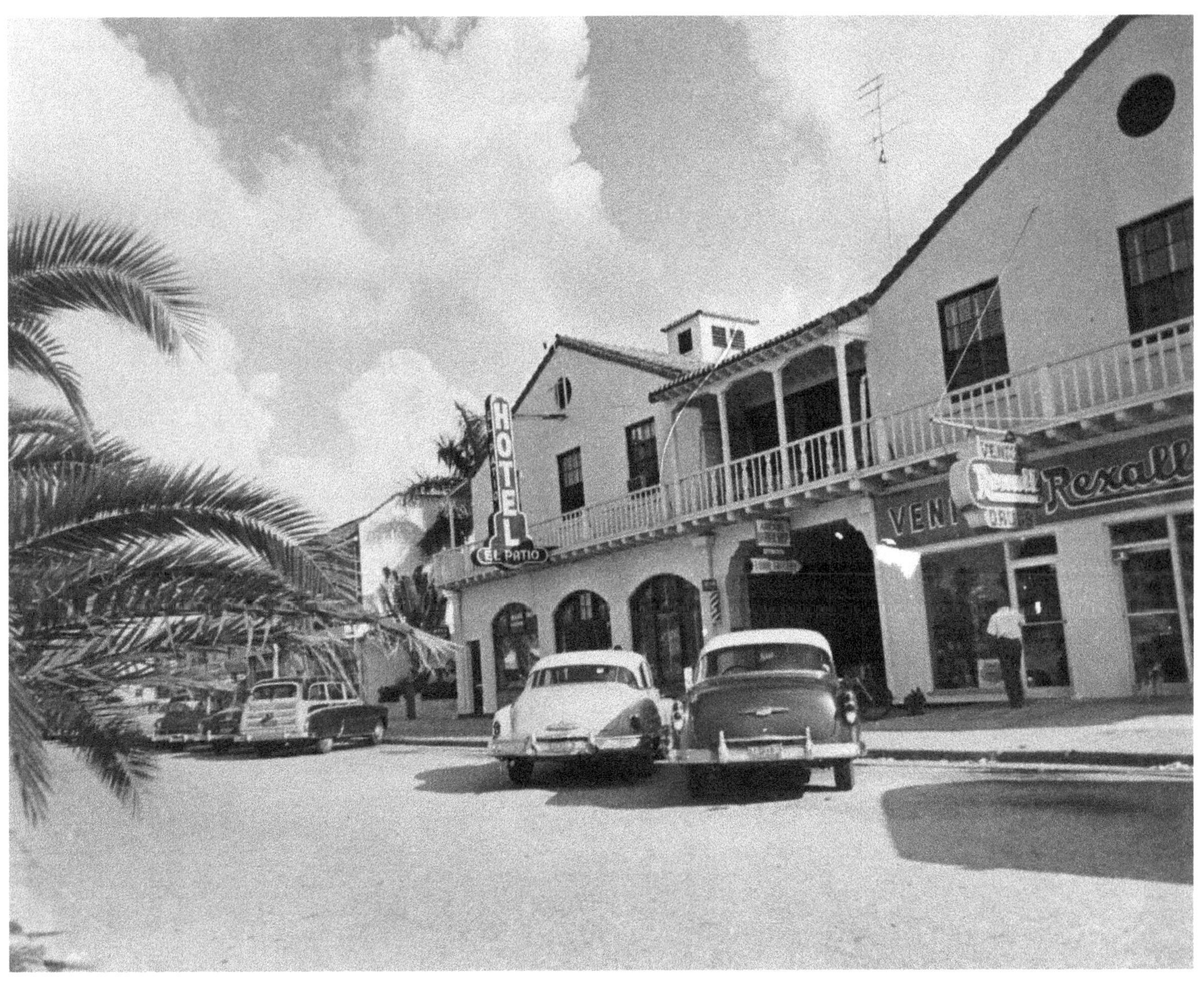

By 1929, hopes for Venice had been dashed, and the city took on a less grandiose appearance than had been envisioned by either Fred Albee or the engineers' union. There was considerable unsold land, and the union was sued several times for breaking promises. Seen here around 1950, this part of the city was still on the mend from the Great Depression.

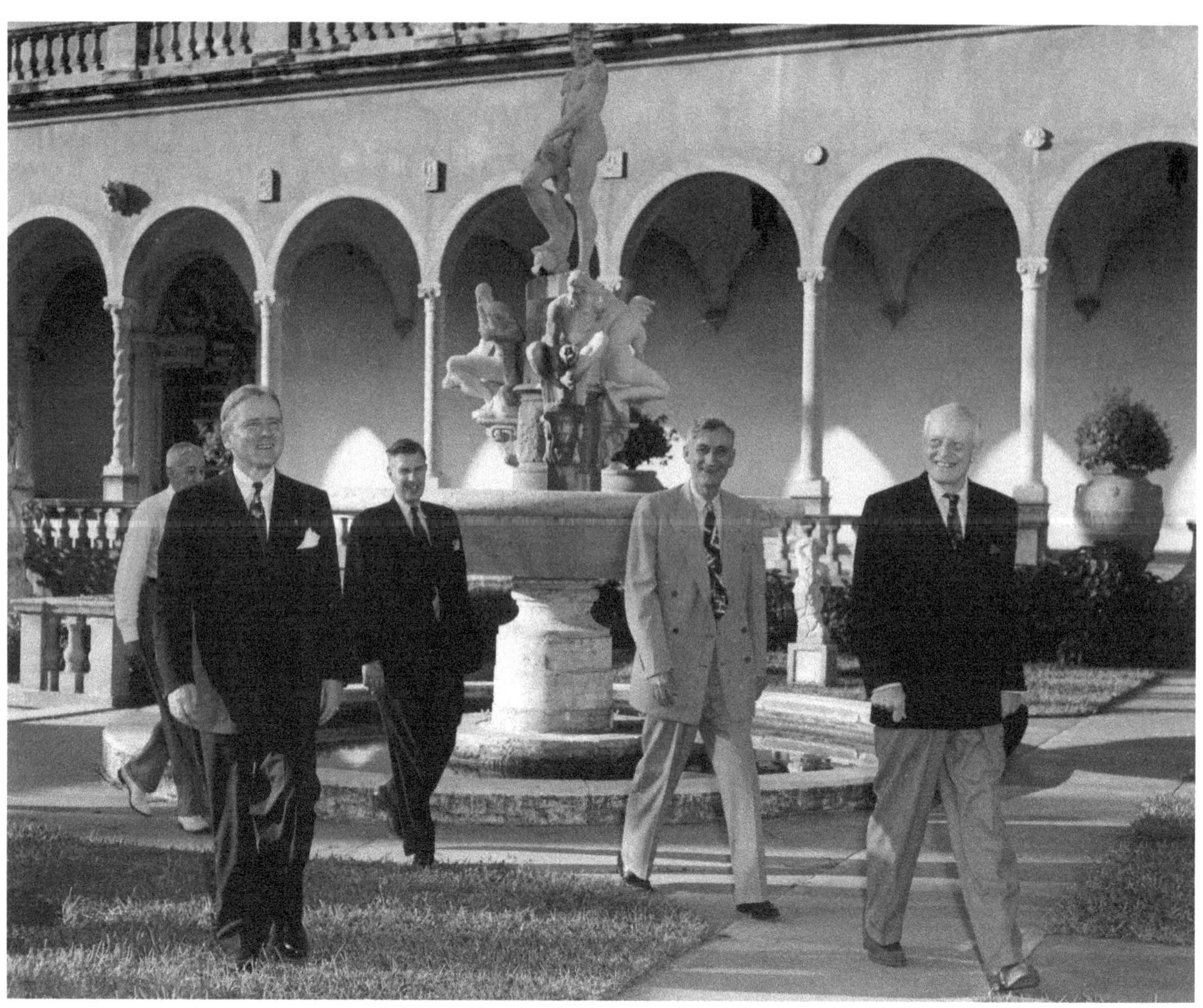

Visiting the Ringling Museum in 1951, Governor Fuller Warren is in the left foreground, along with museum director A. Everett Austine, walking behind him and to his left. The others, from left to right, are museum business manager Colonel J. W. Blanding, state representative James A. Haley, and museum operation committee member Karl Bickel.

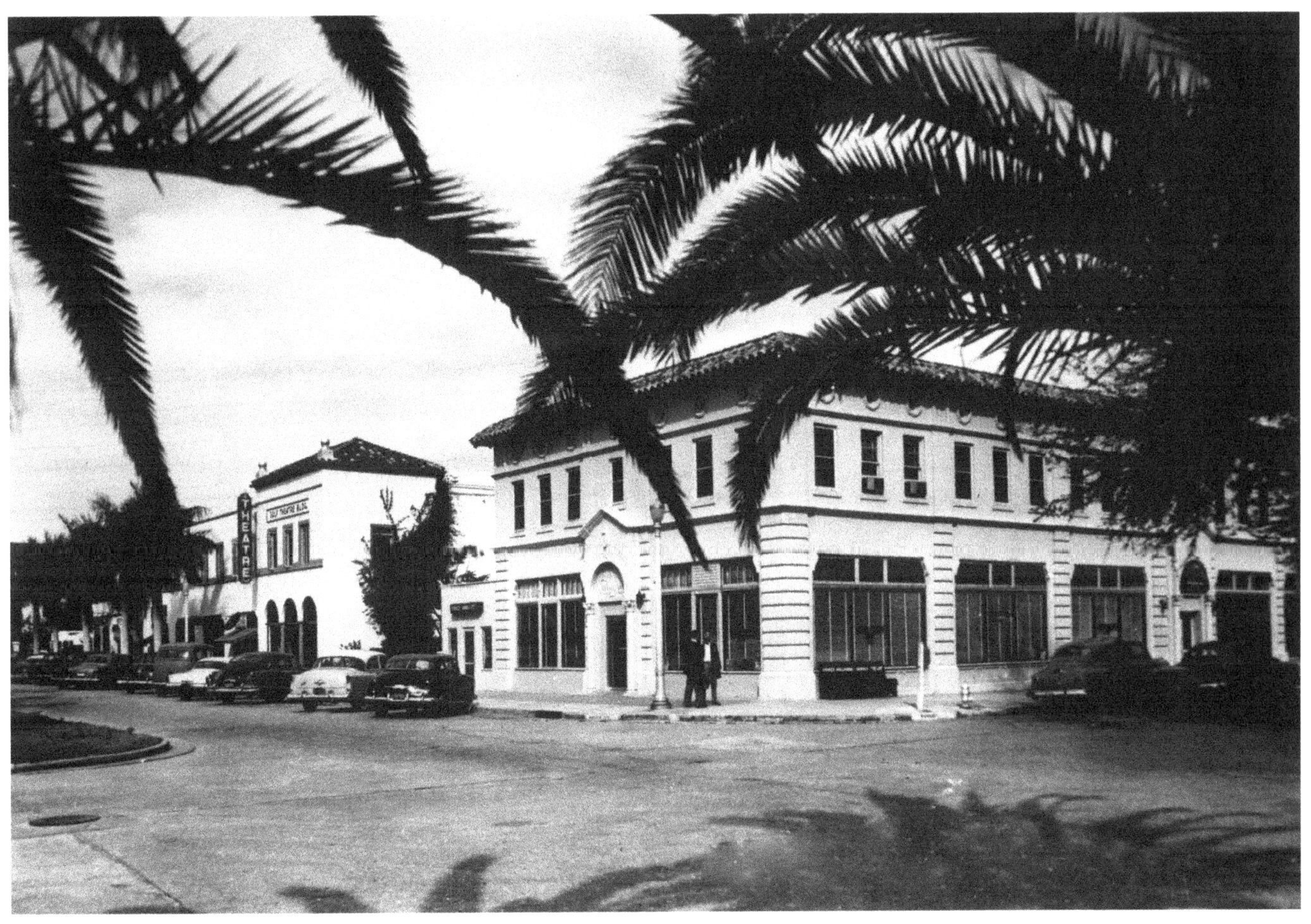

Dr. Fred H. Albee founded the Venice-Nokomis Bank, which opened in this corner building on February 23, 1927. It was the only bank in the county to survive the crash of 1929. The building remains. To its left is the Gulf Theatre, part of a block of stores that stood from the late 1920s until torn down in 1969.

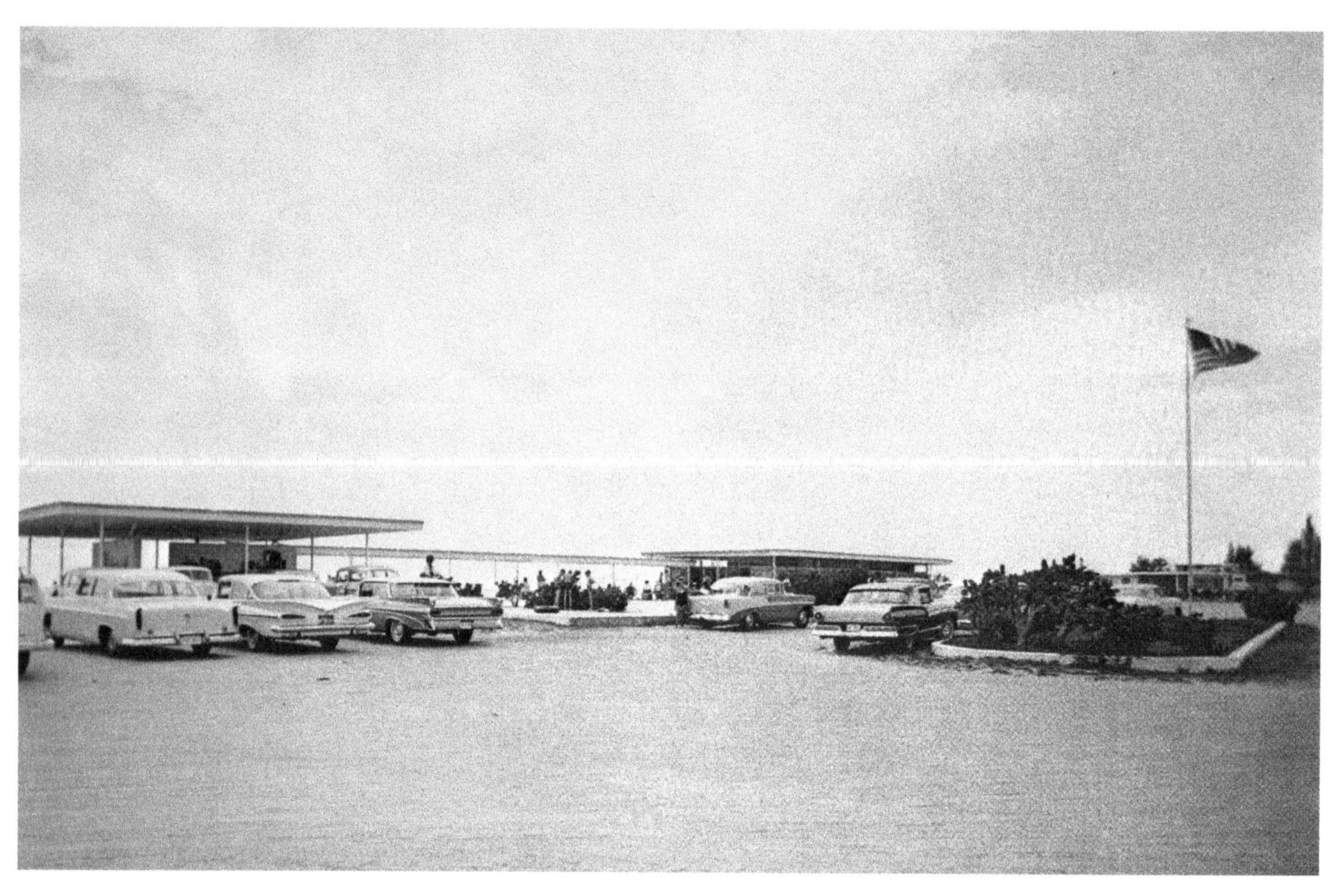

Shown here during the 1950s is the Nokomis Beach plaza, located at the oldest public beach in Sarasota County. The beach's twenty-two acres include a 1,700-foot shoreline along the Gulf of Mexico, and nearly twice that length along the Intracoastal Waterway. The white-sand beach attracts those who wish to swim or just work on their tans.

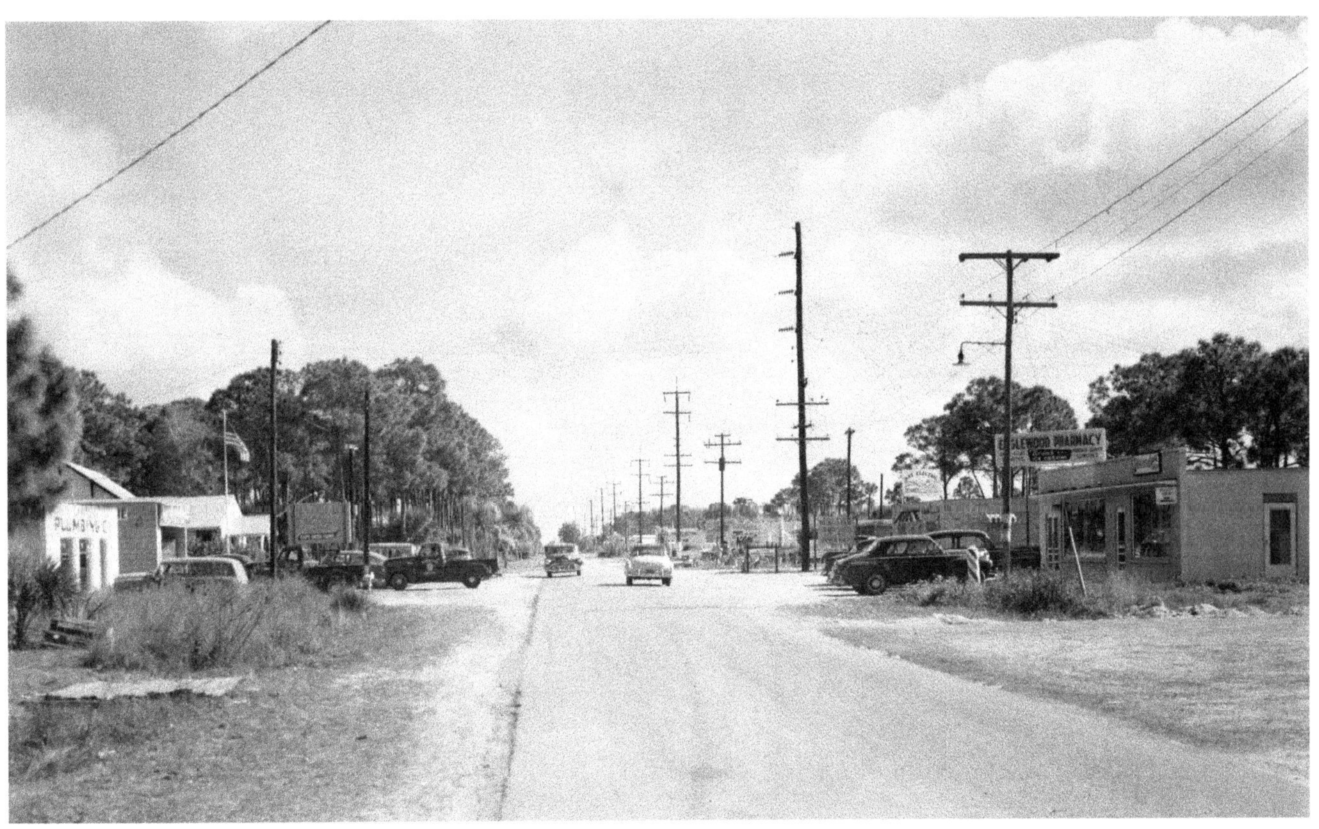

This street began in 1878 when the oxen of William and Mary Goff wore a path through the woods. When the Nichols brothers platted the town of Englewood in 1896, they used that trail as the town's southern boundary and called it Dearborn Street. In 1912, Peter and Florence Buchan built a store and post office on Dearborn, and it became the town's commercial center.

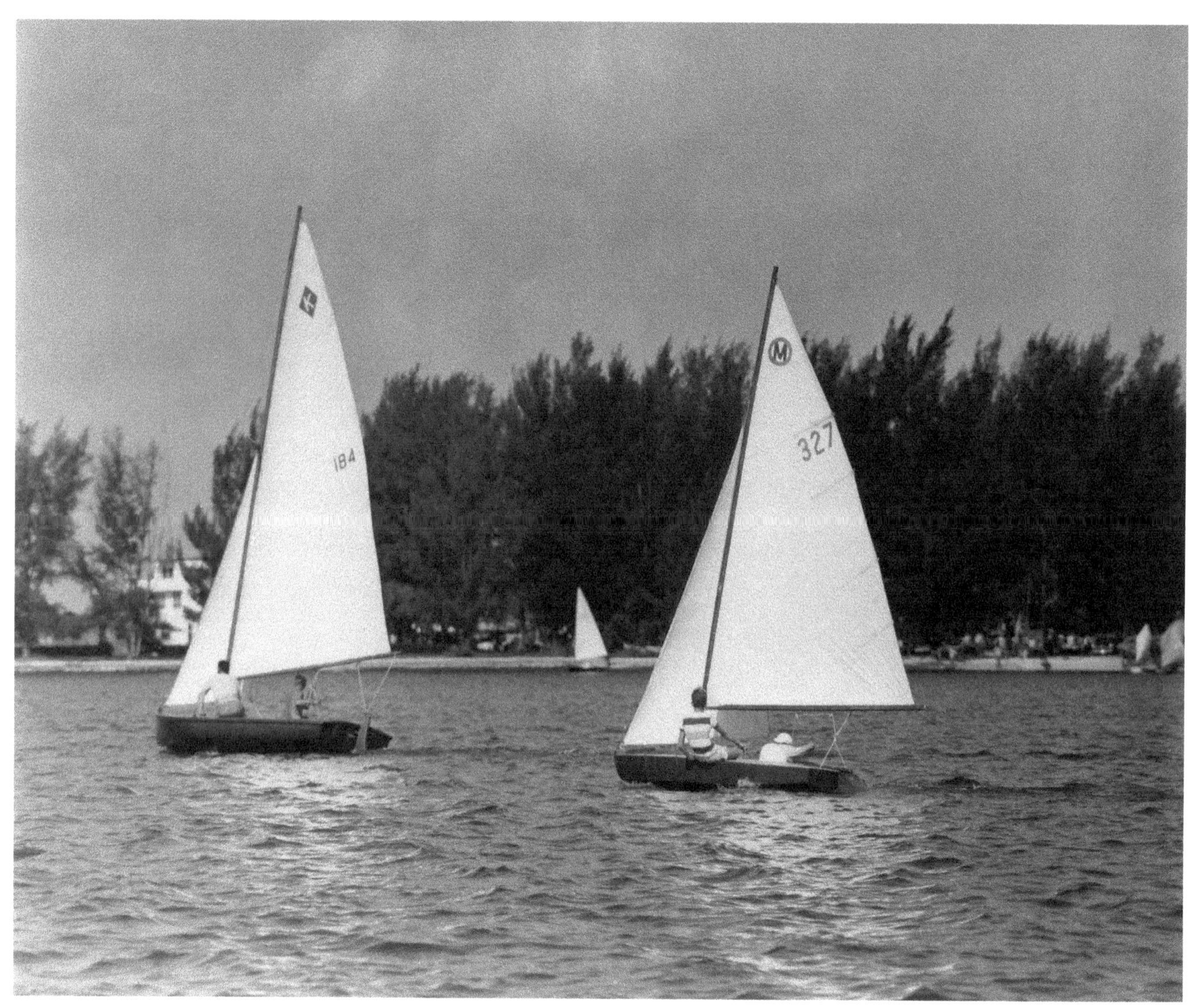

Sailing near Sarasota in 1951, these two boats follow by two decades a group of teens who acquired sloops and began racing them on Saturdays near the city pier. Calling themselves the Sarasota Sailing Squadron, the group went on hiatus in the early 1940s when the members went off to war. Races resumed in the late 1940s, and the Squadron is still going strong.

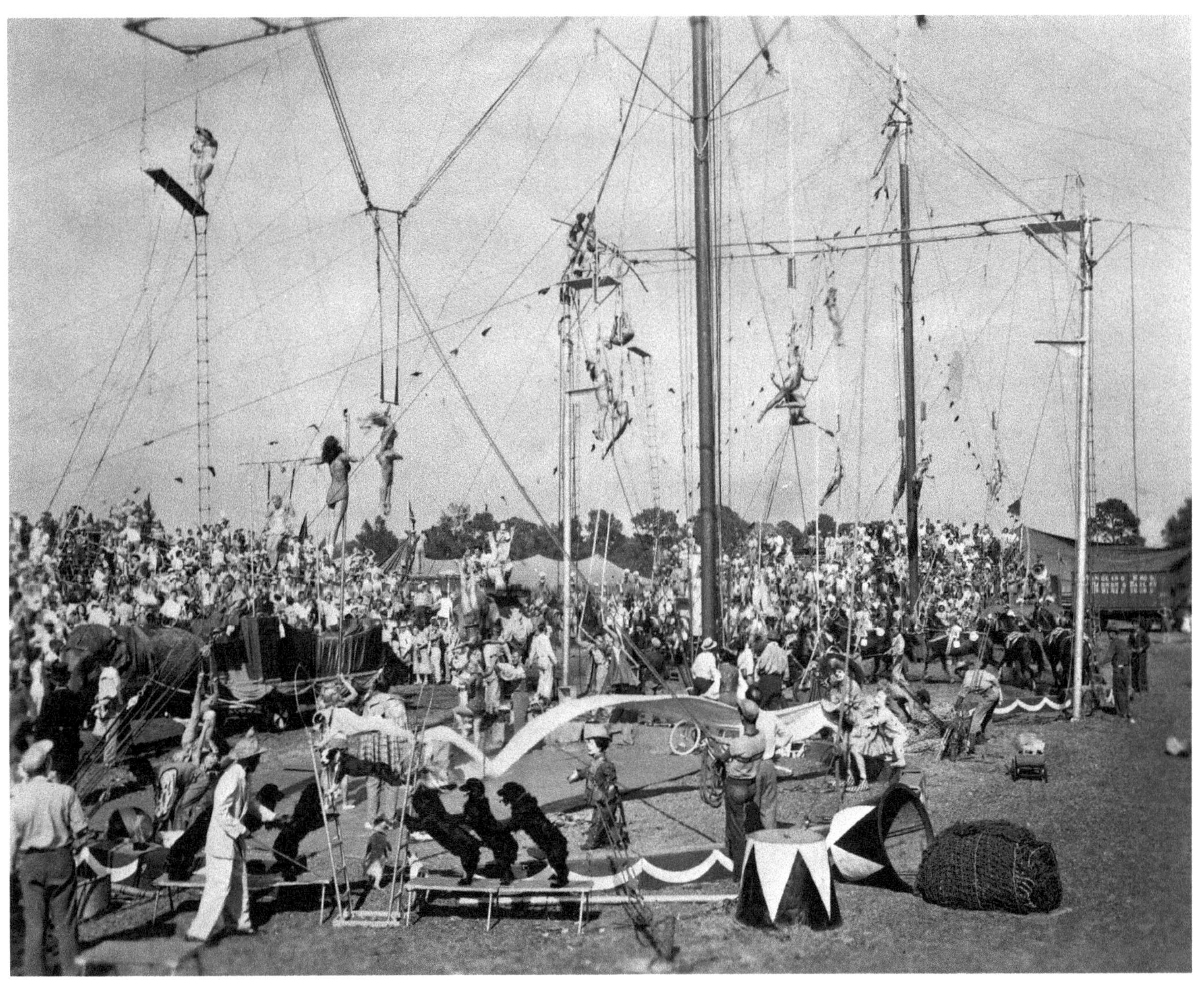

In 1927, Sarasota became winter quarters for the Ringling Brothers and Barnum and Bailey Circus, turning the city into the Circus Capital of the World, after John Ringling was offered 156 acres to bring the circus to town. After the circus moved its winter home to Venice in 1960, Sarasota's connection with the circus became just a little less obvious than here, during the 1951 filming of *The Greatest Show on Earth*.

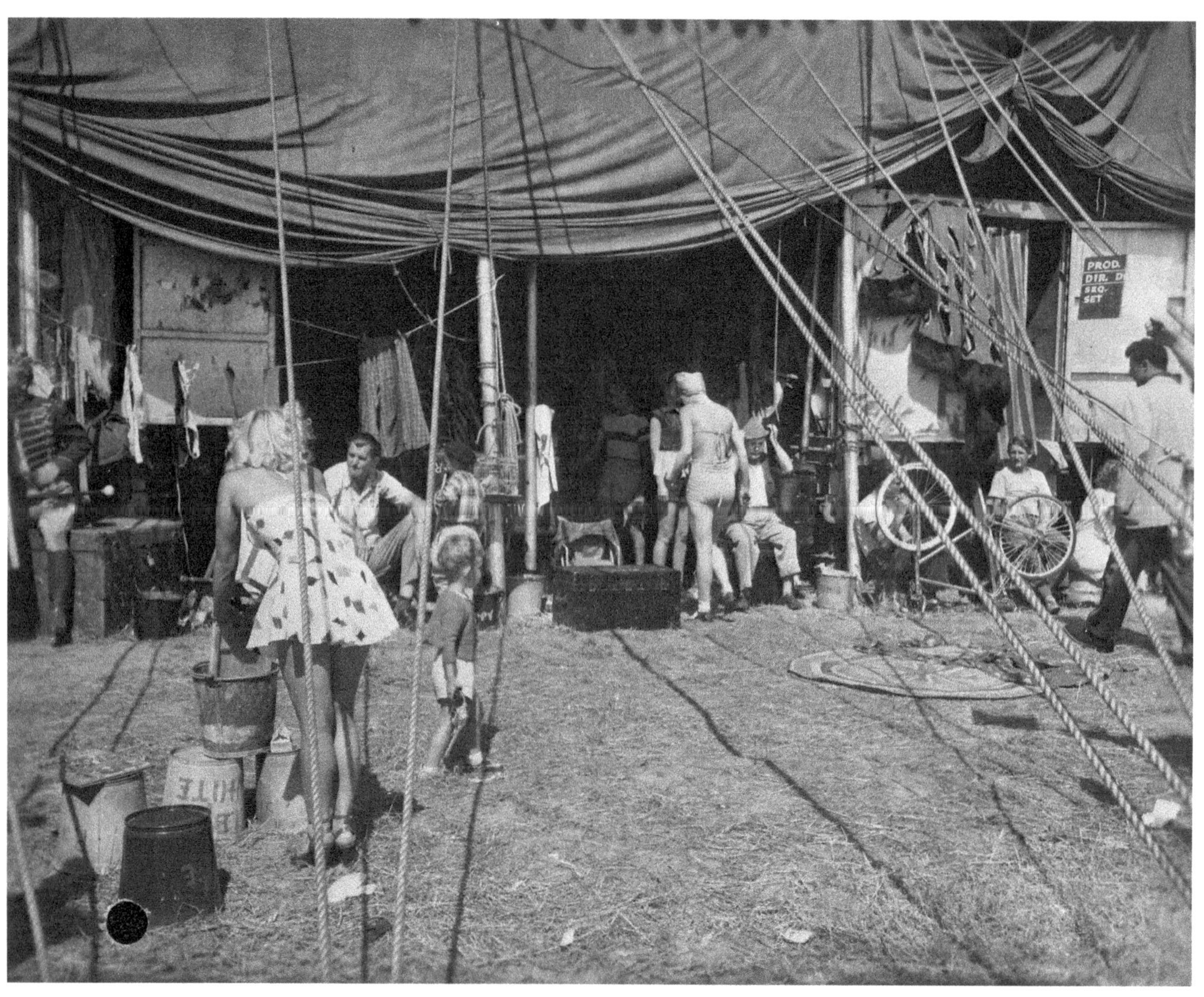

Scenes for *The Greatest Show on Earth,* directed by Cecil B. DeMille, were shot in Sarasota. While Charlton Heston, James Stewart, Dorothy Lamour, and Betty Hutton starred in the picture, many local residents served as extras. Local circus stars advised the actors, and some appeared on film. Circus executive John Ringling North portrayed himself.

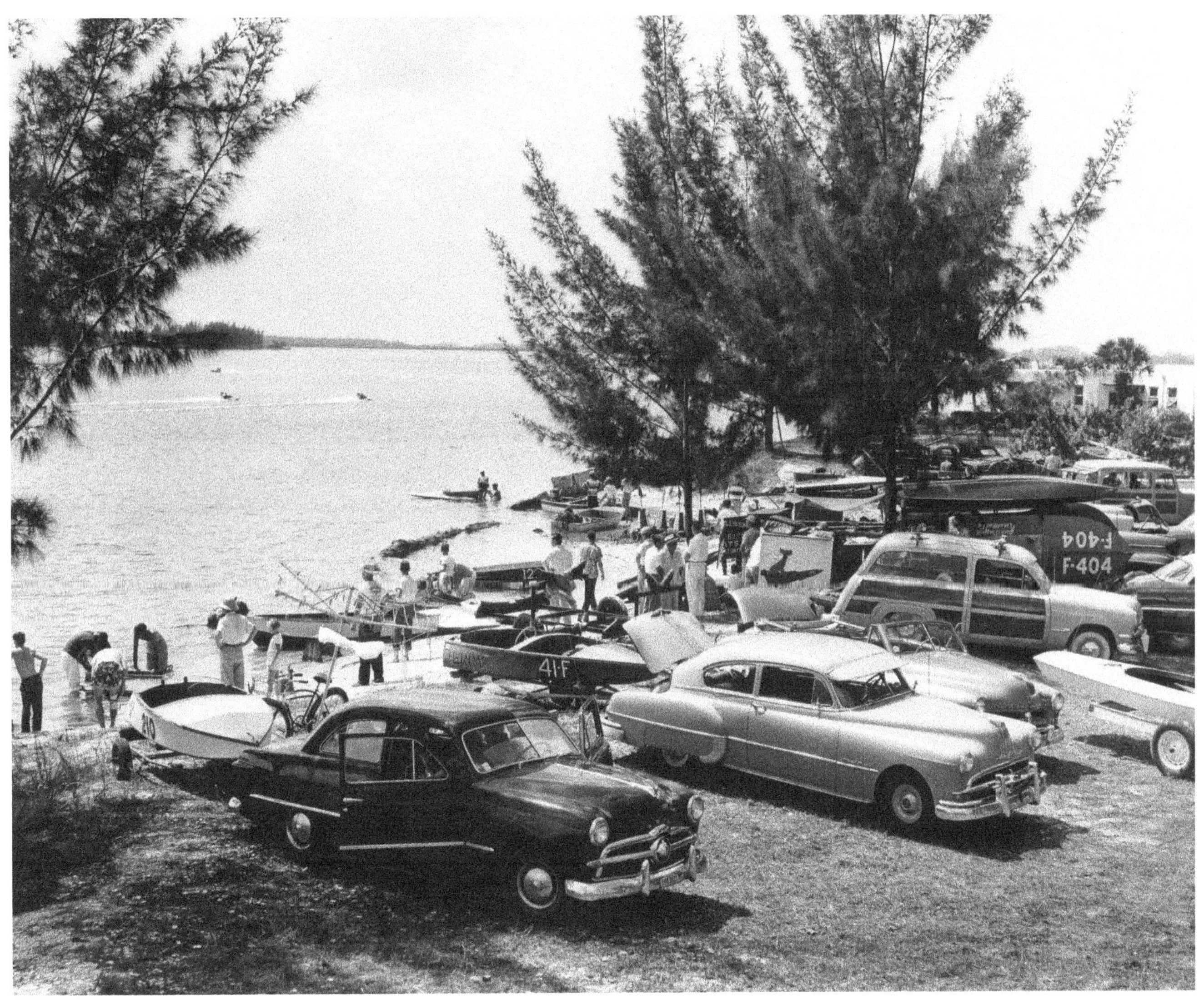

The Labor Day Regatta was begun in Sarasota in 1949 by sailors who had returned from the war. Races highlighted the event and were supported by pit operations along the shore, such as this one in 1951. Regattas have trouble attracting competitors in other parts of the state, but Sarasota's regatta continues to feature over 300 boats in several classes.

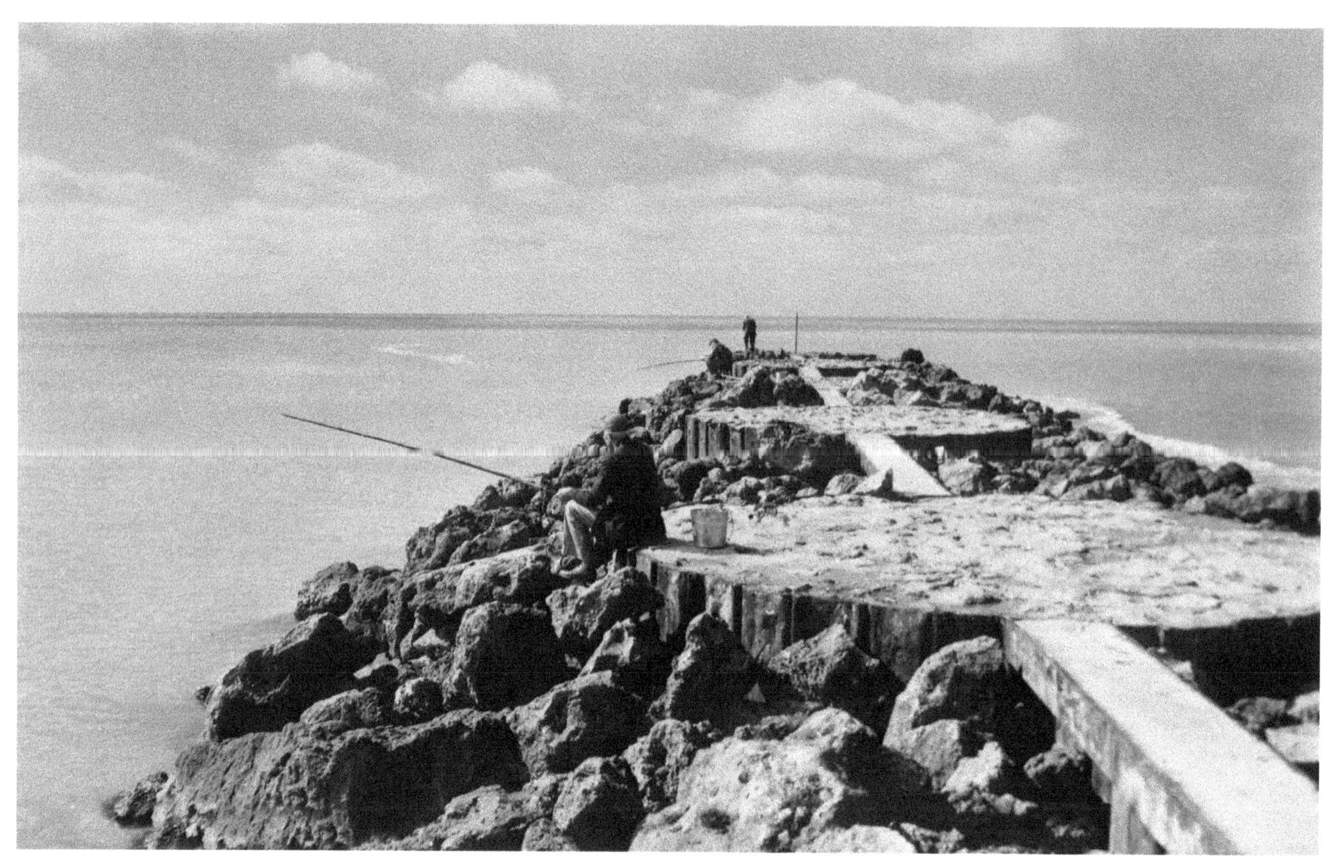

Located near Venice was the Woodmere Lumber Mill and town of Woodmere. Excessive lumber cutting and a 1930 fire killed the town, but parts live on in Venice. Wood from Woodmere was used in Venice's buildings in the 1910s and 1920s, and the Venice jetties built in 1937, one of which is shown here, included foundation stones from Woodmere's buildings.

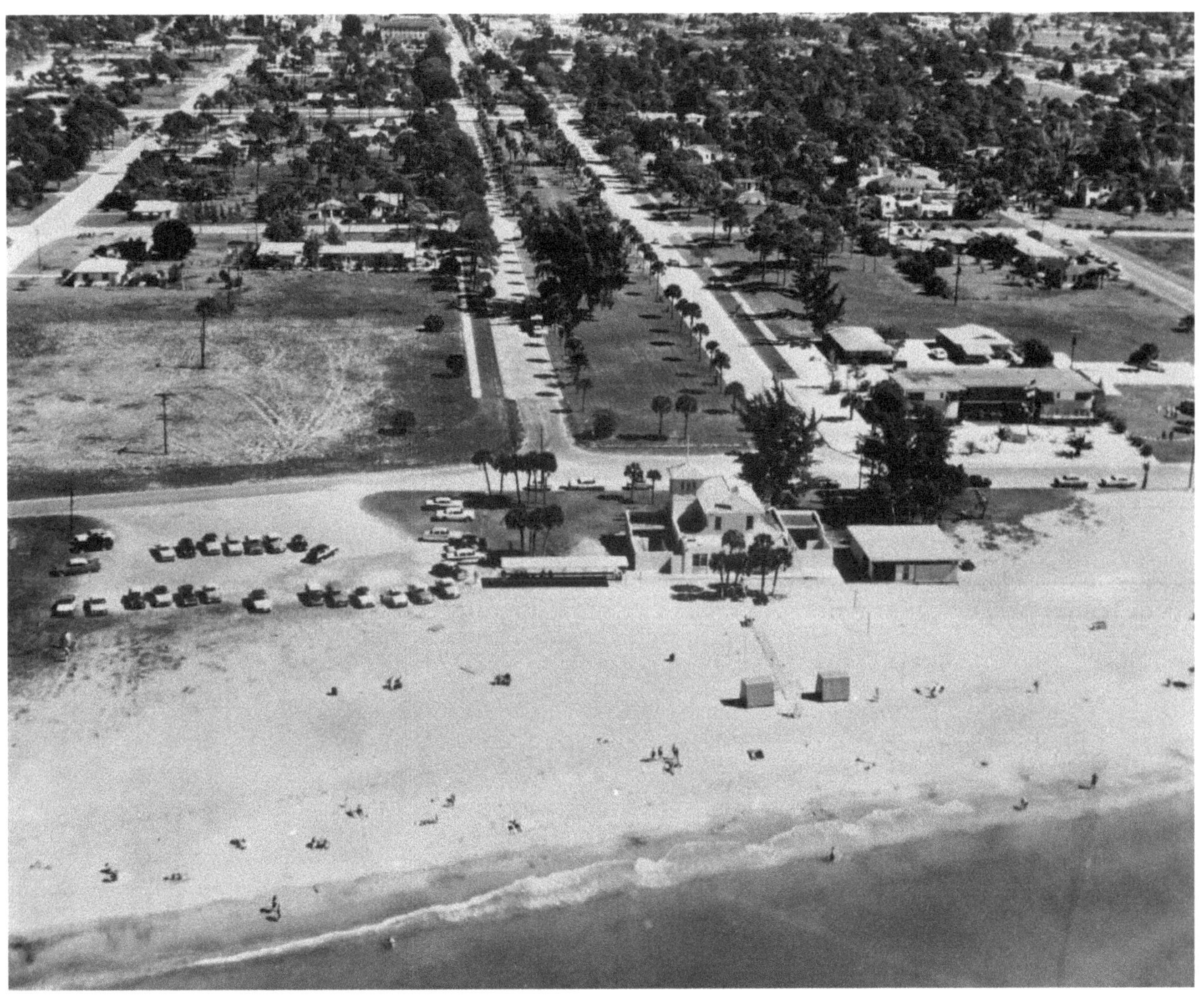

The Sarasota firm of Southern Engineers Incorporated was supposed to implement John Nolen's city plan for Venice. After the Brotherhood of Locomotive Engineers acquired the townsite, it created the BLE Corporation to develop the new city, seen here many years later. BLE replaced Southern Engineers with the engineering firm of Black, McKinney & Stewart of Washington, D.C.

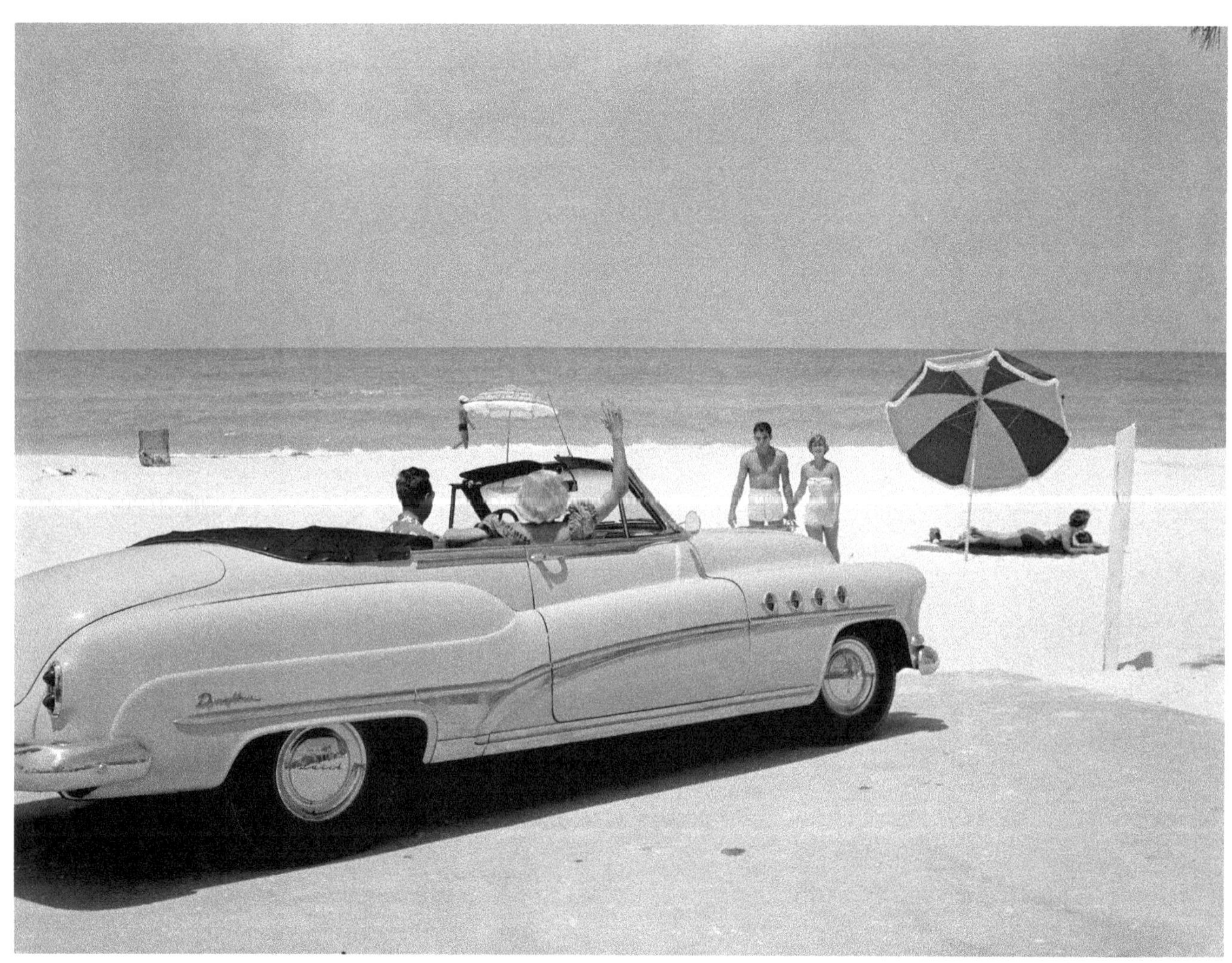

This couple in 1951 is doing something impossible prior to 1926—driving on Lido Beach. Before then, only Siesta Key was accessible by auto. Other islands and their beaches were first reached by a bridge built by John Ringling that connected the mainland to Bird Key, which then connected to Lido and Longboat keys.

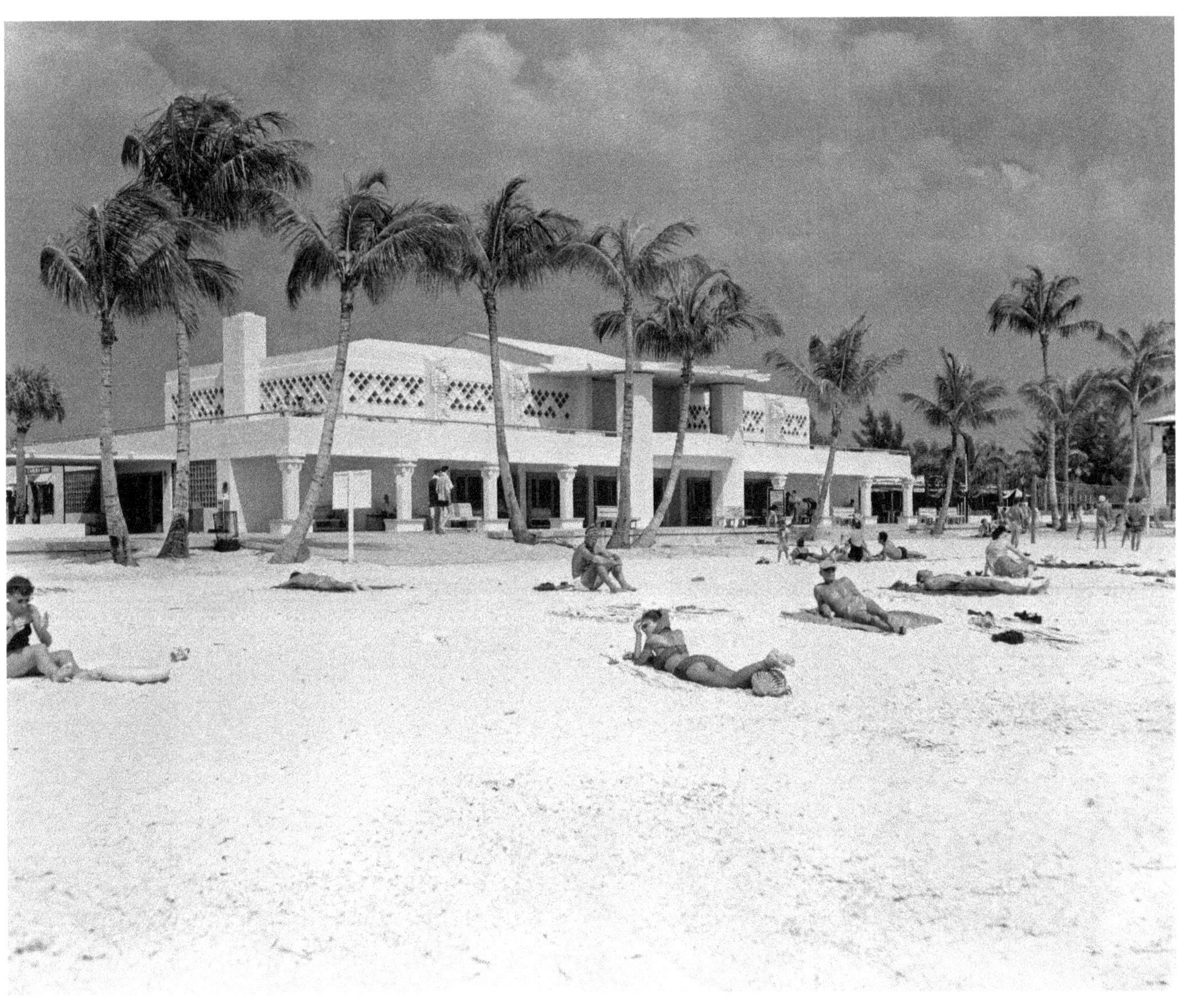

Sarasota's Lido Beach Casino was located on beach frontage acquired by the city from the Ringling estate in 1938 in a tax settlement. The casino was designed by Ralph Twitchell and was initially leased to a private company, but when that didn't work out, the city took over the casino. It closed in 1970 and was replaced by one designed by Tim Seibert.

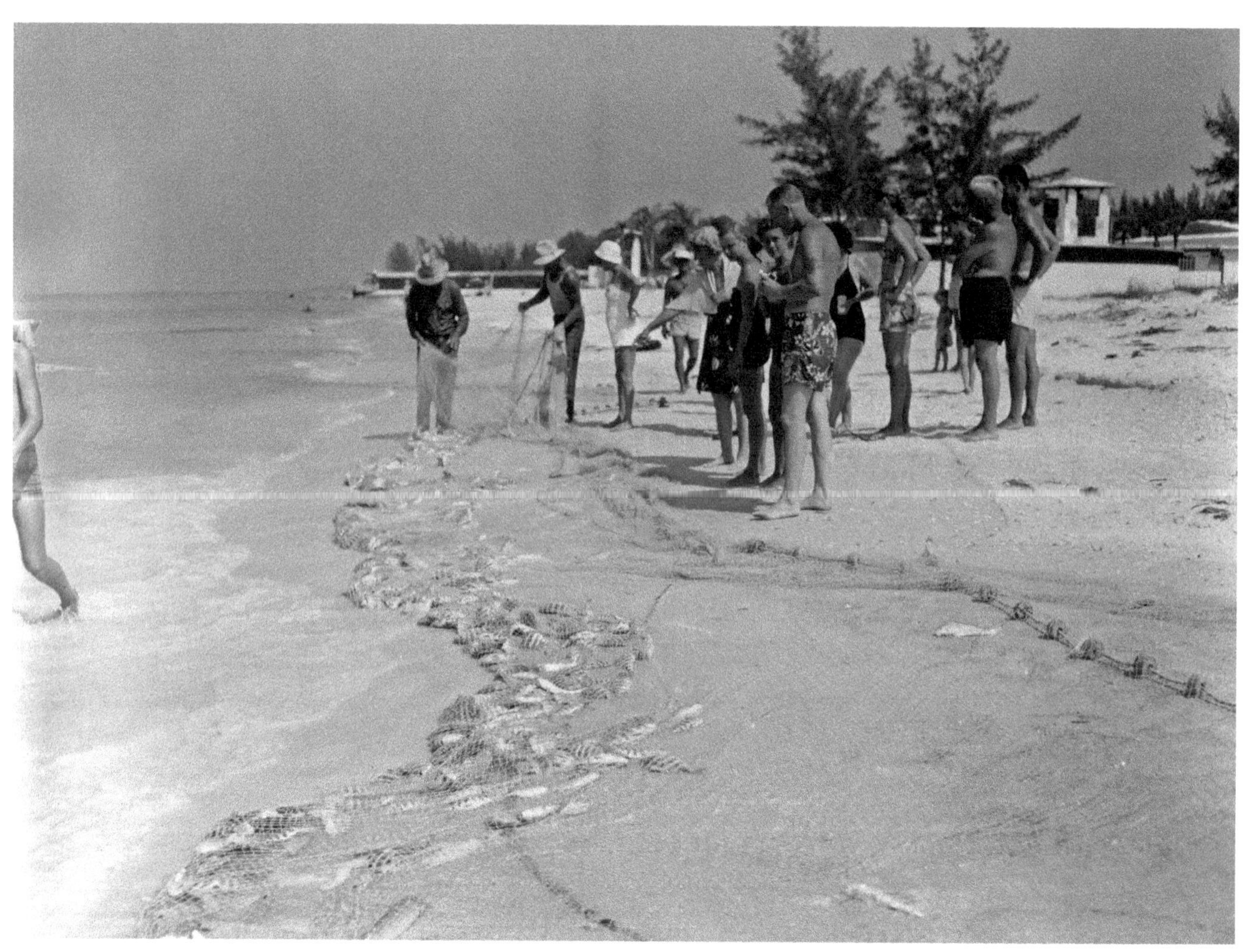

While sport fishermen often come to the area to catch tarpon and kingfish, commercial fisheries also focus on many other varieties. Included in the tons of fish shipped throughout the country are pompano, mackerel, sheepshead, bluefish, channel bass, flounder, drum, and mullet. Some are caught in nets such as this one spread out on a Sarasota beach in 1951.

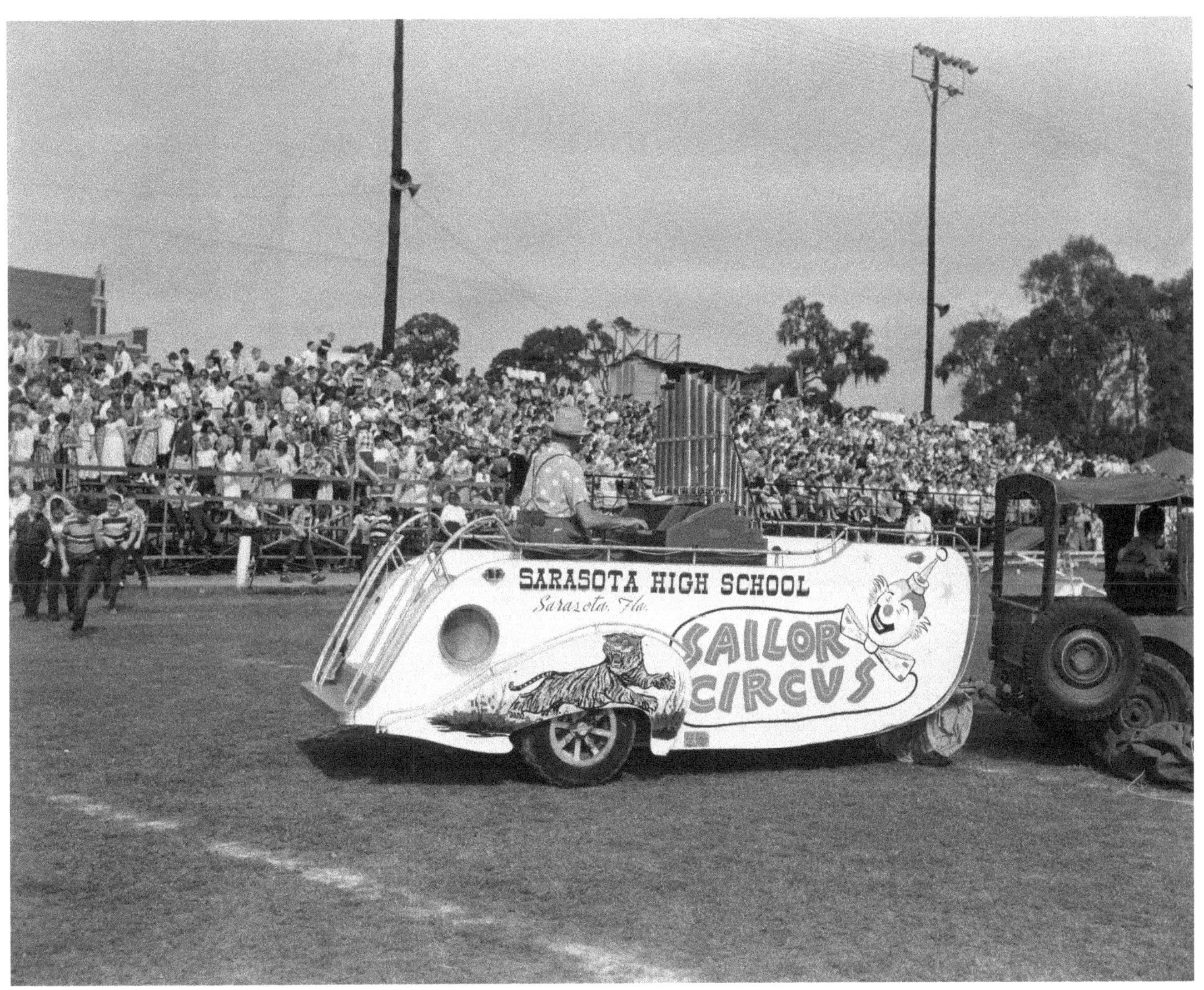

In 1949, the gymnastics program at Sarasota High School was enlarged by Bill Rutland to include circus acts, and the Sarasota Sailor Circus program was begun. Poles were erected at the football field in 1950, and aerial acts were added. Two years later, the program acquired the nickname of the "Greatest Little Show on Earth."

Students from Sarasota High School perform in the Sailor Circus, members of which have appeared on *Ted Mack's Amateur Hour,* the *Mike Douglas Show,* the *Today Show* and have marched in Macy's Thanksgiving Day Parade. Tour destinations have included Alaska, Japan, and Peru. The April show draws visitors from across the country.

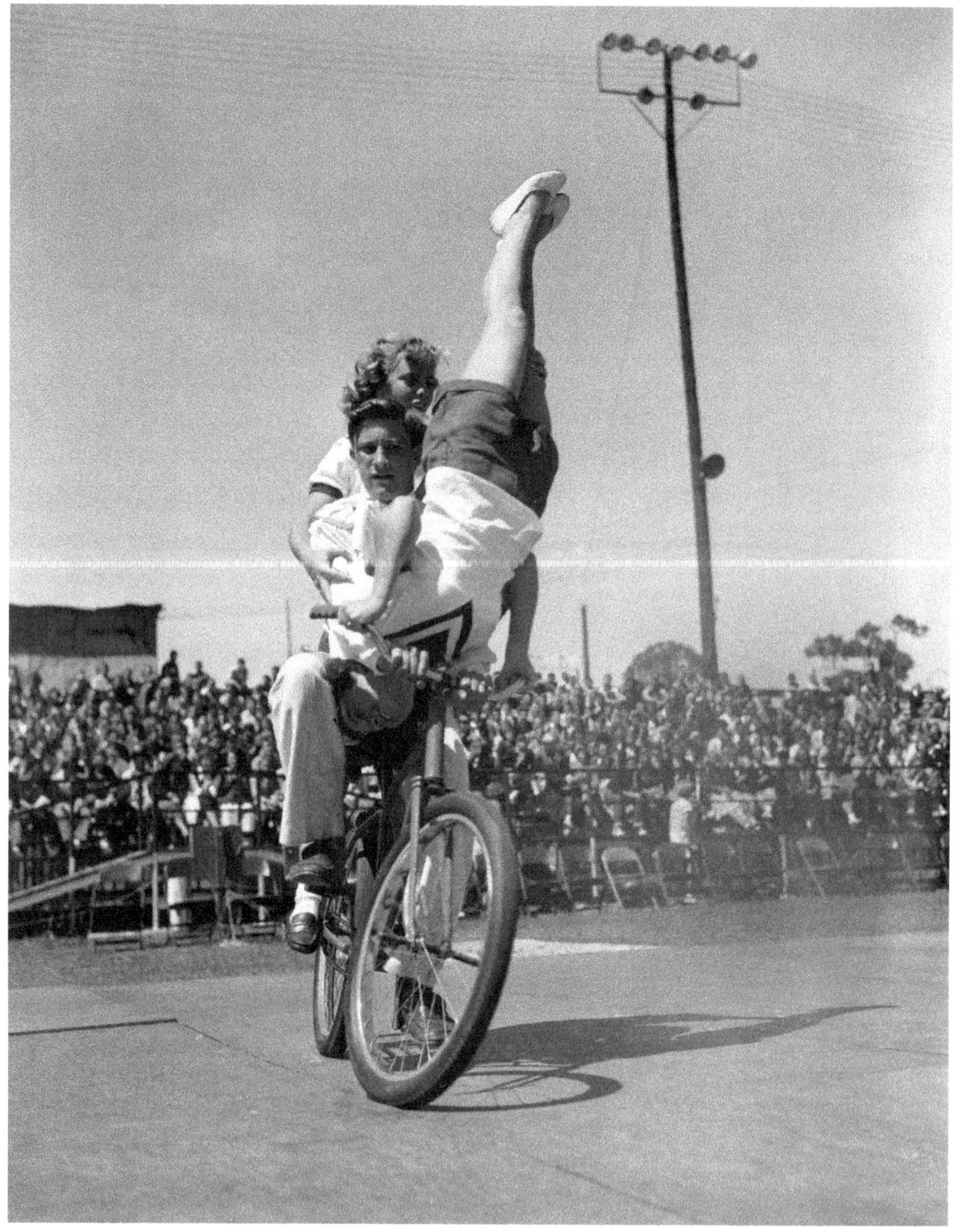

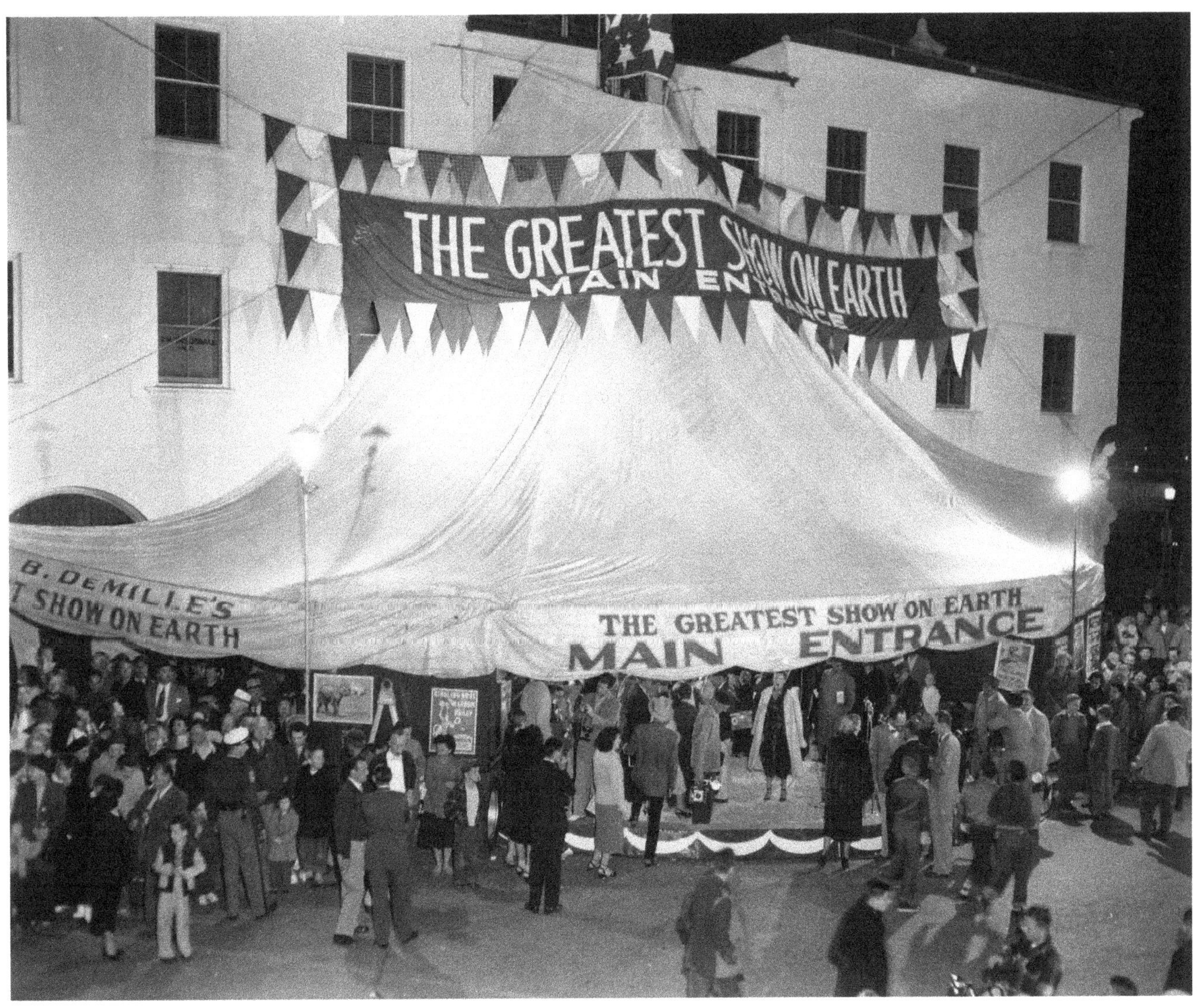

The Greatest Show on Earth premiered after a parade of elephants, giraffes, and human circus performers ended at the Florida Theater, formerly the Edwards Theater. Designed by Roy A. Benjamin and built by Arthur Edwards in 1926, it initially featured vaudeville shows and silent films. In 1936, it was renamed the Florida Theater, then in the 1970s it became the Sarasota Opera House.

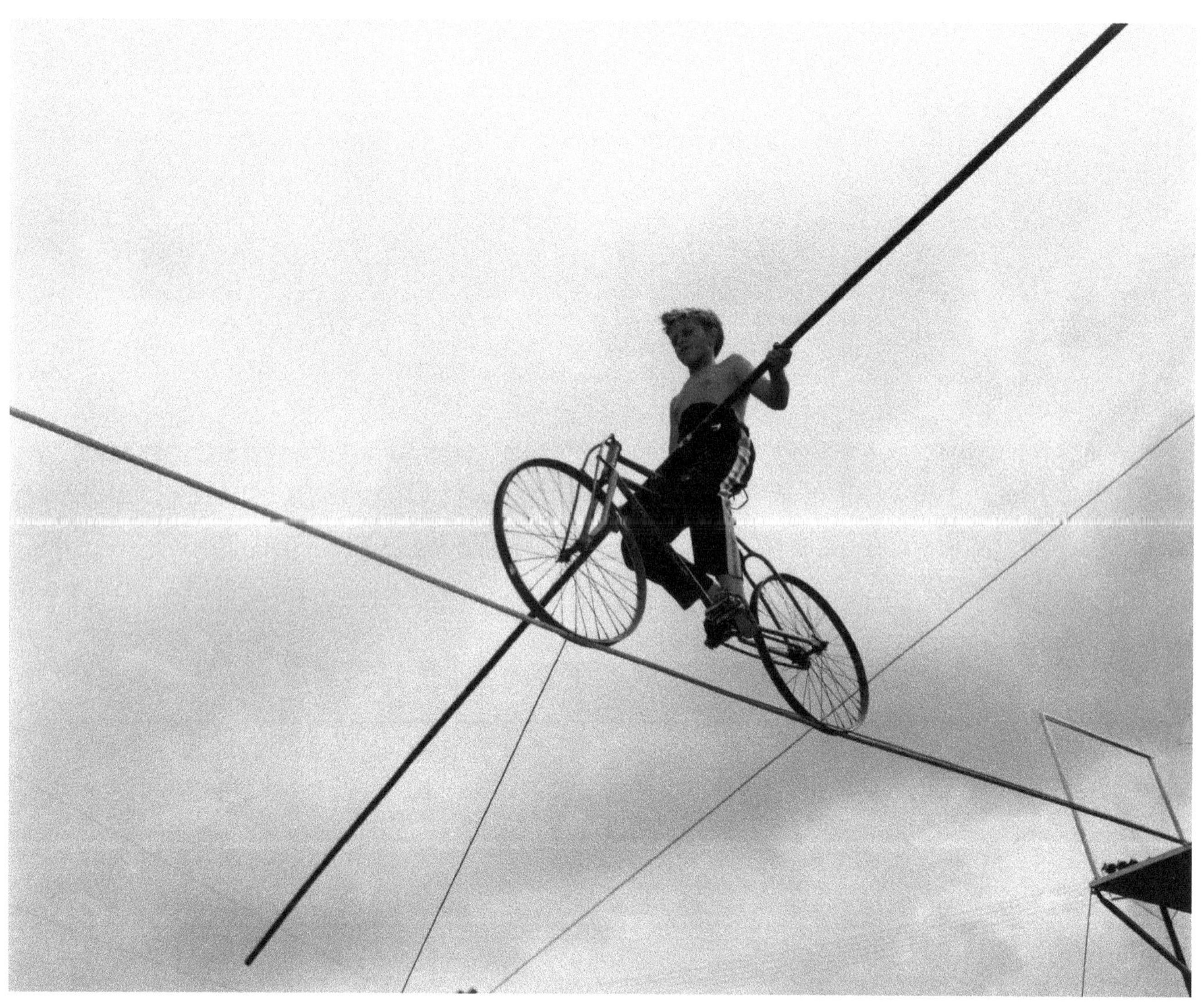

An aerialist performs in the Sailor Circus in 1953, when all of its members attended Sarasota High School. In 1969, the program moved to a new home and expanded to include younger students. In 2004, the program was taken over by the Police Athletic League, and the Sailor Circus became one of the PAL's after-school programs.

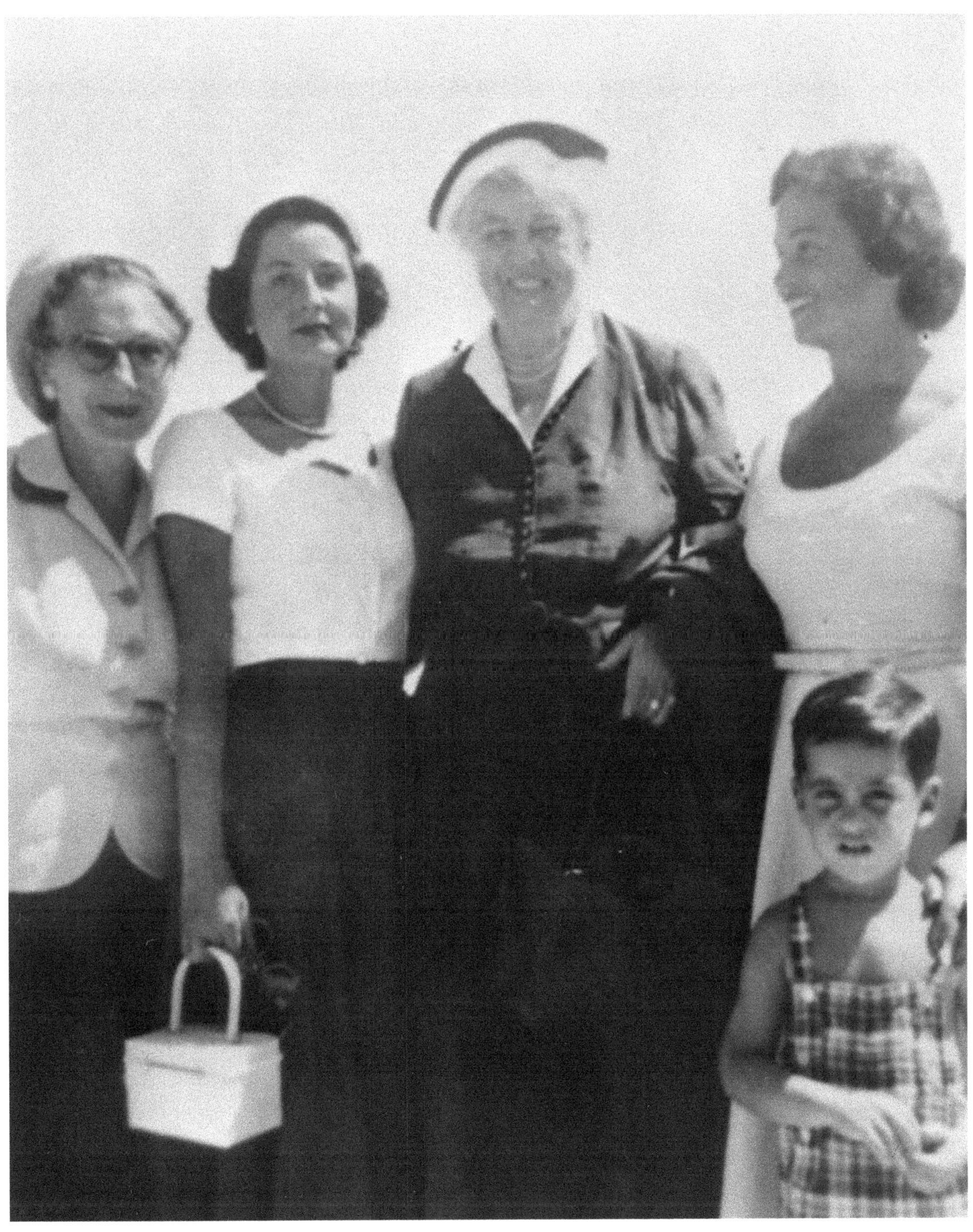

Eleanor Roosevelt visited Sarasota in 1953, between visits to Miami and Bethune-Cookman College in Daytona Beach. Her talks with local officials centered around increasing interest in the United Nations, ending segregation, and selling bonds for Israel. She expressed concern that Sarasota could not reach a decision whether to open a beach for black residents.

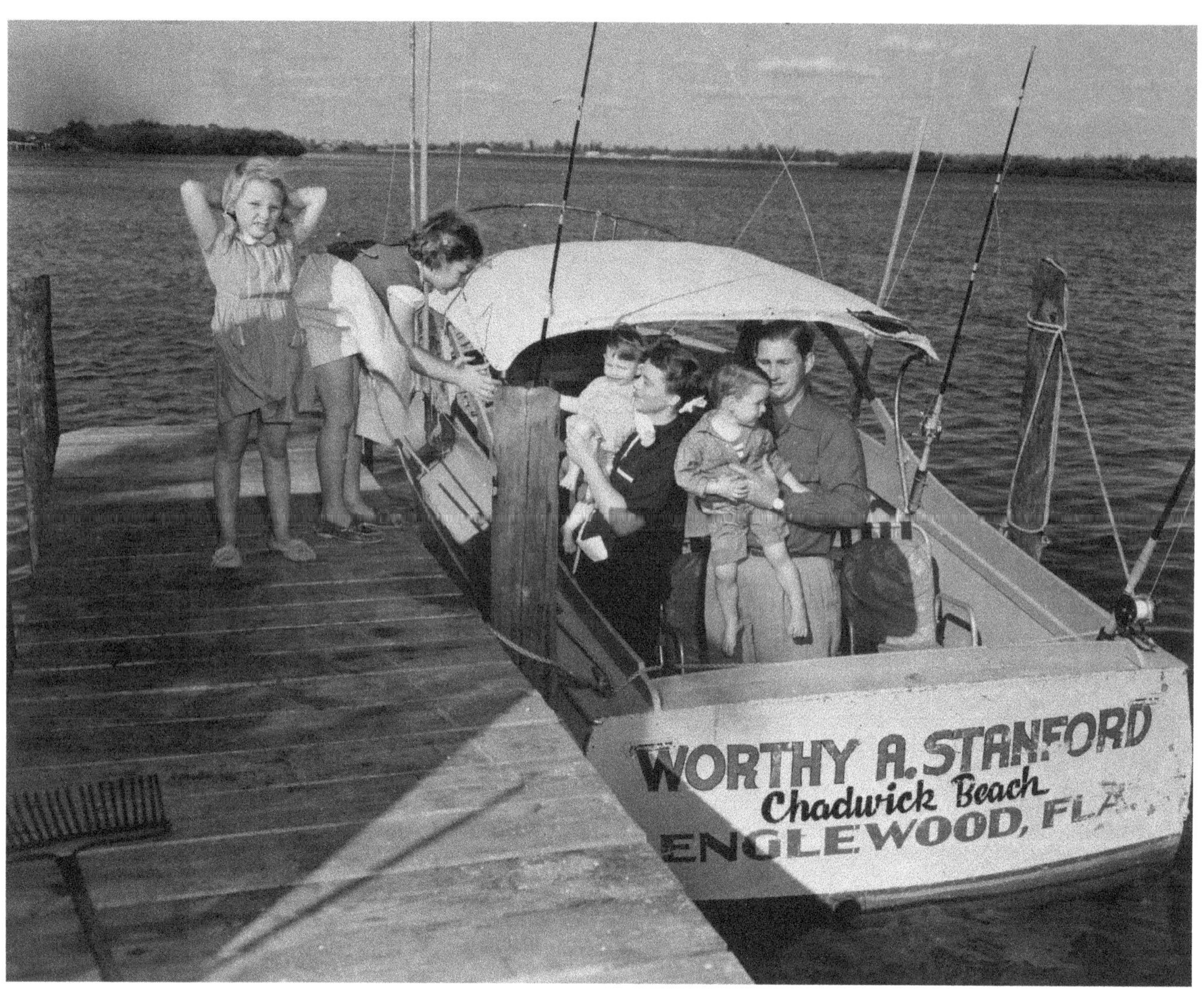

Englewood is known for fishing, and hopeful anglers arrive every year to attempt to land a tarpon in tournaments held at Boca Grande Pass. Those who want to fish from shore also have opportunities, such as on the Bill Ainger fishing pier, created from the old wooden bridge that once joined the mainland to Manasota Key and the gulf beaches.

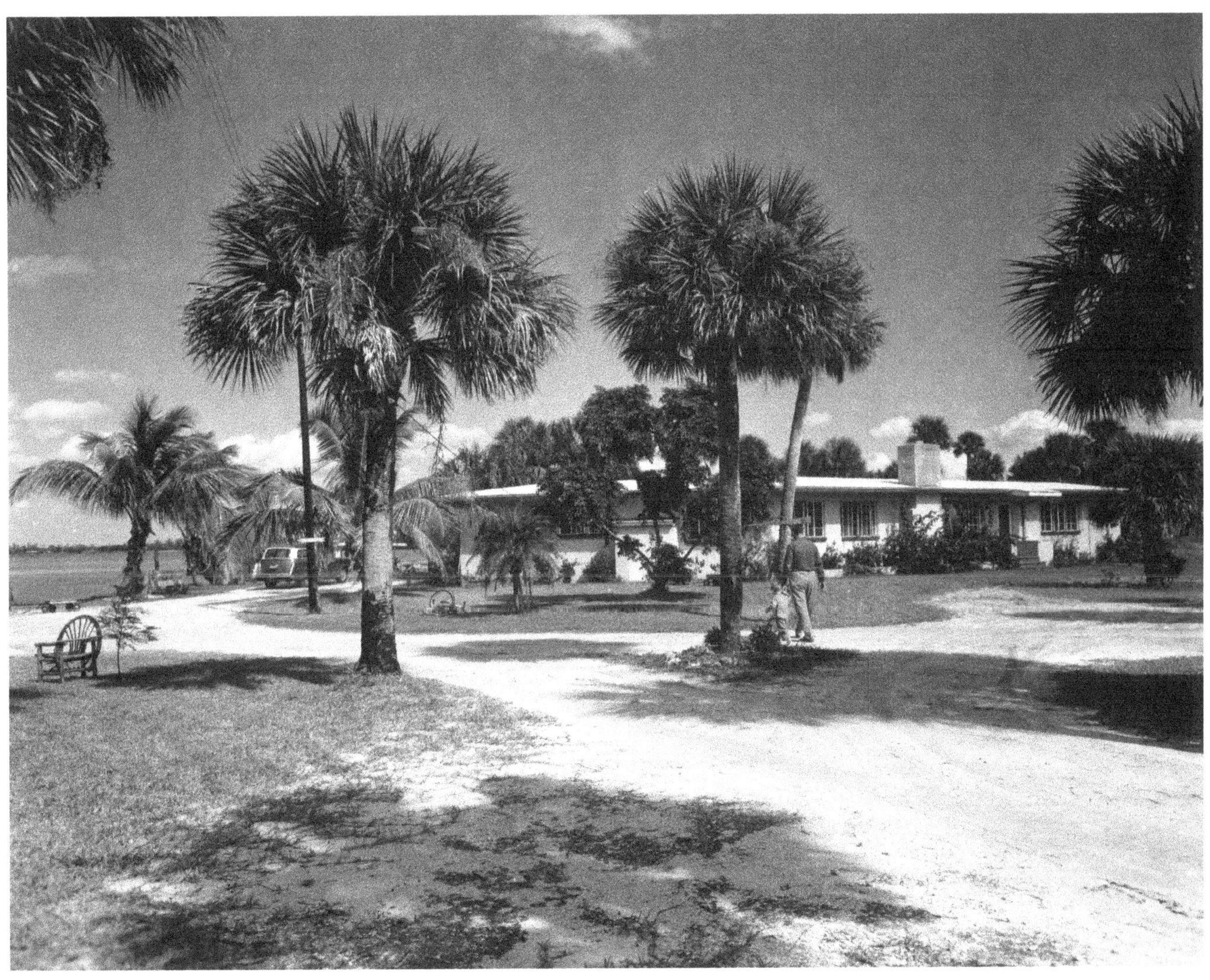

The modern Stanford Fishing Resort run by Worthy A. Stanford, who is seen here in 1953 walking with a young boy, was just one of many businesses to open after Buchan's Landing, which was the hub of activity in early Englewood. P. E. Buchan's general store, post office, and dock served fishermen and schooner captains, and gave the settlement a connection to the outside world.

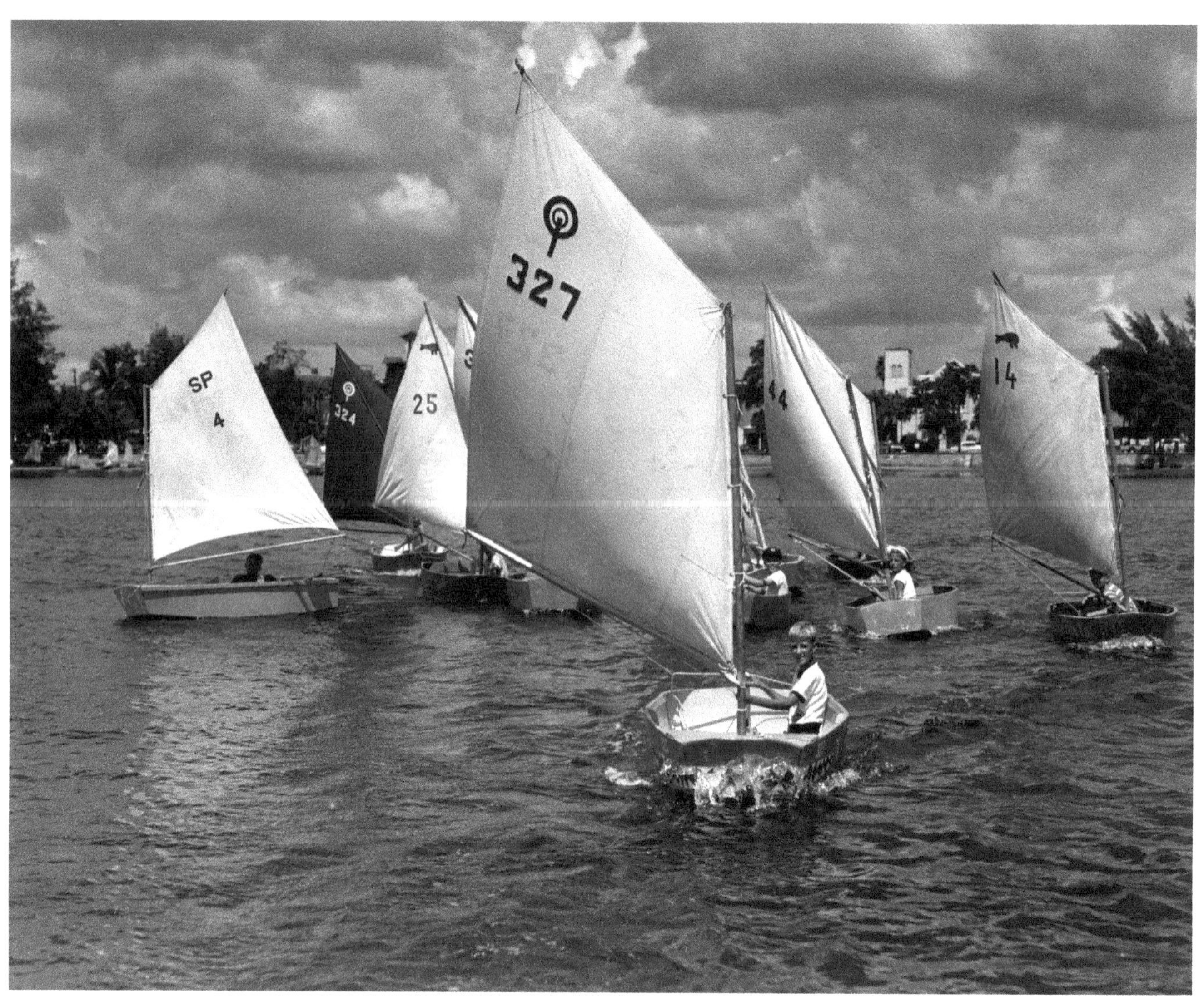

Sarasota County is the home of four yacht clubs and two sailing squadrons. The Sarasota Bay Yachting Association holds several annual races. Shown here are pram-class sailboats participating in one of the Labor Day races in 1954.

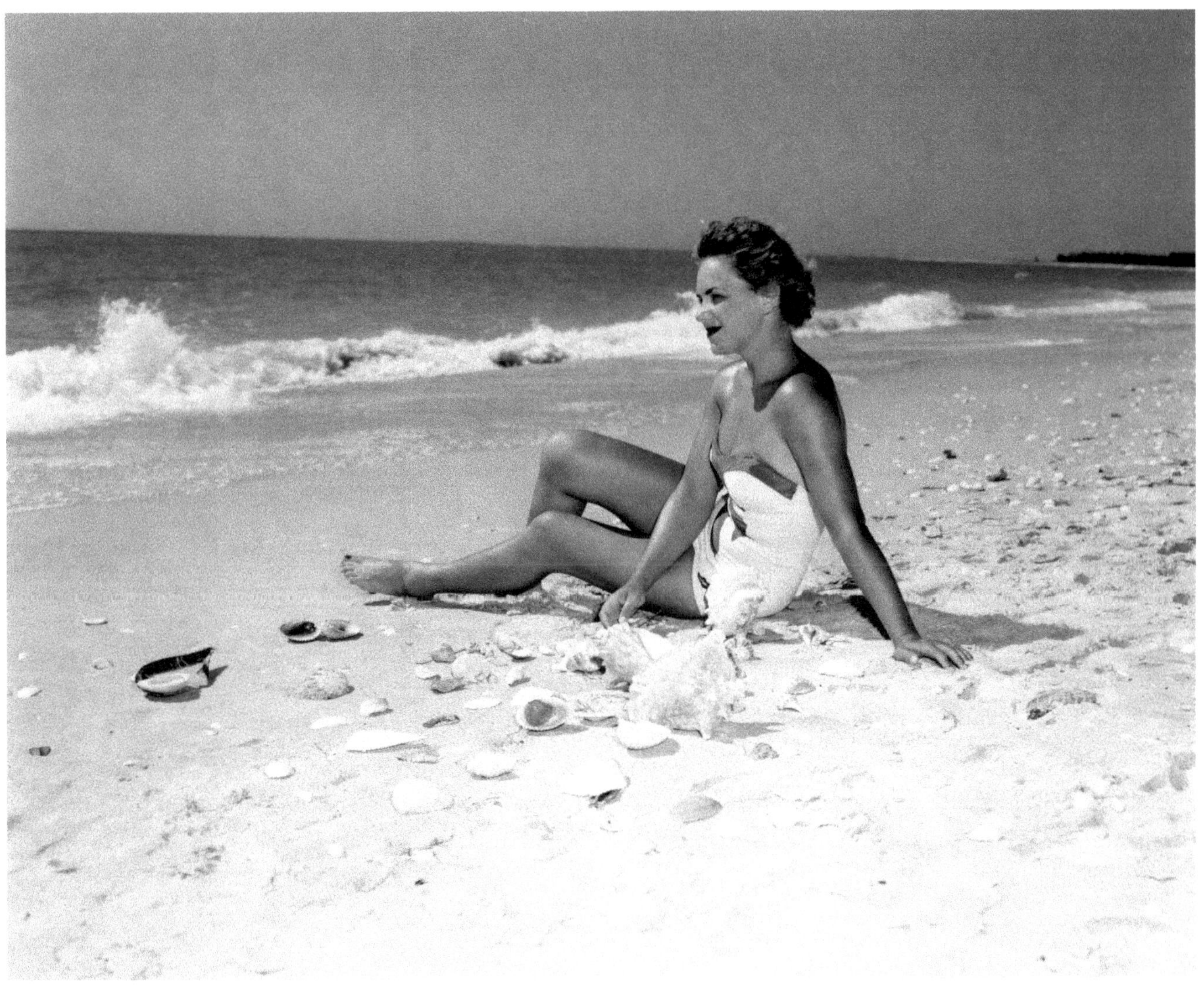

In 1954, Donna Gardner poses on the beach at Englewood with several species of seashells found in the area. Shelling is popular along the gulf coast, and the Sarasota Shell Club has members from Sarasota, Manatee, and Charlotte counties. One of its major events is the annual shell show, where specimens are judged in scientific and artistic categories.

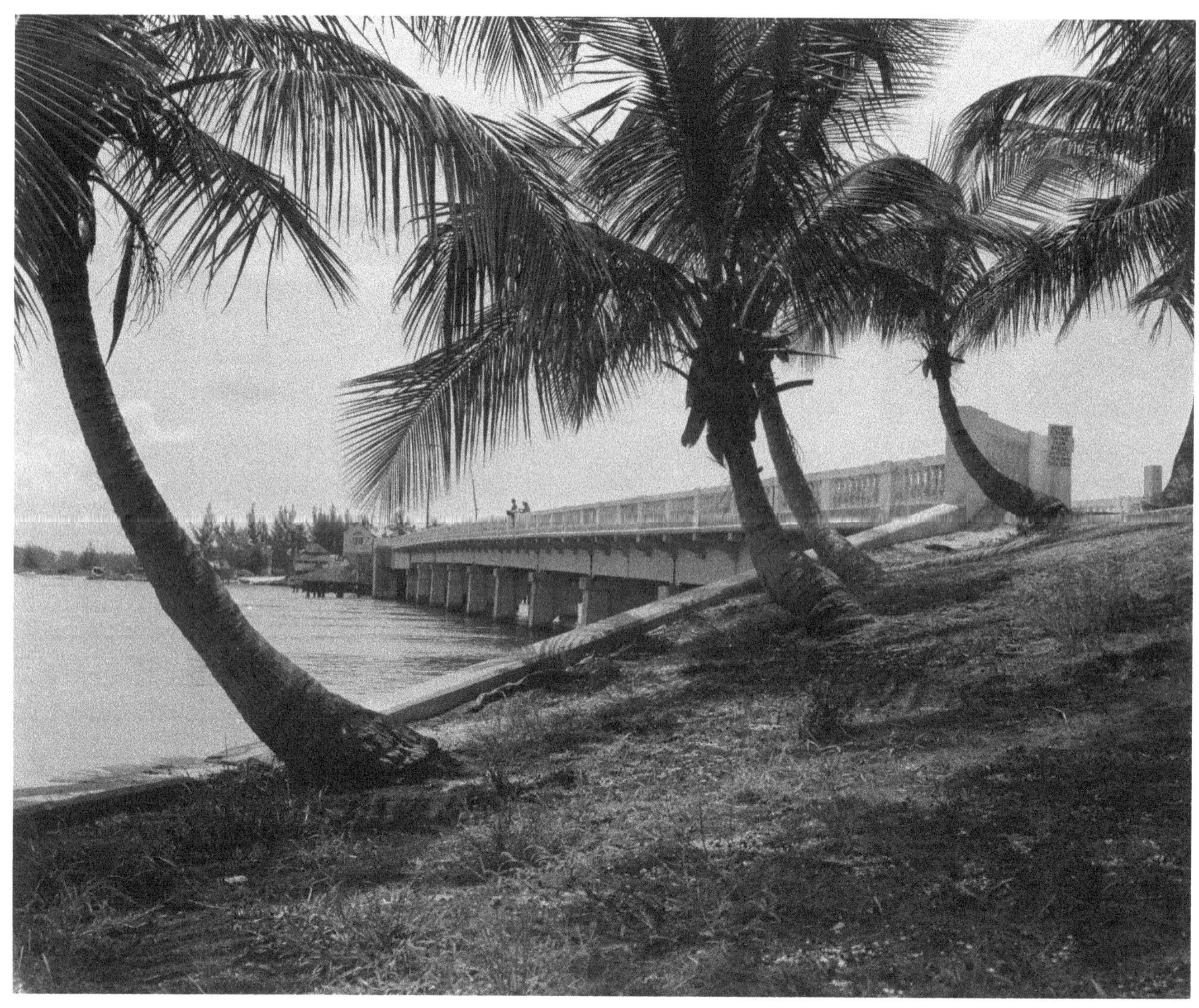

Early settlers on Longboat Key grew guavas, avocados, tomatoes, and citrus, and shipped their crops by steamboat. Farming there was essentially ended by the 1921 hurricane, which flooded the island. The focus of the area then shifted to attracting visitors. The 1950s saw an increase in tourists, most of whom crossed this bridge to reach the key.

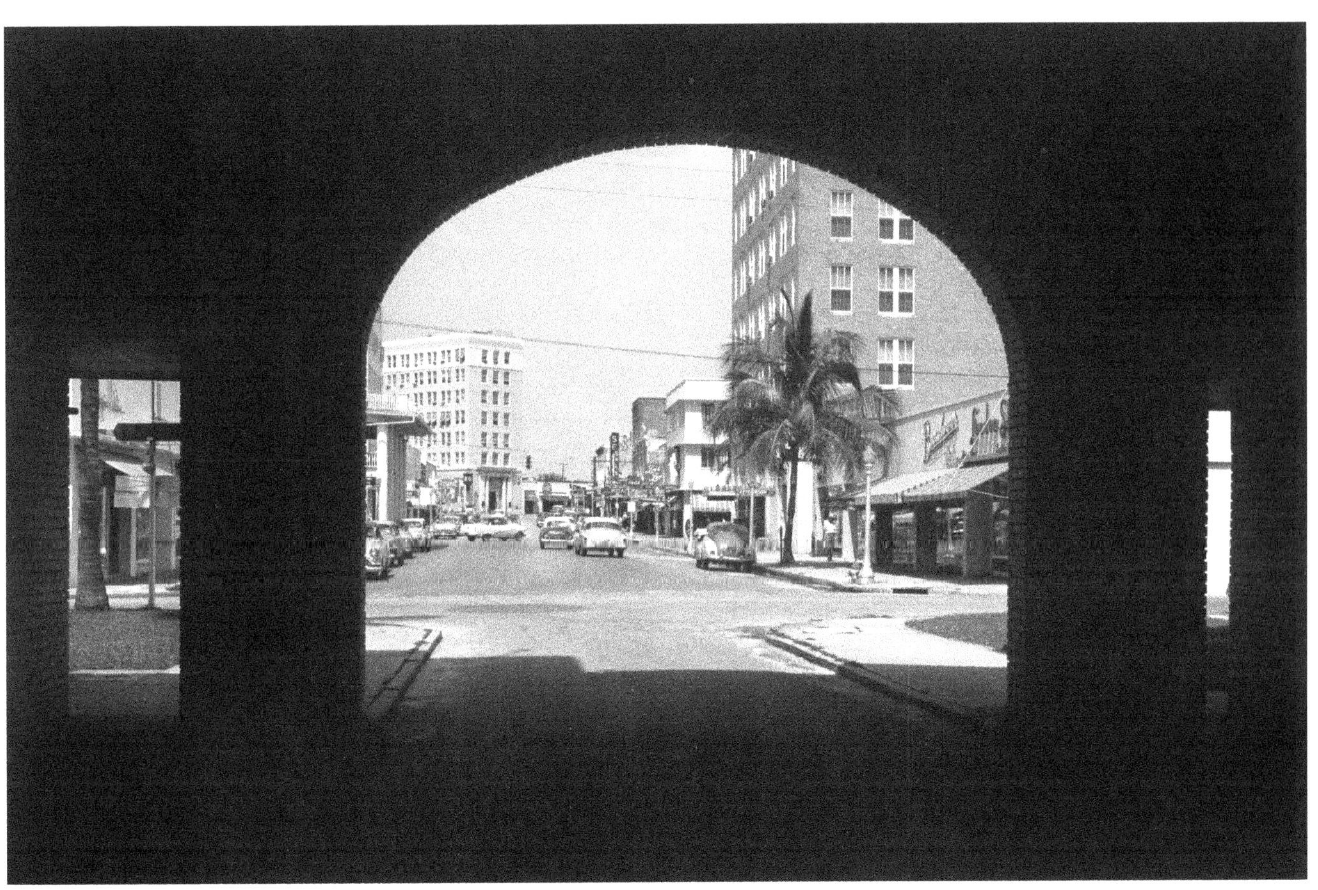

Viewed from the Arcade Building in 1954, the First Bank and Trust Building at the end of the street looks the same as it did when it was built in the 1920s. First Bank closed in 1929 after the stock market crash. Within days, the Palmer Bank was organized by members of Bertha Palmer's family, and the new bank soon moved into the building.

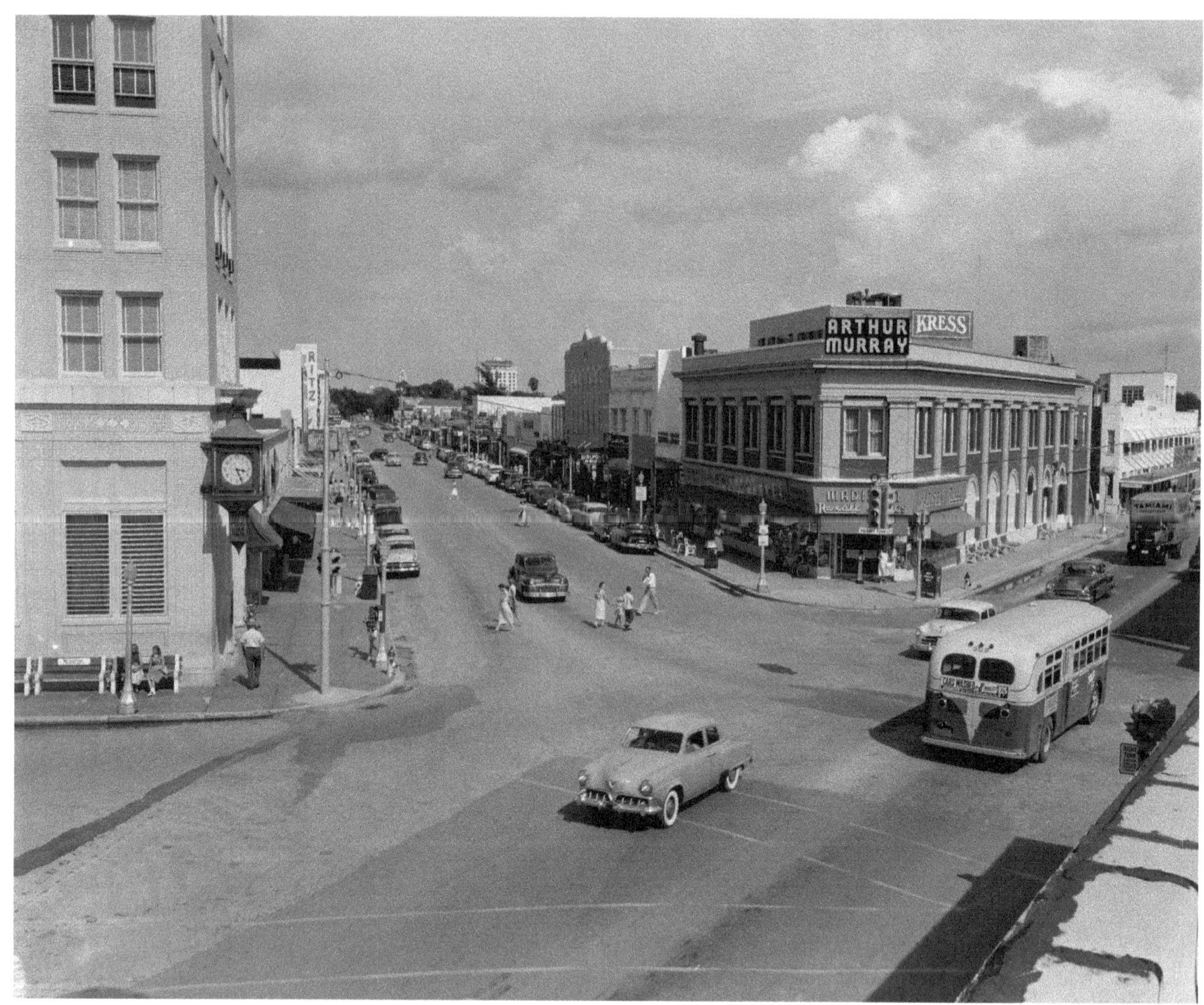

This 1954 view of Five Points includes the art deco Kress Building, located three buildings to the left of the one with the Arthur Murray sign on top. The pointed parapet rises above the name "Kress" still visible on the three-story facade, even though the dime store has not occupied the structure for years. It was built in 1932 with a Spanish theme.

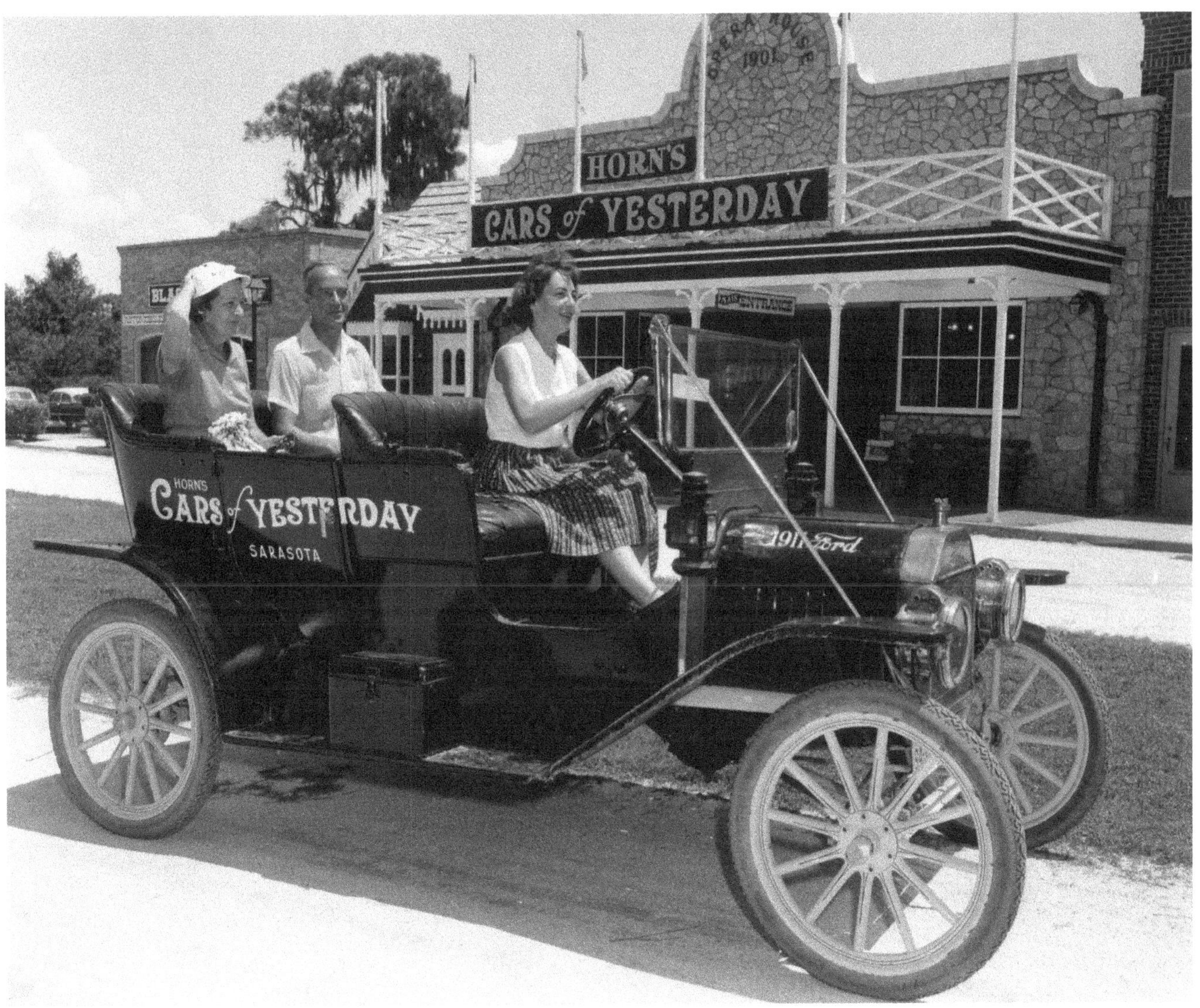

The Florida tourist attraction Horn's Cars of Yesterday opened in Sarasota in 1953. Brothers Bob and Herb Horn of Iowa built it to house their extensive automobile collection, which included a rare Tucker. Also included over time in their hundred or so cars were a pair of 1950s Muntz jet cars, Iso Rivolta sports cars, and several cars once owned by members of the Beatles.

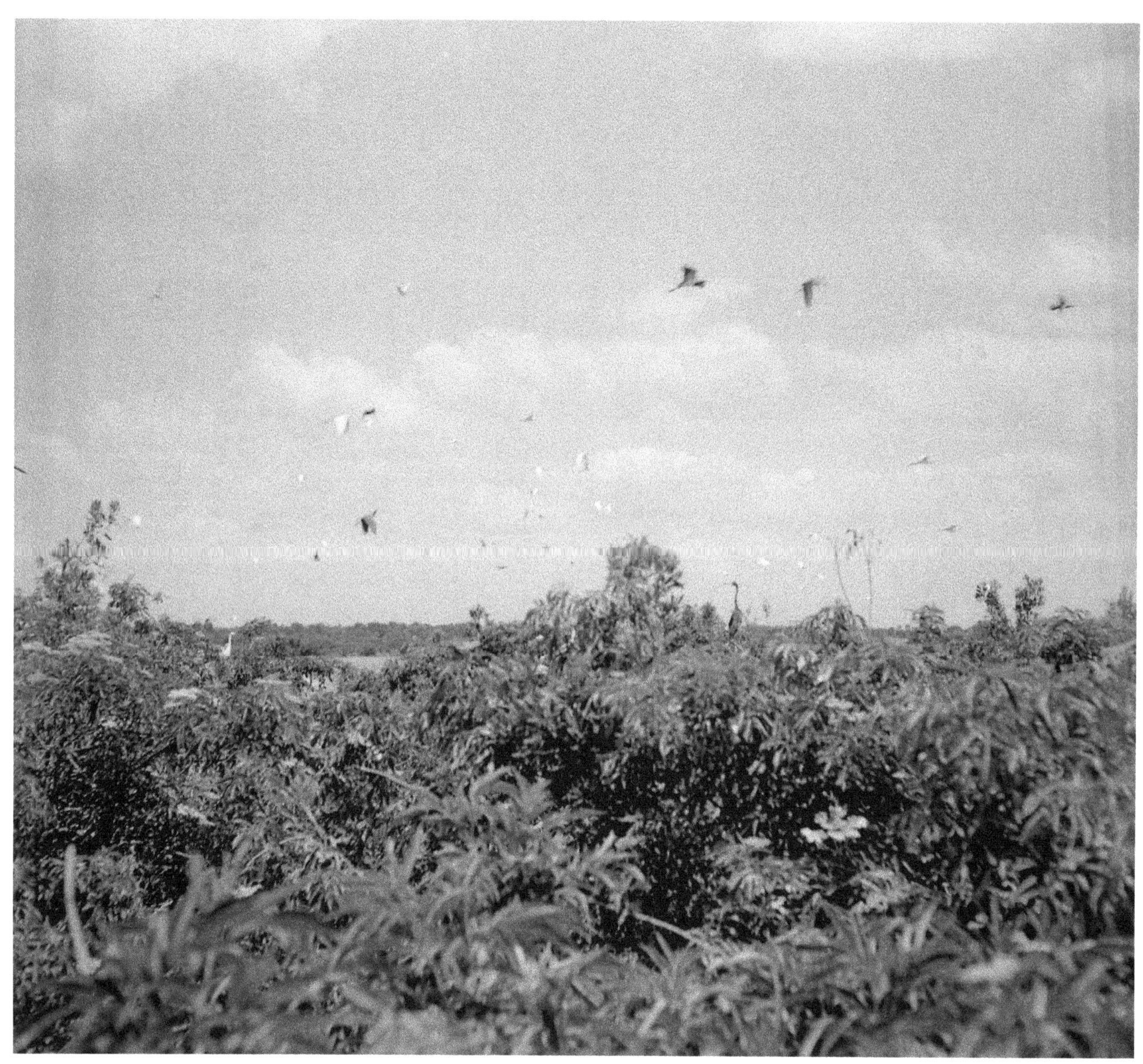

Myakka River State Park opened to the public on June 1, 1942, and became a popular destination for those wanting to hike, camp, or view wildlife such as the birds photographed here in 1955. At the park, one can spend an entire day watching the herons, eagles, ibises, hawks, ducks, and a large variety of smaller birds.

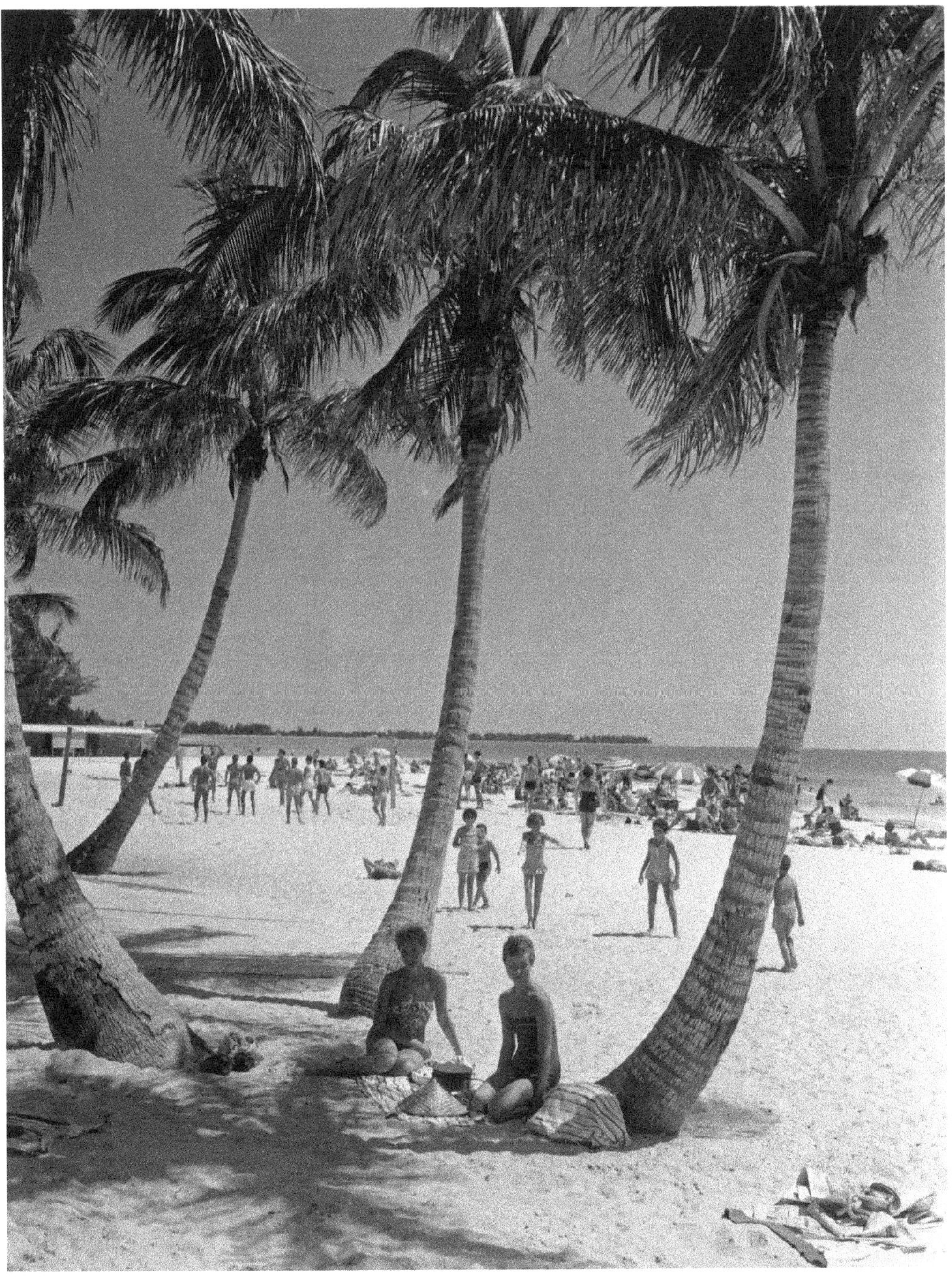

Sarasota's beaches are consistently ranked near the top in the state for overall quality. In 1950, *National Geographic* magazine ranked Siesta Key Beach as one of the four most beautiful beaches in the world. More than likely, those enjoying Lido Beach here in 1955 felt much the same about it.

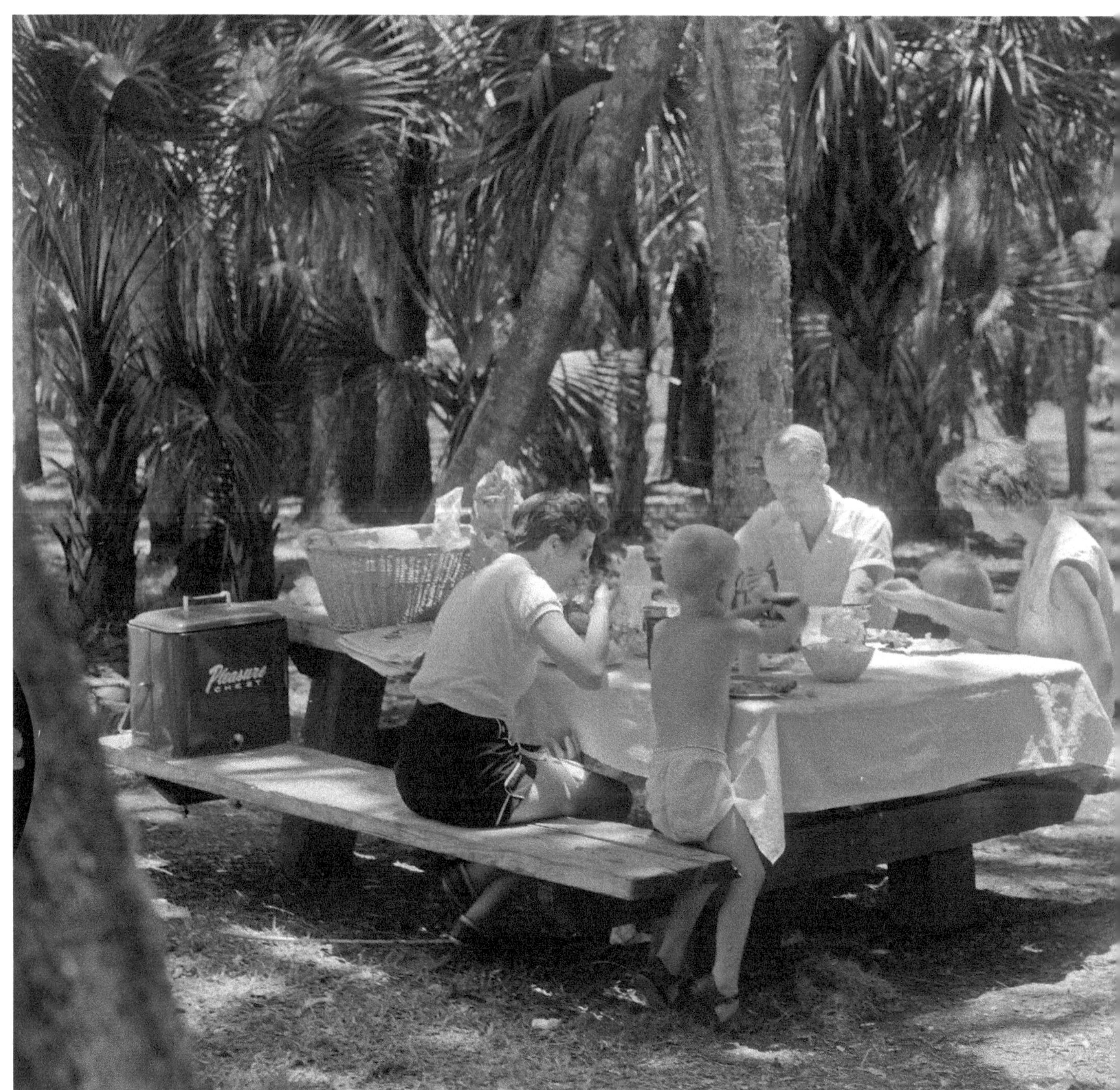
Pleasure
CHEST

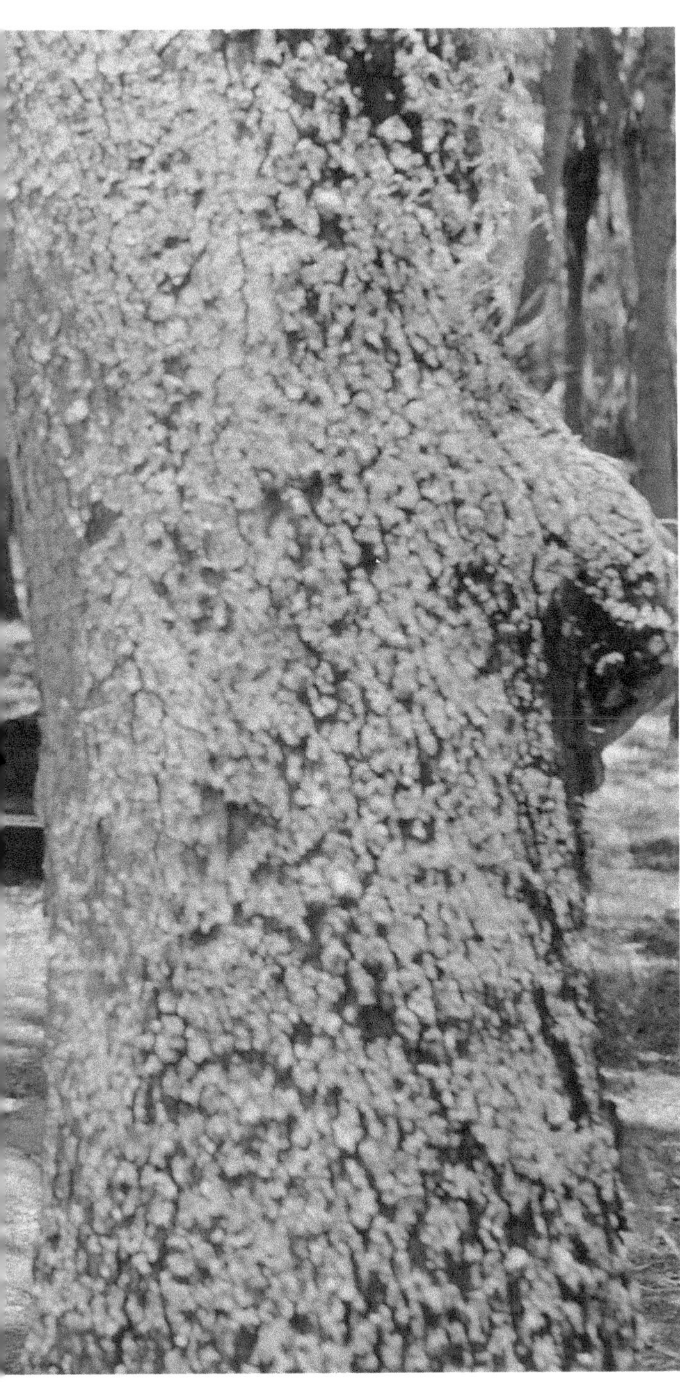

The area where families now picnic at Myakka River State Park used to be part of Bertha Palmer's Meadow Sweet Pastures ranch. To start her ranch, she bought a local herd from Dink Murphy, then she brought in Brahma bulls, which thrived, and Herefords, most of which died of cattle tick fever. Subsequently, Palmer became one of the first in Florida to dip cattle to kill ticks, well before it became mandatory.

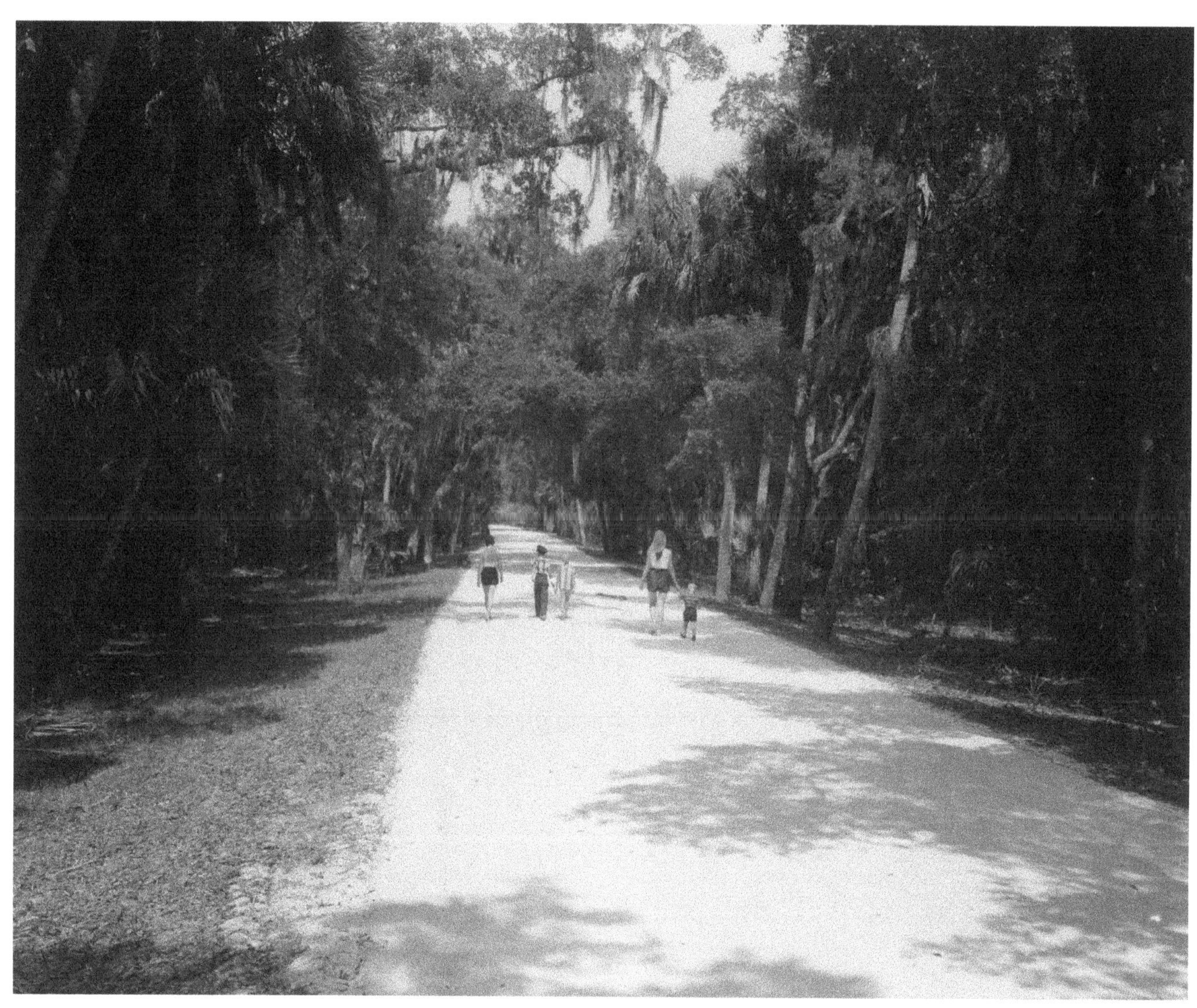

Hiking is a major activity in Myakka River State Park, whether as a leisurely walk, such as this family is taking in 1956, or as a serious trek of nearly forty miles on the Myakka Trail. A variety of walking surfaces are available, including a boardwalk over part of Upper Myakka Lake, and an elevated canopy walkway that passes through treetops.

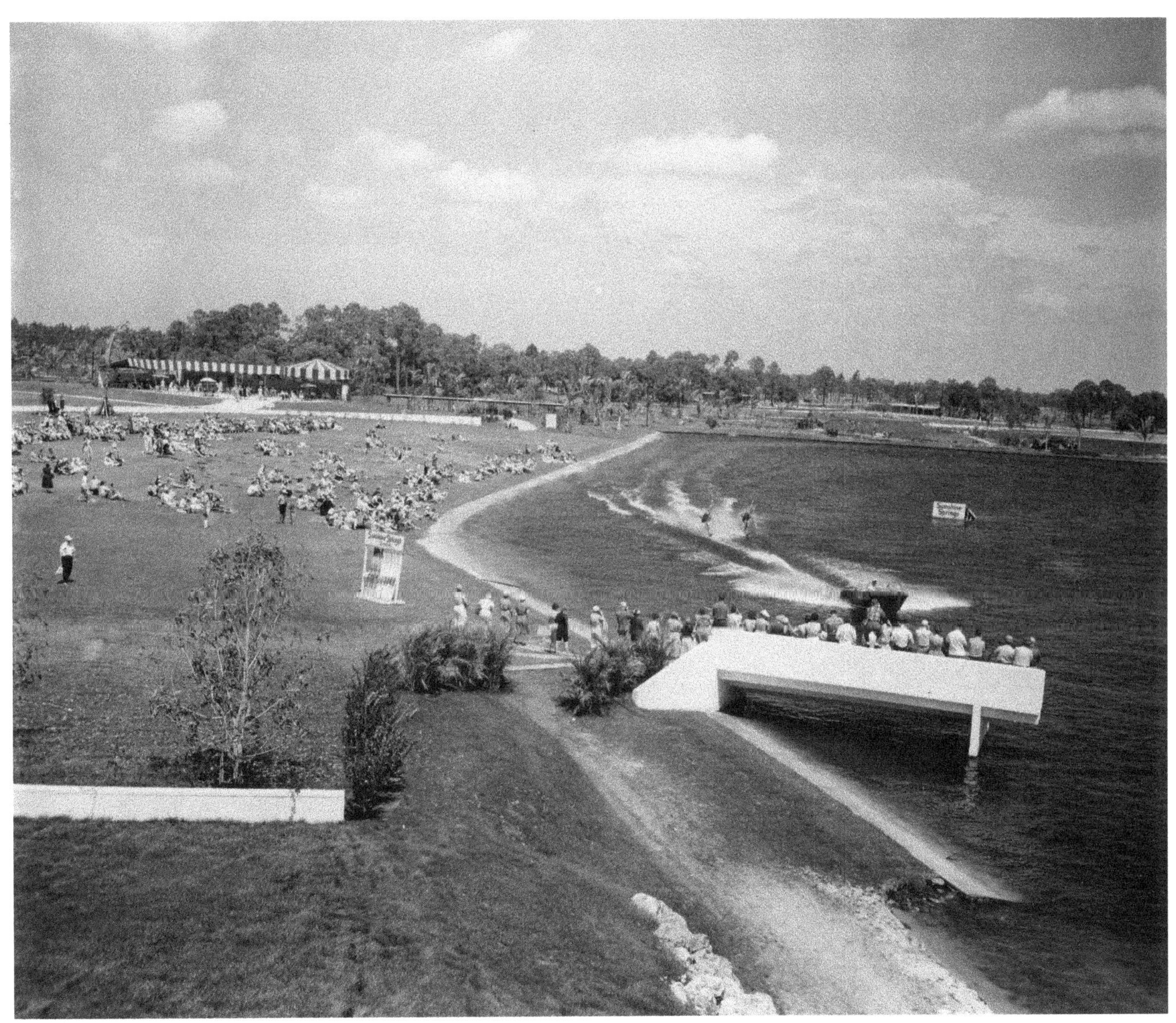

In the last half of the 1950s, Sarasota had an attraction known as Sunshine Springs and Gardens, seen here in 1956. On its twenty acres near Proctor Road were beautifully landscaped gardens viewed from swan boats that sailed along its canals. A 400-acre lake featured water-ski shows with jumping boats, female "aquabelles," and a skiing elephant.

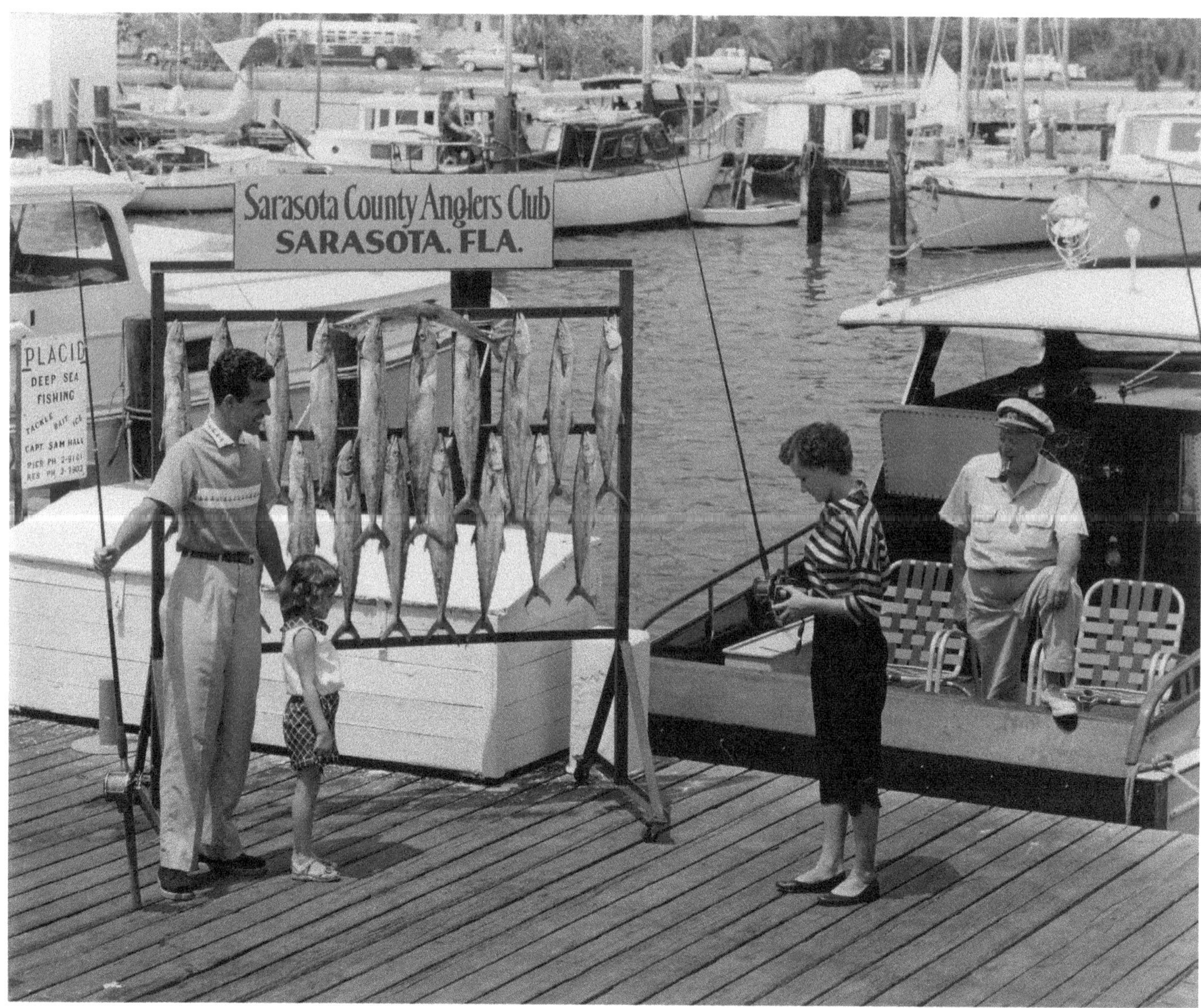

Some said tarpon were so abundant in early Sarasota that you could catch all you wanted just by rowing into the bay and hitting them with a club. Other varieties, such as the king mackerel shown in this 1956 advertisement photo, have remained popular with professional fishermen and tourists alike. The group posed here are Duane, Janenne, and Mary Lou Roberts.

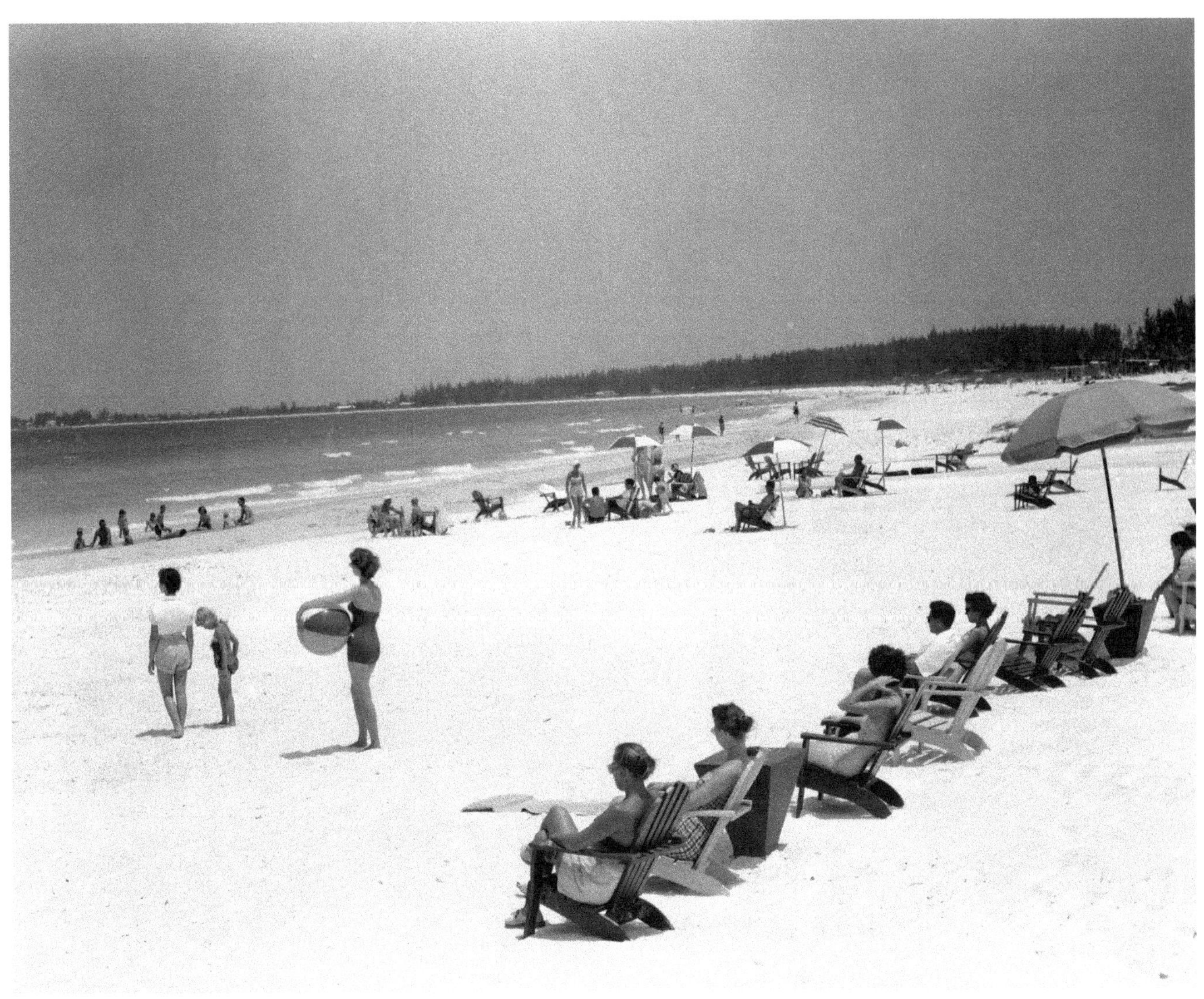

In 1956, sunbathers enjoy the beach at Siesta Key, formerly called Little Sarasota Key. One of the first residents of the island was "Uncle Ben" Stickney, who lived there in the late 1890s and who had briefly run the DeSoto Hotel. The area was later laid out for development by Henry Higel, who dredged a cutoff channel and separated Bay Island as a separate piece of land.

Posing against a palm tree on Longboat Key in 1956 is Barbara Jean Laney, a resident of nearby Bradenton. A model and television actress, she worked in the 1950s show *Sky King*, a popular program about a former military pilot, portrayed by Kirby Grant, who patrolled his ranch in a small airplane.

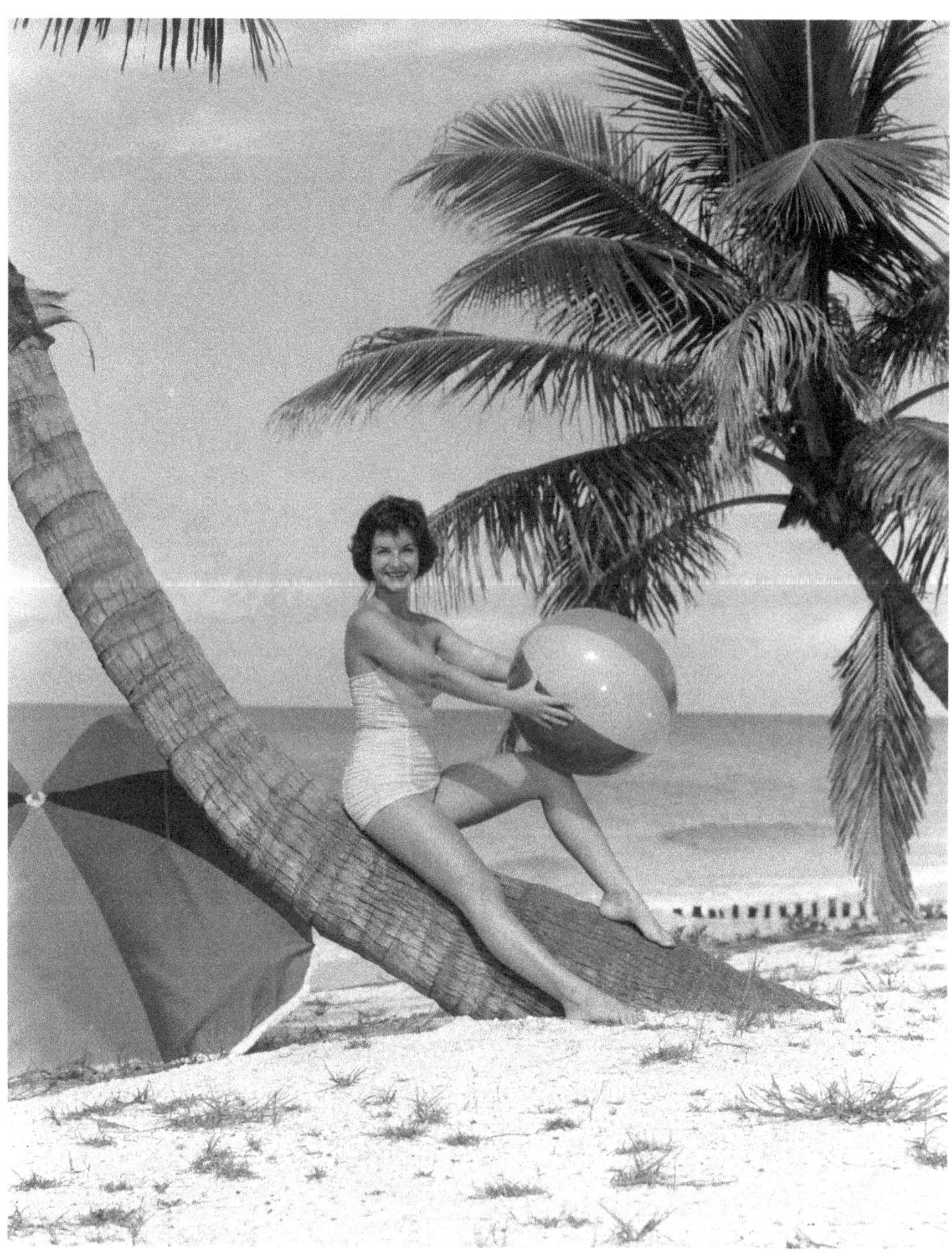

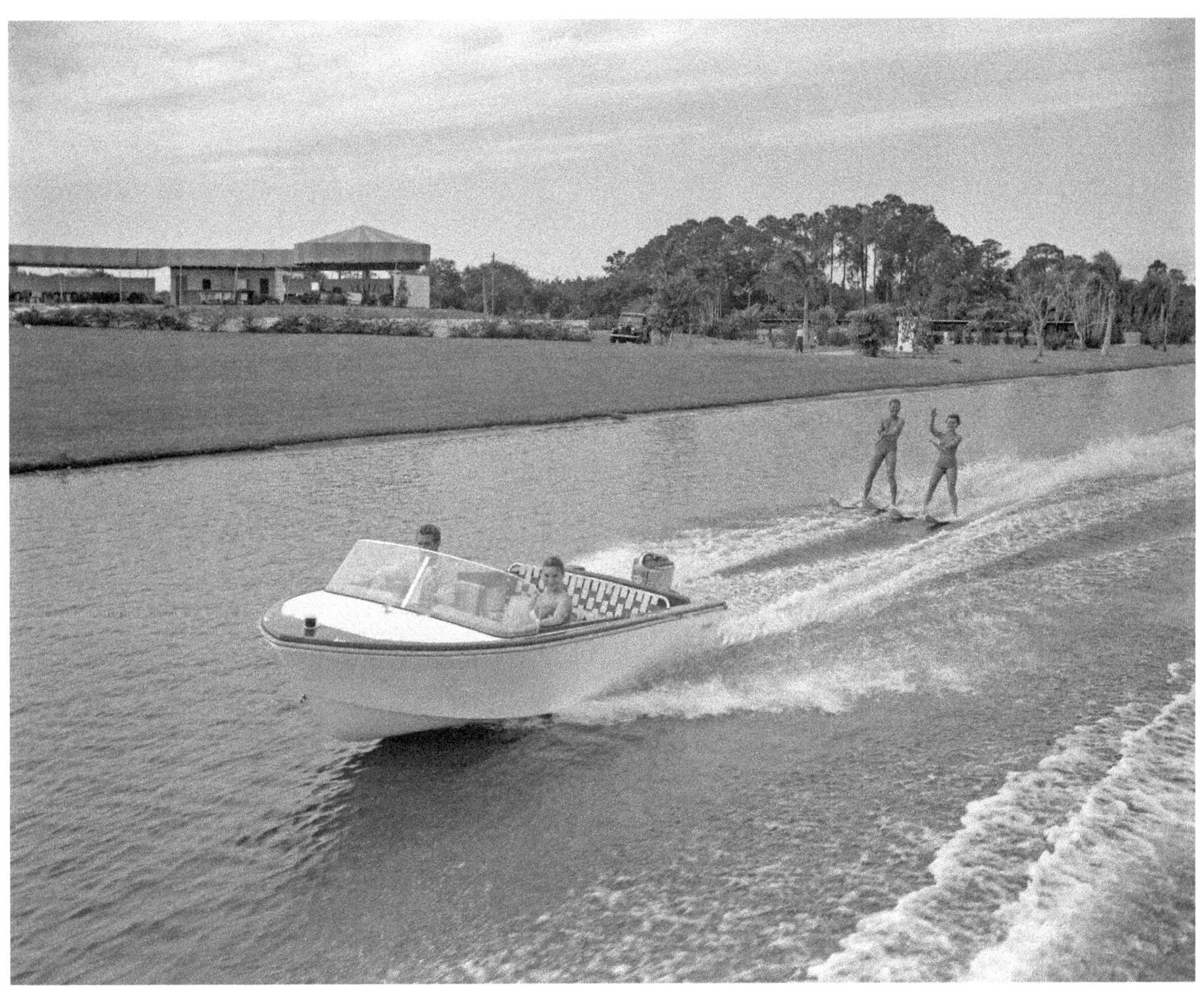

Although named Sunshine Springs, the aquatic attraction was not a real spring. Leonard Tanner bought ranchland and capitalized on the names of several other springs that attracted tourists. Sunshine Springs hosted the Miss Florida pageant but fell upon hard times, and in 1960 the land was sold for redevelopment.

David B. Lindsay bought ten acres of Sarasota swampland in the 1930s and brought in thousands of plants from around the world to create Sarasota Jungle Gardens. By 1936, it was promoted as a major destination for tourists, who came to see its lagoons, Gardens of Christ, Tiki Garden, and plants such as the rare Australian nut tree and strangler fig. These young visitors in 1958 appear most interested in the flamingos.

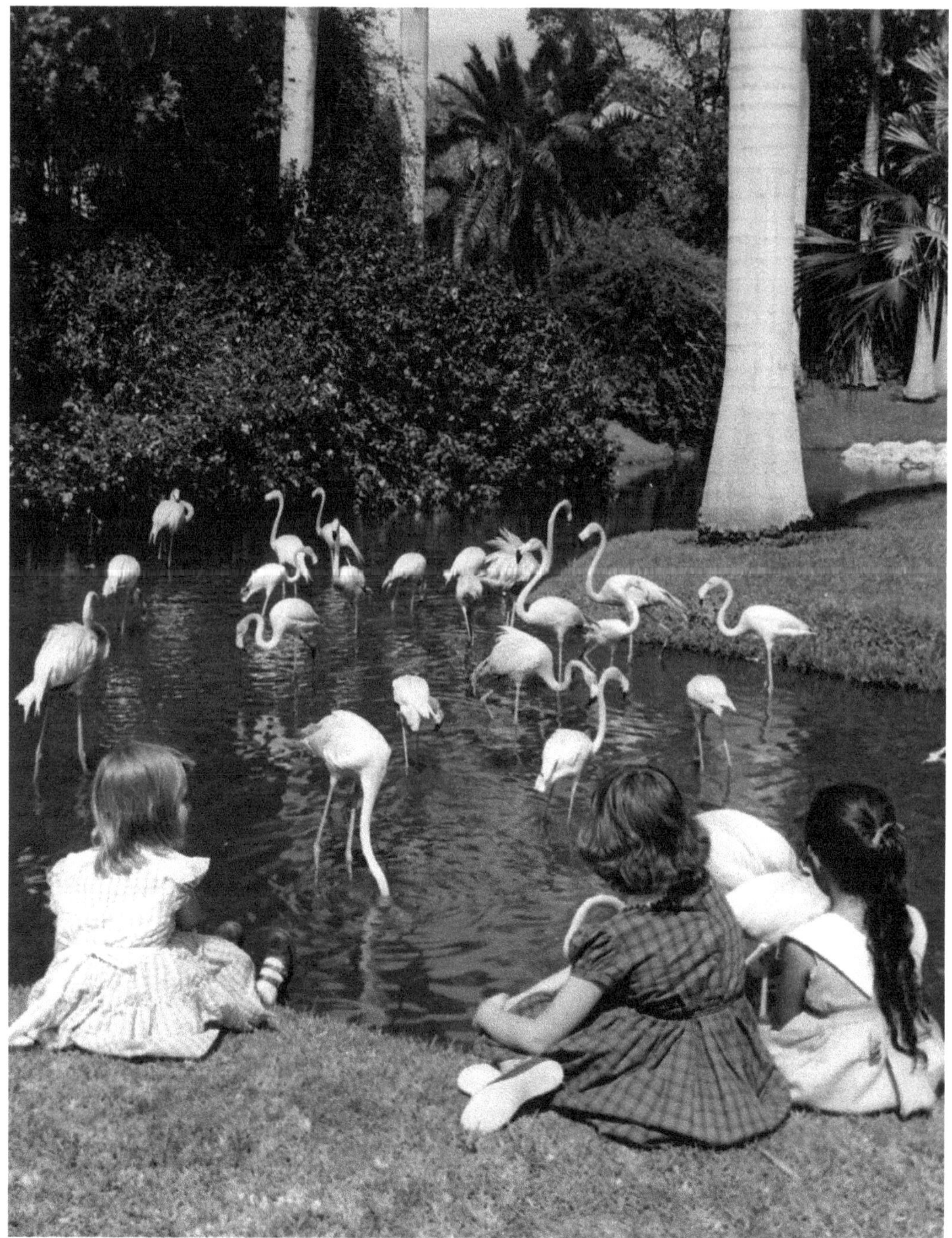

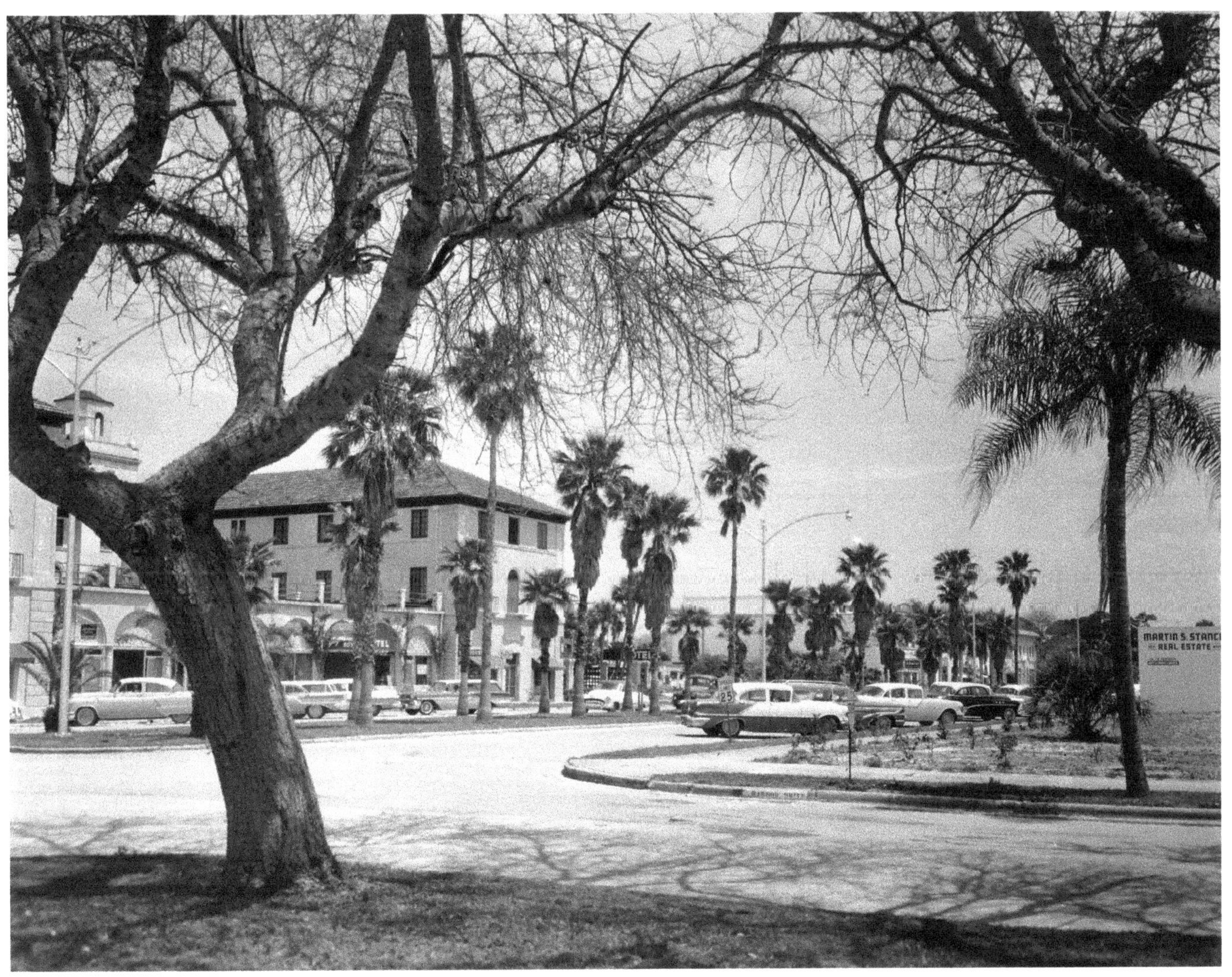

Seen here in 1958, Venice's main thoroughfare was Venice Avenue, a 200-foot-wide boulevard with a wide, tree-lined parkway in the center. Along Venice Avenue were the first residences built for members of the Brotherhood of Locomotive Engineers, begun in July 1926 in the Gulf View subdivision. Those three homes were the most expensive to be built within the city.

John Ringling bequeathed his museum and other properties to the state of Florida. The state operated them for several decades, but after a long period of deterioration their management was transferred to Florida State University. Major renovation has restored the properties' original grandeur.

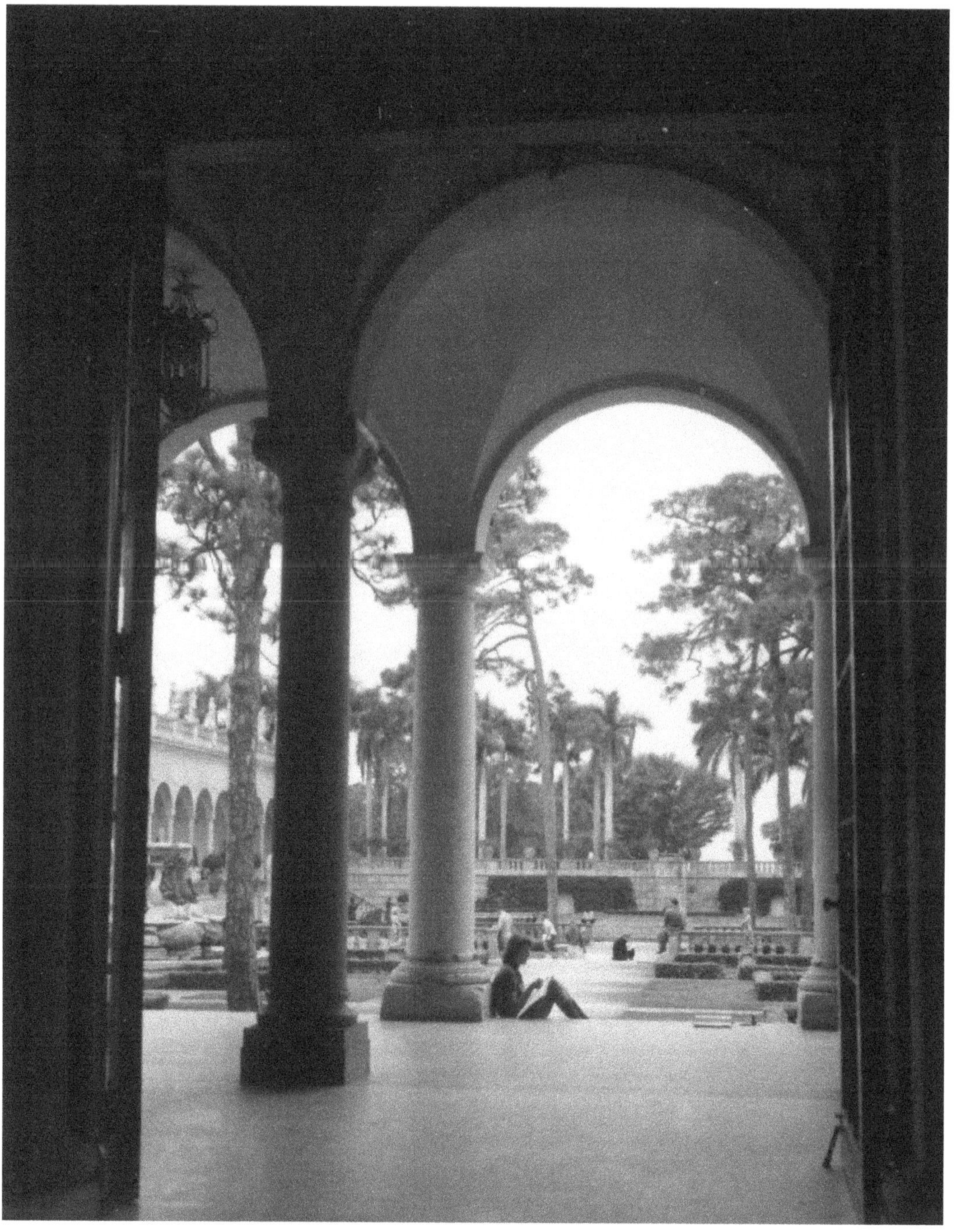

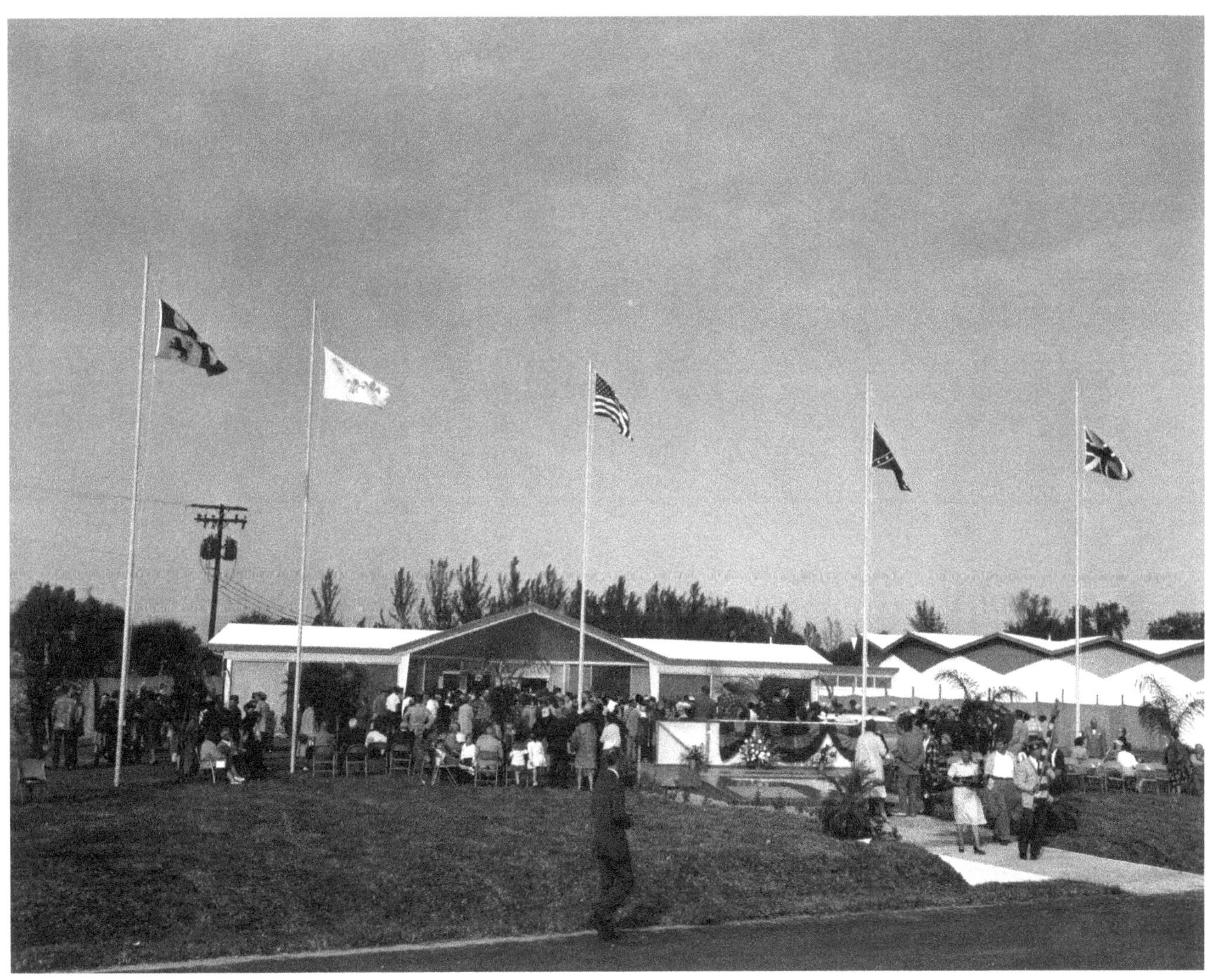

Florida held a Quadricentennial Festival in 1959 to commemorate the expedition of Tristán de Luna y Arellano, who tried to set up a permanent colony along Pensacola Bay. His effort was abandoned after two years. Warm Mineral Springs, shown here, hosted the festival because according to Florida legend it is one of the locations of the Fountain of Youth.

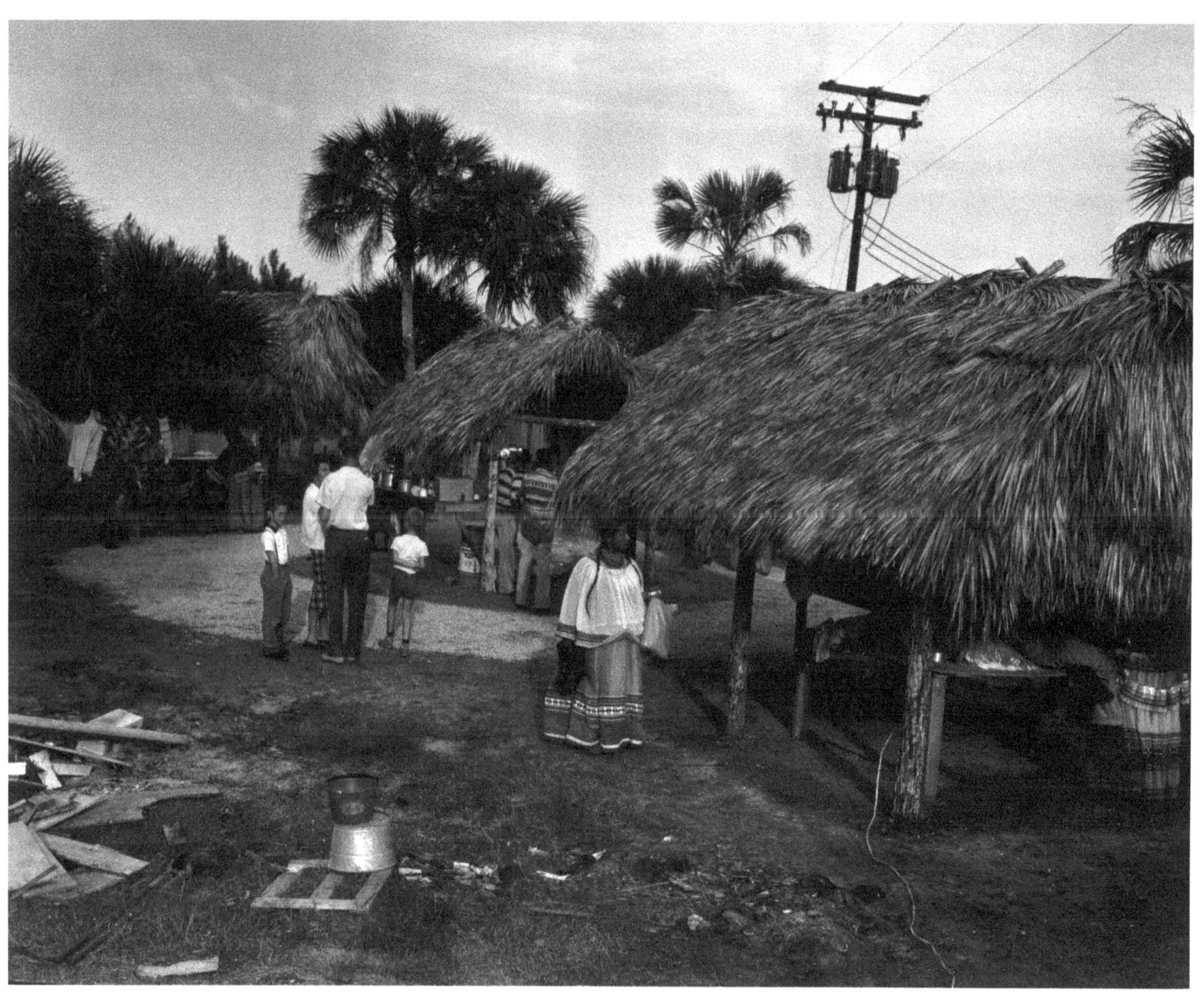

In addition to the Spanish theme of the Quadricentennial celebration at Warm Mineral Springs, exhibits and events recalled other major influences on the local culture. Shown here is an exhibit focusing on the Seminoles, while others chronicled the English and French presence, the local Scottish settlers, and the circus.

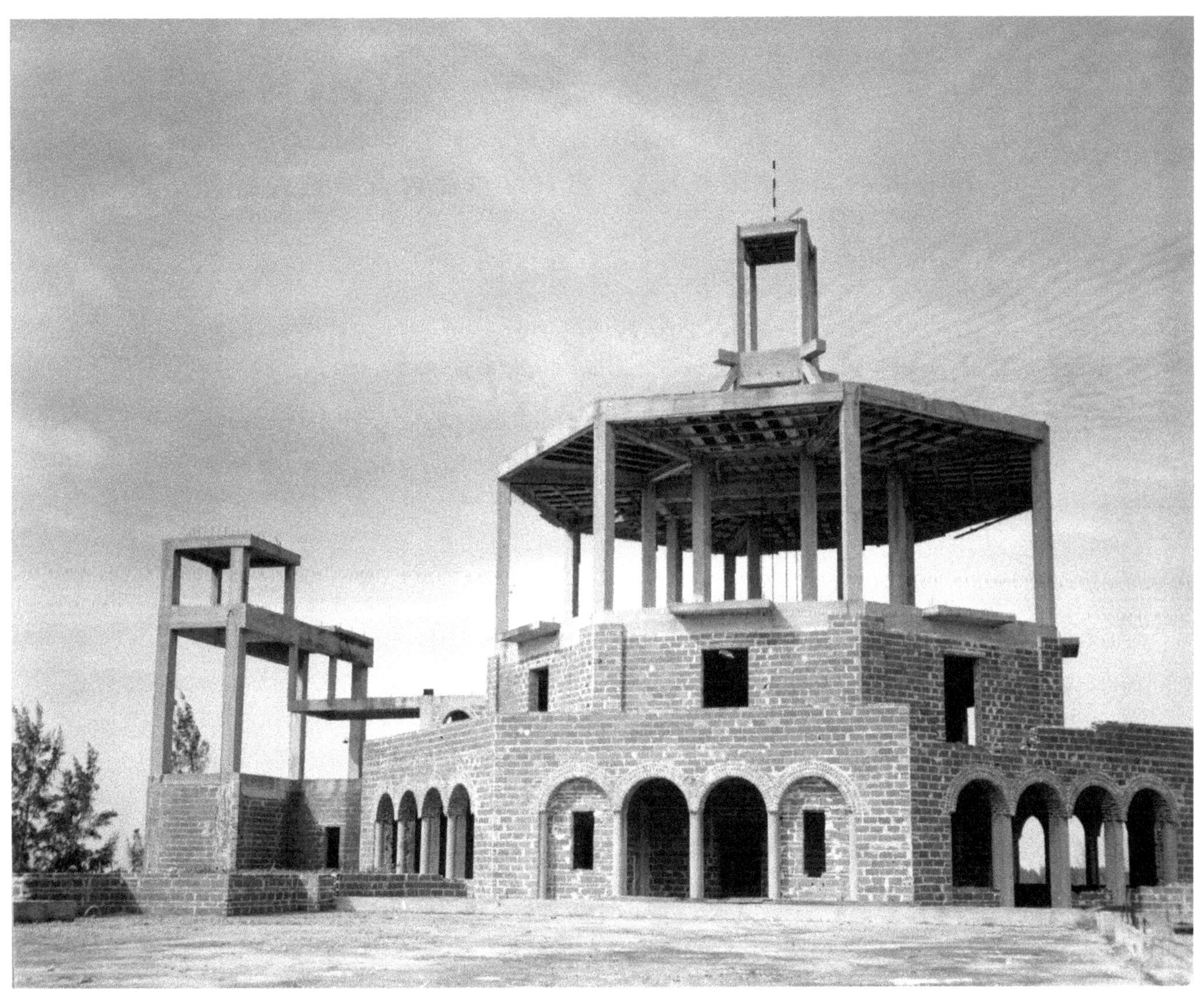

John Ringling began building a luxury hotel in 1926 on Longboat Key. More than $650,000 was spent on the project, which was incomplete when the land boom went bust and the stock market crashed. Shown here is the shell of the "ghost hotel" 33 years after it was begun and just before it was razed by the Arvida Corporation.

Beaches and Skyscrapers

(1960–1970s)

The beaches of Sarasota County have an international reputation, and tourists come from everywhere to enjoy the pure white sand and calm waters of the Gulf of Mexico. The north and south ends of Lido Key are particularly well known. One can choose from crowded areas patrolled by lifeguards or areas intentionally kept near-private by limiting parking.

Having defeated all other entries in a 1987 competition called the Great International White Sand Challenge, Siesta Beach offers hardpacked sand for walkers and runners, and soft areas to spread towels and relax in the bright Florida sun. At the south end of Siesta Key, large groups and families can picnic, hike, and generally enjoy the outdoors. Casey Key features private beaches and areas that are reached most easily by private boat.

The city of Sarasota's attractions include the Ringling School of Art and Design, the Caples campus of New College, the Marie Selby Botanical Gardens, the Selby Library, and the John and Mable Ringling Museum of Art. Osprey attracts visitors with its Historic Spanish Point.

The first condominium in Venice opened in 1959. Located on Tarpon Center Drive and providing a great view of Venice Beach, it signaled a trend away from the single-family homes and small apartment buildings of the past, and toward the avenues of modern high-rise lodgings along the gulf shore. The small beachside homes on the barrier islands began to be overshadowed by high-rise towers, such as the 28-story Plymouth Harbor development on St. Armands Key, which opened in 1966.

The appearance of condominiums spread from Sarasota and Venice to other communities, including Osprey and Nokomis, leaving little resemblance to the original fishing and agricultural settlements. The beachside cities now look like many other developed areas along the Florida shores.

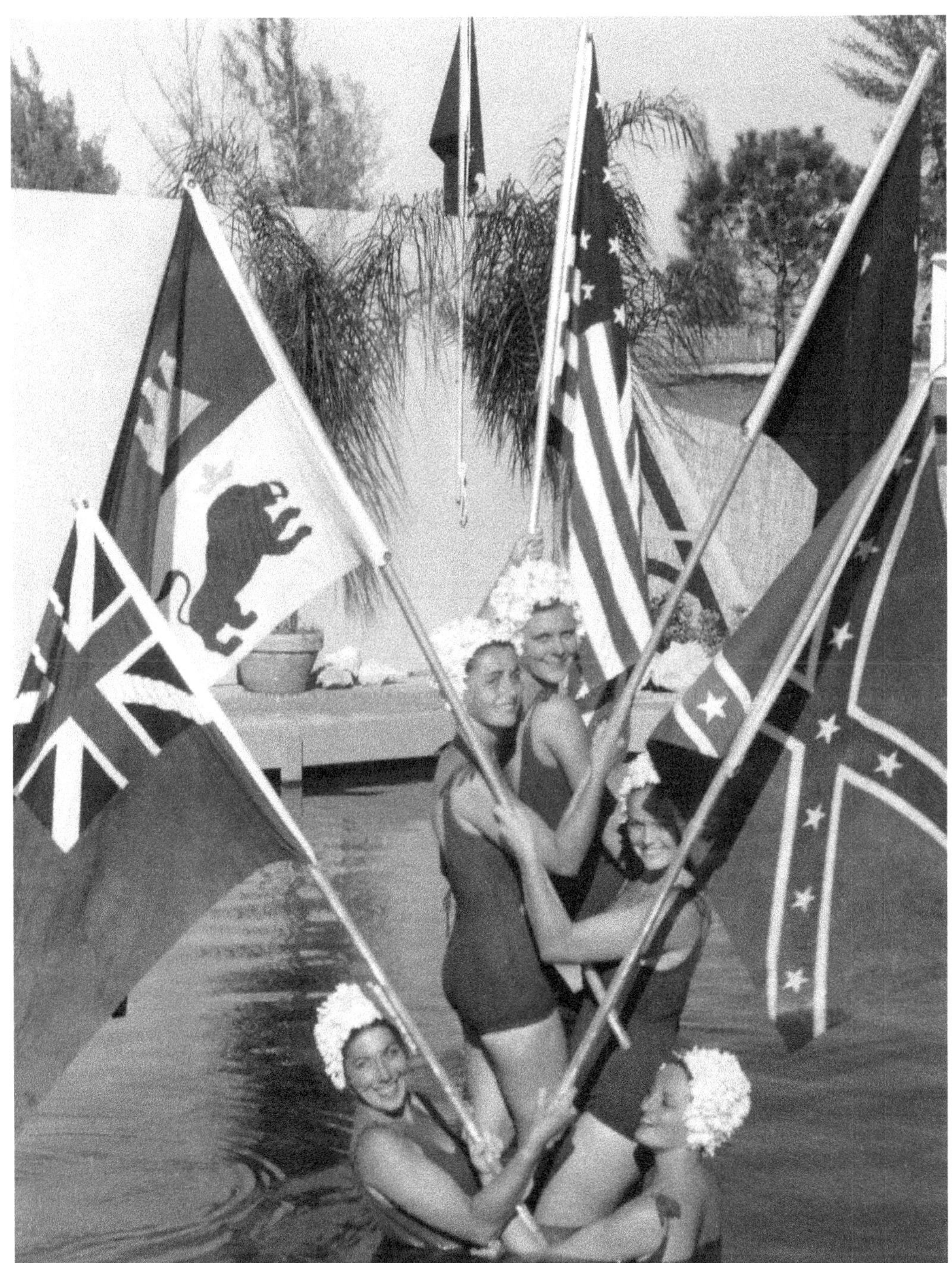

The Quadricentennial Festival ran until April of 1960 at Warm Mineral Springs and celebrated four centuries of Florida under the flags of Spain, France, England, the Confederate States of America, and the United States. The biggest exhibit was the Cyclorama, a mural of the travels of Ponce de León complete with theatrical lighting and sound.

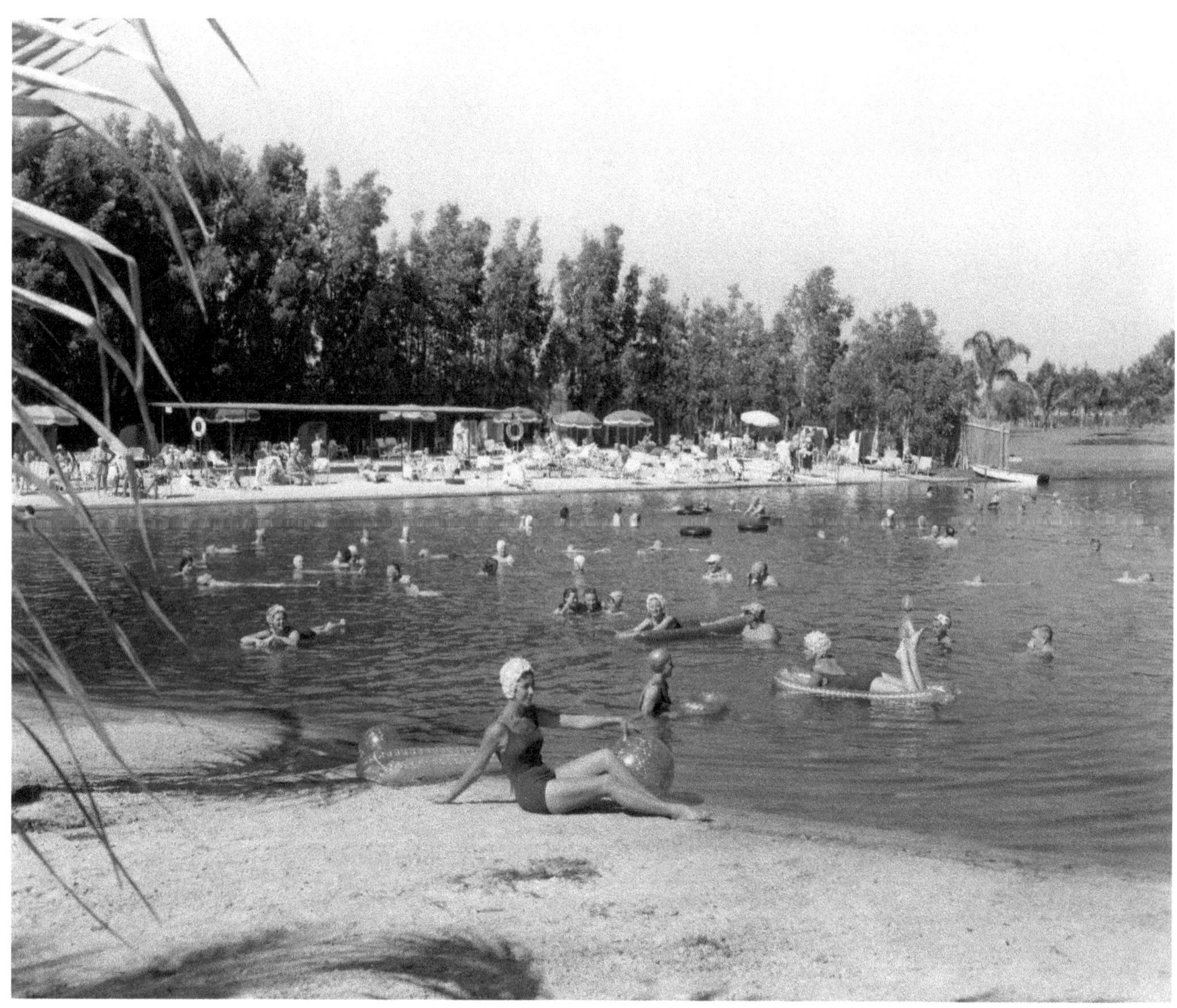

Near the Myakka River is Warm Mineral Springs, a naturally free-flowing mineral spring that fills a sinkhole with 87-degree mineral water. Visitors such as these in 1960 come to reap the benefits of the minerals. Below the water's surface are stalactites and stalagmites, which indicate the presence of a formerly dry cave.

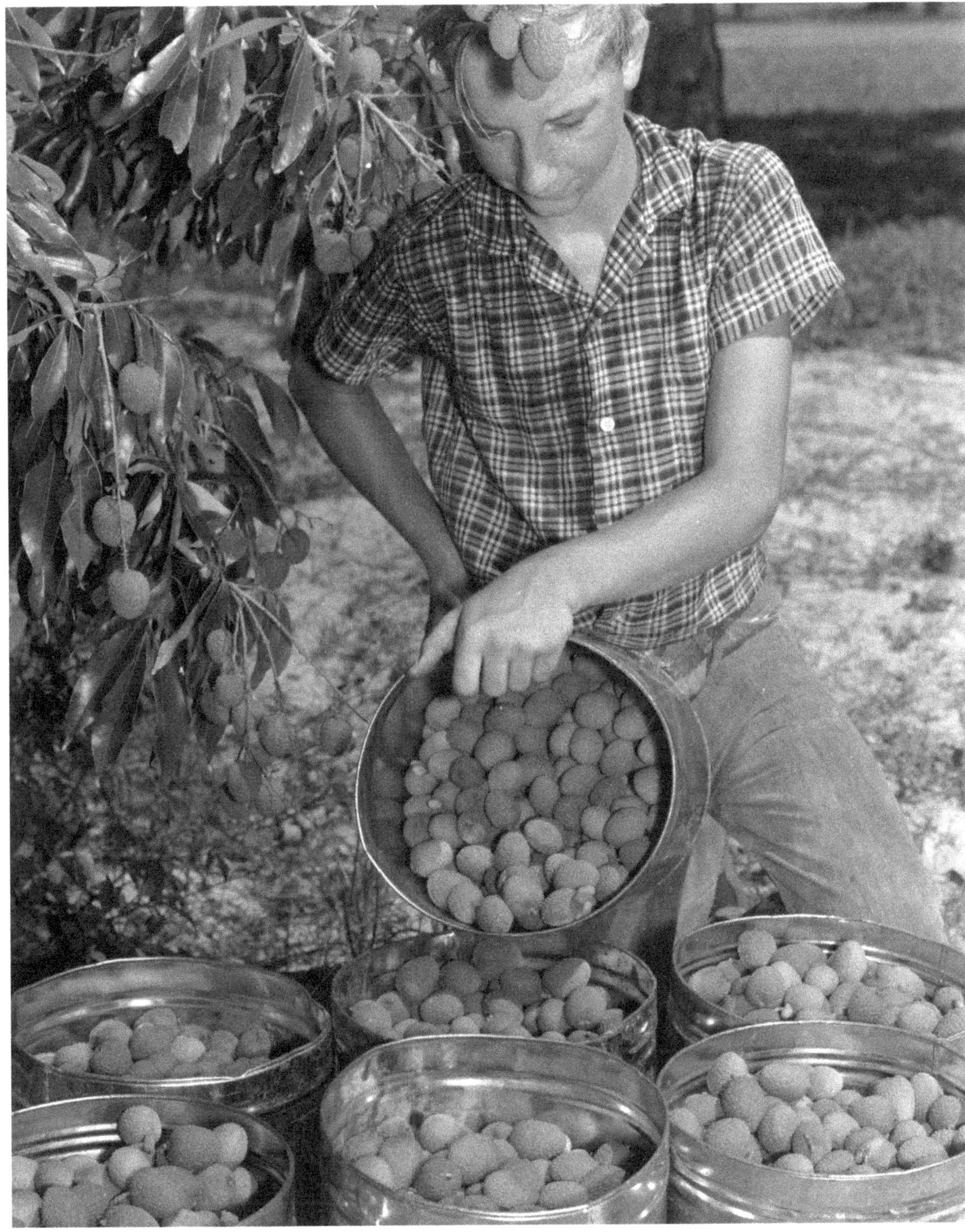

A boy pours a load of picked lychees at Palmer Nurseries in Osprey, formerly part of the estate of Chicago socialite Bertha Honoré Palmer. The lychee experiment did not produce a major crop, for two reasons: people weren't excited about lychees, and therefore bought few, and the lychees turned out to be very sensitive to even a slight amount of cold weather.

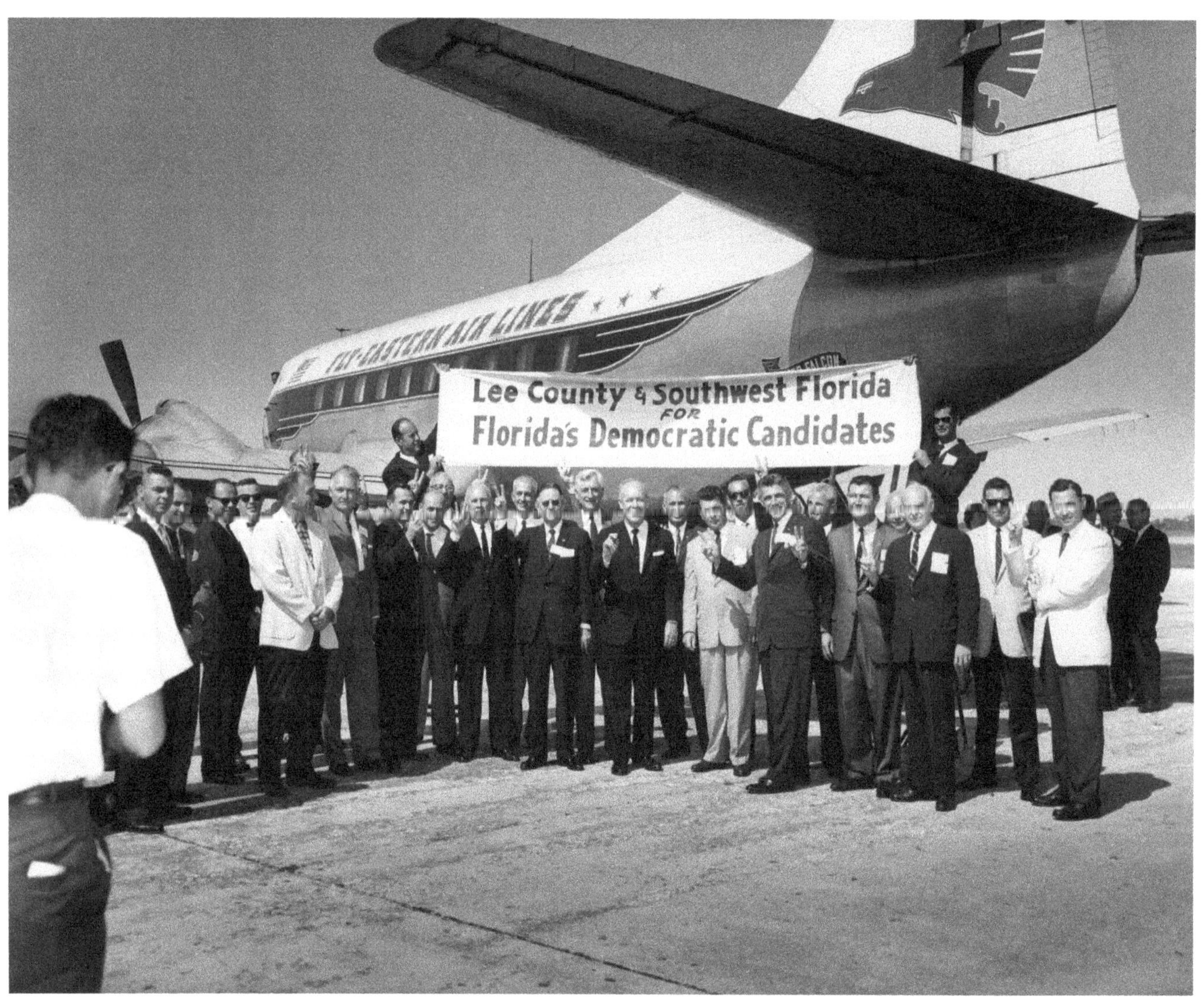

In 1960, a group of Democratic candidates stopped at the Sarasota airport to seek support in the upcoming election. Among those photographed are, left to right, Richard W. Ervin, Jr., Doyle E. Conner, Ray E. Green, Thomas D. Bailey, James A. Haley, Farris Bryant, Edwin L. Mason, and J. Edwin Larson. All were elected or reelected to various positions.

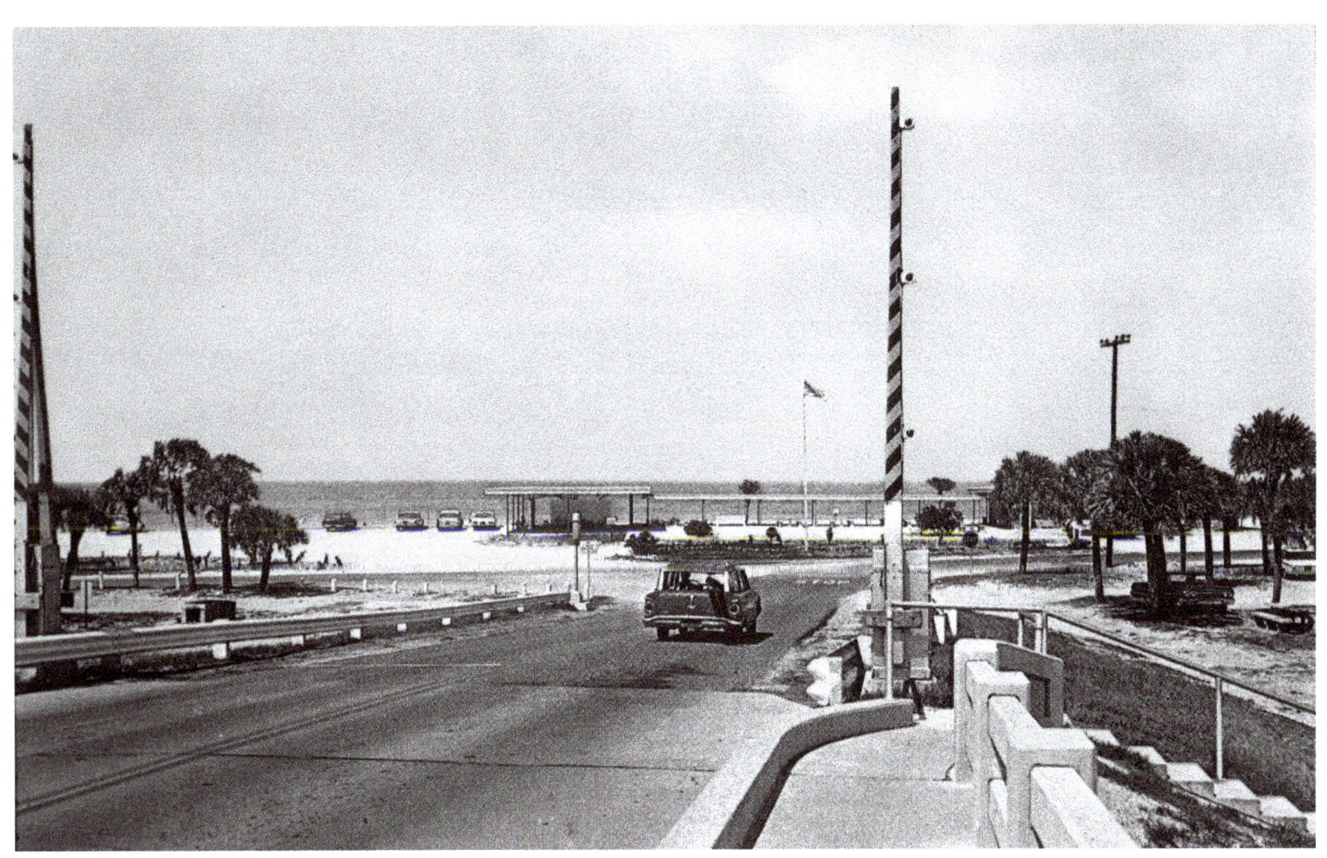

Located between Siesta Key and Venice, Casey Key is one of the few islands reachable by causeway that has not been developed with chain hotels. Rather, small inns are found near the marina rental areas and public beach access. Along the island's tree-canopied roads are expensive homes with great views of the Gulf of Mexico or Little Sarasota Bay.

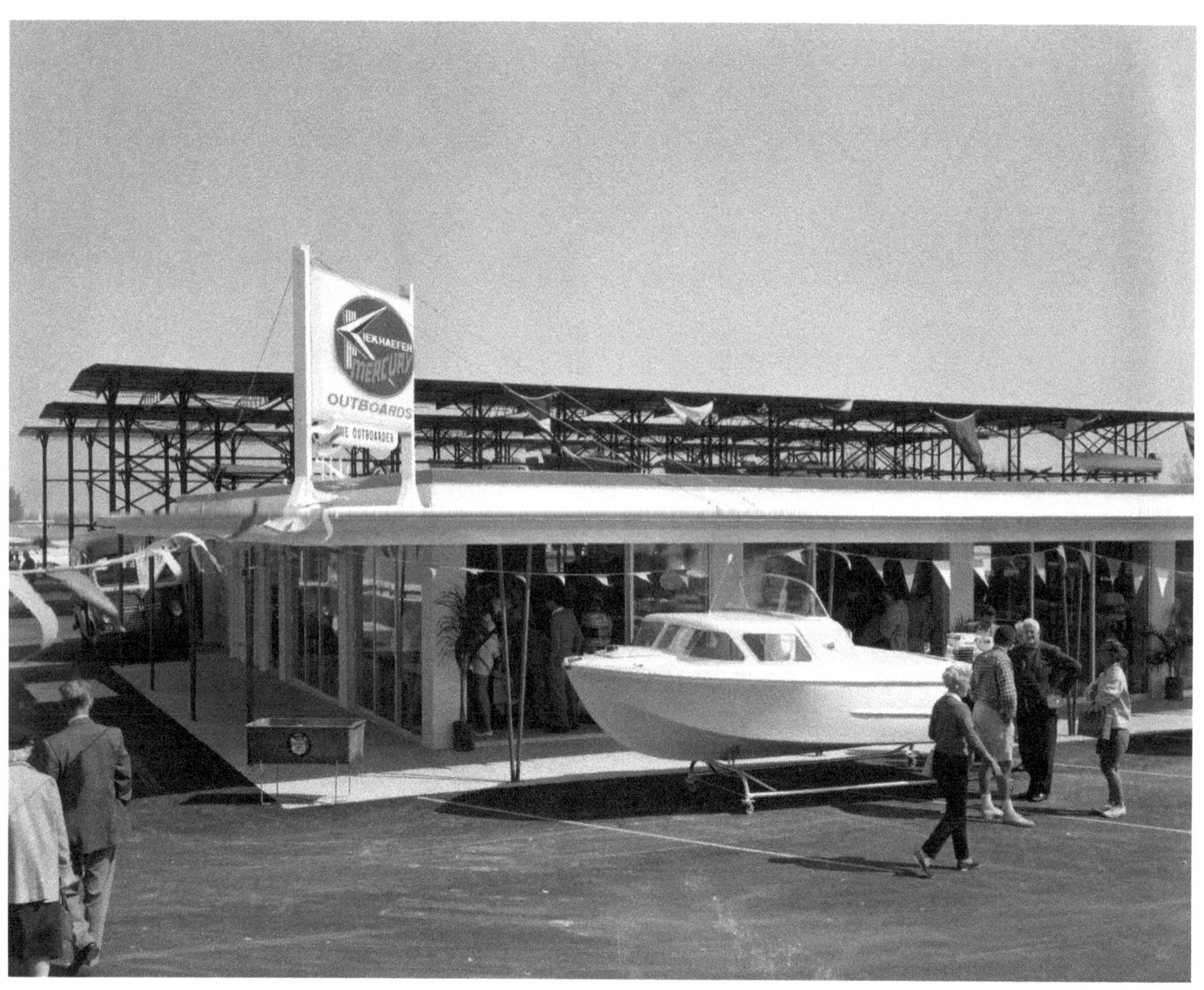

Seen here is the Outboarder of Sarasota, one of several marinas that have served the area over the years to accommodate the needs of fishermen, divers, and sightseers. Incorporated in 1966, it was renamed Gulfwind USA in 1997. The corporation went inactive in 2000.

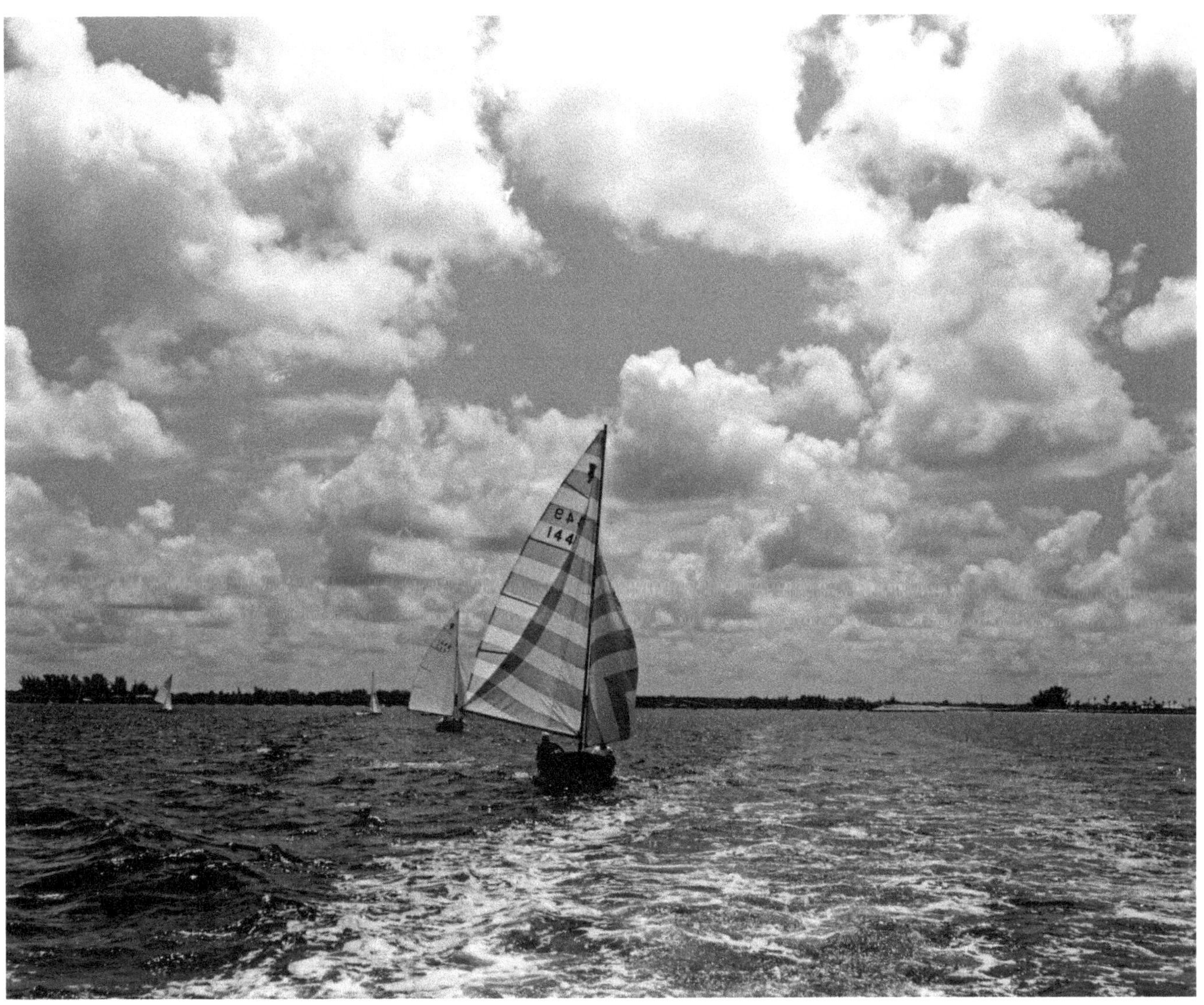

These sailboats are racing on Labor Day 1961. Sailors often join one of the local clubs. Sarasota has the Sarasota Yacht Club, the Sarasota Sailing Squadron, and the Sarasota Power Squadron. Bird Key has its own yacht club. One of the activities of the Venice Sailing Squadron and the Venice Yacht Club is the Shark's Tooth Regatta.

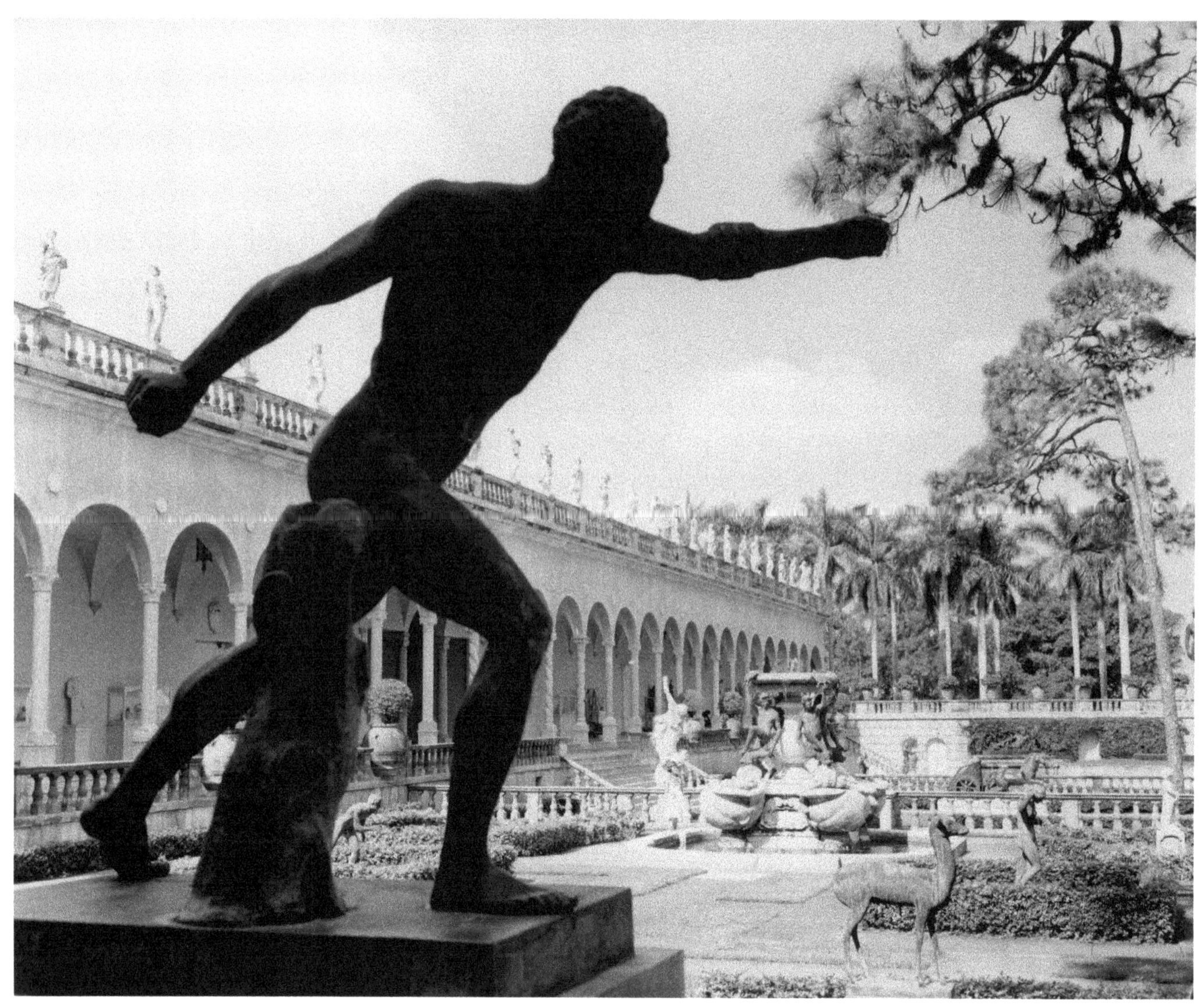

During the 1920s, John Ringling often attended art auctions in London and New York, seeking works for his collection. His favorite painters were Titian, Peter Paul Rubens, Frans Hals, Diego Velázquez, and Paolo Veronese. He also purchased a collection from the Metropolitan Museum of Art that included works from Rome, Cyprus, and Greece.

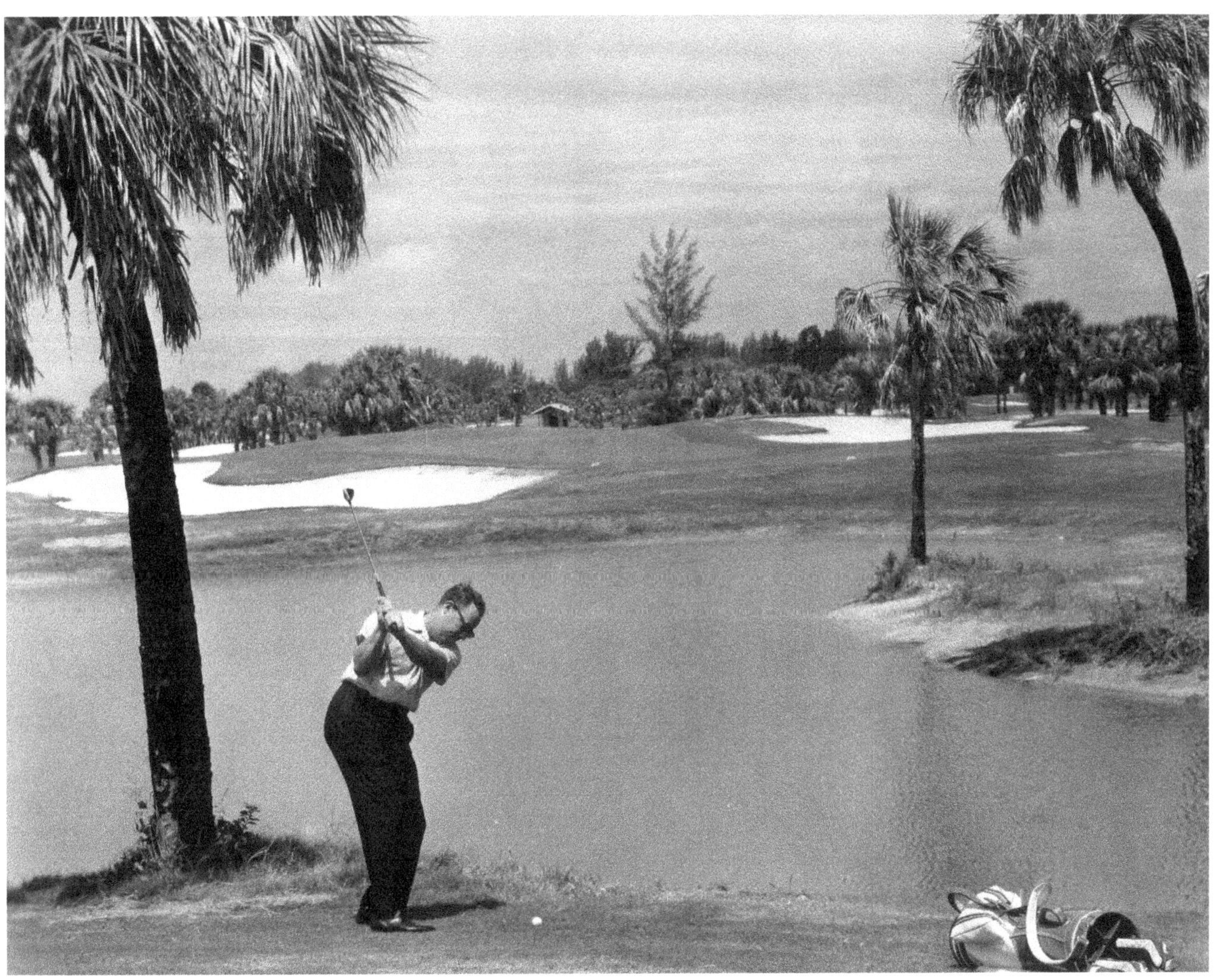

Ever since J. Hamilton Gillespie built his golf course, the game has been an important part of life in Sarasota. In 1927, Bobby Jones cut the ribbon at the opening of a new municipal course designed by Donald Ross, then played the course and had the best score of the day. Later, the course was named in Jones's honor. The golfer seen here in 1961 is playing a course on Longboat Key.

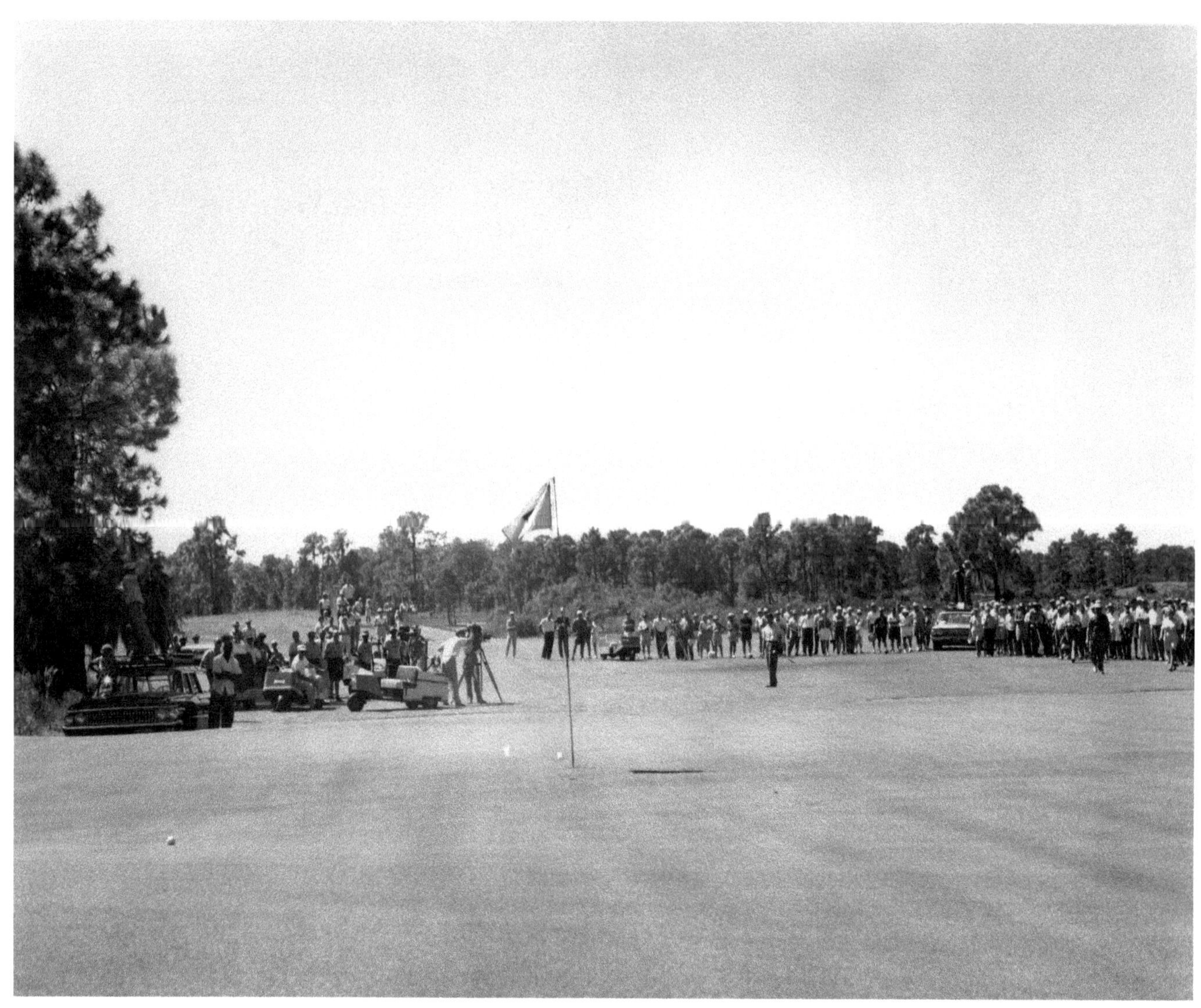

Filming here in Sarasota, the television show *All-Star Golf* featured Sam Snead, Gene Littler, Arnold Palmer, and others competing on a variety of golf courses for up to $52,000 in prize money. Airing from 1957 to 1963, the show was variously hosted by Jim Britt, Dick Danehe, and Jimmy Demaret on ABC until 1961, then moved to NBC.

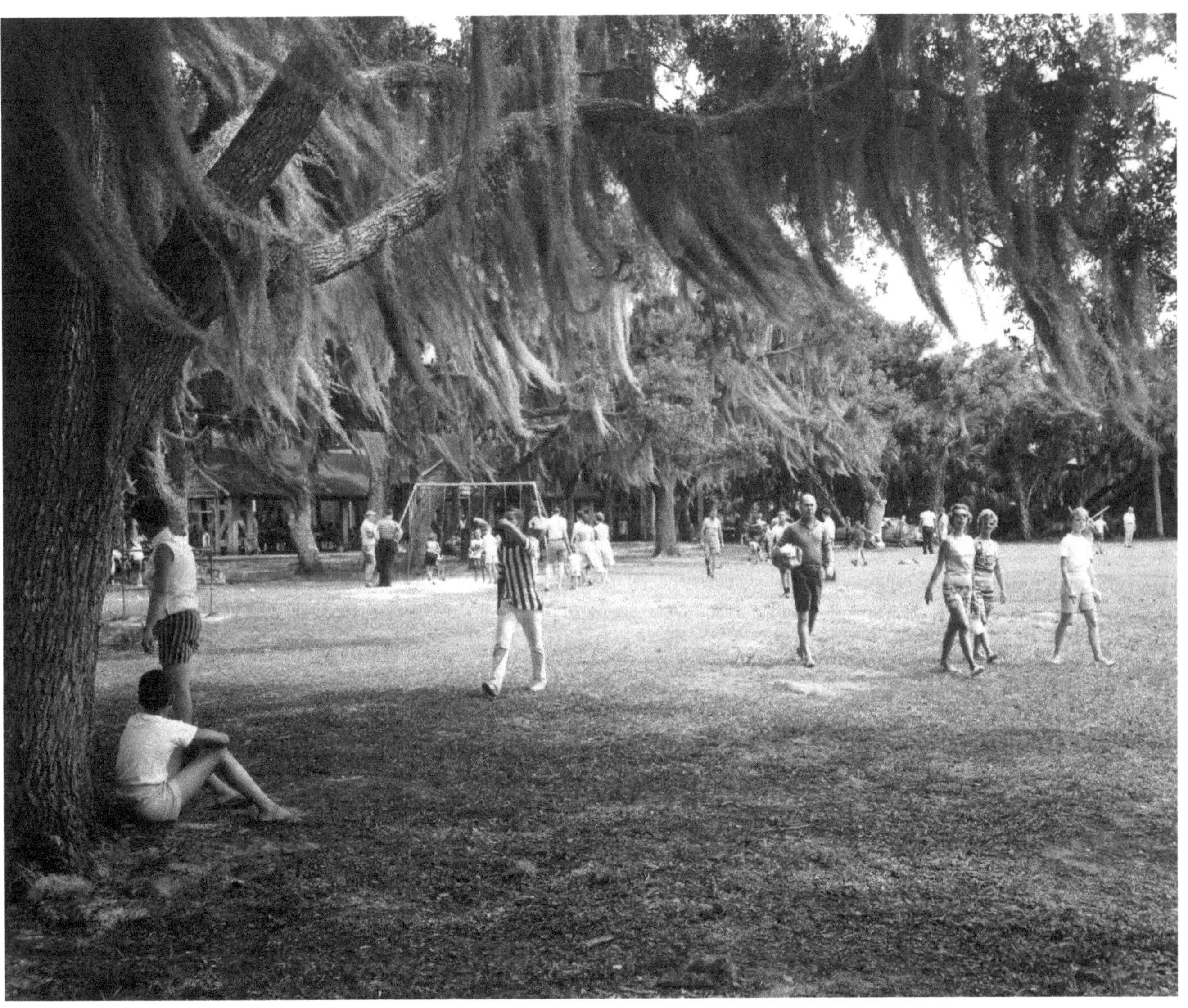

Myakka River State Park, seen here in 1962, is one of the oldest and largest Florida state parks. Offering memorable opportunities for visitors to get close to nature on the trails, rivers, and lakes, the park also includes playgrounds, a concession stand, a visitor center, and modernized cabins for those who prefer not to sleep in tents.

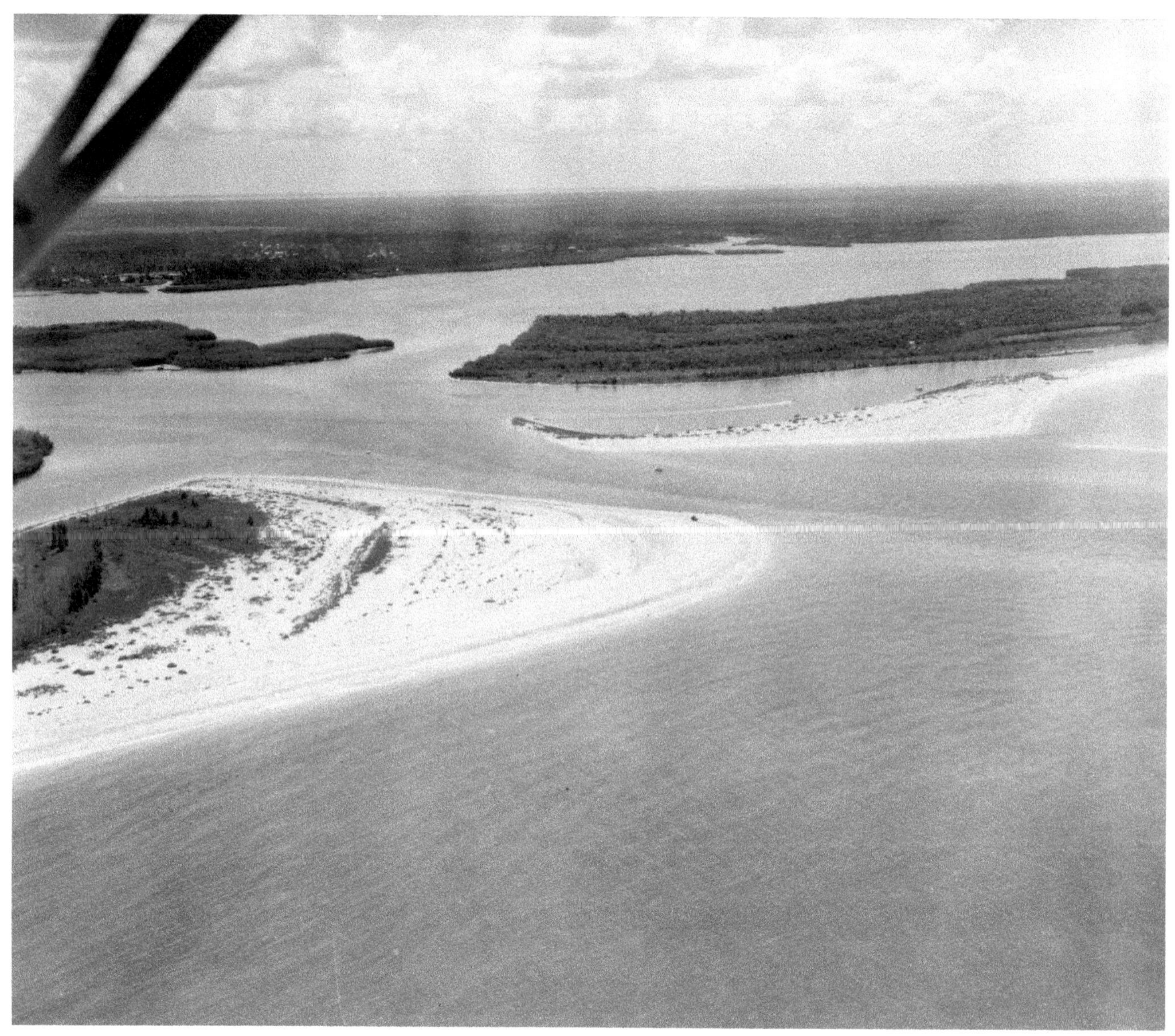

Viewed from overhead in 1964, Stump Pass Beach on Manasota Key remains one of the least-crowded beaches in the Sarasota area. It's also one of the better ones for seeking seashells and shark's teeth. Manasota Key has a look from an older time, with souvenir shops and restaurants but not much traffic.

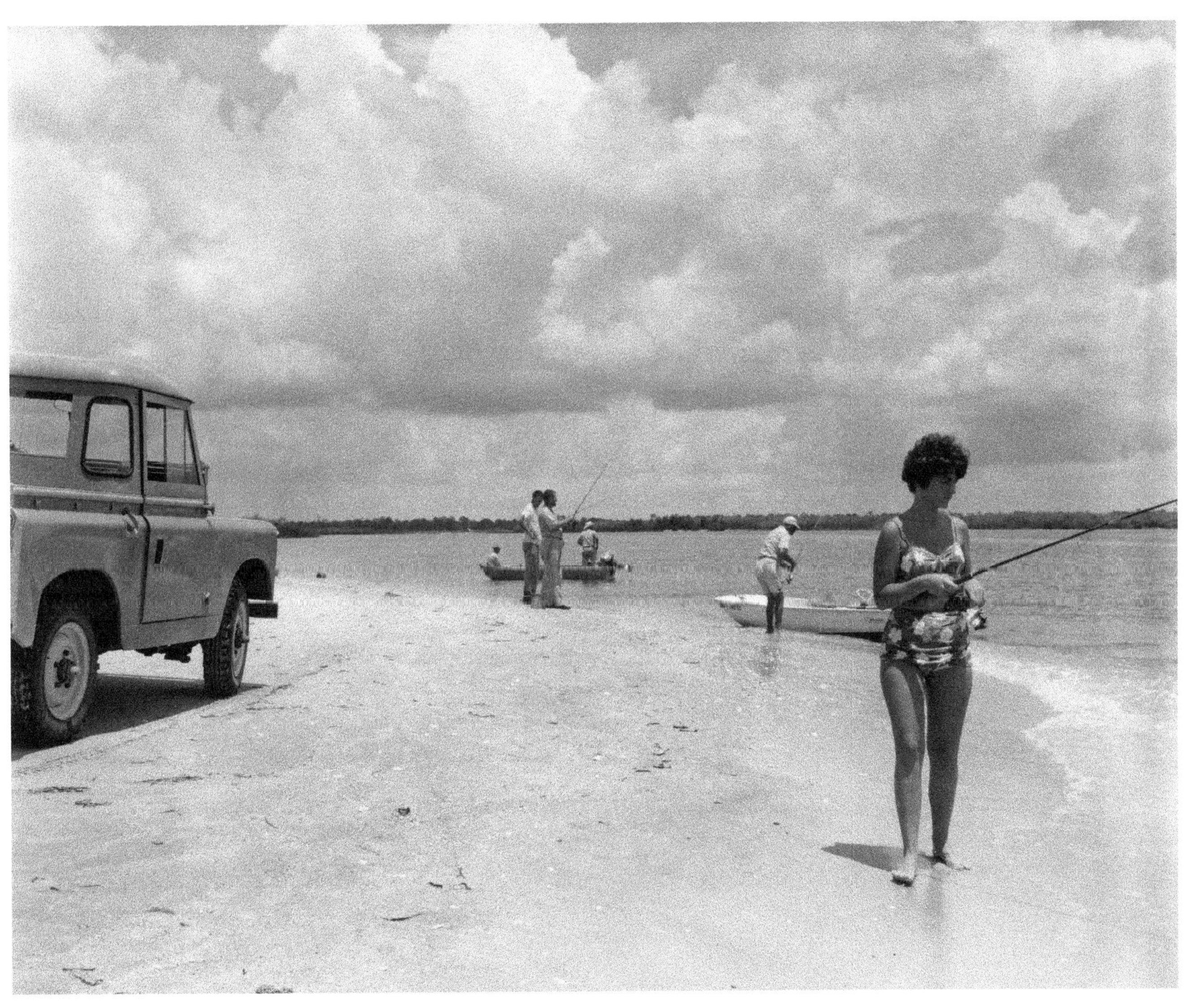

At the southern end of Manasota Key is Stump Pass Beach State Park, a popular place for hiking and fishing in the surf, as shown here in 1964. Wildlife available just for viewing includes manatees, terns, egrets, gopher tortoises, and frigate birds.

The Marblehead Putter Company had a brief existence in Sarasota, from 1962 until 1966. Here, one of its employees, Jim Taylor, works on a golf club. Marblehead clubs were used not only on the local courses, but also throughout the country.

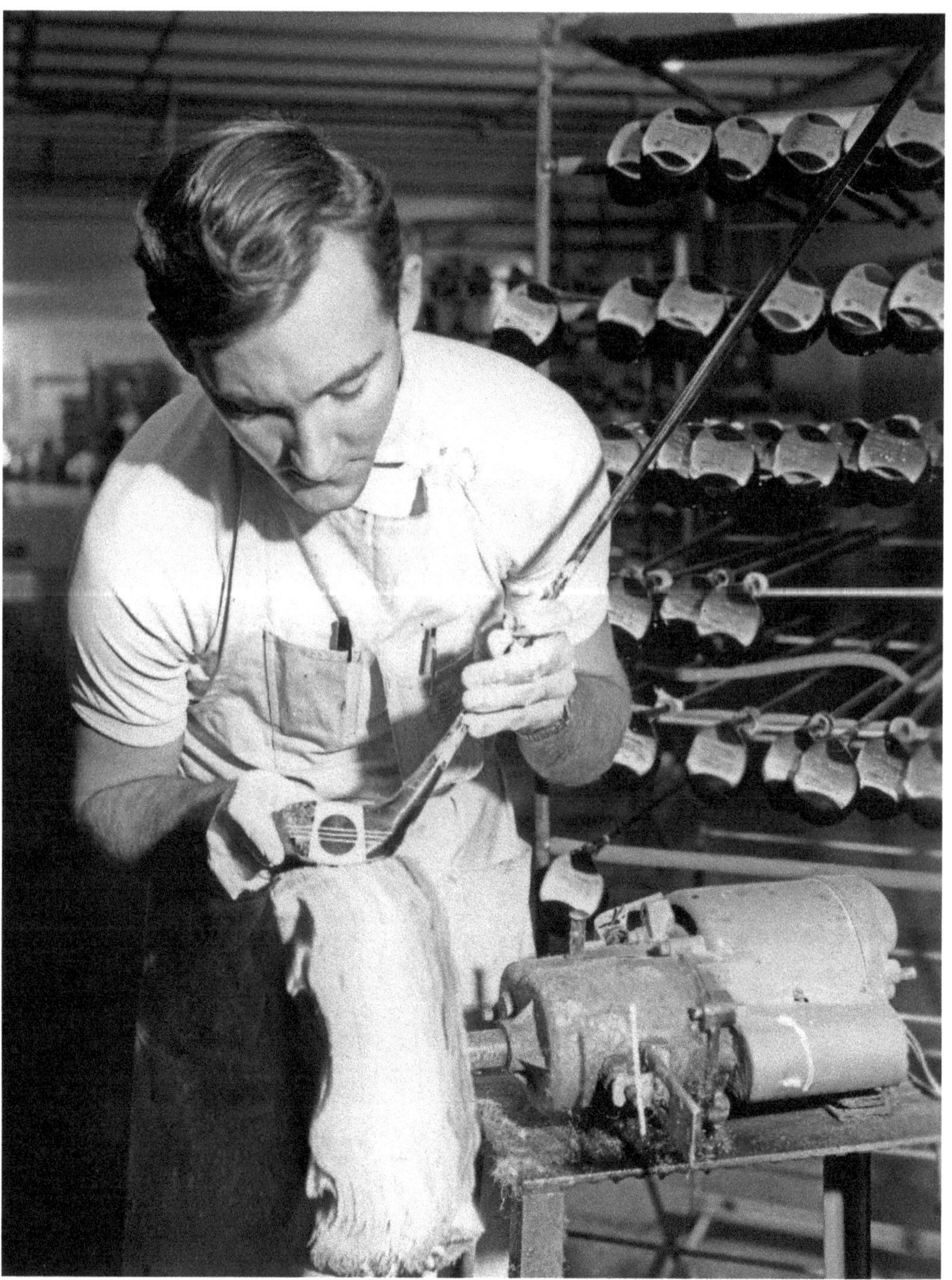

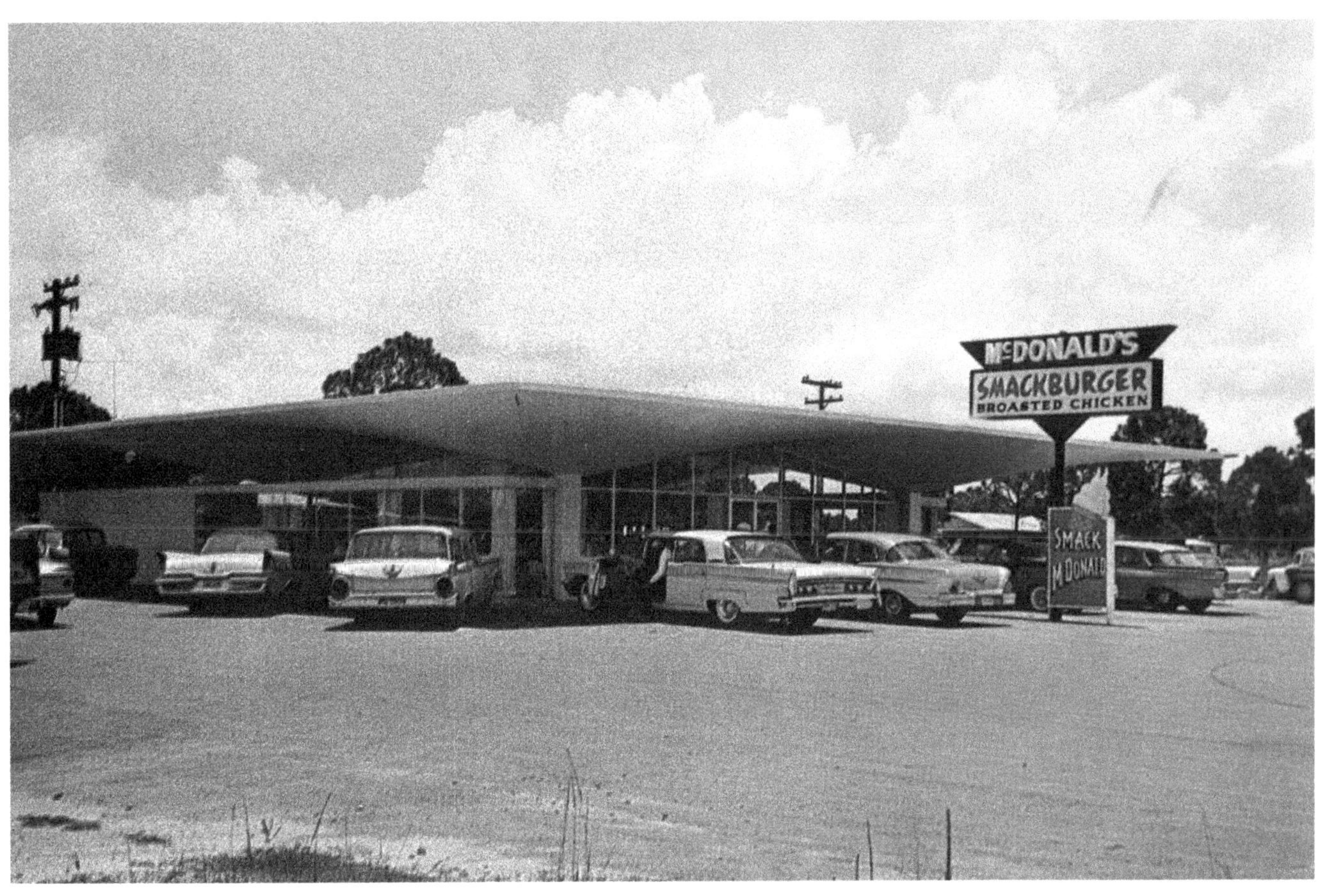

In 1932, Mack McDonald acquired Sarasota's Duckie Wuckie hamburger stand and renamed it the Smack Restaurant. Smackburgers were the signature menu items. The McDonalds sold the business in 1956, moved to Venice, and there in 1961 opened this Smack Restaurant, which lasted until 1969.

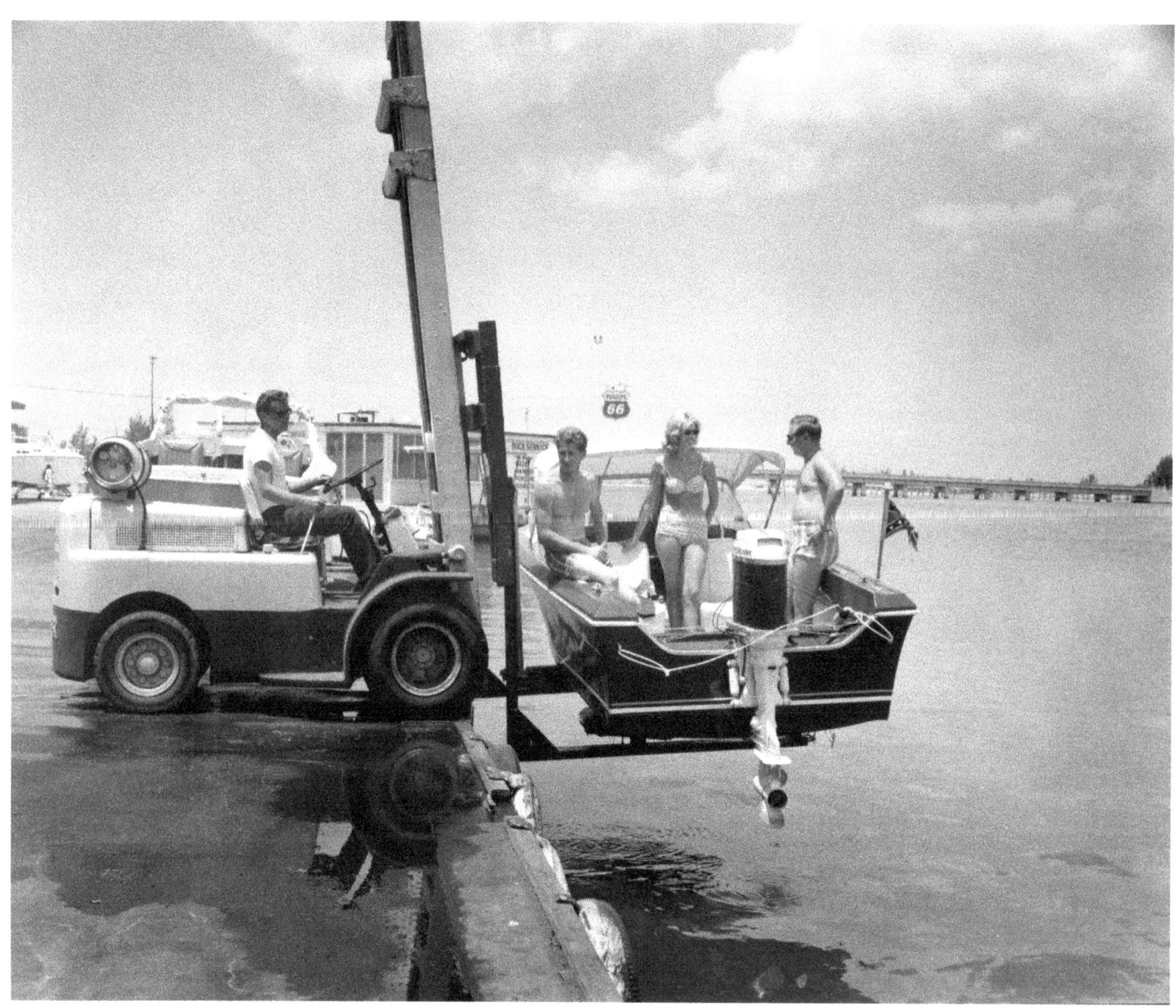

Throughout Sarasota County, numerous boat ramps allow boat owners to put in and spend a day cruising among the mangroves, keys, and other maritime attractions. However, in 1965, this marina on Longboat Key had another way of launching a small boat: with a forklift to lower the boat with its passengers to the surface of the water.

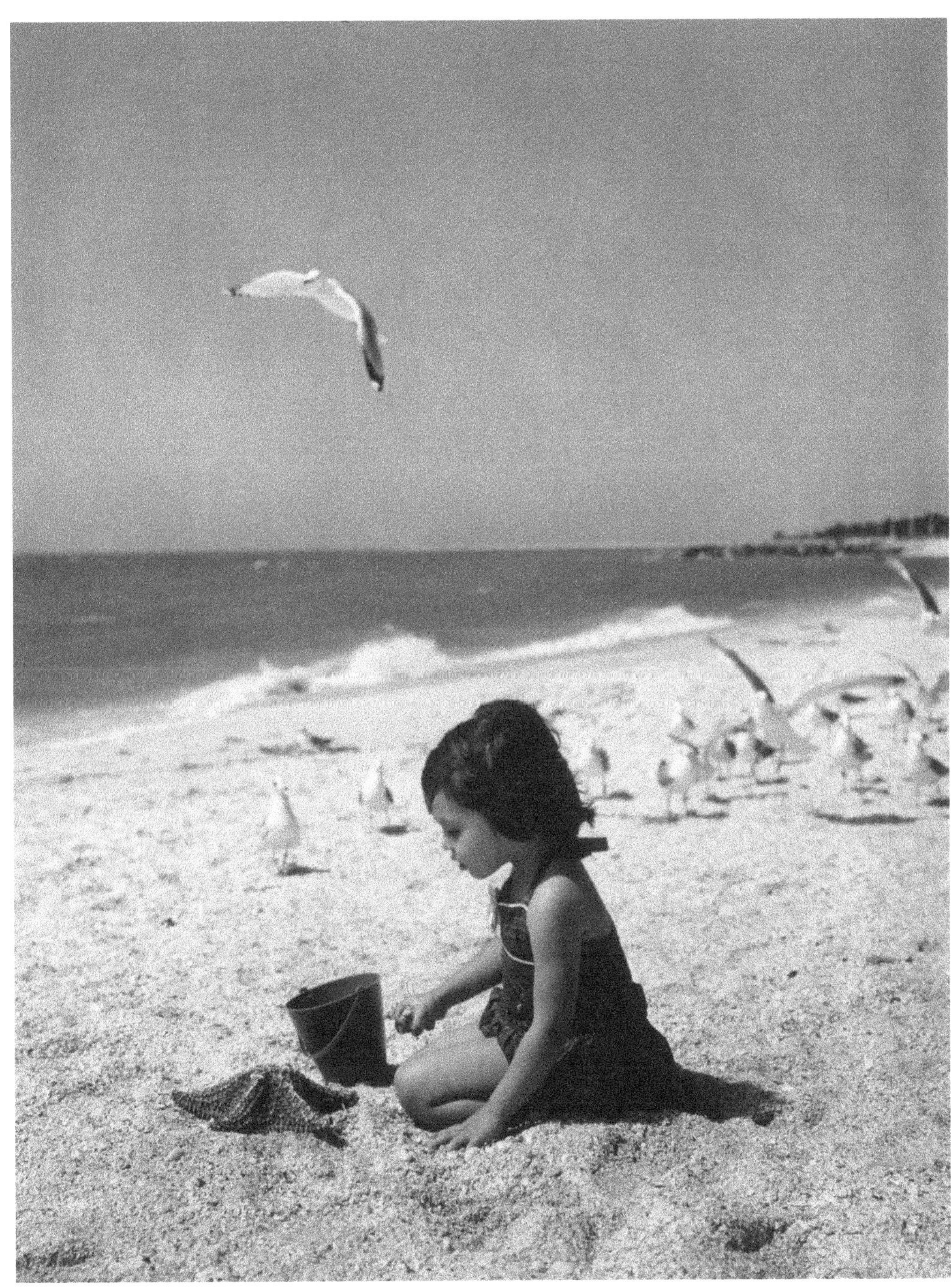

Sarasota's beaches have always been popular for all types of activities, even for just gazing at a starfish, as young Donna Walwork is doing in this 1965 photo. The photo may have been taken at Siesta Beach, purchased by the city in 1954 for use as a public beach. The name of Siesta was taken from a 1907 residential development on the island.

A themed tourist attraction known as Floridaland opened in Osprey in December 1964. Owner Philip Smashey promoted the theme of "Everything Under the Sun." Especially popular were a jumping dolphin show and this western town. In keeping with its attempt to attract tourists of varied interests, Floridaland also featured a petting zoo and colorful birds.

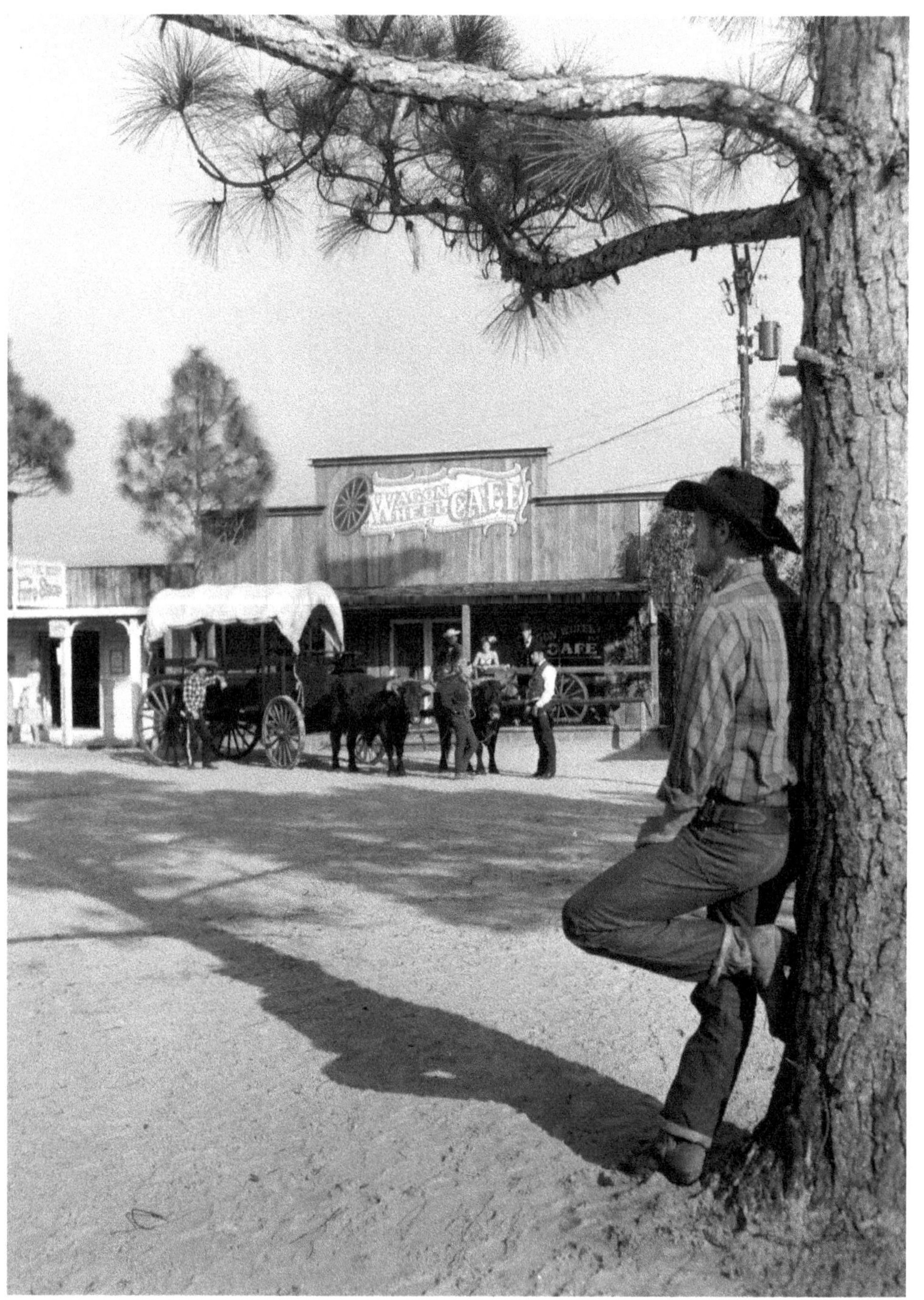

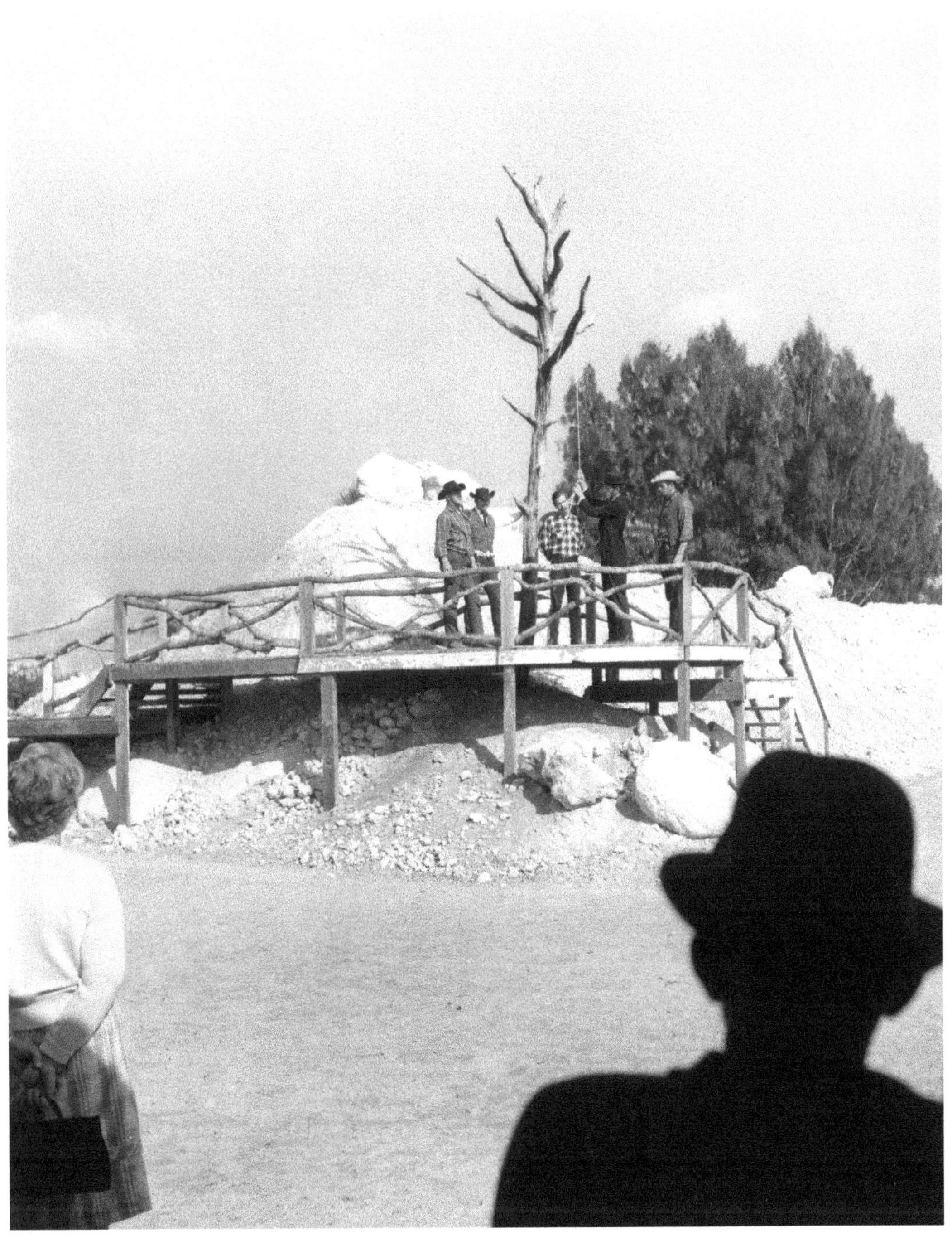

One of Floridaland's popular theatrical shows was held at Hangman's Hill, where the "bad guy" was mock-executed, often after a staged shootout on the streets of the western town. Another western feature was the saloon show. Floridaland bit the dust in the early 1970s, when small attractions were being eclipsed by huge theme parks such as Walt Disney World.

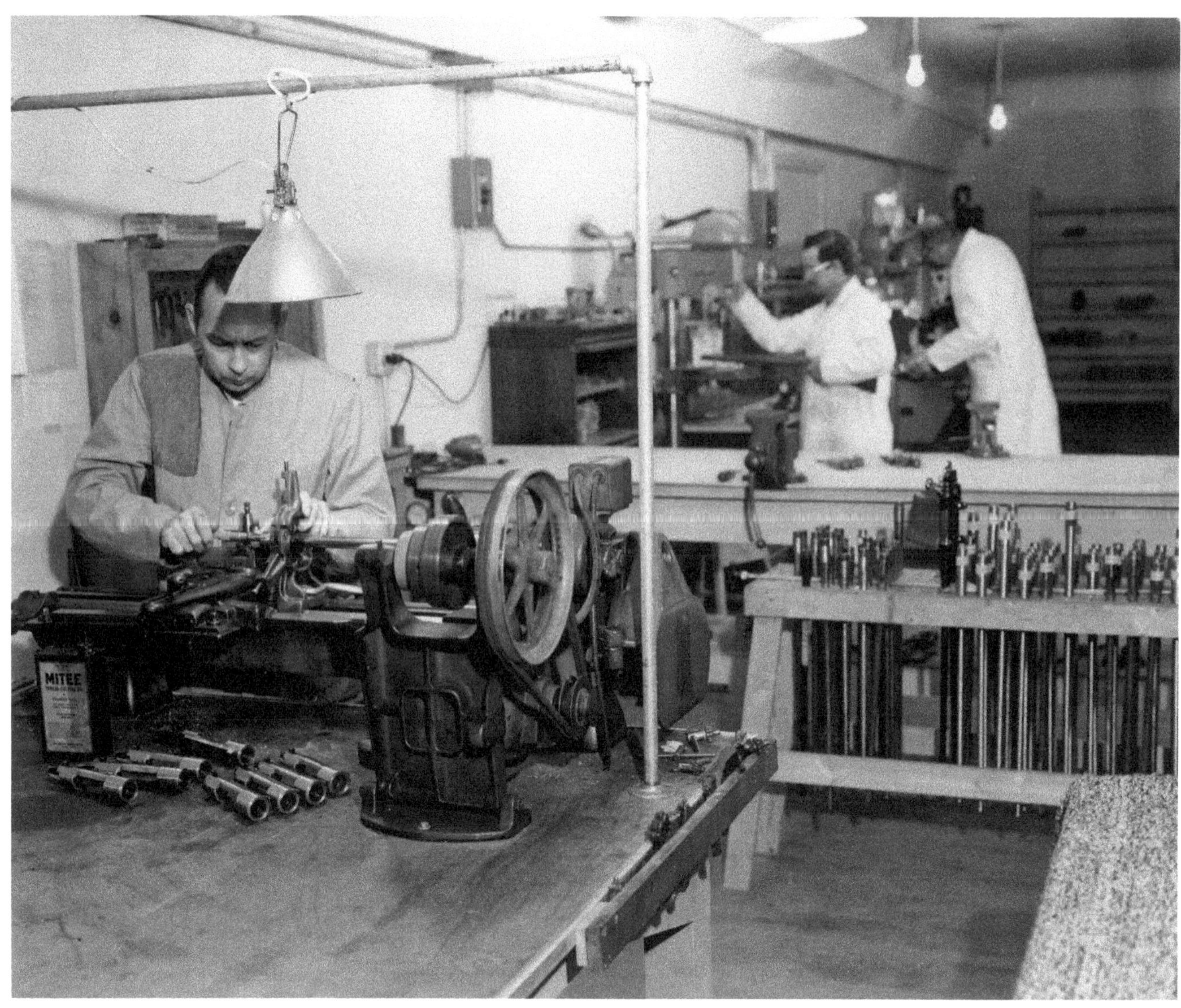

An Osprey gunsmithing business was incorporated in 1962 as the Safari Custom Rifle Corporation, then two years later was renamed the Winslow Arms Company. It was led by John C. Winslow of Osprey and remained in business there until the late 1970s.

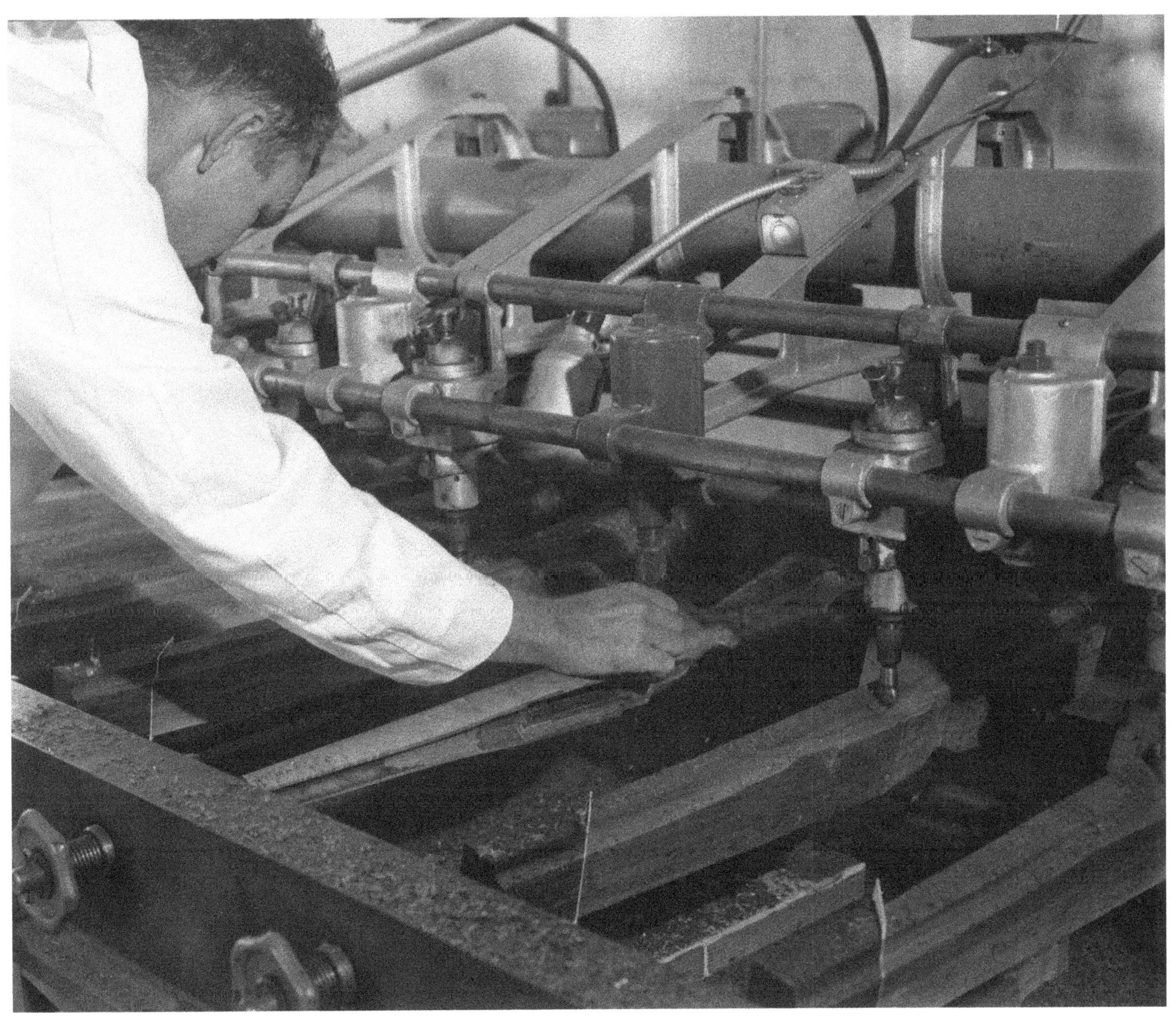

In the 1960s and 1970s, the Winslow Arms Company located in Osprey produced "long guns" (rifles and shotguns). One of the models prized today is the Winslow Model 70, similar to the Winchester Model 70 rifle.

One of several circus-related sites in Sarasota was the Circus Hall of Fame, which opened in 1956 with an opening crowd of more than 5,000. In addition to exhibits on the history of the American circus, the attraction featured live acts such as the trapeze artist shown here in 1966. At that time, the attraction was drawing about 80,000 visitors annually.

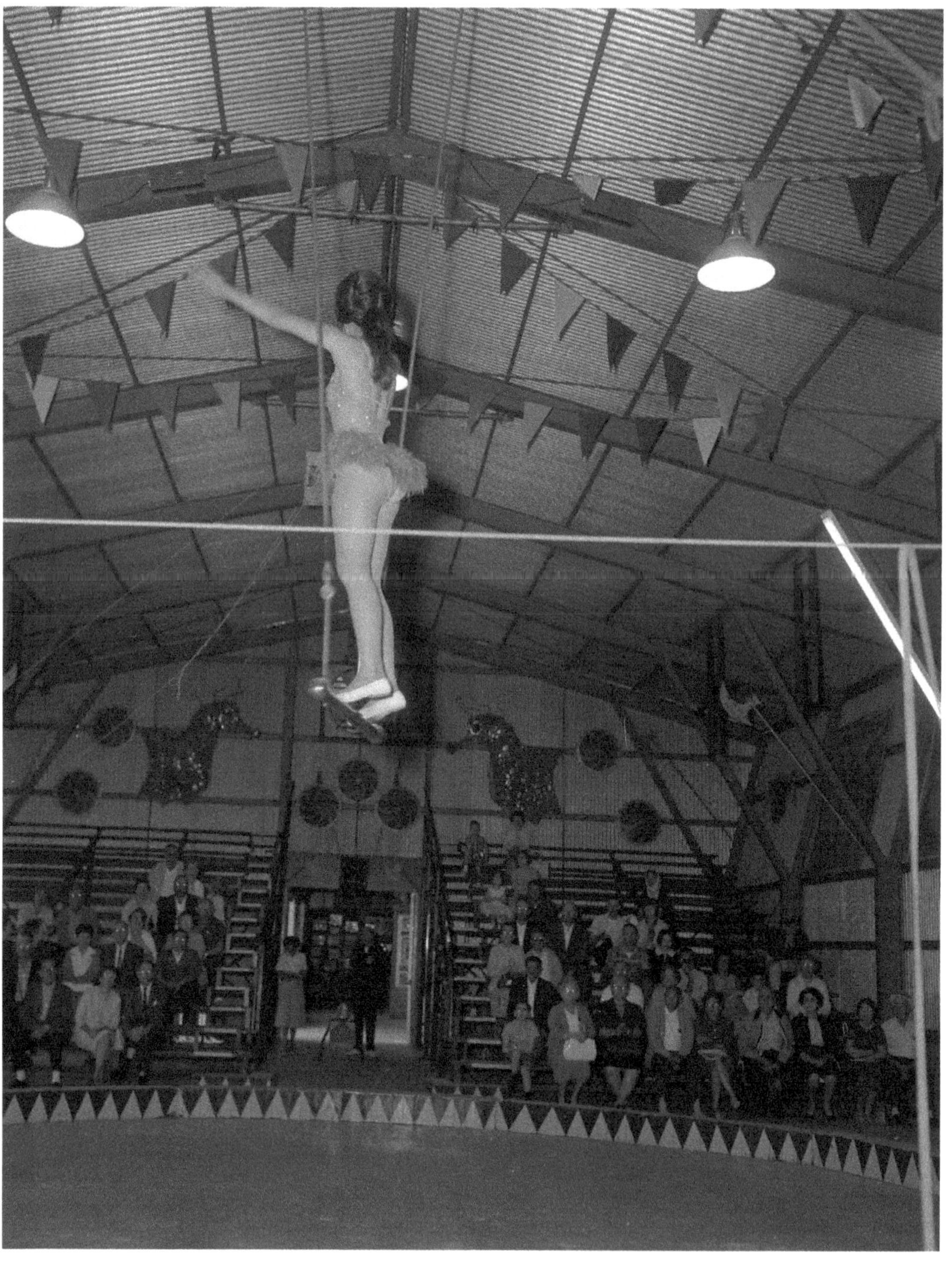

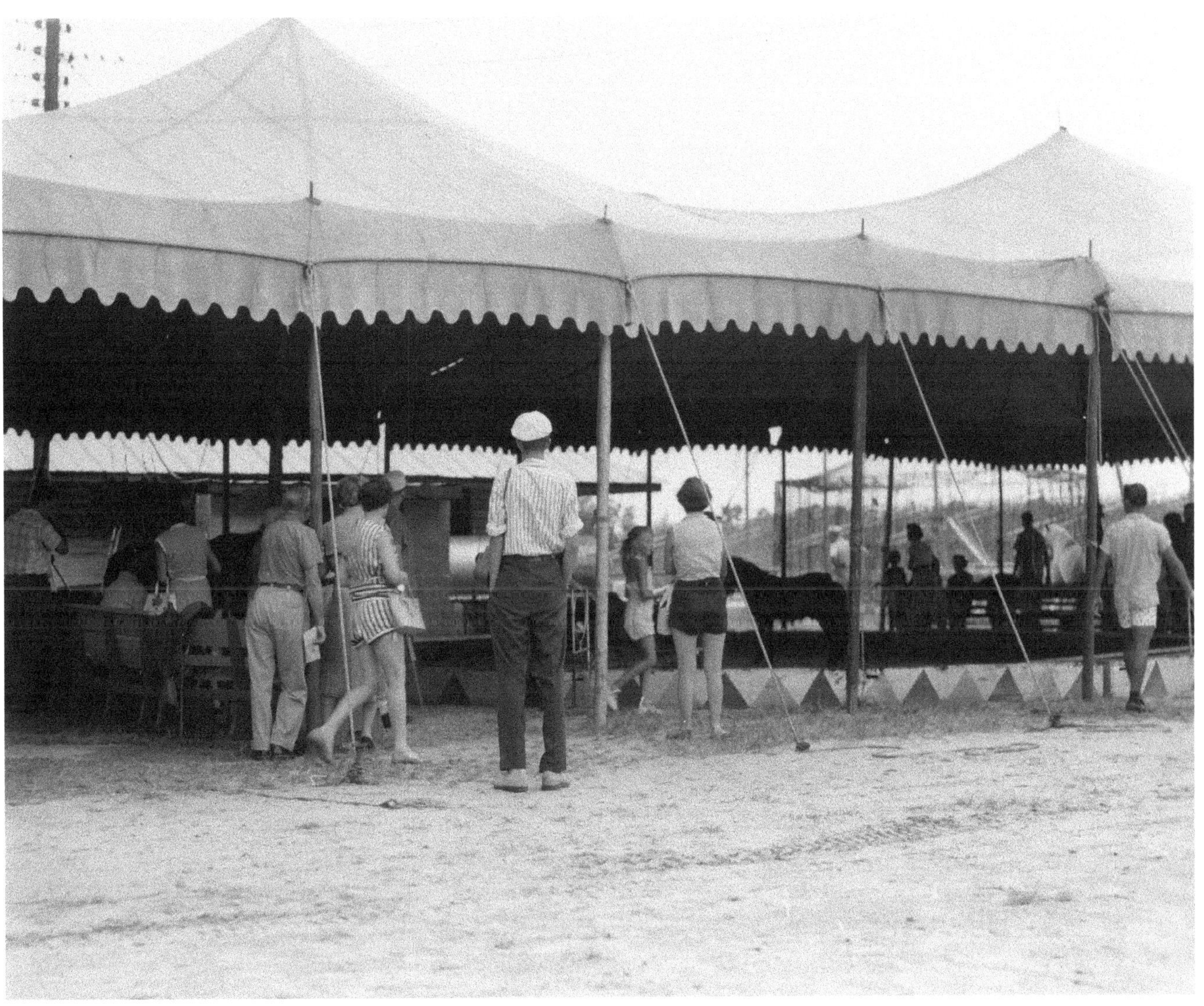

In 1960, the Ringling Brothers and Barnum and Bailey Circus moved its winter headquarters from Sarasota to Venice. Performances were given there until 1991, when the Venice location was closed down. Evidence of the circus connection, including a life-size statue of animal trainer Gunther Gebel-Williams, can still be found throughout the city of Venice.

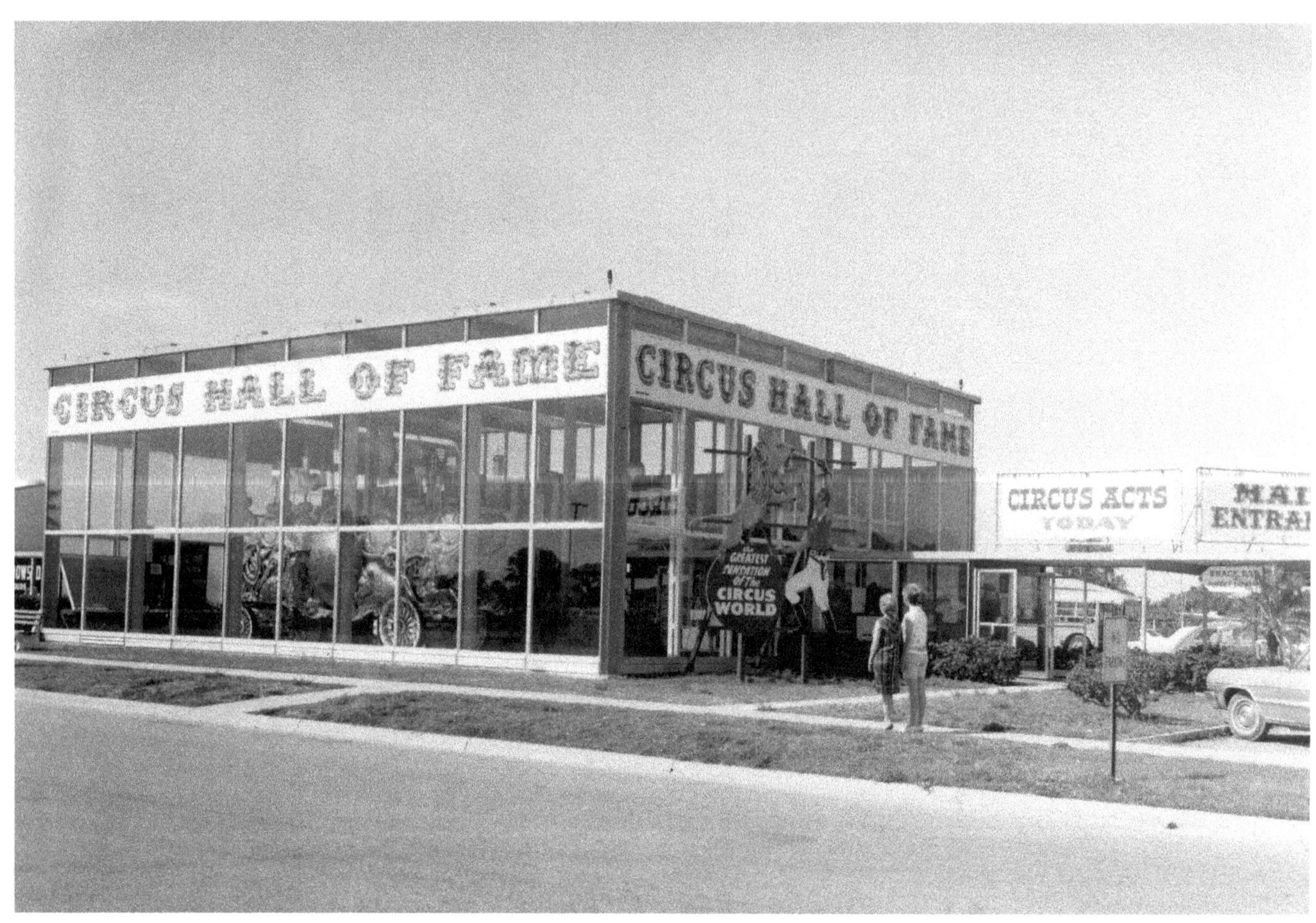

Seen here in 1966, the Circus Hall of Fame was located in leased buildings, rather than on a site that it owned. In 1979, the land was sold and the lease terminated. The Hall of Fame's collection of circus memorabilia was purchased for $450,000 by a group from Peru, Indiana. The Hall of Fame was then moved to the group's hometown and was expanded both in size and in scope.

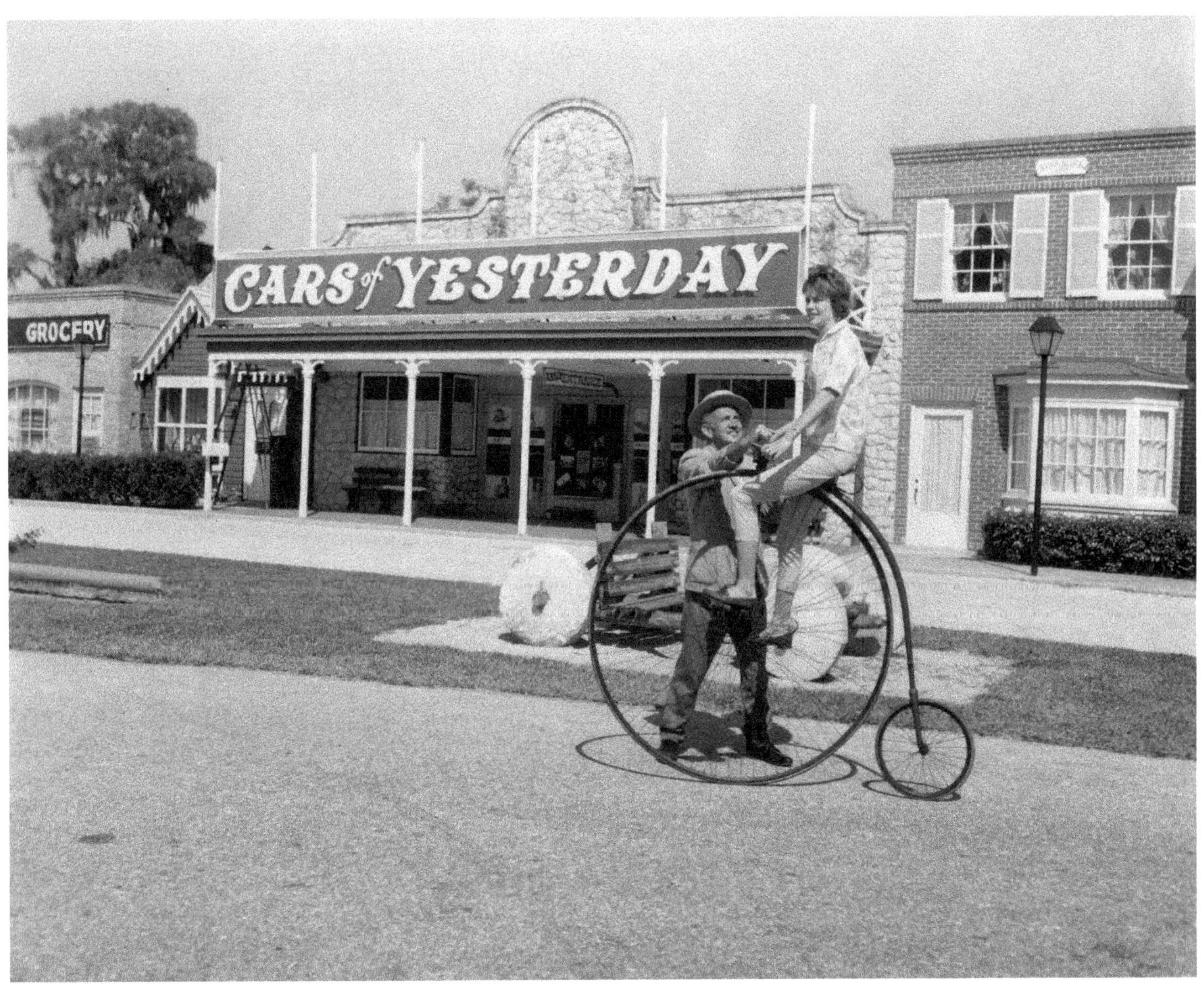

Walter Bellm approached the Horn brothers, owners of Horn's Cars of Yesterday, and tried to buy a rare Tucker automobile. The Horns said no, since it was part of a collection they did not want to break up. Bellm got the Tucker anyway by purchasing the entire attraction, which he renamed Bellm's Cars and Music of Yesterday in the 1960s.

By the time this photo was taken in 1966, the face of Sarasota bore no resemblance to that seen by J. Hamilton Gillespie or John Ringling. Gone were the small beachside homes and piers, and most of the early homes of the well-to-do. In their place, concrete-and-glass condominiums and offices typical of nearly every Florida beachside city were being built.

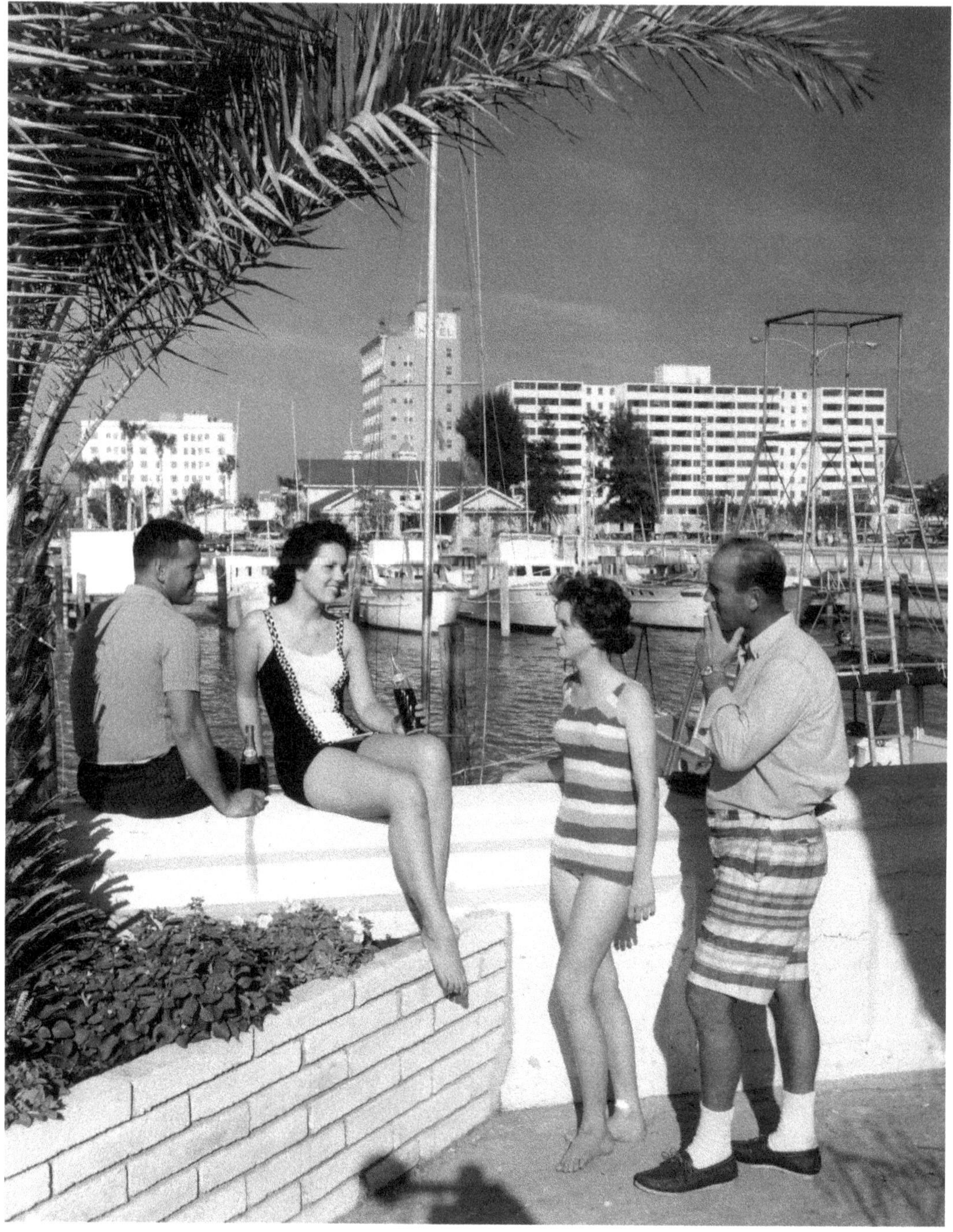

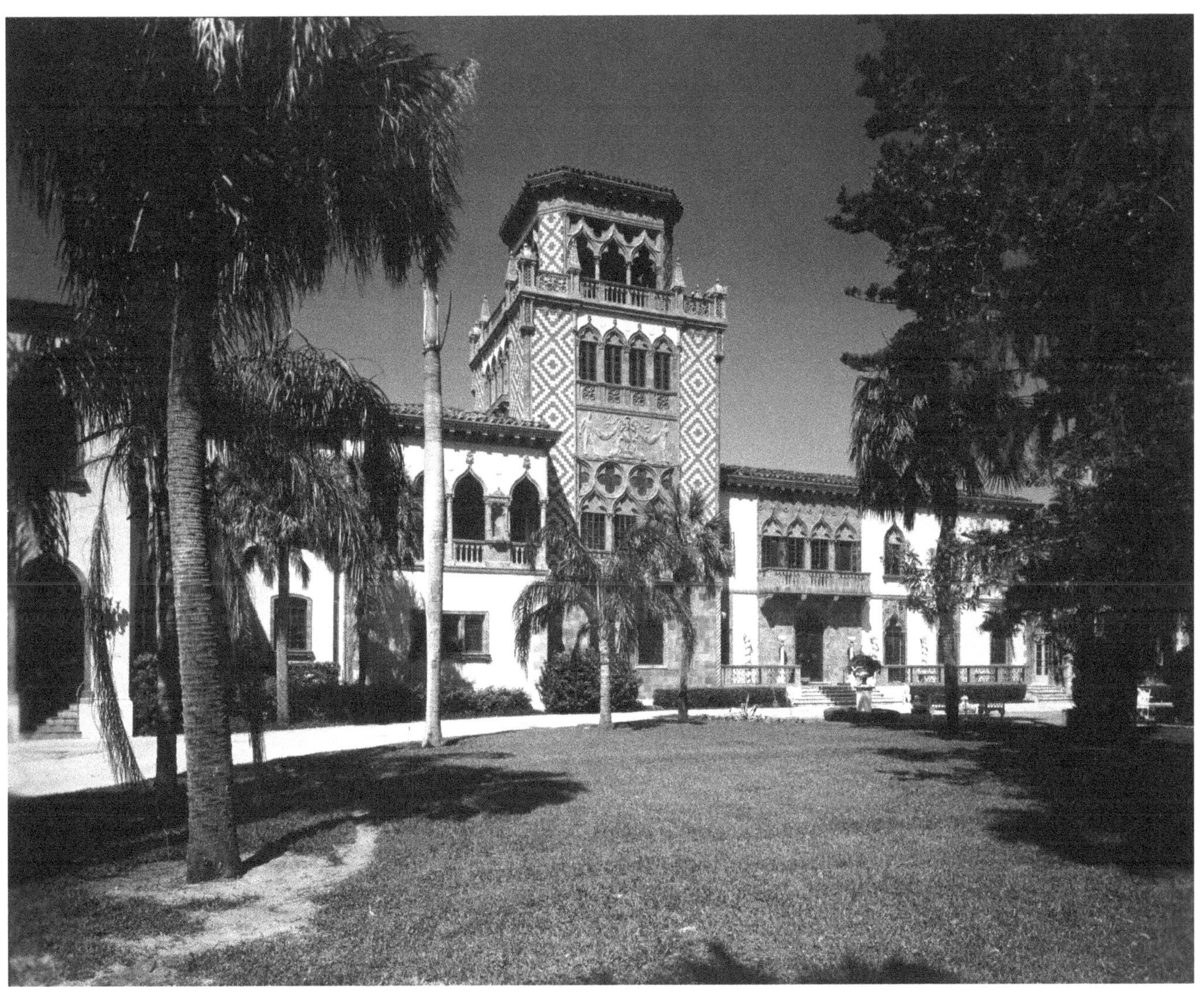

In 1925, John Ringling hired John Phillips to design a building worthy of the art collection he had amassed. Utilizing elements from Italian Baroque and Renaissance museums and palaces, the museum opened in October 1931 and is seen here as it appeared 35 years later. Ringling's collection of paintings by Baroque masters is considered to be one of the country's finest.

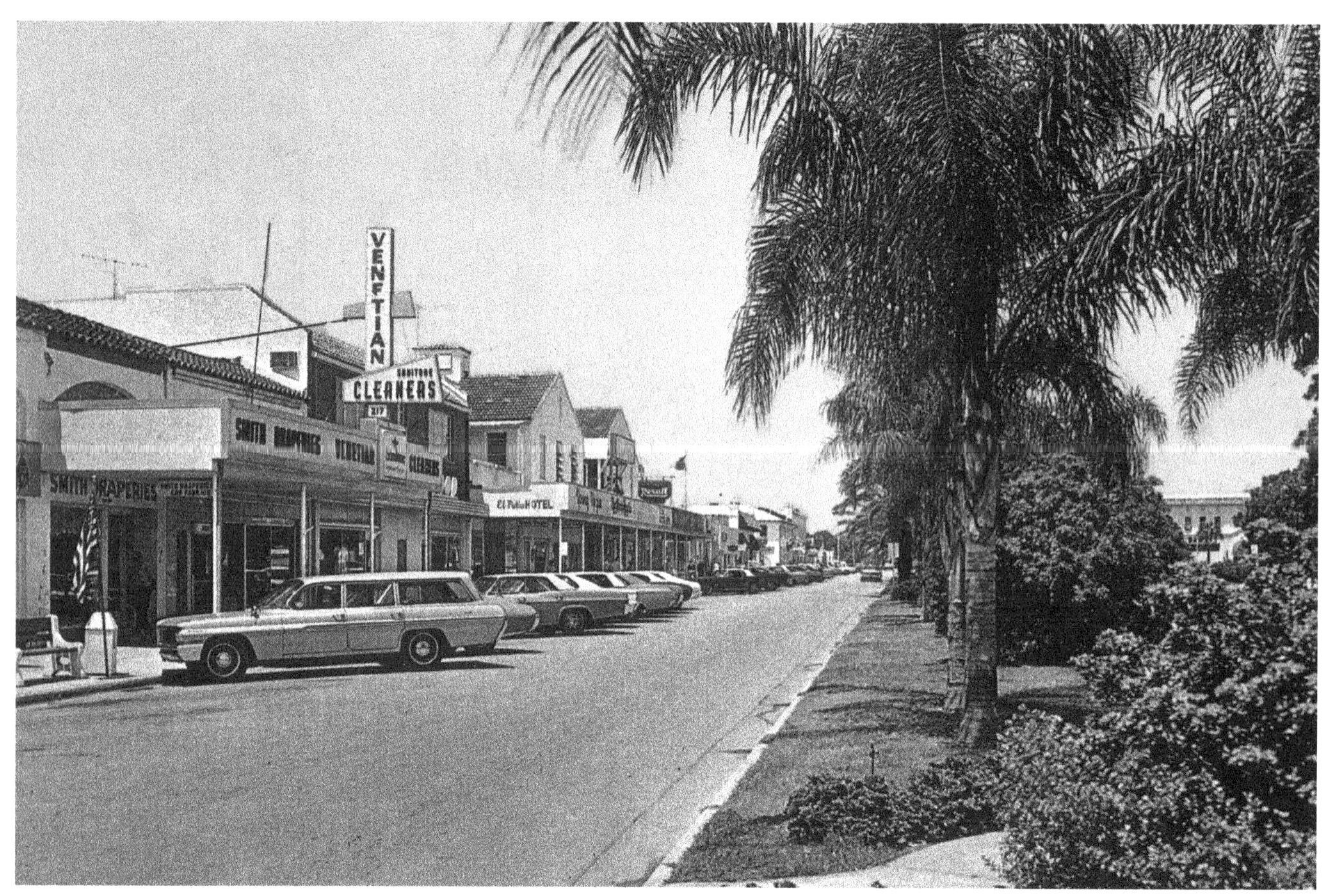

When the Brotherhood of Locomotive Engineers moved out of Venice in 1929, the architectural requirement of a Northern Italian Renaissance style was abandoned. As a result, Venice turned into a city with a wide variety of building styles and materials.

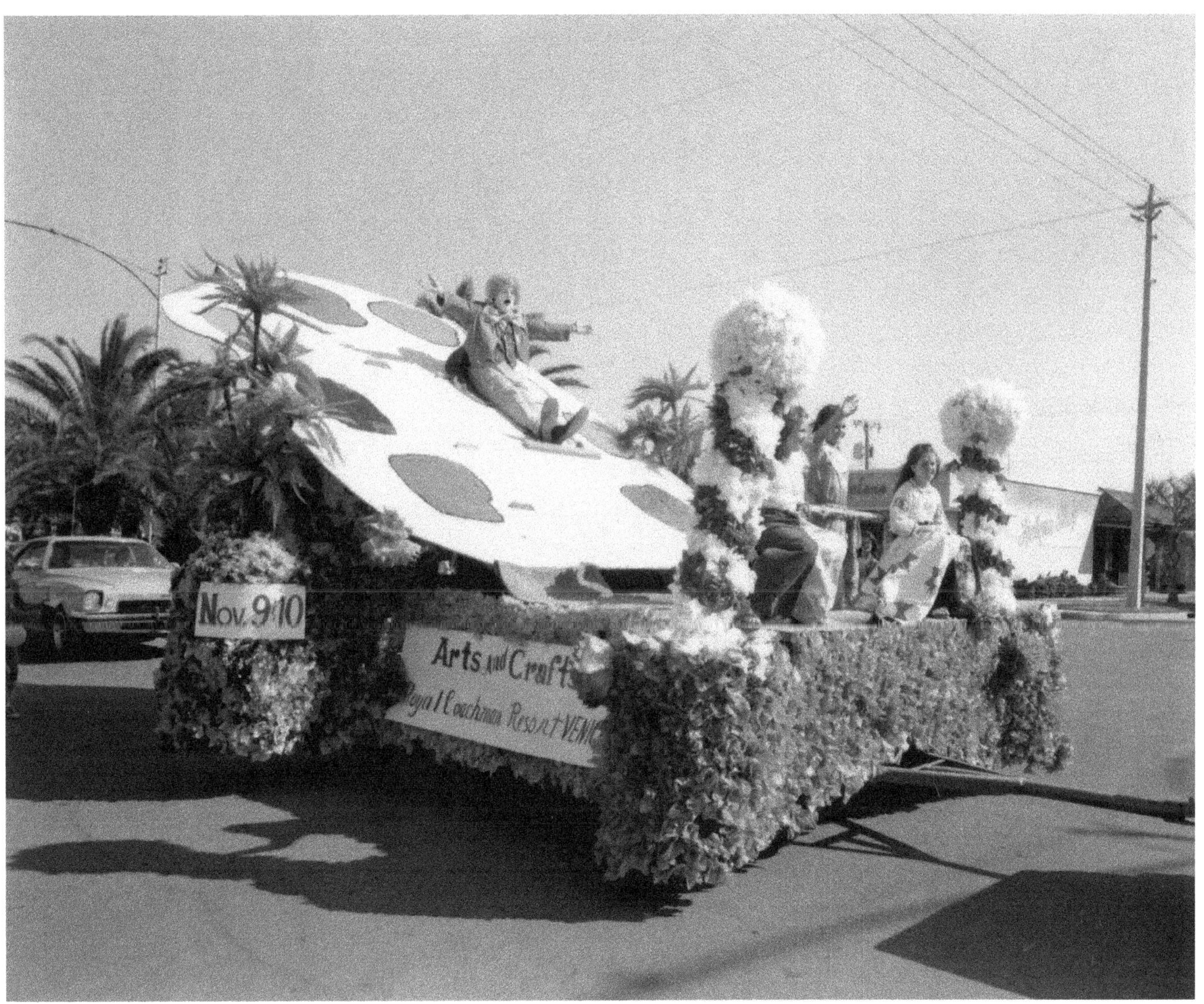

This parade float celebrates children's arts and crafts, and implies Venice's circus connection by the clown seated on the oversized pallet. The float was sponsored by the Royal Coachman Resort, which opened in 1969. Located on Laurel Road in Nokomis, the Royal Coachman is a mobile home resort with wooded campsites and plenty of amenities.

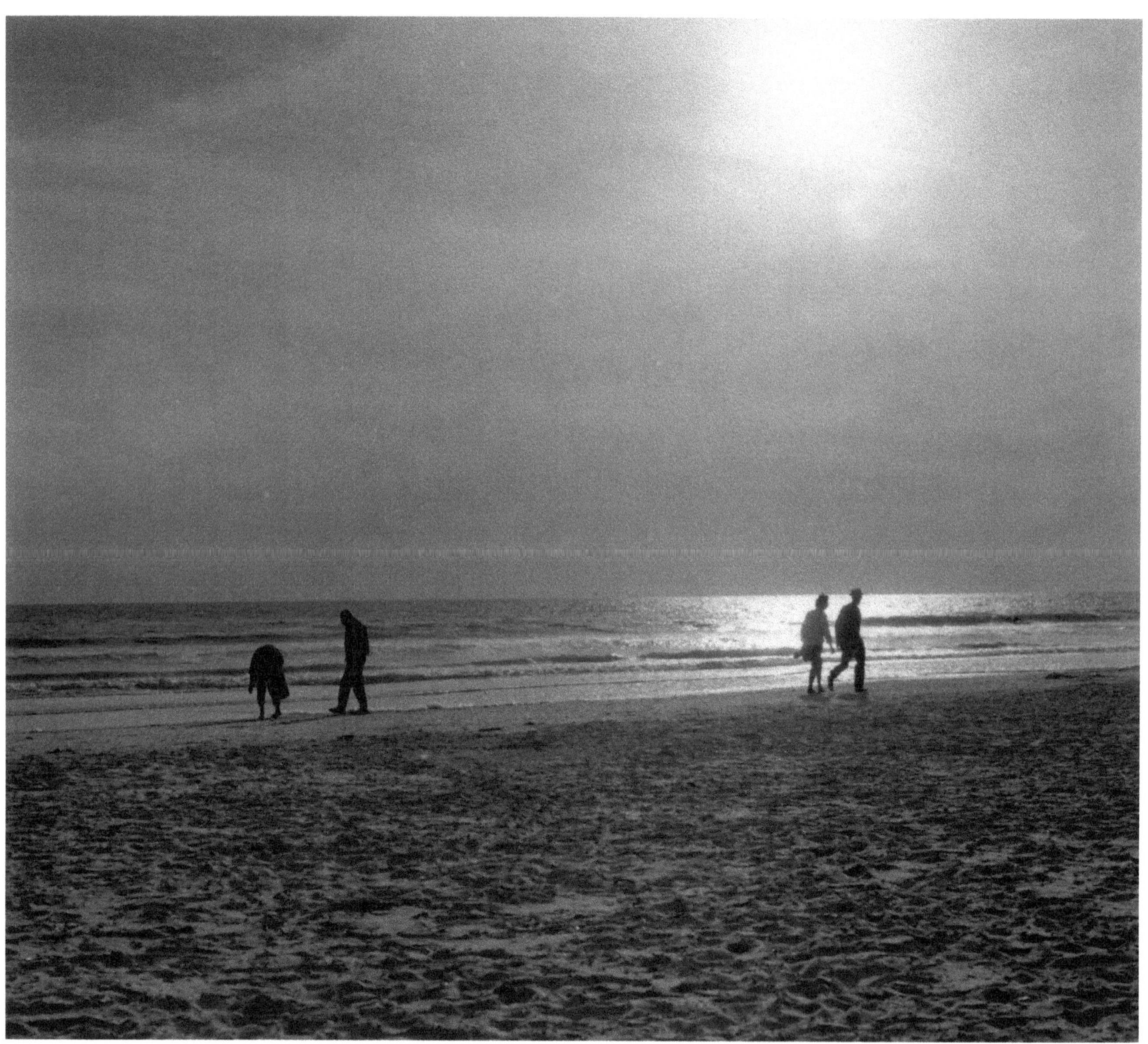

Sarasota's beaches boast some of the whitest, softest, and purest beach sand to be found and receive superior reviews from the travel industry. For example, Siesta Beach was named Best Overall in the 1987 Great International White Sand Challenge. It ranks in the top ten nationally, largely because the beach is 99 percent quartz, with almost none of the crushed shells, rocks, or lava found elsewhere.

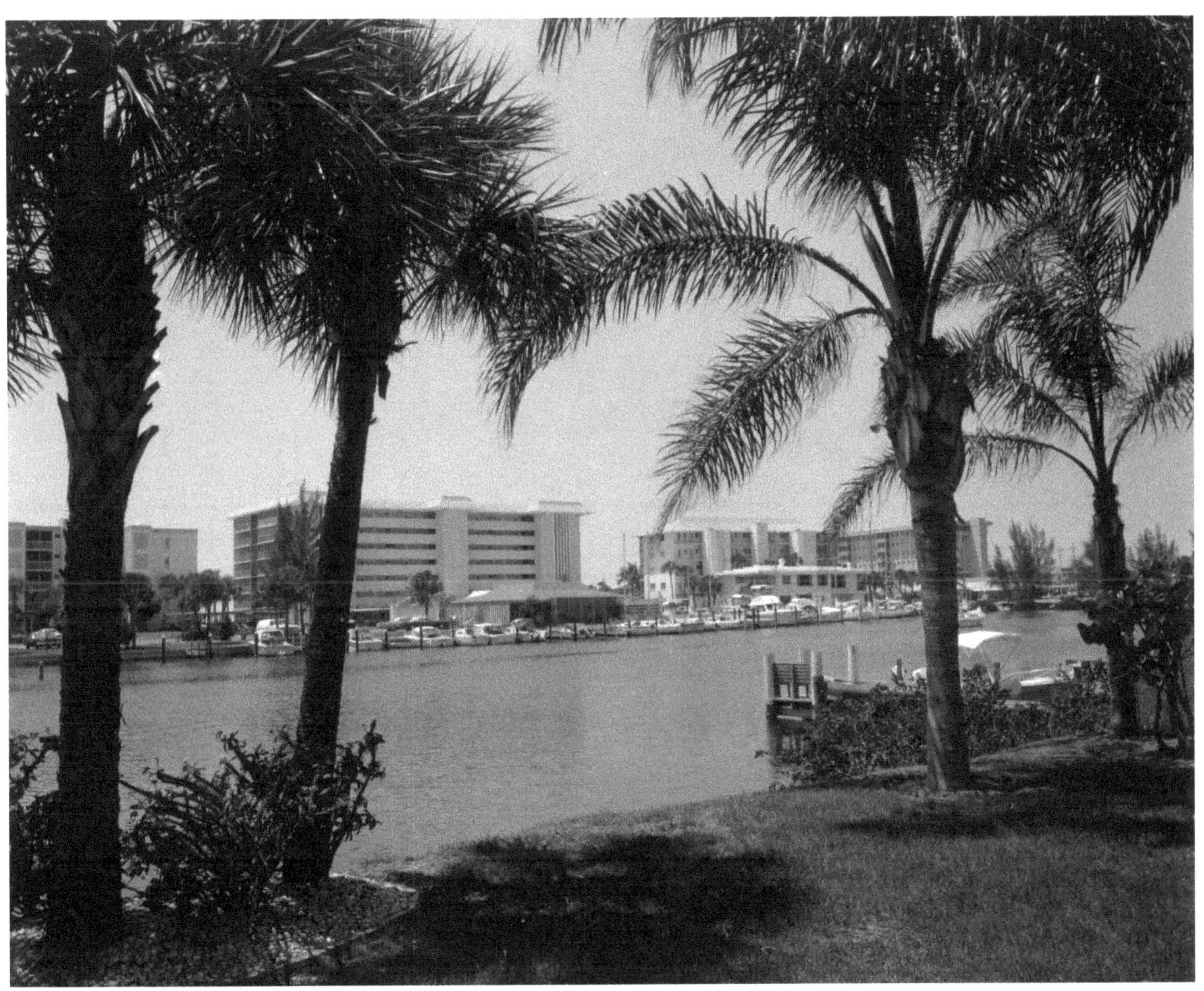

The first condominium project in Venice appeared in 1959. A high-rise along Tarpon Center Drive, it provided its residents with a magnificent view of Venice Beach and the Gulf of Mexico, but it signaled a new era in the city, which now resembles many other Florida coastal cities whose beachfront properties are crowded with residential towers.

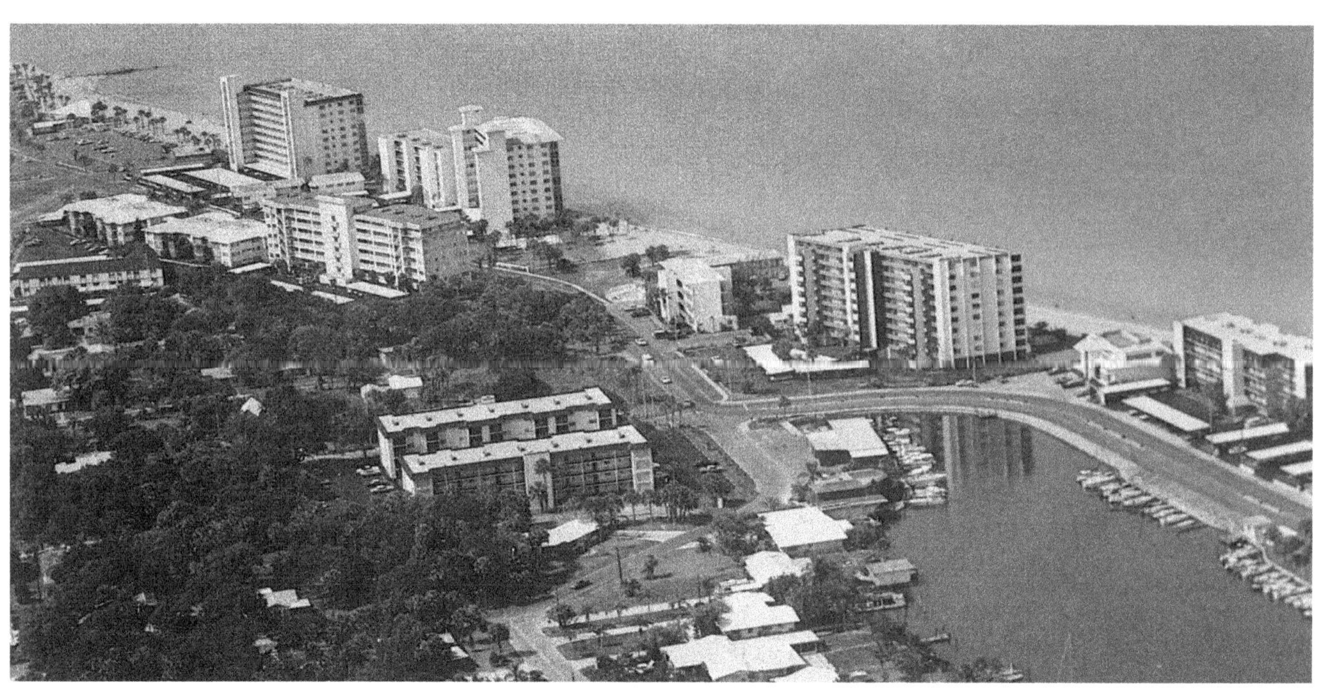

Shown here are apartment buildings lining the esplanade in Venice. The waterfront had always been important to Venice and became more so with the construction of the 150-mile Intracoastal Waterway. Dredging began in 1960 at the rate of two miles per month, and the Waterway was dedicated in 1967. Part of the project involved creation of the island of Venice.

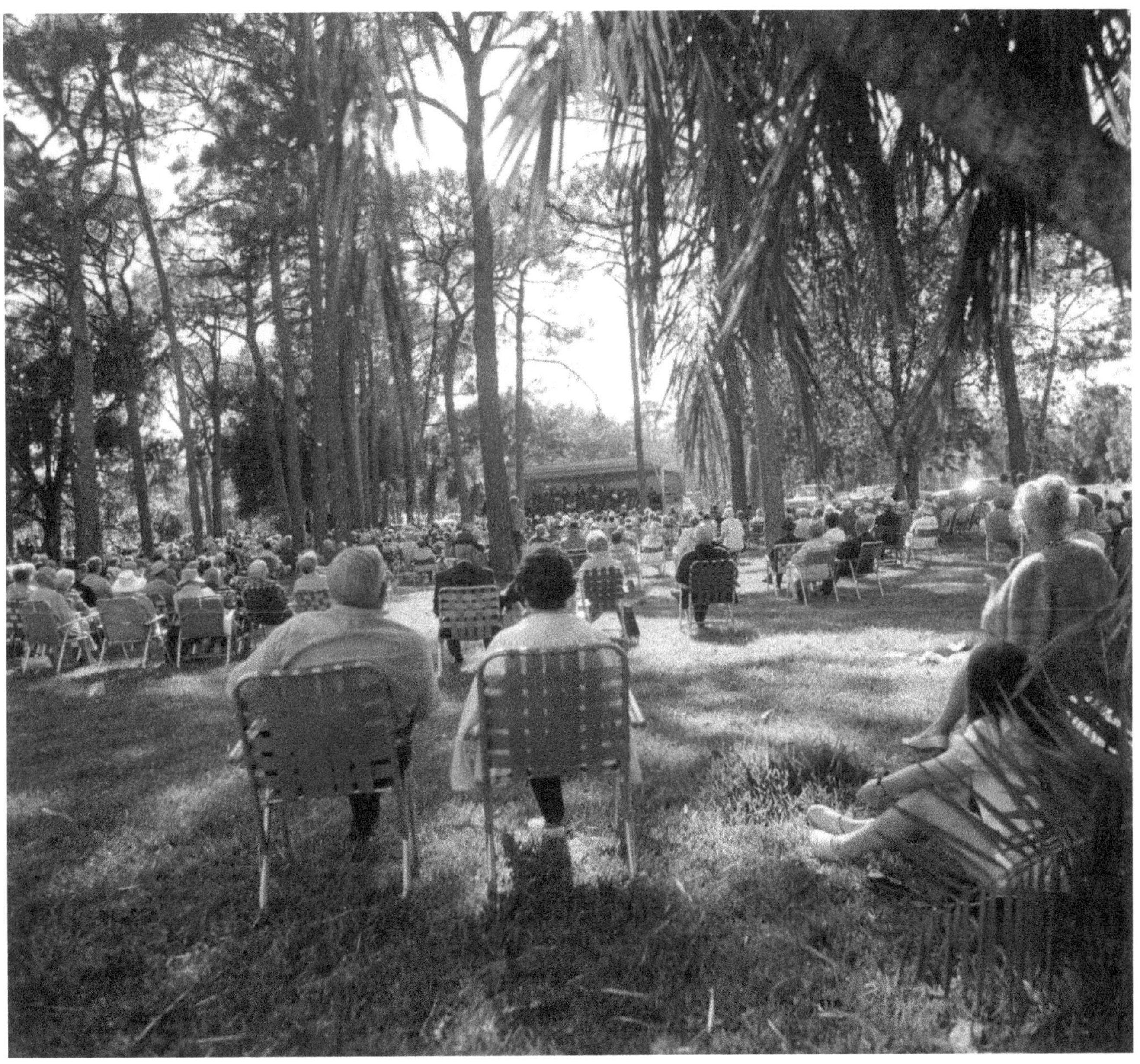

Over the years, Mosquito eradication programs have made the gulf coast a pleasant location for outdoor events such as this 1971 concert. Today, outdoor concerts can still be enjoyed at the Sarasota Polo Club, Phillippi Estate Park, Van Wezel Bayfront and other venues.

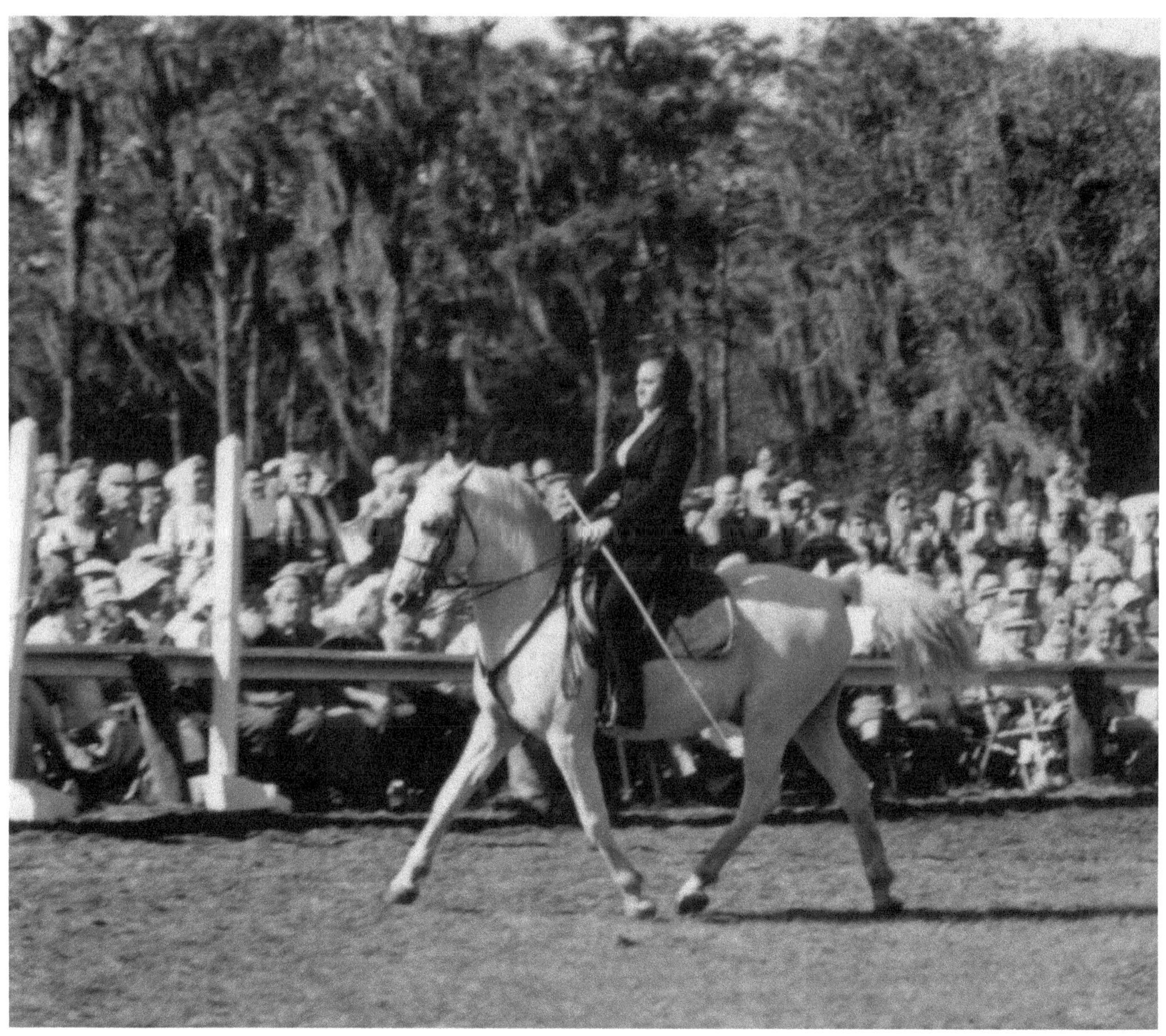

At the end of World War II, General George Patton rescued 250 Lipizzaner stallions, and in 1962 Ottomar Herrmann of Austria brought several to his adopted home near Sarasota. It became their winter base where the horses would be trained before leaving on spring tours to delight crowds around the country. The Myakka City training ranch is itself a tourist attraction.

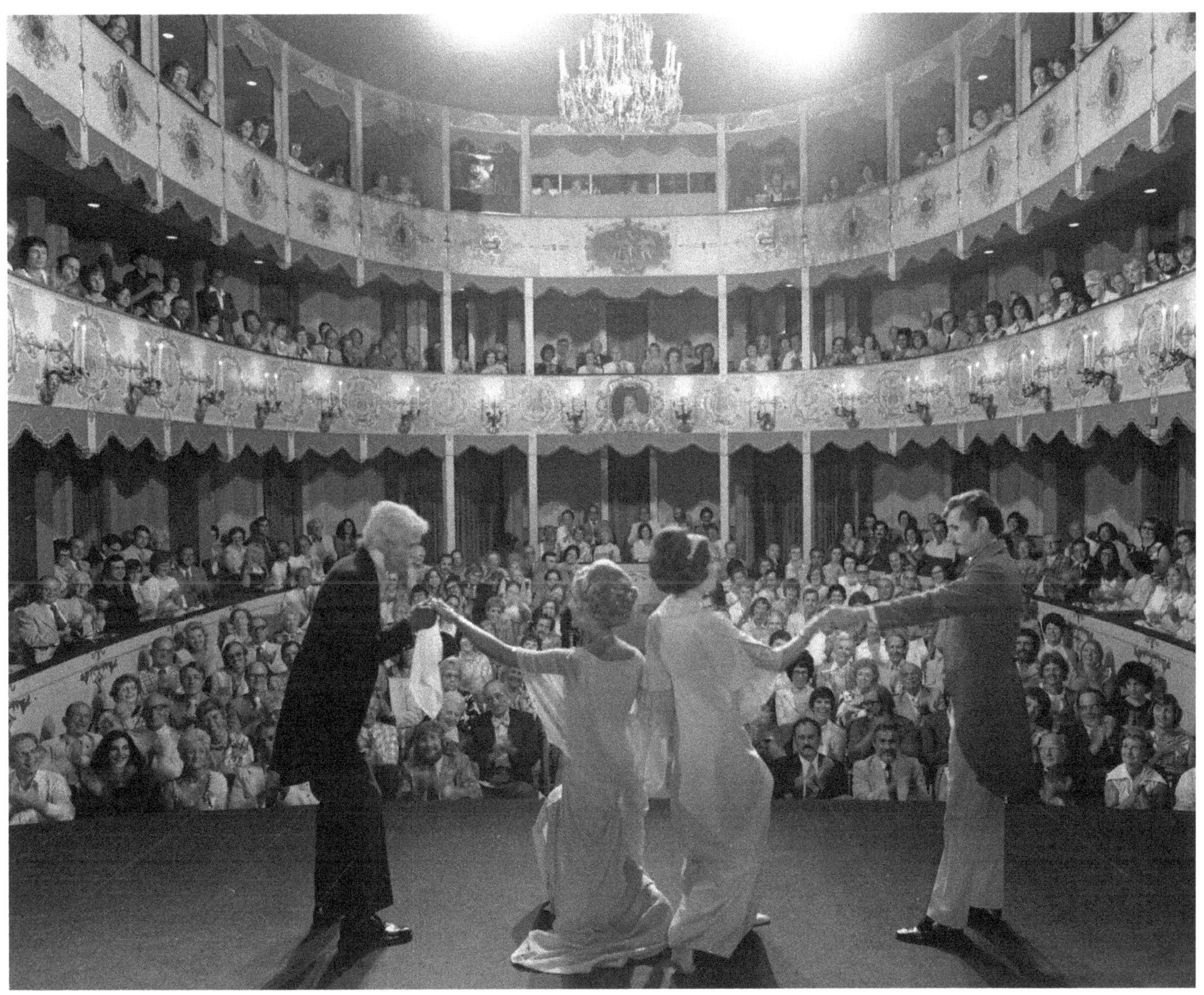

In 1798, this theater was built in Italy to honor a former queen of Cyprus. Dismantled in the 1930s, the building was stored in Venice, Italy. A. Everett "Chick" Austin saw portions of it in 1937, and when he became the director of the Ringling Museum of Art, in 1946, he arranged for the building's acquisition. It was reassembled in Sarasota and opened in 1952 as the Asolo Theater.

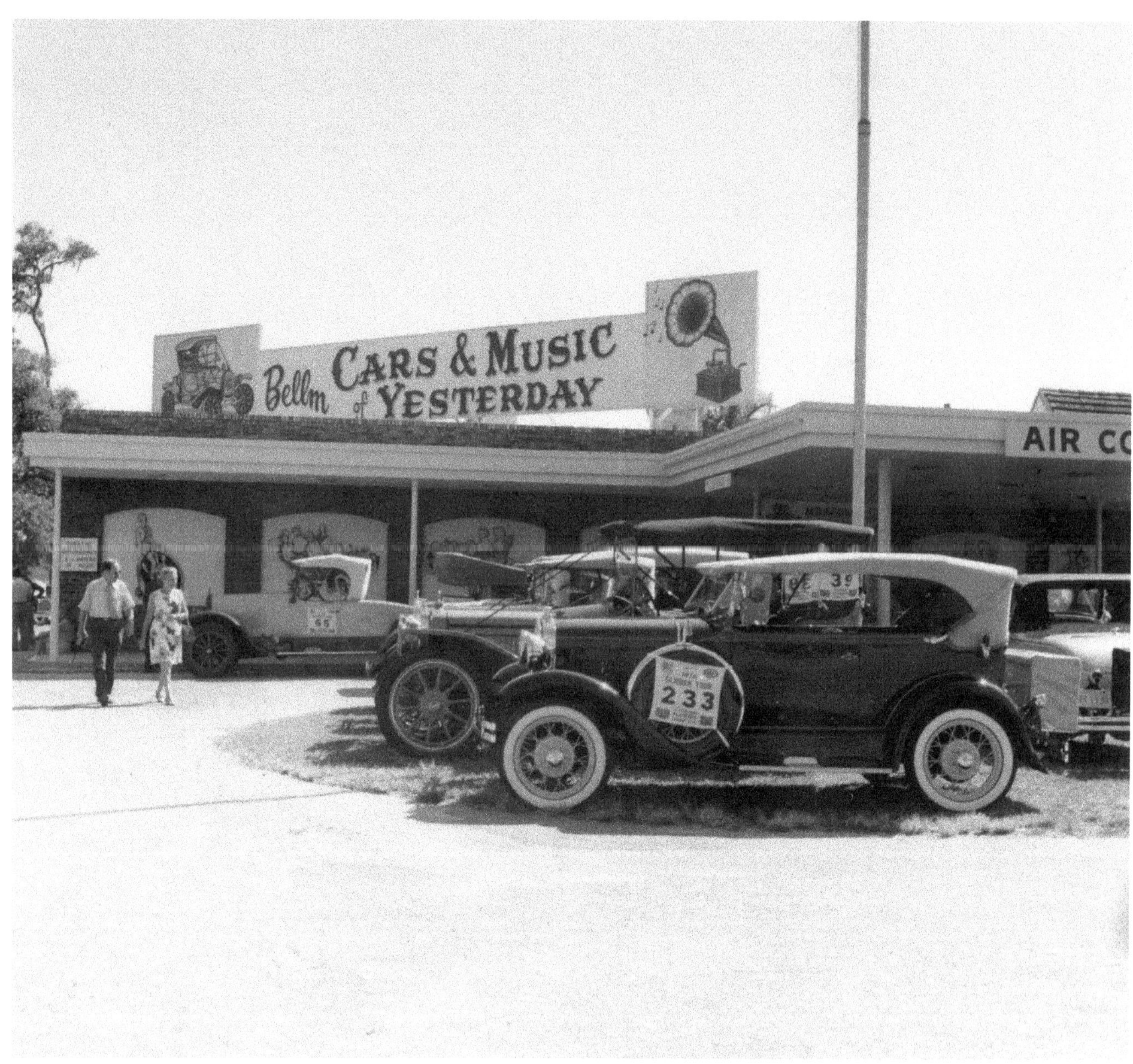

Bellm's Cars and Music of Yesterday featured vehicles such as those shown here in 1974 and a collection of mechanical music devices known around the world. One of the attraction's most prized items was the Gypsy Queen Gasparini fair organ crafted in Paris in about 1895. Walter Bellm eventually sold the museum, and it was renamed in 1999 as the Sarasota Classic Car Museum.

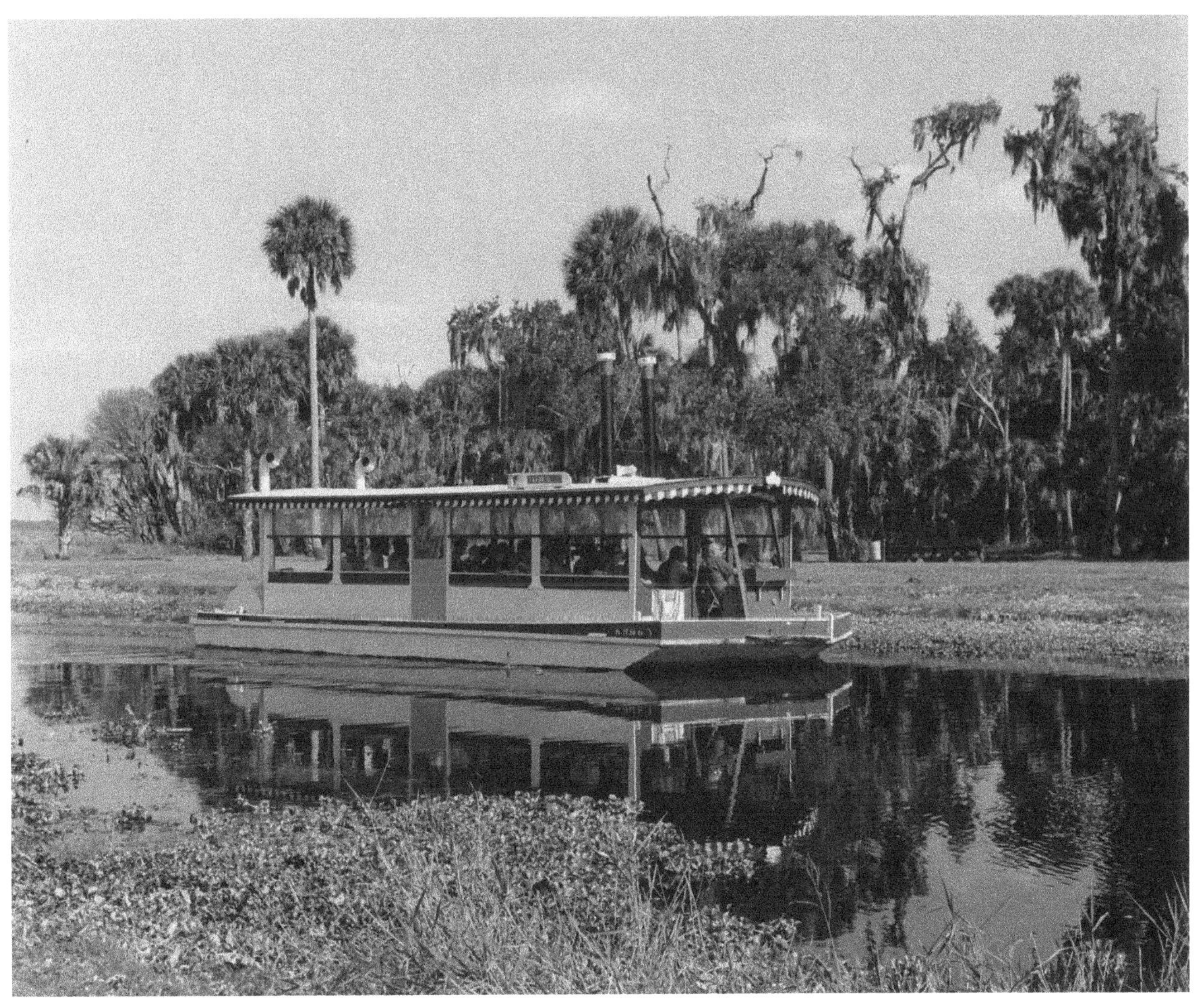

The Myakka River, which flows 14 miles through the large park of the same name, has been designated a Florida Wild and Scenic River. Enjoyed here in the 1970s by visitors on a boat tour, the river and scenery can be accessed today by canoe, kayak, or the popular airboats *Myakka Maiden* and *Gator Gal.*

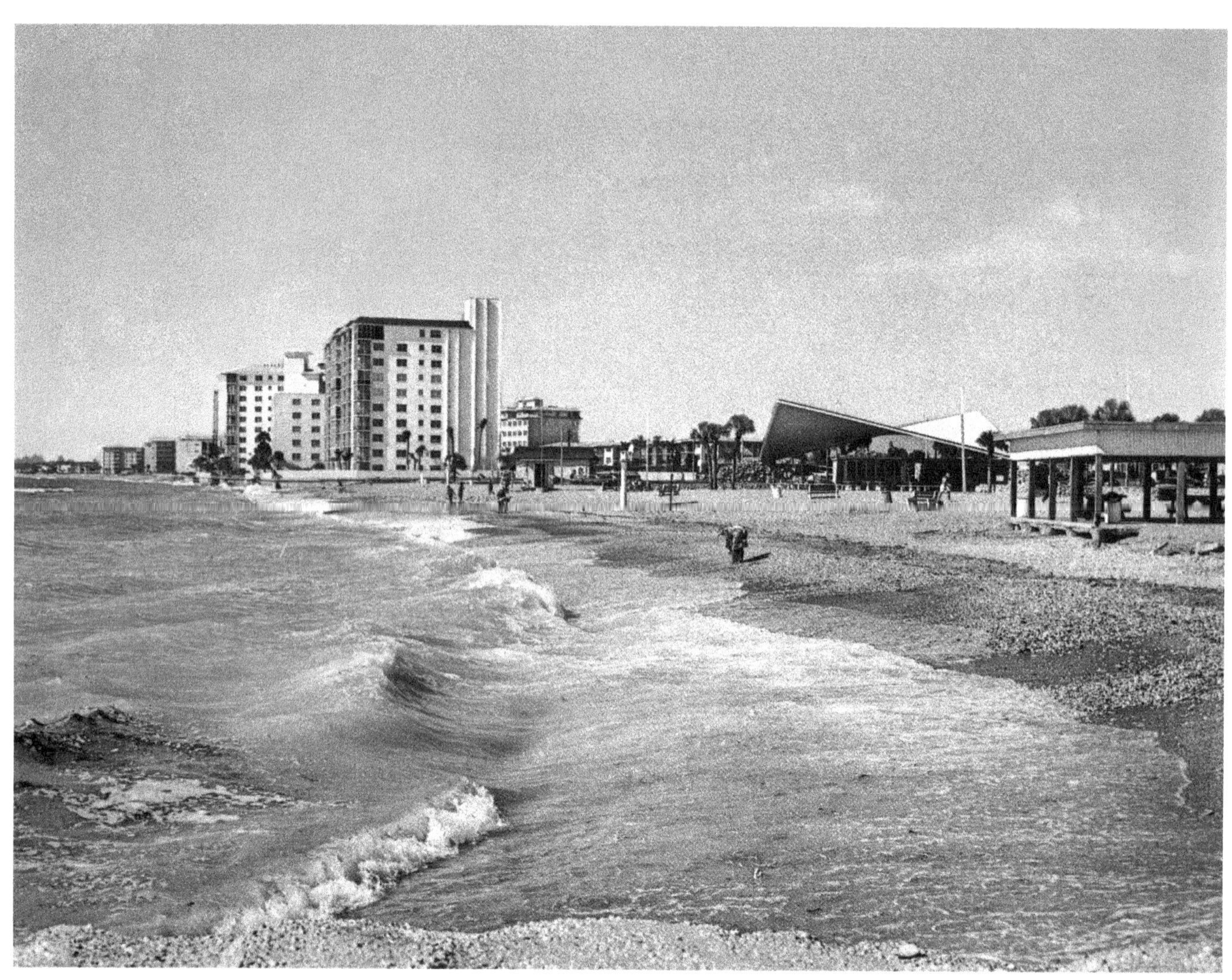

The Venice beach starts at the northern boundary of the city, where a waterway connects the Intracoastal Waterway to the Gulf of Mexico, and continues south for miles to the county's Caspersen Beach Park. Along the beach can be found seashells and so many shark's teeth that one of the city's nicknames is "Shark's Tooth Capital of the World."

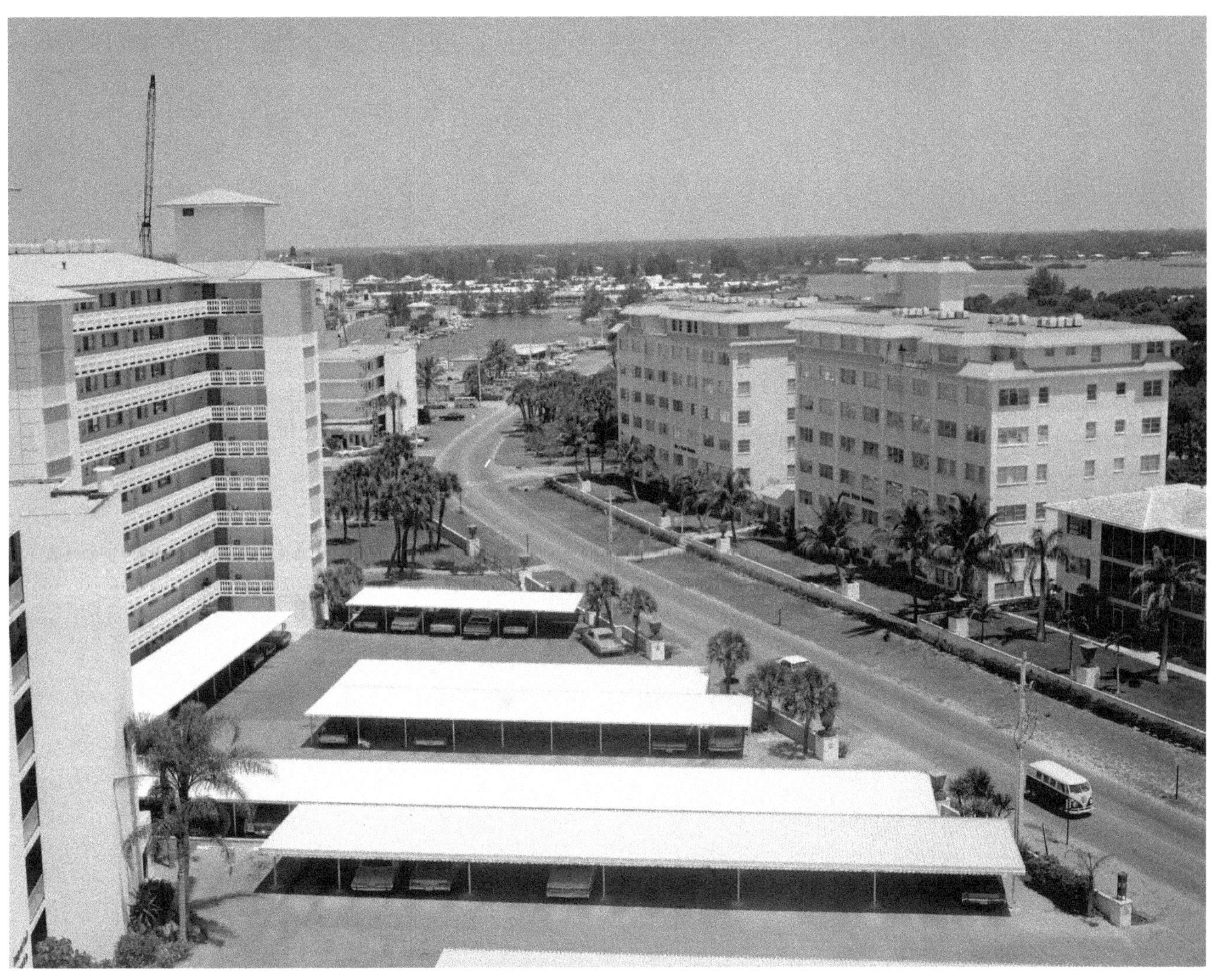

In 1974, with buildings such as these, the look of Venice was moving away from the Northern Italian Renaissance style favored during the 1920s for a retirement town built for a labor union.

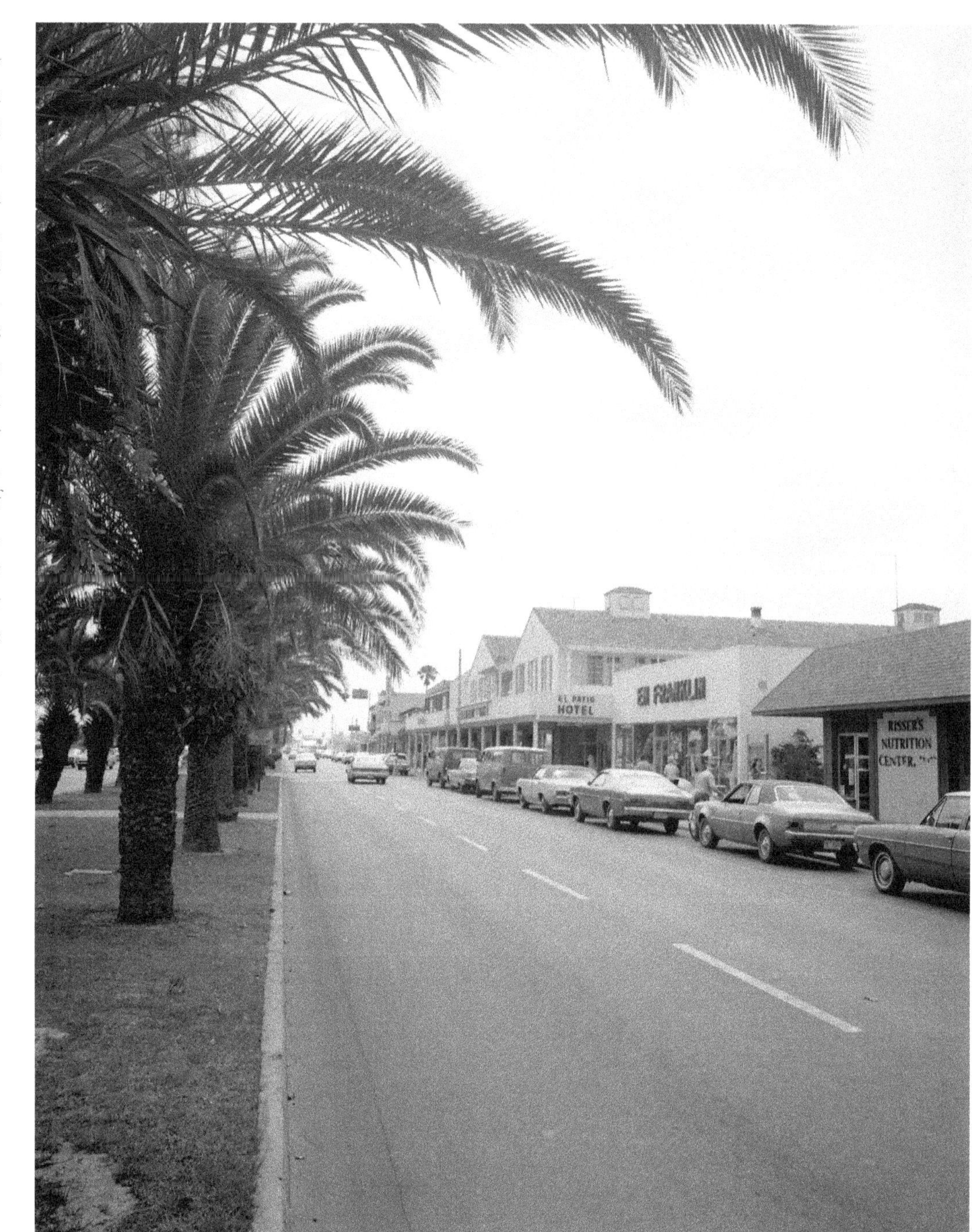

Built in 1926 by Stanton and Elizabeth Ennes and called the Ennes Arcade, the structure with the chimney, center, originally contained the Hotel Valencia. Since 1936, it has been the El Patio Hotel. It had an attractive balcony and arched entrance, but by the time of this 1974 street view, those features were obscured by a rather plain canopy over the sidewalk.

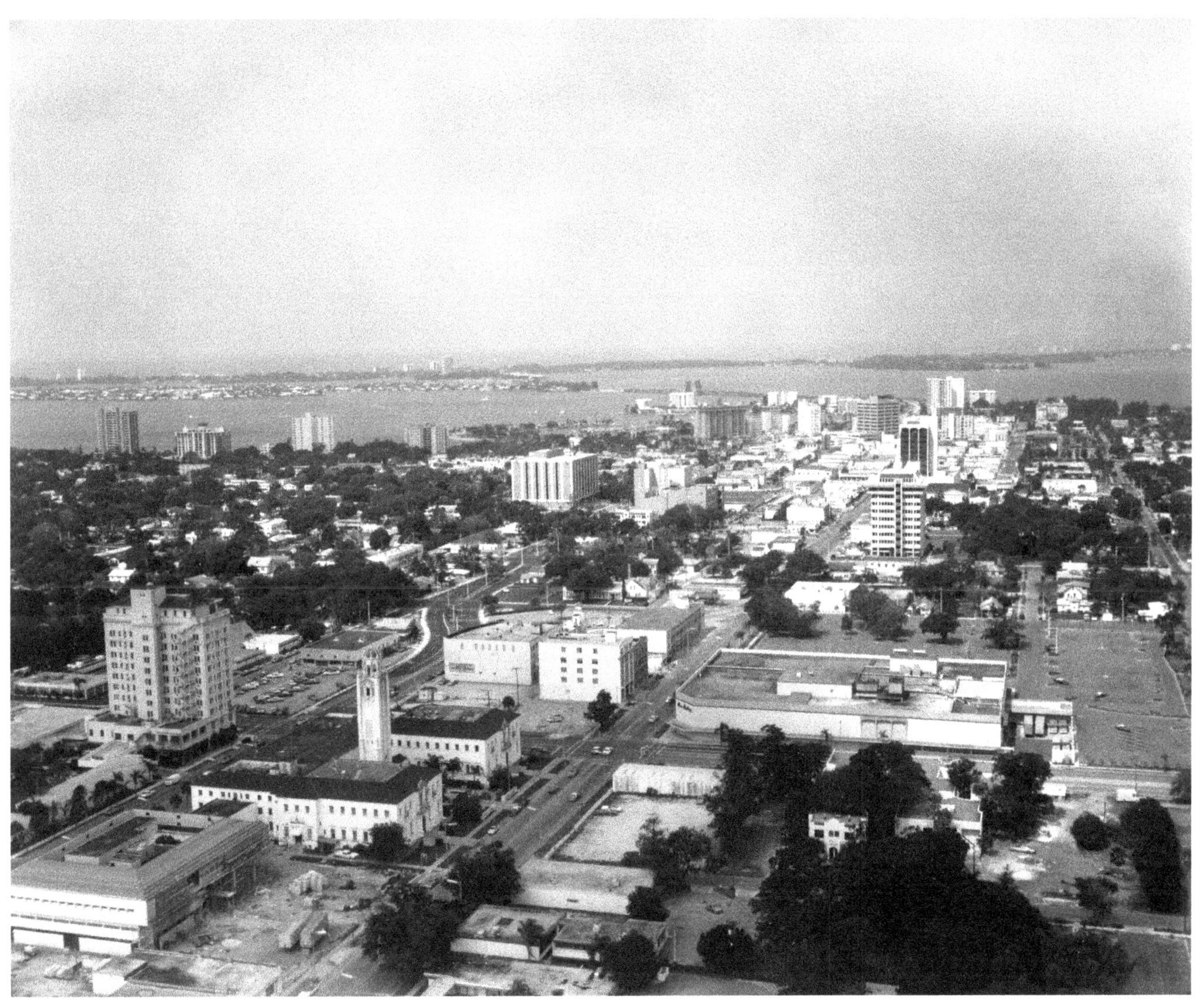

In this 1975 view of Sarasota, skyscraper residences and office buildings have been added to the skyline. But in the left foreground sits the Sarasota County Courthouse, completed in 1927. Its tower and reflection pool are flanked by a pair of Mediterranean-style wings to represent a balance of power between administrative and judicial functions.

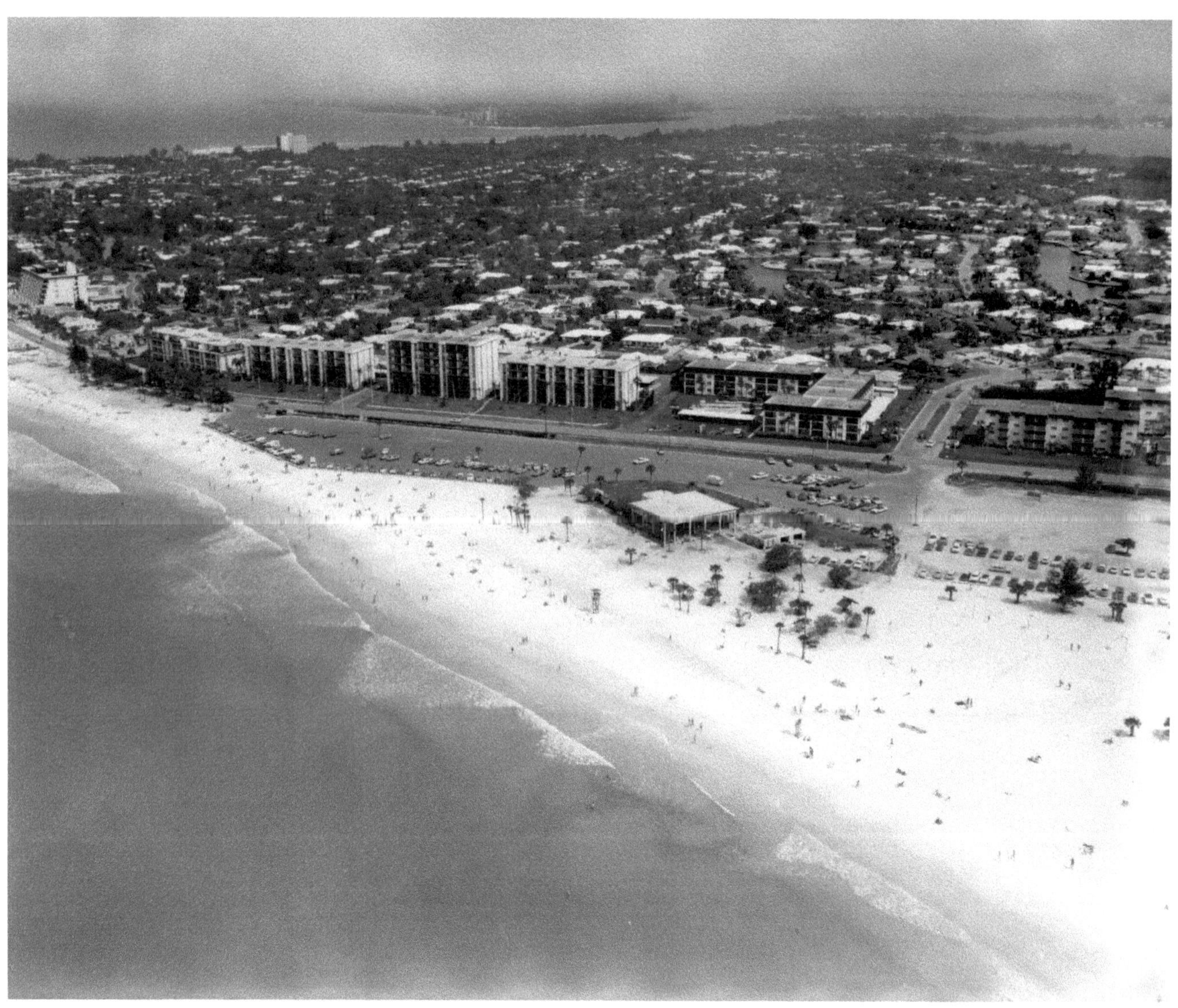

Originally, the Siesta Key seen here in 1975 was known as Sarasota Key. Thomas Edmondson and Louise Whitaker purchased more than a hundred acres on the key, becoming one of the first families to settle there. One of its major roads is Ocean Boulevard, named for Ocean Roberts, the wife of Louis Roberts, who enlarged his home there in 1906 and operated it as a hotel.

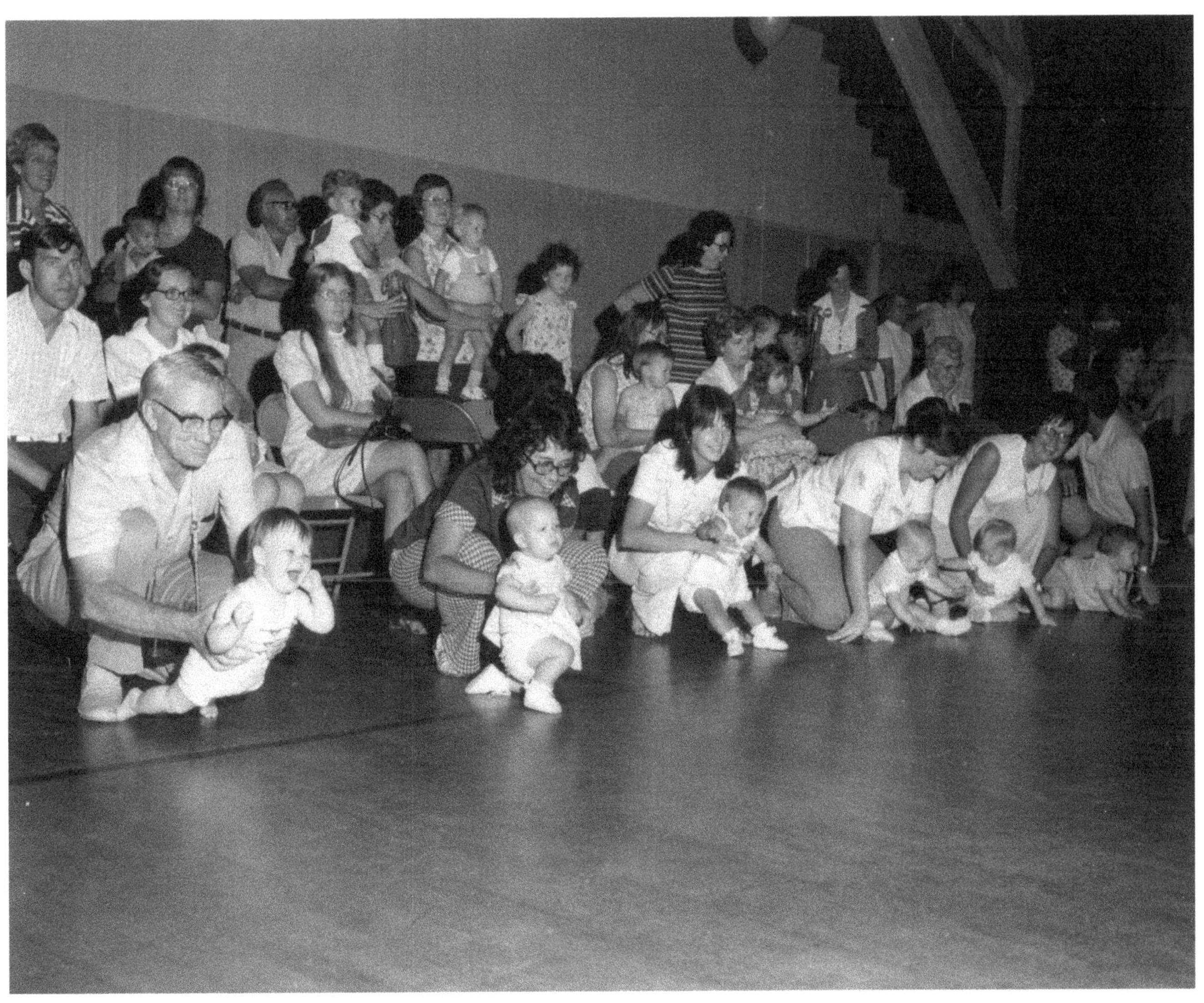

According to a local legend created by winter visitor George Chapline, explorer Hernando de Soto had a daughter, Sara, who was buried in Sarasota Bay. Sarasota held a pageant in 1916 to commemorate her, and in 1964 the annual festival was renamed the King Neptune Frolics. Events have included the diaper derby shown here in 1975.

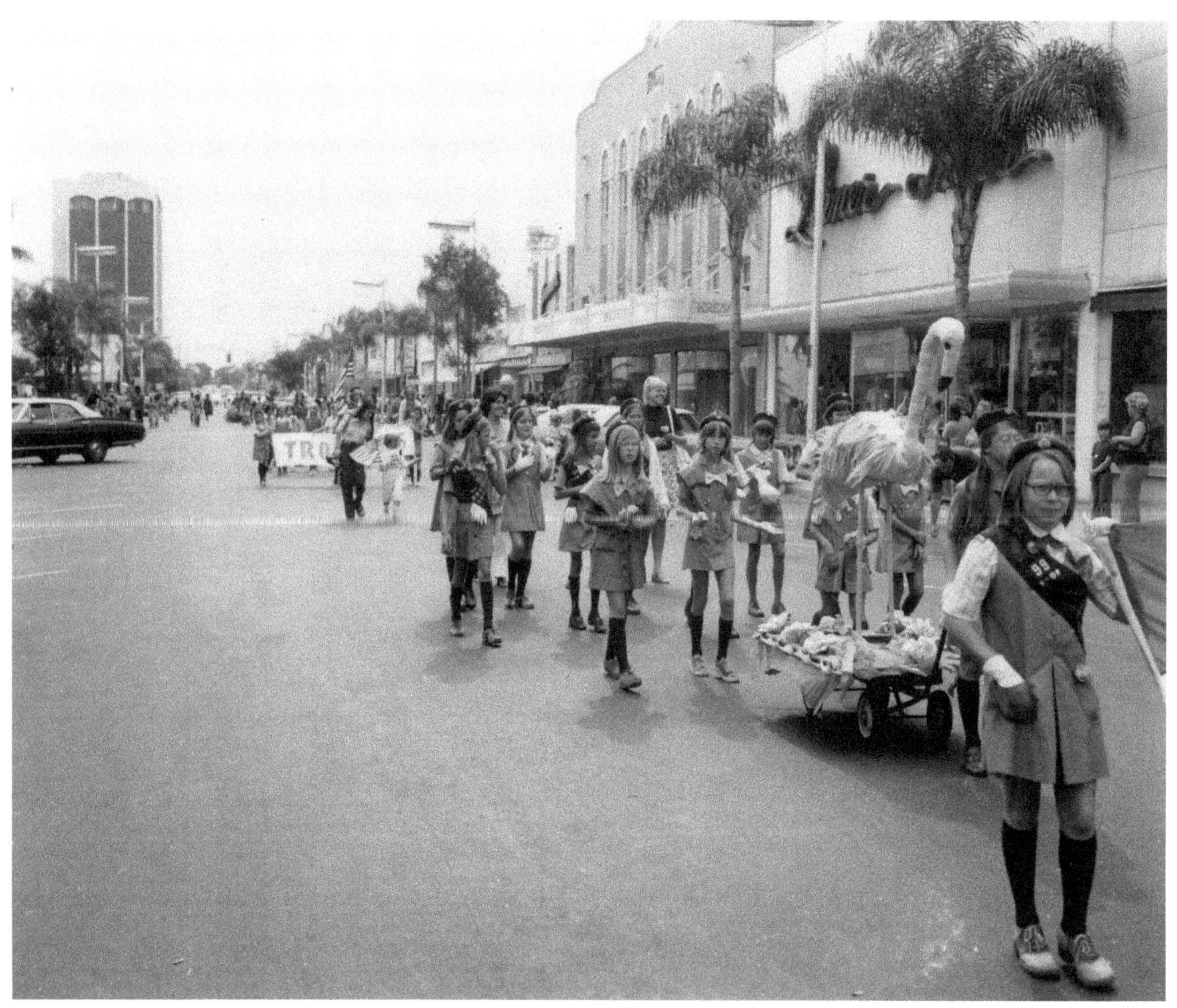

The original 1916 pageant lasted five days. Carnival rides were set up, and athletic events were held. Over the years, events such as "spearing the ring," contested by riders on horseback, were replaced by food and souvenir concessions and parades such as this one in 1975, in which Girl Scouts towed a fake flamingo through downtown Sarasota.

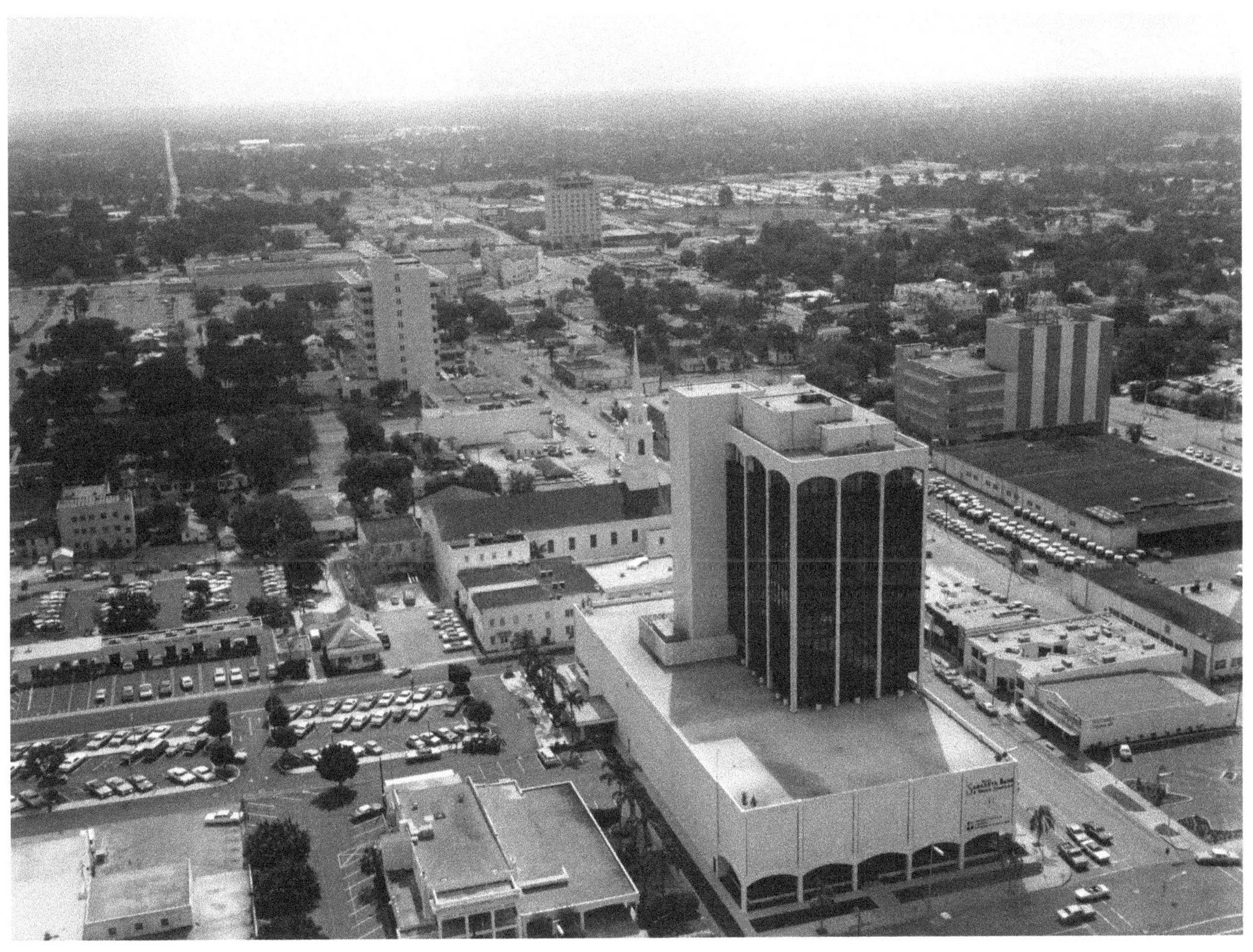

The tall building in the foreground was known as Ellis Sarasota Bank & Trust Company. When it was founded in 1939 by J. J. Williams, Jr., and J. C. Cardwell, it was known as Sarasota State Bank. In 1951, it was renamed Sarasota Bank & Trust Company and advertised itself as the "Friendly Bank." It moved to this 14-story building in 1969.

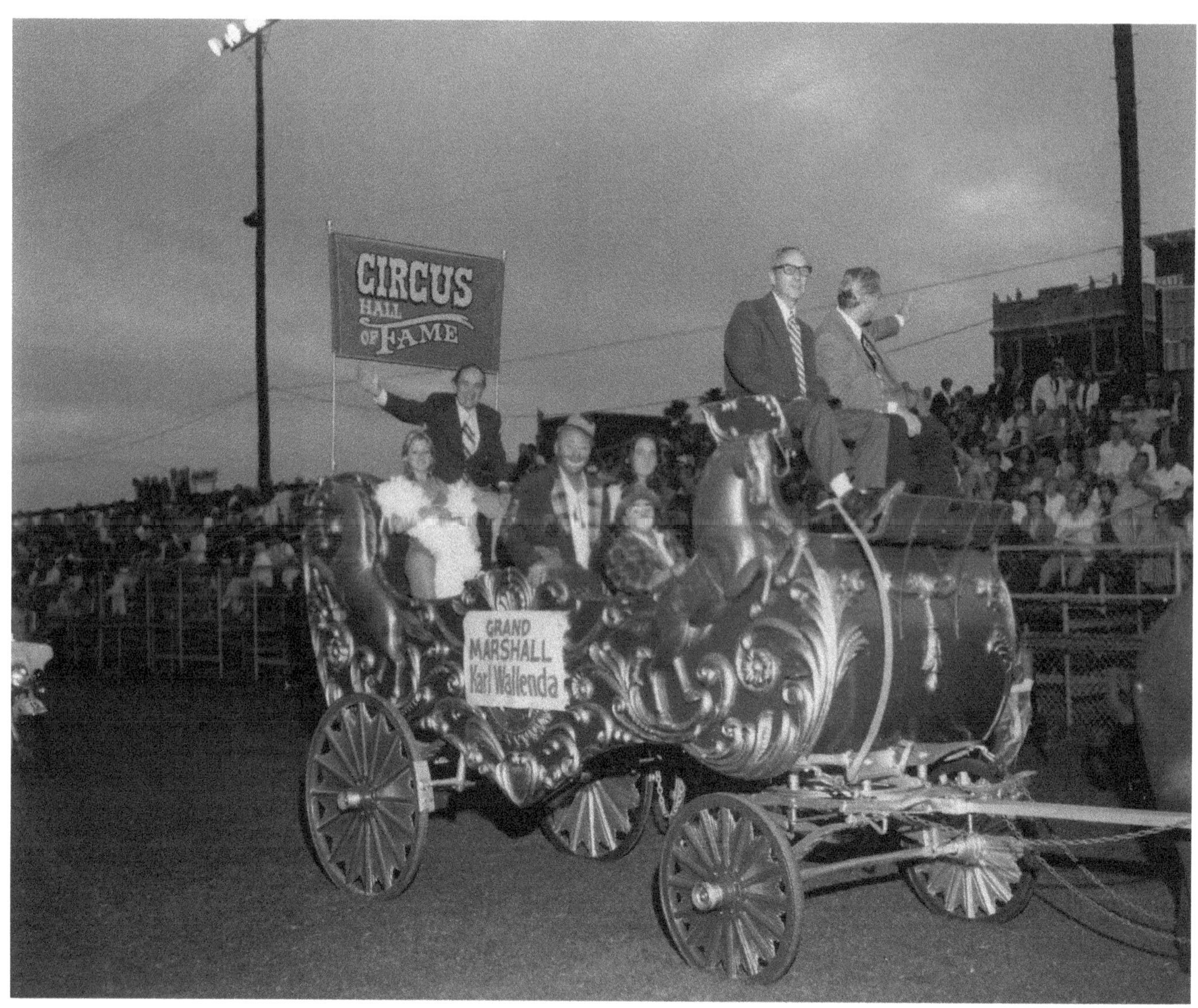

The King Neptune Frolics parade sought celebrities to serve as grand marshal. Shown here in 1975 is Karl Wallenda, patriarch of one of the most famous circus families of all time, the Flying Wallendas. A family of high-wire performers, the Wallendas dazzled audiences in Europe and the United States with dangerous stunts undertaken without a safety net.

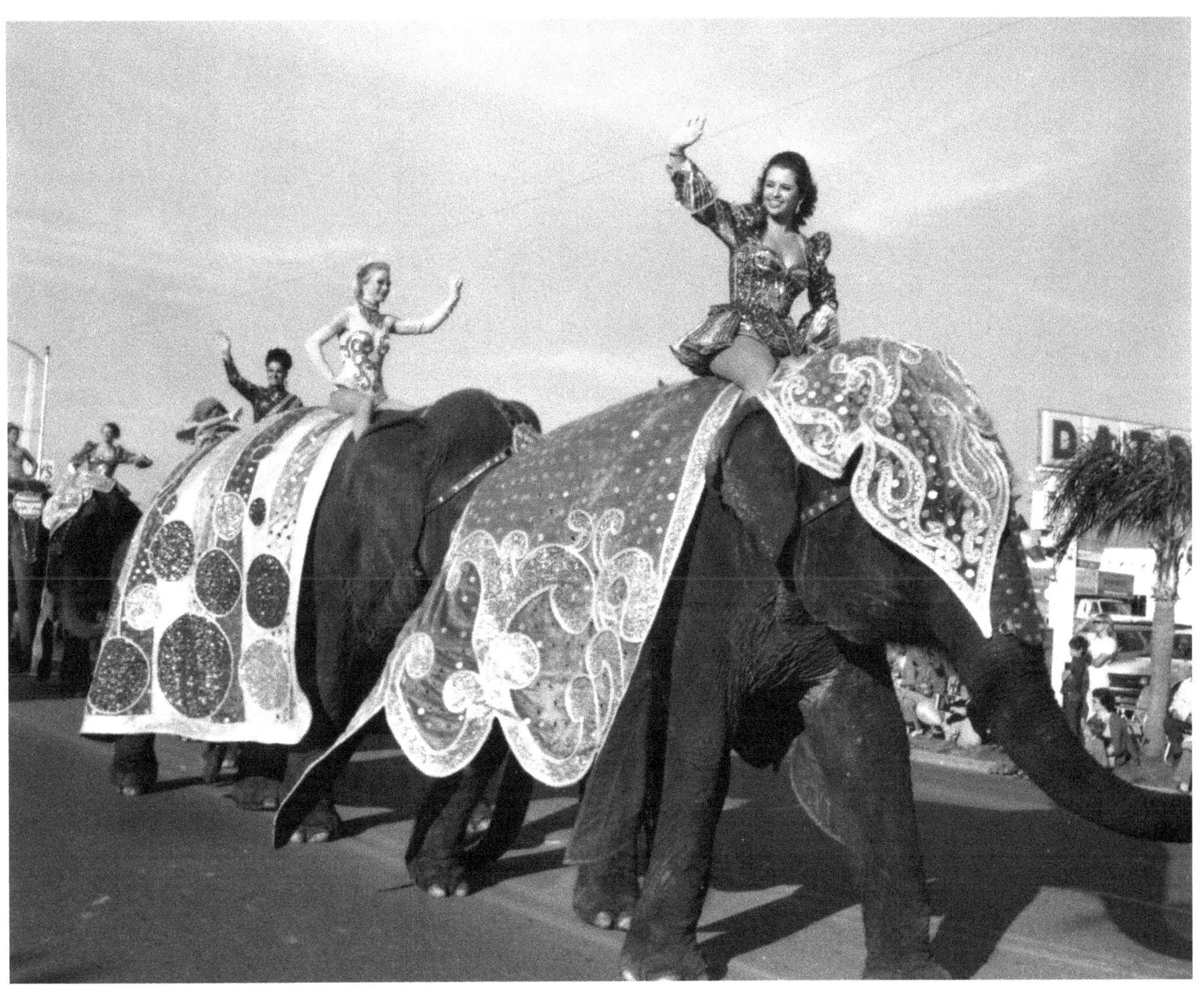

Prior to the 1927 move to Sarasota, the Ringling Brothers Circus wintered in Baraboo, Wisconsin, and Barnum and Bailey's circus wintered in Bridgeport, Connecticut. In Venice, site of this 1976 circus parade, a 5,000-seat arena was constructed for performances that became the city's top tourist attraction for more than three decades beginning in 1960.

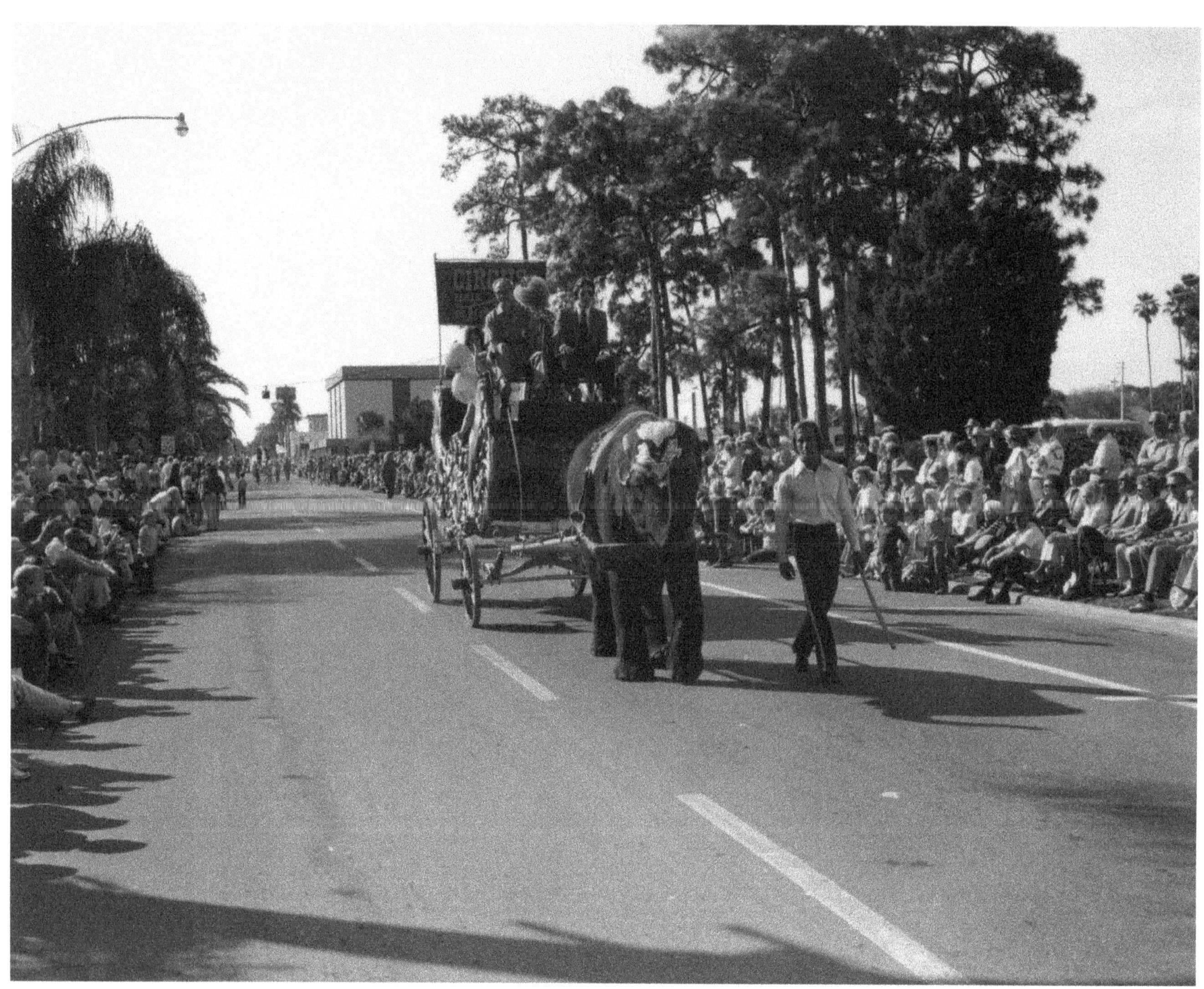

The first circus train of performers and other employees arrived in Venice in 1960 and was greeted by a crowd of more than 10,000. But in 1992, the Seminole Gulf Railroad announced the abandonment of the deteriorating ten miles of train track into Venice. Because the circus needed railroad transportation, it moved from Venice that year.

Notes on the Photographs

These notes, listed by page number, attempt to include all aspects known of the photographs. Each of the photographs is identified by the page number, photograph's title or description, photographer and collection, archive, and call or box number when applicable. Although every attempt was made to collect all available data, in some cases complete data was unavailable due to the age and condition of some of the photographs and records.

II **Belle Haven Inn**
State Archives of Florida
RC13799

VI **Crew Working on Railroad**
State Archives of Florida
RC01846

X **Military Academy Students and Drum Corps**
State Archives of Florida
RC01862

3 **Nellie Abbe Whitaker and Children**
State Archives of Florida
MS25856

4 **Central Street and Pineapple Avenue**
State Archives of Florida
RC01856

5 **Walter, Jim, and Luther Manson**
State Archives of Florida
RC02828

6 **View from the DeSoto Hotel**
State Archives of Florida
RC01845

7 **Travel by Wagon**
State Archives of Florida
RC02826

8 **DeSoto Hotel**
State Archives of Florida
RC01848

9 **DeSoto Hotel**
State Archives of Florida
FR0757

10 **South Gulf Stream Avenue**
State Archives of Florida
RC02444

11 **Baptist Convention**
State Archives of Florida
RC01866

12 **Felix Pinard House**
State Archives of Florida
RC02140

13 **The Palms Hotel**
State Archives of Florida
RC02132

14 **Palms Hotel Porch**
State Archives of Florida
RC02141

15 **First Methodist Church**
State Archives of Florida
RC01844

18 **The Palms Hotel**
State Archives of Florida
RC01863

19 **John Savarese's Steamship *Mistletoe***
State Archives of Florida
N040699

20 **Louis Roberts Fishing Boat**
State Archives of Florida
RC02145

21 **Colonel J. Hamilton Gillespie**
State Archives of Florida
RC01851

22 **Railway Employees Laying Track**
State Archives of Florida
RC01849

24 **Dr. Leffinwell and Dr. Warren Fishing**
State Archives of Florida
RC01859

25 Steamboat *Vandalia*
State Archives of Florida
N040852

26 Sarasota High School
State Archives of Florida
N040316

27 Sarasota Jail
State Archives of Florida
N040297

28 Stately Home on Bay Shore Drive
State Archives of Florida
RC13798

29 Early Sarasota Hotel
State Archives of Florida
N040275

30 Early Machine Shop
State Archives of Florida
RC14041

32 Englewood State Bank
State Archives of Florida
N030307

35 Edson Keith, Jr., and Wife
State Archives of Florida
N040287

36 Venice-Nokomis Bank
State Archives of Florida
PR13153

37 Venice Avenue
State Archives of Florida
RC00-175

38 Mira Mar Hotel
State Archives of Florida
PR09801

39 Bronze Replica Statue of *David*
State Archives of Florida
N038832

40 Kiwanis Band
State Archives of Florida
N040288

41 Watrous Hotel
State Archives of Florida
N040320

42 Sarasota City Hall
State Archives of Florida
RC08755

43 Nettie and Frederick Keith
State Archives of Florida
N040286

44 Jimmy Keith
State Archives of Florida
RC12563

45 Phillippi Mansion
State Archives of Florida
N040311

46 Keith Bathhouse
State Archives of Florida
N040262

47 Mira Mar Hotel
State Archives of Florida
PR09802

48 Sarasota Yacht and Automobile Club
State Archives of Florida
RC07698

49 Nokomis Flooding
State Archives of Florida
N035910

50 1926 Hurricane Damage
State Archives of Florida
N035903

51 Nokomis Home after 1926 Hurricane
State Archives of Florida
N035909

52 Methodist Episcopal Church
State Archives of Florida
RC19784

53 Five Points
State Archives of Florida
RC07695

54 First Bank and Trust Building
State Archives of Florida
RC07696

55 Venice Shopping Area
State Archives of Florida
RC00-195

56 Construction of Venice
State Archives of Florida
RC21580

57 Construction Workers
State Archives of Florida
RC21579

58 Venice Street Construction
State Archives of Florida
RC00-178

59 Venice's Bays
State Archives of Florida
RC00-192

60 Drinking Tea at the Oasis
State Archives of Florida
RC00-196

61 Venice Bridge
State Archives of Florida
PR20692

62 Park View Hotel
State Archives of Florida
PR13151

63 **Venice Deluxe Coaches**
State Archives of Florida
RC00-169

64 **Treasure Island**
State Archives of Florida
GE0944

65 **Train on Palmer's Former Land**
State Archives of Florida
PR09325

66 **Venice-Nokomis United Methodist Church**
State Archives of Florida
N035906

67 **Drilling of First Well**
State Archives of Florida
GE2206

68 **Tourist Lodgings**
State Archives of Florida
PR12558

69 **The Venice Hotel**
State Archives of Florida
RC00-290

72 **Sarasota Beach**
State Archives of Florida
GE1260

73 **Sarasota's First Railroad Station**
State Archives of Florida
N040295

74 **Casino**
State Archives of Florida
RC21581

75 **The Kentucky Military Institute**
State Archives of Florida
N044317

76 **Tin Can Tourist Convention**
State Archives of Florida
N028614

78 **American National Bank**
State Archives of Florida
N040274

79 **Alex and Bob Rosin with Bobo**
State Archives of Florida
PR02795

80 **John and Mable Ringling Museum of Art**
State Archives of Florida
PR09439

81 **Tin Can Tourist Band**
State Archives of Florida
N028611

82 **P-40 Flying Tiger**
State Archives of Florida
N047605

83 **Lieutenant Jerry Jacobs**
State Archives of Florida
MS26223

84 **Venice Street**
State Archives of Florida
PHA019

85 **Florida Medical Center**
State Archives of Florida
RC21269

86 **P-51 Mustang**
State Archives of Florida
N046191

87 **A-29 Hudson Bomber**
State Archives of Florida
N046186

88 **View from the Terrace Hotel**
State Archives of Florida
C006324

89 **Decorating a Christmas Tree**
State Archives of Florida
N028609

90 **Tarpon Tournament**
State Archives of Florida
C005457

91 **The Venice Shuffleboard Club**
State Archives of Florida
C002957

92 **Bingo at Trailer Parks**
State Archives of Florida
C002949

93 **One of Sarasota's Beaches**
State Archives of Florida
C006290

94 **Myakka River**
State Archives of Florida
C011681

95 **Baby Snooks**
State Archives of Florida
C011686

96 **Poolside on Lido Beach**
State Archives of Florida
C007042

97 **In Front of Lido Beach Casino**
State Archives of Florida
C007140B

98 **Esther Williams**
State Archives of Florida
N035543

99 **BRIDGE BUILT BY THE CIVILIAN CONSERVATION CORPS**
State Archives of Florida
C011694

100 **SWIM TEAM RUNS ON LIDO BEACH**
State Archives of Florida
C007138A

101 **SARASOTA REPTILE FARM AND ZOO**
State Archives of Florida
C010203

102 **SARASOTA COUNTY FAIR HORSE RACE**
State Archives of Florida
C009626

103 **PALMER NATIONAL BANK**
State Archives of Florida
GV008572

104 **BATHING BEACH**
State Archives of Florida
C009733

106 **THE HOVER ARCADE**
State Archives of Florida
C008136

107 **AUTOMOBILE OF MRS. CHARLES BELL**
State Archives of Florida
C008943

108 **AERIAL VIEW CAPTURED BY SHERMAN M. FAIRCHILD**
State Archives of Florida
PR15208

109 **SARASOTA COUNTY COURTHOUSE**
State Archives of Florida
PR02187

110 **THE RINGLING MUSEUM**
State Archives of Florida
PR09442

113 **HOTEL AFTER THE GREAT DEPRESSION**
State Archives of Florida
PR13160

114 **GOVERNOR FULLER WARREN**
State Archives of Florida
GV035093

115 **VENICE-NOKOMIS BANK**
State Archives of Florida
PR13155

116 **NOKOMIS BEACH PLAZA**
State Archives of Florida
N035900

117 **DEARBORN STREET**
State Archives of Florida
N030308

118 **SAILING NEAR SARASOTA**
State Archives of Florida
C015181

119 **CIRCUS CAPITAL OF THE WORLD**
State Archives of Florida
N040280

120 **THE GREATEST SHOW ON EARTH**
State Archives of Florida
N040278

121 **THE LABOR DAY REGATTA**
State Archives of Florida
C015118

122 **VENICE JETTY**
State Archives of Florida
N044286

123 **AERIAL VIEW**
State Archives of Florida
PR13157

124 **DRIVING ON LIDO BEACH**
State Archives of Florida
C015093

125 **LIDO BEACH CASINO**
State Archives of Florida
C015216

126 **NET FISHING STATE ARCHIVES OF FLORIDA**
C015230

127 **SARASOTA SAILOR CIRCUS**
State Archives of Florida
C016148

128 **SAILOR CIRCUS PERFORMERS**
State Archives of Florida
C016132

129 **THE GREATEST SHOW ON EARTH PREMIERE**
State Archives of Florida
C015943

130 **AERIALIST PERFORMS IN THE SAILOR CIRCUS**
State Archives of Florida
C018490

131 **ELEANOR ROOSEVELT**
State Archives of Florida
MS26031

132 **FISHING PIER**
State Archives of Florida
CWH0662

133 **STANFORD FISHING RESORT**
State Archives of Florida
CWH0667

134 **PRAM-CLASS SAILBOATS**
State Archives of Florida
C019794

135 Donna Gardner
State Archives of Florida
CWH0887

136 Bridge to Longboat Key
State Archives of Florida
C019699

137 First Bank and Trust Building
State Archives of Florida
C019701

138 View of Five Points
State Archives of Florida
C019702

139 Horn's Cars of Yesterday
State Archives of Florida
C022015

140 Myakka River State Park
State Archives of Florida
FPS00684

141 Lido Beach
State Archives of Florida
C021992

142 Family Picnic Area
State Archives of Florida
FPS00683

144 Hiking in Myakka River State park
State Archives of Florida
C023347

145 Sunshine Springs and Gardens
State Archives of Florida
C023042

146 King Mackerel
State Archives of Florida
C023069

147 Sunbathers at Siesta Key
State Archives of Florida
C023351

148 Barbara Jean Laney
State Archives of Florida
C023841

149 Sunshine Springs
State Archives of Florida
C026868

150 Sarasota Jungle Gardens
State Archives of Florida
RC27051

151 Venice Avenue
State Archives of Florida
C027036

152 Ringling Museum
State Archives of Florida
C028597B

153 Quadricentennial Festival
State Archives of Florida
C031337

154 Warm Mineral Springs
State Archives of Florida
C031335

155 Ghost Hotel
State Archives of Florida
C029451B

157 Quadricentennial Festival
State Archives of Florida
C031948

158 Warm Mineral Springs
State Archives of Florida
C031798

159 Boy Picking Lychees
State Archives of Florida
C033438

160 Democratic Candidates at Sarasota Airport
State Archives of Florida
RC19257

161 Casey Key
State Archives of Florida
N035896

162 Outboarder of Sarasota
State Archives of Florida
C031895

163 Sailboats Racing on Labor Day
State Archives of Florida
C037161

164 John Ringling's Art Collection
State Archives of Florida
C037205

165 Golf Course
State Archives of Florida
C037444

166 All-Star Golf
State Archives of Florida
FPS01413

167 Myakka River State Park
State Archives of Florida
C039312A

168 Stump Pass Beach
State Archives of Florida
C640479

169 Stump Pass Beach State Park
State Archives of Florida
C640469

170 Marblehead Putter Company
State Archives of Florida
C650288

171 Smack Restaurant
State Archives of Florida
N044288

172 Forklift Launching Boat at Marina
State Archives of Florida
C650411

173 Donna Walwork on Beach
State Archives of Florida
C650271

174 Floridaland
State Archives of Florida
C650014

175 Hangman's Hill at Floridaland
State Archives of Florida
C650019

176 Winslow Arms Company
State Archives of Florida
C651637

177 Winslow Arms Company Machine
State Archives of Florida
C651638

178 Circus Hall of Fame
State Archives of Florida
C660579

179 Ringling Brothers and Barnum and Bailey Circus
State Archives of Florida
C023700

180 Circus Hall of Fame
State Archives of Florida
C660583

181 Bellm's Cars and Music of Yesterday
State Archives of Florida
C660571

182 1966 Scene of Sarasota
State Archives of Florida
C660526

183 John Ringling's Building Designed by John Phillips
State Archives of Florida
C660513

184 Venice Street Scene
State Archives of Florida
N044319

185 Parade Float
State Archives of Florida
C682180

186 Sarasota Beach
State Archives of Florida
C677819

187 Condominium Project in Venice
State Archives of Florida
C681737

188 Apartment Buildings Lining the Esplanade in Venice
State Archives of Florida
N044310

189 Outdoor Concert
State Archives of Florida
C678089

190 Lipizzaner Stallions
State Archives of Florida
C681157

191 Asolo Theater
State Archives of Florida
PR09437

192 Bellm's Cars and Music of Yesterday
State Archives of Florida
C682079

193 Visitors on the Myakka River
State Archives of Florida
FPS1219

194 Venice Beach
State Archives of Florida
N044287

195 The 1974 Look of Venice
State Archives of Florida
C681738

196 Ennes Arcade
State Archives of Florida
C681739

197 Sarasota Skyscrapers
State Archives of Florida
C682539

198 Siesta Key
State Archives of Florida
C682496

199 Diaper Derby
State Archives of Florida
C682548

200 Girl Scouts Towing Fake Flamingo
State Archives of Florida
C682611

201 Ellis Sarasota Bank & Trust Company
State Archives of Florida
C682538

202 King Neptune Frolics Parade
State Archives of Florida
C682607

203 Ringling Brothers Circus
State Archives of Florida
C683479

204 Circus Parade
State Archives of Florida
C683480

HISTORIC PHOTOS OF SARASOTA COUNTY

The settlements along Florida's gulf coast that now comprise Sarasota County—including Venice, Osprey, Englewood, and Sarasota—started out with economies reliant on cattle, citrus, and fish. The communities grew with the arrivals of immigrants from Scotland, transplants from among the socially prominent of Chicago, and others looking for a better place to live.

The story of the county is of people such as Bertha Palmer, who was able to have a town moved, and John Ringling, who made the area the "Circus Capital of the World." It is also the story of agricultural towns evolving into cities sought by tourists.

Historic Photos of Sarasota County traces the region's growth from the small wooden homes and fishing piers of old to the modern high-rise condominiums of today. In vivid black-and-white, the book offers historic images of the early pioneers in the wilderness, the "Tin Can Tourists" arriving in trailers, and sunbathers on the broad white beaches.

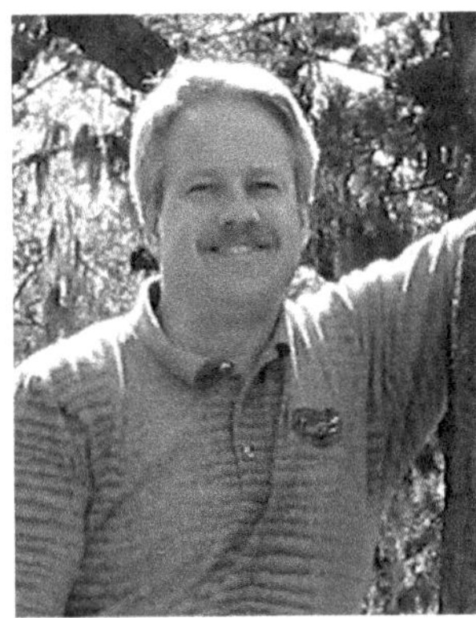

Steve Rajtar has authored 16 books, each dealing with history, particularly that of Florida. He has written *Historic Photos of Florida Attractions* and *Historic Photos of Gainesville,* both available from Turner Publishing. He grew up near Cleveland, Ohio, and after graduating from the University of Central Florida and the University of Florida, he entered the practice of law. He continues in that profession today.

A love of the outdoors and a fascination with local history has resulted in one of his hobbies: leading historical tours in the communities of Florida. Thousands of individuals have attended hundreds of tours he has led through historic neighborhoods, downtowns, and cemeteries. This book is a virtual tour, not only through the neighborhoods of Sarasota County, but also through the decades of its growth into a major tourist destination.

www.ingramcontent.com/pod-product-compliance
Lightning Source LLC
LaVergne TN
LVHW060614110826
845154LV00003B/83
9781684420261